HISTORY OF THE SWEDES OF ILLINOIS ...

8 888006 791168

HISTORY OF THE SWEDES OF ILLINOIS ...

Vol. Pt1

Ernst Wilhelm Olson , Martin J. Engberg , Anders Schön

HISTORY OF THE SWEDES OF ILLINOIS ...

Vol. Pt1

Ernst Wilhelm Olson , Martin J. Engberg , Anders Schön

ISBN : 8888006791168

First Published 1908, reprint 2017 in India by

Facsimile Publisher
12 Pragati Market
Ashok Vihar, Ph-2
Delhi-110052, India
E-mail: books@facsimilepublisher.com

CHAPTER VIII

The Swedish Lutheran Church

Lars Paul Esbjörn, Founder and Pioneer

THE Swedish Methodists had already organized two congregations and the Swedish Episcopalians one, when the first Swedish Lutheran clergyman began religious work in Illinois in a modest and unassuming way. It did not take many years, however, until the Lutherans had outdistanced both the Methodists and the Baptists, who soon appeared in the field. Born and raised as members of the state church of Sweden, a large part of the Swedish immigrants eagerly embraced the opportunity to group themselves into congregations around former ministers of that same church who, out of interest in the spiritual welfare of their fellow countrymen in the West, had sought them out to preach to them the word of God and administer the sacraments. Its many faults notwithstanding, the Swedish state church was still dear to the hearts of serious-minded persons among them, and they were all the more willing to adhere to the faith defended by the blood of their fathers since they could here organize their congregations independently of the government and without any form of state supervision. The innate force of the Lutheran Church here, as earlier among the German Lutherans in the East, got an opportunity to develop under the benign influence of untrammeled religious freedom, and the result has been wonderful indeed. In a very short time Swedish Lutheran churches were organized not only in various parts of the state of Illinois but also in the adjoining states of Iowa and Indiana. This was the comparatively small beginning of the large and powerful Swedish Lutheran Church of America, known as the Augustana Synod, which, in little more than half a century, has extended its work and influence over a large part of the United States, over parts of Canada and to Alaska and Porto Rico.

The first Swedish Lutheran minister in Illinois was Lars Paul Esbjörn. With the exception of Peter Wilhelm Böckman, in Wisconsin, and Carl Peter Agrelius, in New York, both of whom were failures as such, Esbjörn was also the first Swedish Lutheran preacher in America in modern times. He may properly be styled the father of the Swedish Lutheran Church in this country. He not only founded the Augustana Synod, but also began the Swedish educational work in the United States. As a pioneer and founder, Esbjörn 'for all time will! hold first place in the annals of Swedish-American Lutheranism.

Lars Paul Esbjörn was born in Delsbo parish, in Helsingland, Oct. 16, 1808. His parents were Esbjörn Paulson, a country tailor, and Karin Lindström, his wife. When the boy was five years old his mother died, and two years afterward he lost his father. An old maid-servant named Stina took the motherless boy in charge before the death of his father and was a tender foster-mother to him until he reached his twelfth year. It was she who taught him to read, and after she discovered the boy's aptness in his studies, she did not rest until she had him entered, in the fall of 1820, in a school in the city of Hudiksvall. Like all other poor boys, he suffered great privations in trying to get an education. Being a boy of weak constitution, want had a telling effect on him, yet he proved a diligent and hard-working pupil, who stood high in the estimation of his teachers. With good scholarship marks he entered the gymnasium at Gefle in 1825, and there took up astronomy, higher mathematics and navigation alongside of his prescribed studies. Having taken notice of his predilection for mathematics, his guardian advised him to join the topographical engineering corps of the army in order to raise funds for continued study, but Lars Paul was fixed in his resolve to become a minister, and nothing could swerve him. He had inherited three hundred crowns from his parents, but that sum did not go far. His noble-hearted foster-mother, however, exerted herself to the utmost to provide the necessary means and his home parish gave him assistance in the same way that Luther was helped when a boy. He was accustomed at Christmas time to make a round of the well-to-do farmers, singing a stanza or two of some hymn at every house, and received in compensation various gifts, according to the circumstances of the giver, ranging from money and grain down to dried meat and tallow candles.

At midsummer, 1828, aged nineteen, Esbjörn passed examination for admission to the University of Upsala and was enrolled as a theological student of the university. After completing a four-year course in theology, he was ordained minister June 11, 1832, probably in the Upsala Cathedral by Archbishop Carl von Rosenstein, and became assistant pastor in Öster-Våhla parish, in Upland, where he served for three years. Subsequently he was chosen pastor for the Oslättfors factory and also school-teacher in Hille, Gestrikland, filling both positions for fourteen years.

During this time he was perceptibly influenced by Rev. George Scott, the English Methodist preacher at Stockholm, not, however, in a sectarian sense, but in the direction of deepening his religious convictions. From this time on Esbjörn was a strict and earnest pietist of the old school, and he became known as a zealous "läsareprest" (revivalist preacher), while still a strict conformist to the church. The earnest

Rev. Lars Paul Esbjörn

and gifted young pastor early devoted himself to literary work, partly original, partly translations and revisions of older religious books and tracts. In the early forties, when the great temperance agitation stirred the country, Esbjörn became one of the foremost temperance advocates in northern Sweden, contributing by speaking, writing and forming temperance societies toward that change of public sentiment which ultimately made it possible for the lawmaking power to stop the

private distillery system and thereby stem the flood-tide of drunkenness.

Actuated by his great enthusiasm in behalf of temperance, Esbjörn
at times probably went too far, for instance in forcibly depriving farmers whom he met in the road of the whiskey kegs they were bringing
home. But even where he acted with the utmost caution he did not
escape bitter persecution, for the dram was dear to the hearts of the
people and whiskey was a power in the land. His enemies sought in
every way to make trouble for him, and even went so far as to threaten
his life. One night when Esbjörn attended a religious meeting, several men lay in ambush for him under a bridge he was expected to
cross, evidently for the purpose of beating or killing him. Luckily for
him, the meeting lasted so long that the ruffians got tired of waiting
and went home, thinking that their man had been forewarned and had
taken another route.

As a consequence of his stern piety and strict ideas on temperance,
Esbjörn aroused much opposition among the clergy of the archbishop-
ric, who did everything to prevent his obtaining a rectorate. Having
passed the pastoral examination in 1839, he was nominated for that
office in several places, such as Regnsjö, Söderhamn and Loos, but in
every instance he was bitterly opposed by the whiskey interests. In
the last-named place it is claimed he received a majority of the votes,
but was deprived of the position by trickery.

No wonder, then, that this energetic and profoundly earnest minister of the gospel wearied of the ungrateful treatment accorded him
at home and began to look about for another field. He had no difficulty in finding one. The emigration of the first party of Erik Jansson's
followers to America in 1846 had directed the attention of all
Sweden to the great western land of promise. In the years next following one large party of emigrants after another had embarked for
America. Esbjörn could not have failed to notice this movement, for
it was in his own native district that Erik Jansson obtained his principal following and whence the sect gradually emigrated in larger or
smaller parties, which were soon followed by others of their countrymen who longed for America for economic reasons equally as urgent
as were the religious considerations of the Erik Janssonists. The latter
class of emigrants, who were still devoted to the creed and doctrine of
the Swedish Lutheran Church, in letters to their friends and relatives
at home complained bitterly of their religious needs, their situation
being all the graver as they were surrounded on all sides, not only by
the Erik Janssonists and the Swedish Methodists but by all sorts of
American religious sects with which they did not wish to affiliate, and

in this predicament they did not have one single Lutheran pastor to minister to their spiritual wants.

Realizing the pressing needs of these people, Rev. Esbjörn decided to emigrate and become their pastor. The question of earning a livelihood from the start caused him a great deal of worry. His knowledge of Methodism, gained from Rev. Scott of Stockholm, had given him a high opinion of the unselfish motives of that church, and he seems to have had assurance that the same church in America would be found equally unselfish, relying on it to render some aid in his work as a Lutheran pastor. A correspondence appears to have been carried on between him and Rev. Jonas Hedström of Victoria on this subject, Hedström being known to him through letters from emigrants. But this did not lead to any direct results, wherefore Esbjörn turned to the Swedish Mission Society with a petition for official recognition and financial aid from that source. He received both, the financial aid, however, being quite insufficient.

After having received leave of absence to engage in clerical work in foreign territory, Esbjörn, accompanied by 140 emigrants from the provinces of Gestrikland and Helsingland, embarked June 29, 1849, on the sailing vessel ''Cobden,'' bound from Gefle for New York. The voyage, besides being fraught with difficulty and peril, craved the life of one of Esbjörn's children, and the body was interred in Helsingborg, where the vessel touched. This was but the first of a series of sorrows and reverses that were to follow. The party arrived at New York in the latter part of August or early in September, with the intention of proceeding to Victoria, Ill. Their plan was frustrated, however, for when Esbjörn met Rev. O. G. Hedström in New York he was informed that the American Methodists would give him no aid as a Lutheran minister, but only on condition that he join the Methodist Church. This Esbjörn would by no means consent to do. In his predicament he turned to the headquarters of the American Board of Home Missions in New York with an inquiry whether they would for a time support him in his work among the Lutherans. Having apparently received a favorable reply, he had no further reason to look up Rev. Jonas Hedström in Victoria, but began to make inquiries for some other western settlement where he might take up missionary work. He did not have to look long for just such an opportunity. While in New York, he had the fortune to meet the aforementioned Captain P. W. Wirström, who for a short time had been living in the new Swedish settlement at Andover, in Henry county. Wirström seems to have been the agent of the land company in New York that founded Andover, and it was no doubt through his influence that this company promised Esbjörn ten acres of land for a church on condition that he and his party would settle there.   After careful consideration, Esbjörn resolved to go to Andover to stay.

With Captain Wirström as guide and adviser, the party now started on their tedious journey westward.   They traveled by canal-boat to Buffalo and thence by steamer to Chicago.   Shortly after having passed Detroit, another of Esbjörn's children died and was buried in a very primitive coffin in a sandbank on the shores of Lake St. Clair.   Rev. Esbjörn himself took sick with the cholera and was compelled to stop in Chicago with his family, only two of his sons going with the rest of the party to Andover.   Three weeks later, when Esbjörn arrived there he discovered to his great sorrow that the alert Jonas Hedström had already been there and succeeded in persuading most of the newcomers to leave Andover and come with him to Victoria. Before, this same Hedström had recommended Andover as a suitable place of settlement for the Swedes, but now that he had learned of Esbjörn's unwillingness to become a Methodist he changed his tone, disparaging the place and doing everything to induce his countrymen to move away.

In Andover Esbjörn had to contend with all the customary trials and reverses of pioneer life, such as sickness, poor shelter and lack of suitable food.   He succeeded in renting for himself and family a couple of small, stuffy rooms in the attic of Captain Mix's place, a farmhouse situated just outside of the little village, and now owned by the widow Anna Lovisa Gustafsson from Östergötland.   The first Sunday Esbjörn preached in Andover, the Francis schoolhouse serving as the meeting-place, he was still so weak that he had to speak seated in a chair.   He spoke with intense feeling, taking the words, "In my weakness I am strong," as the text for his introductory remarks.   During the ensuing winter, Esbjörn occupied the crowded and uncomfortable quarters aforesaid, but in the meantime he purchased a little farm of ten acres, with primitive buildings, situated south of the timber, down toward Edwards Creek, and moved there in the Spring of 1850.

The Swedish Lutheran Church at Andover

In his work as Swedish Lutheran pastor at Andover, Esbjörn from the very start met with bitter opposition from Jonas Hedström, the Swedish Methodist pastor, who naturally was desirous of retaining the advantage he enjoyed on account of his long term of service in this vicinity.   Nor did he miss a single opportunity to poison the minds of the settlers against Esbjörn and his work.   In conversations held with individual members of his flock he would make the assertion that the Lutheran Church was spiritually dead; that it was the Babylonian harlot, which every one must shun who would be saved; that the new

Swedish pastor had come to put the free settlers under the bonds of the Swedish state church; that there were no Lutheran congregations in America; that the Methodists were the true Lutherans, etc. Clearly, these and similar utterances from a man who had gained the confidence of the settlers in both wordly and spiritual matters would gain credence among them to a certain extent and hurt Esbjörn in his work. Hedström had the advantage of being backed by the American Methdist Church, from which he received a salary, small as it was, while there was no Lutheran congregation, conference or synod of any kind in this part of the country from which Esbjörn could get aid and advice. He stood entirely alone, and was thrown on his own resources both as to the methods and the means by which to prosecute the work.

In this isolated and difficult position, Esbjörn was obliged to turn to the Illinois branch of the Congregational American Board of Home Missions, at Galesburg, with a request to be taken care of and to get the recommendation of the mission board for aid from its funds. This was in December, 1849. His request was given favorable consideration, and after Esbjörn had personally met with the board, explaining his religious tenets and showing his credentials, the Central Association for its part granted the petition on the following conditions: that Esbjörn, as a member of the association, was to be responsible to that body; that he was to work as a Lutheran pastor, preaching and administering the sacraments, and that his assigned field was Andover and Galesburg, where respectively 180 and 100 Swedes already had settled. It is especially worthy of notice that the association did not impose the condition that Esbjörn should join the Congregational Church, but that he was permitted to continue a Lutheran pastor. An appropriation of $300 was recommended by the association and referred to the mission board in New York which in turn granted the request of Esbjörn. In its letter, dated Jan. 14, 1850, the board stipulates that Esbjörn be appointed to preach the gospel to the Swedish people in Galesburg, Andover and surrounding country for a term of twelve months, under the direction of the Mission Board of the Central Association. The Swedish people in this district were expected to contribute $100 to his support, making a total salary of $400 for the year. He was directed to make a report of his work at the end of each quarter. This appointment was accompanied by a personal letter from Dr. Milton Badger, corresponding secretary of the board of missions, with instructions to Rev. Esbjörn not to admit as members of any congregation persons unable to give evidence of the new birth nor permit such to participate in the Lord's Supper. In his communication Dr. Badger criticises the German Lutherans for admitting members to their congregations by confirmation.

On the ocean voyage and on the journey inland Rev. Esbjörn had preached twice every Sunday to his fellow passengers and daily conducted morning and evening prayers accompanied by brief biblical expositions. This practice he continued after the arrival at Andover, and soon extended his ministerial work to Galesburg, Berlin (Swedona) and Rock Island. At the end of February, 1850, he reported to the aforesaid mission board in New York that he had preached every other Sunday at Andover and Galesburg, respectively, usually twice at each place, conducted evening prayers and Bible exegeses in the private homes, visited the families and the sick, held monthly mission meetings and temperance lectures and circulated religious tracts. From this it appears that from the very outset Esbjörn entered upon his duties with great zeal. In this same report he says that the people in Galesburg had begun to build a Swedish Lutheran meeting-house, toward which $550 already had been subscribed. He expressed the hope that a similar edifice would soon be erected in Andover. He complained, however, about the poverty which was general among his countrymen, causing them so great worry over the question of earning a living that their minds were not sufficiently open to the truth of the gospel; also of the general exodus to California of goldseekers, a movement creating such a stir among the people that they found no time to think about the salvation of their souls. Another cause for complaint was the open avowal of Rev. Jonas Hedström of his purpose to convert all the Swedes to Methodism and bring them into his congregation. Furthermore, former Erik Janssonists living in Galesburg were giving him much trouble by their self-righteousness and spiritual pride.

In the first part of March of the same year Esbjörn could report that the number of persons attending the public services were, at Andover about 70, at Galesburg 80, at Rock Island 30, at Berlin 12, of whom 12 to 15 could be regarded as true Christians; that a temperance society with 43 members had been organized in Andover, and that the proposed Swedish church in Galesburg was in course of erection.

These reports show the actual condition among the people about the time that Esbjörn, on the 18th of March, 1850, in the house of Widow Anna Lovisa Gustafsson, organized the Swedish Lutheran Church of Andover, the first of its kind since the time of the Delaware Swedes. The first members were only ten in number, viz., Rev. Esbjörn and his wife, Jan Andersson, Mats Ersson, O. Nordin, Sam. Jansson, And. Pet. Larsson, Mrs. Jansson, "Christina at Knapp's" and Stina Hellgren. The small number shows how anxious Esbjörn was to follow out his instructions with respect to church membership. But on the 23rd of the same month there was an addition of 30 to 40 members. Among these were Captain Wirström and his wife, also Eric Ulric

Norberg, known for his prominence in the schisms of the Bishop Hill Colony. In the beginning of December the church numbered 46 members and its meetings were attended by an average of 50 to 60 persons. Sunday schools were organized both in Andover and Galesburg simultaneously with the churches.

At first the meetings were held in Esbjörn's home, south of the timber, where the audiences were accommodated in two or three rooms provided with chairs and improvised benches, or else in the Francis schoolhouse. Occasionally, prayer meetings were conducted at the house of Mrs. Gustafsson, known as Captain Mix's place. These people were actuated by a certain degree of religious zeal, a kind of imitation of the enthusiasm of the Methodists. The order of service conformed in the main to that of the Swedish state church, and Rev. Esbjörn retained the ministerial garb of that church. The prayer meetings were frequently attended by Methodists, but the spiritual arrogance displayed by them made their appearance rather disagreeable to Esbjörn. His dependence on the American Congregationalists as well as the fact that he was surrounded by Methodists who lost no opportunity to decry everything that savored of the Swedish state church, caused Esbjörn gradually to accommodate himself to the Reformed order of service to the extent of discarding for a time certain portions of the Swedish church ritual as well as the use of the Pericopes. Not until the early sixties, after the Swedish Lutherans had become an independent church, did Esbjörn resume the position he held at the time of his arrival, that of a strict conformist to the practices as well as the doctrines of the Swedish church. His departure from those practices under the circumstances should not be too severely judged. It was the result more of necessity than of inclination. He was never a noisy revivalist, his religious convictions and Christian experiences being deeper and more temperate than those of his puritanical American associates.

Despite opposition, the little congregation at Andover steadily grew and soon the question of a church building arose. The members were all poor settlers, unable to defray the cost without outside aid. Consequently, Rev. Esbjörn, according to the common custom, was obliged to start out on a soliciting tour. In April, 1851, he left on a trip through Ohio, Pennsylvania, New York and Massachusetts. During the eleven weeks he was out he succeeded in raising not less than $2,200, of which sum Jenny Lind, the renowned Swedish singer, contributed $1,500. Upon his return home in July, he at once began preparations for building. All the members of the church, men and women, were set to work making brick, and the foundation was laid for a structure 45 feet long and 30 feet wide, with basement designed

for school room and sacristy. It was hoped to get the basement ready
by Christmas, but rainy weather prevailing during the summer and
fall interfered with this plan. The brick was spoiled by the rain and
the sawmills in Andover were damaged by floods, whereby the congregation was compelled to go elsewhere for its building material, pay-

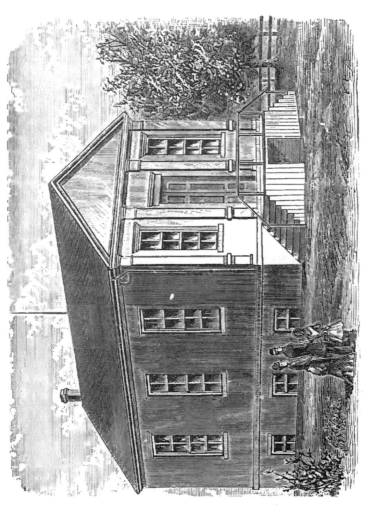

The First Swedish Lutheran Church in America, 1854

ing a high price for it, besides having to haul it a distance of thirty
miles. Cold weather soon put a stop to the work, but not until the
basement had been so nearly finished that services could be held there
during the ensuing winter. The basement was still unplastered and
only partly under roof, no floor having been laid above and a large
opening having been left for the tower.

The next summer work was resumed but under still more unfavorable conditions. The corn crop failed, no work was to be had, and, to add to the misery of the settlers, a terrible cholera epidemic broke out in the community, making such inroads among the settlers that much of the lumber bought for the church had to be used for coffins for the victims of the scourge.

On Advent Sunday, Dec. 3, 1854, after more than three years of work and sacrifice, the congregation finally dedicated its church edifice, now almost finished. This was a day of great rejoicing, praise and thanksgiving being offered by grateful hearts to the Highest. The church, which seated 300 persons and could accommodate a larger number in an emergency, was considered a great structure for the times, although quite insignificant as compared with the large, handsome Swedish-American churches of our day. It was not built according to any particular style of church architecture, the congregation being contented just so they had a house of worship of some kind. The church was in the form of a long rectangle. The basement was like a dark cave; but was nevertheless used to house newcomers, many of whom died there of the cholera. The pulpit, placed at the middle of one end of the building, and surrounded by a semi-circular altar railing, resembled an old-fashioned Swedish scullery. The upper part of the pulpit, not much larger than a salt barrel cut in half lengthwise, stood crowded back against the wall.

This old church still stands, and, having been recently remodeled, now serves as schoolhouse and meeting hall for the young people's society. When it was proposed several years ago to tear down the old landmark the women pioneers still living arose in protest, calling attention to the part played by them in its construction, and thus the old relic was spared. In front of the church lies the old churchyard where rest so many of the Swedes of Andover.

Up to the autumn of 1852, Esbjörn was the only Swedish Lutheran minister in Illinois. He was then in charge of a pastorate extending about fifty miles from end to end, including Andover, Galesburg, Knoxville, Henderson, Moline and Rock Island. He spent a great deal of time traveling between these points. Roads were bad and bridges few, and traveling in all kinds of weather and under contingent difficulties had a bad effect on his health. In the fall of that year he received well-needed assistance in the work when T. N. Hasselquist arrived from Sweden and took charge of the Galesburg field and a lay preacher named C. J. Valentin was stationed in Moline and Rock Island. Thereby Esbjörn's field was practically limited to Andover and vicinity. But the Andover congregation even then was scattered far and wide over the prairies, including, as it did, Berlin (Swedona), La Grange (Orion), and Hickory Grove (Ophiem), or, in short, all the Swedish Lutheran settlers in the neighborhood of Andover. Berlin and La Grange soon were made separate charges and subsequently independent congregations. In the fall of 1853 the church numbered 210 communicant members, who contributed a total of $80 to the salary of the pastor.

Rev. Esbjörn and his parishioners at the outset had many bitter feuds with the Methodists led by Rev. Hedström, and several other religious groups. Ere long, however, the Lutherans and Methodists had to stop fighting between themselves and turn toward their common opponents and competitors, the Baptists, who in the summer of 1852 commenced operations, led by Gustaf Palmquist, a former schoolmaster, who had come over the year before and at first served as Lutheran preacher in Galesburg. Palmquist made a few converts among the Lutherans, but the principal harvest was reaped among the Methodists. Although the hotbed of the Baptist movement was at first Galesburg and afterward Rock Island, the Andover congregation did not entirely escape being influenced. But Rev. Esbjörn proved to be a wide-awake shepherd who successfully thwarted the efforts made to scatter his little flock.

After a series of hot encounters with Methodists and Baptists, from which the Lutheran pastor and his flock seem to have emerged with a deepened sense of the worth of the evangelical Lutheran confession, the congregation grew both in numbers and in inward stability. The order of service and ecclesiastical practices of the old country were more fully adhered to, while greater importance was attached to soundness in spiritual life. Peace having eventually been restored in the church, renewed disturbances occurred when one B. G. P. Bergenlund, in the summer of 1855, after having been appointed assistant pastor and school teacher, began to cast aspersions on Rev. Esbjörn and his work, at the same time giving offense and scandalizing the church by conduct unbecoming a pastor and a Christian. Bergenlund, apparently a native of Ignaberga, in the province of Skåne, and a man of education, had come to this country in January, 1853, stopping in Jamestown, N. Y. There and in Sugar Grove, Pa., he began preaching to his fellow countrymen and in the fall of the same year came to Illinois at the suggestion of Rev. Hasselquist. Having passed examination, he was licensed by the Synod of Northern Illinois as a regular preacher, whereupon he returned to Jamestown and Sugar Grove. By his unseemly behavior he spoiled his reputation in less than a year and was forced to leave. In May, 1855, he appeared in Moline, where he took ministerial charge of the Swedish Lutheran congregation without notifying Esbjörn. When the congregation showed a disinclination to receive him, he left for Andover where he insinuated himself into the confidence and friendship of the people by going from house to house. In this manner

Esbjörn had forced upon him an assistant whom he had not asked for and did not want, but whose functions he endeavored to restrict by means of written instructions. Bergenlund, who had so little regard for the proprieties that he would preach high mass in highly inappropriate dress, including heavy gloves, nevertheless gained a firm foothold in the community and soon began to act in total disregard of his written instructions. At the annual meeting of the Synod of Northern Illinois in 1855, Esbjörn was appointed traveling solicitor of funds for a Scandinavian professorship at the Illinois University at Springfield, the theological school of that synod. From the early part of the year 1856, when Esbjörn engaged in that work, Bergenlund had free hands. Tiring of the arrogant and arbitrary actions of this man, Esbjörn after a couple of months resigned his pastorate. In March he was seriously considering a removal to the new Swedish settlement of Stockholm, now Lake Pepin, Wis., but later in the spring he received a call from the Swedish Lutheran Church in Princeton, Ill., which he accepted, removing there in August. Bergenlund continued operations in Andover, but before the end of the year the parishioners had their eyes opened to the eccentricities of their pastor and resolved to call Rev. M. F. Hokanson, of New Sweden, Iowa. Bergenlund still had a small party back of him, which made it possible for him to hold on for a short time, but he had lost confidence generally. In the summer of 1857, he was compelled to leave Andover and the next fall the Synod of Northern Illinois refused to renew his preacher's license. After drifting about from place to place, mostly in Minnesota, he came back in 1860, after the Scandinavian Lutherans had separated from the Synod of Northern Illinois and formed the Augustana Synod. He was then re-admitted into the Synod of Northern Illinois and ordained minister. He now began to make vehement attacks on the Augustana Synod, but more particularly on Esbjörn. After a few years he returned to Sweden where he succeeded in gaining admittance to the state church and obtain a charge in the bishopric of Göteborg, where still perserving in his erratic ways he gave old Bishop Björk a great deal of annoyance.

The Andover church, having been disappointed in Bergenlund, called as its pastor Rev. P. Petersson of the bishopric of Vexiö, Sweden, who promised to accept, but was unable to keep his promise. After having been served temporarily by Rev. O. C. T. Andrén of Moline, the church in the spring of 1858 issued a call to Rev. Jonas Swensson of Sugar Grove, Pa., who had arrived from Sweden two years before. After due consideration, he accepted the call and removed to his new field in September of that year. His arrival marked the beginning of a new epoch in the history of the Andover church. But before entering on that period we will briefly review the further career of his predecessor.

Rev. Esbjörn's Later Career

From Andover Esbjörn removed to Princeton. Here he remained only two years. During this short period he accomplished much, including the work in connection with the erection of a church. In spite of illness, he worked strenuously and with marked success for the spiritual development of his congregation. The people became more interested in churchly affairs and listened more attentively to the sermons; furthermore, the services were made still more attractive by means of better singing, resulting from earnest practice, encouraged by the pastor himself, not to mention other improvements.

At the task of collecting funds for the Scandinavian professorship of the seminary, Esbjörn, who was an experienced solicitor, succeeded admirably. When the time arrived to appoint the incumbent of that chair, Esbjörn was chosen as the most suitable man available and assumed the position in the fall of 1858. After two years a combination of circumstances compelled him to resign. He then went to Chicago in April, 1860, accompanied by all but two of the Scandinavian students, and there continued teaching. Dissatisfied with their relations with the Synod of Northern Illinois, the Scandinavian Lutherans in June of that year met near Clinton, Wis., and organized an independend synod, called the Augustana Synod, and resolved to establish a theological school of their own in Chicago, the Augustana Theological Seminary, virtually a continuation of the school conducted for the past few weeks by Esbjörn. Rev. Esbjörn was formally chosen head of the institution, continuing his work as teacher with good results for three years.

With all his soul Rev. Esbjörn had thrown himself into the work of raising his fellow countrymen in America to a higher level, and in his tireless endeavor in various fields he scarcely took notice of the rapid flight of time. At first he had felt no symptoms of homesickness, being too busy to think of that, but with advancing years—he was now past fifty—he began to long back to the country of which he was part and parcel through birth and early training. There were also economic reasons for his home-sickness. For all these reasons Esbjörn in 1863 returned to his native land after fourteen years of fruitful work among his countrymen in America. During this period great changes had taken place in Sweden. That temperance legislation for which Wieselgren, Fjellstedt and, last but not least, Esbjörn had fought was now an accomplished fact, the private distillery system having been abolished by the riksdag of 1854, and the work for spiritual enlightenment no longer meeting with the same stubborn resistance as before. Thoroughly tried in life's battle, the stern reformer, who before his departure from Sweden failed to obtain a certain pastorate on account of his temperance views and other "newfangled notions," was now met with open arms and was given the very lucrative rectorate of Öster-Våhla parish, in Upland, thus being recompensed even in a pecuniary way for all his privations in a foreign land. In this quiet spot he labored for seven years, dividing his time between his pastoral duties and private study and research, which had been his hobby from early youth, such as mathematics, chemistry and astronomy, besides theology. In the meantime he closely followed the rapid progress made by the church he had founded in America, and nothing gave him greater pleasure than a visit by some one of his former co-workers in this country.

Esbjörn was the author of ten published books and pamphlets on various topics.

The burden of years grew steadily heavier, health and bodily vigor gave way, and soon the eve of rest for this indefatigable laborer had arrived. After only a month of actual illness Rev. L. P. Esbjörn passed away in the Öster-Våhla parsonage, July 2, 1870, in the sixty-second year of his life, and was buried in the parish churchyard. A few years ago a handsome monument was erected on his grave to mark the last resting-place of this eminent Swedish-American pioneer.

The sermons of Rev. Esbjörn were highly edifying, but he was by no means an orator in the ordinary sense of the term. His voice was ruined in the early part of his career through sickness and over-exertion, and he never affected eloquence. His discourses were nevertheless very captivating by dint of his lucid logic, his clear and profound ideas and the simplicity of his diction. He was a man of clear and well-balanced mind, pre-eminently fitting him for the profession both of preacher and educator. As a man Esbjörn was devout and warm-hearted, unselfish almost to a fault, righteous, unaffected and without pride or vainglory. He was translucent, so to speak, and in his character there was nothing to hide. Although not really credulous, and being a good judge of men, he would sometimes be imposed upon, owing to his sheer goodness of heart.

Before emigrating to America, Esbjörn was married to Miss Amalia Maria Lovisa Planting-Gyllenbåga, a devout and refined lady, who held the same religious views as he. Poverty, illness and numerous reverses had given her a despondent and melancholy disposition. Their children were: Paul, who died in the Civil War in 1861, while on duty in Missouri; Johannes, who returned to Sweden in 1863, entered the railway service and is now living in Karlskrona; Joseph, who also served in the Civil War, was retired as captain, and is now living in Minneapolis, Minn.; Maria, who married a German Lutheran clergyman named Schnur, and died many years ago, and two sons, twins, who died on the voyage to America. July 11, 1852, Mrs. Esbjörn died in Andover and lies buried in the old churchyard. Subsequently, Esbjörn was twice remarried, first to Helena Catharina Magnusson, who was born at Sund, Östergötland, June 29, 1827, and died in Andover, Sept. 15, 1853; afterward to her sister Gustafva Albertina Magnusson, born at Sund in 1833. The children of the latter union still living are: Rev. C. M. Esbjörn, Ph. D., minister of the Augustana Synod; Prof. C. L. E. Esbjörn, of Augustana College, at Rock Island, Ill.; and two daughters, Maria and Hanna. Another son, Paul Oscar Esbjörn, a physician of Stanton, Ia., died in 1908.

Rev. Jonas Swensson

Jonas Swensson, who supplanted the erratic Rev. Bergenlund as pastor of the Andover church, where he labored for a long term of years, is another pioneer and early leader of the Swedish Lutheran Church in America. He was born at Snollebo, parish of Våthult, Småland, Aug. 16, 1828. His parents were Sven Månsson and his wife Catharina Jonasson. In the parental home he received a careful Christian training, the foundation for his subsequent career. In his early youth he had a desire to study for the ministry, but such a course seemed to have been closed to him by his father's death when he was but nine years old, together with the fact that there were six other children in the home to be provided for. But later on the outlook cleared. After his confirmation he became a blacksmith's apprentice, but abandoned that occupation to enter the teachers' seminary at Vexiö in 1846. While there, his early plan was revived and that summer he took up private studies in theology with his teacher, Rev. Josef Bexell, and in 1847 continued these studies for the curate of Bredaryd parish. At the end of August he went to Jönköping, entering the rector's class at the school in that city, and was very 'favorably received by the rector, Rev. Fileen. In two terms he finished his courses and entered the gymnasium at Vexiö in the fall of 1848. Here he studied for two years, until September, 1850, when he passed his final examinations. July 29, 1849, in the Hemmesjö church, Swensson preached his first sermon, and after that he frequently, while still a student, filled the pulpits of other churches in Småland.

Sept. 24, 1850, he was graduated into the university of Upsala with high standing. He at once took up the theological course at the university and passed final examination in June, 1851. The following October he was examined for entry into the ministry before the Vexiö chapter and, on the 8th of the month, was ordained minister and assigned as curate to Rector Andrén at Unnaryd. Swensson's exceptional capacity for study is shown by the fact that he finished both elementary and theological studies in about five years. Many who had known the tall and sturdy youth as a blacksmith's apprentice or as a pupil at the elementary school at Vexiö were greatly surprised to find him in the ministry in so short a time. At Unnaryd and Jälluntofta Swensson now labored for four and one-half years, till the spring of 1856.

Himself an earnest Christian from his school days, Swensson strove zealously to awaken and maintain the new life among the members of his church. His own Christianity being most profound, he had little sympathy for the superficial new evangelism that was gaining ground in Sweden about this time. From the very beginning of his pastoral career he carefully prepared his sermons and committed them to writing, thereby laying the foundation for that system and order which characterized his work throughout life. From many neighboring parishes people flocked to hear him, and, young as he was, he became the spiritual father and counselor of many. In spite of a severe affection of the lungs, he continued his work with undiminished vigor and was eventually restored to health, contrary to the expectations of himself and his friends.

His reputation as an earnest and devout preacher had crossed the ocean with the emigrants, and on the 24th of June, 1855, he received a letter from Dr. Peter Fjellstedt containing a call for him to become pastor of the Swedish Lutheran congregation at Sugar Grove, Pa. His first thought was to decline positively, but the more he considered the matter, the more clearly he discerned it as his duty to accept. In August the same year he had a personal meeting with Dr. Fjellstedt, when that devout and warm-hearted divine urged him to go to the assistance of his countrymen in the West. Dr. Fjellstedt promised to help him procure the needed funds and to render every assistance. Finally Swensson, after much trepidation, decided to accept the call, although still very much worried over the pecuniary phase of the situation, which seemed all the more grave as he was about to marry his betrothed, Miss Maria Blixt of Unnaryd.

The marriage took place March 29, 1856, and on April 6th he preached his farewell sermon in the Unnaryd church, followed by similar sermons in various churches in the vicinity. Everywhere his many friends contributed more or less freely toward his traveling expenses, so that on reaching Göteborg with his bride he had no less than 800 crowns at his disposal, without having borrowed a penny. Here the young couple were detained from April 22nd to May 20th, before embarking on the ship "Minona" for America. With prayers and blessings for friends left behind, he sailed away from his native land which he was never to see again. After a voyage of six weeks' duration, they reached New York on the very birthday of the republic, July 4th. The 11th of the same month he arrived at Sugar Grove, and preached his first sermon there two days later. His first impression of the people was not entirely favorable. Even those who confessed themselves Christians seemed strange to him. On every hand liberty seemed to have been turned into license. All this set him wondering whether, after all, his field of greatest usefulness did not lie in the old country.

His doubts as to his calling and the resultant melancholy were somewhat relieved when in the fall of the same year he visited Illinois

Rev. Jonas Swensson

and here met elder brethren whose acquaintance and fellowship gave him new courage. During the conference and synod meetings he attended he sat quietly listening to the proceedings, never uttering a word. But no one followed the transactions more attentively than he. After having preached in several of the Swedish churches here, he returned to the East and took up his work with renewed energy.

In Sugar Grove a little frame church had been built before Rev. Swensson's arrival, but it was not yet finished, and the parsonage was still in course of erection. In Jamestown, where Swensson was also to preach, there was no church edifice. Strife and differences existing with respect to the temporal affairs of the churches were a constant source of worry and sorrow to a man of his sensitive nature, but what affected him still more was the spiritual indifference and the bitter partisanship stirred up by the aforesaid Bergenlund and by the Methodists. Such a condition naturally revolted against Swensson's strict sense of propriety and his devotion to good order in the church. His concern for the welfare of the congregations, however, kept him at his post. Not even the flattering call to become assistant to Rev. Erland Carlsson of the Immanuel Church in Chicago could induce him to leave.

But there came a time when he thought it his duty to leave his first field of labor in this country. The church at Andover was about to be torn asunder by internal dissensions fomented by the intrigues of Bergenlund, and stood in great need of an able and energetic pastor. Such a man was found in Rev. Swensson, to whom a call was extended in June, 1858. At the earnest solicitations of his brethren, who were familiar with the sad state of affairs, he accepted the call and removed to his new charge the following September. Here, as in Sugar Grove and Jamestown, he had to reap the bitter fruits of Bergenlund's operations. With his installation as pastor of the Andover church Sept. 19th, Swensson's main life work began. For fifteen years he remained here, doing a great work not only for the local church but also in behalf of the entire Augustana Synod. For this reason the Synod classes Rev. Jonas Swensson as one of its founders and pioneers. The Andover congregation which had a membership of 356 when Rev. Esbjörn left, had increased to 400 when Swensson arrived. The settlement developed rapidly in every direction. As early as 1858 a church was built in that part of the locality known as Berlin, situated eight miles away, and on the 17th of February, 1859, a congregation was organized at that place. Next in order the Woodhull congregation was organized in 1868, followed by the New Windsor church in 1869, that of Orion in 1870, and finally the Cambridge congregation in 1875. At all these places Rev. Swensson alone preached for many years. At Berlin he held services regularly every other Saturday until 1866 when the church obtained a pastor of its own. Considering that Swensson usually preached two or three times each Sunday, held catechetical meetings at certain seasons of the year in the various districts of the settlement, made numerous visits to the sick, attended synods, conferences and other church conventions, often visited and preached in vacant congregations, and also looked out for the financial interests of his own church, meanwhile being almost constantly hampered by sickness in his own family, it appears that Swensson was a very busy man. The wonder is that he found time for it all. During the last three years of his life, he was also president of the synod, an office which alone would give the average clergyman all that he could do. For several years prior, Swensson held the position of synodical secretary.

Although in good health, it seems a miracle that Swensson, strenuously as he worked, did not give out much earlier than he did. It never occurred to him to husband his strength. He considered it his

The Present Swedish Lutheran Church, Andover

duty to sacrifice himself in the service of the church and at no time could he be persuaded to take a few months' rest. Often, after spending eight or nine hours in church, preaching, catechising and administering the sacraments, as on confirmation days, he would sit up till twelve o'clock with a few intimate friends, talking, singing and playing; yet the next morning would find him up at four and busy currying the horses in order to be ready to start out on his official rounds immediately after breakfast.

The little church which had been erected during Rev. Esbjörn's term of service at Andover, shortly after Rev. Swensson's coming was found too small, and in 1864 it was decided to erect a new one. The work on the new building, which was not begun until 1867, gave Rev. Swensson, as well as the church council and the building committee, a great deal of additional work and worry. On Nov. 15, 1868, the congregation moved into the new edifice, this being made the occasion of an impressive jubilee celebration. The new church, however, was not finished until 1874, the year after Rev. Swensson's death, when it was dedicated with solemn ceremonies on the 23rd day of August. The church completed represented an outlay of $30,985, not counting the work performed gratuitously by members of the congregation. This church still stands as a fitting monument to Rev. Swensson and his noble endeavors, in the same sense that the old one was a testimonial to the energy of his predecessor, Esbjörn. During the last year of Swensson's life, the congregation attained to a membership of 1,855, of whom 951 were communicants.

As a preacher, Swensson was always popular. When he got thoroughly warmed up on a certain text, he would preach for two or three hours without a sign of physical exhaustion or waning interest in his topic. He never affected oratory or poetic flights of imagination, his sermons, simple and logical, addressing themselves to the reason and not to the feelings of his audience. His preaching was principally of the didactic order, bearing a striking resemblance to that of the famous Swedish preacher Anders Nohrborg. Swensson had an aversion to preaching or speaking at public celebrations and festive occasions. He was a model shepherd of his flock. The sick he visited with a regularity prompted by large-hearted sympathy rather than a sense of official duty, and he was never known to neglect a sickbed on account of inclement weather, bad roads or unseasonable hours, day or night. In his frequent travels between the distant points under his spiritual charge, he became an expert driver, with few rivals in the art of handling horses. He was generally in a hurry, this good parson, and when he whizzed by on his regular tours between Andover and Berlin, puffing great clouds of smoke from his pipe, he bore more than a remote resemblance to a railway locomotive going with a full head of steam. He was equally conscientious and businesslike in his attention to his duties as president of the synod. Its sessions were conducted in an orderly, parliamentary manner and with scrupulous fairness to all sides. He had a tender heart and, although a man of meager income, he would invariably give a helping hand to those in need. Swensson was of tall stature and fine build, and possessed a powerful, though rather inflexible and unmusical voice, which carried well even in as large an auditorium as that of the new Andover church. In his personality he combined dignity with artlessness and simplicity. He abhorred hypocrisy and affectation. While reticent in a crowd, he was a good talker and an entertaining companion among his intimate friends.

During his later years, Swensson was subject to attacks of gout accompanied by spasms, followed by fainting spells. This affection caused his death. He passed away in his home at Andover Dec. 20, 1873, at the early age of forty-five. His wife survived him by only one year. A monument erected by the congregation marks the spot in the old church-yard where reposes this energetic and faithful pastor of the Andover church. He left four children, three sons and one daughter, viz., Rev. Carl Aron Swensson, Ph. D., renowned as the founder and president of Bethany College, at Lindsborg, Kans., who died in Los Angeles, Cal., Feb. 16, 1904; John Swensson, manager of the Gustaf Adolf orphanage at Jamestown, N. Y.; Luther Swensson, former postmaster at Lindsborg, Kans., and Mrs. Anna Carlsson of Lindsborg.

Rev. Swensson's duties as preacher and pastor left him no time for literary work. A modest little pamphlet on a religious topic, published by him while still in Sweden, is the only published product of his pen.

Omitting details, the further story of the Andover church may be briefly told. After a vacancy of one and one-half years, Rev. Swensson's place was filled in the spring of 1875 by Rev. Erland Carlsson, of Chicago, another of the venerable pioneers of the Swedish Lutheran Church of America. He had charge until 1884, when ill health compelled him to resign. In 1875 a parsonage was built at a cost of $3,600.

Rev. Carlsson devoted himself to the watering of the spiritual seed sown by Swensson in this field, and in this as well as in his efforts to educate the children and keep the young people in the church he succeeded remarkably well. After being three years without a permanent pastor, the church in 1887 called Rev. Victor Setterdahl who labored here for a period of eighteen years, or until the spring of 1905. In March, 1900, the fiftieth anniversary of the Andover church was celebrated with festivities befitting the occasion. The successor of Setterdahl is Rev. Carl P. Edblom. In 1906, the church had a total membership of 1,120, of whom 684 were communicants.

The Andover church is not only the oldest of the Swedish Lutheran churches in this country but also one of the richest, most stable and most conservative. It would be hard to find a church anywhere whose members are so generally well-to-do and financially independent as are the parishioners of Andover. A visitor today does not easily realize that little more than half a century ago the first Swedish settlers began to build homes in this locality, organize themselves into a congregation and erect a church, all this under the most discouraging conditions.

Rev. Tuve Nilsson Hasselquist

The second in order of the ministers of the Swedish state church who came over during the pioneer days in order to minister to the spiritual wants of their poor and widely scattered fellow countrymen in Illinois was Rev. T. N. Hasselquist from Skåne. He came here in the autumn of 1852 and for almost forty years aided in framing and up-building the Swedish Lutheran Church of America in various capacities, as pastor, as editor of the church paper and for a period of thirty years as president of its college and theological seminary. Esbjörn and Hasselquist are the central figures around which are grouped all the principal events of the early days of the Swedish Lutheran Church of this country. While the work of Esbjörn, the founder, is of primary importance to Swedish Lutherans in Illinois and all America, that of Hasselquist was no less significant, including, as it did, both the task of developing and establishing the church on the foundations already laid and of taking up new lines of work, for instance, the founding of the first Swedish newspaper in the United States as the organ of that church.

Tuve Nilsson Hasselquist was born in the parish of Ousby, in northern Skåne, March 2, 1816. His parents were country folk of the substantial sort. Their sons were given a fairly thorough education at home. Rev. Collin, the rector of the parish, having noticed that the boy Tuve had a good head for study, urged his father to send him to school to fit him for a learned career. Consequently, at the age of fourteen, he entered a school at Kristianstad and there adopted the name of Hasselquist, from that of his native place Hasslaröd.

After only five years, young Hasselquist passed the examination for admission to the university of Lund, where he began his theological studies after being engaged for some time as a private tutor. He was examined for the ministry by the Lund chapter and ordained by Bishop Faxe the day before midsummer, in 1839, being at once appointed curate of the parishes of Everlöf and Slimminge. Here he remained for one year, and was subsequently assigned to Kristianstad. After another year, he was transferred in 1842 to the parishes of Glimåkra and Örkened in the northeast corner of the province.

Young as he was, Rev. Hasselquist was already widely known for his true Christian character and his devotion to his pastoral calling. His sermons were full of spirit and power. Not confining himself to the Sunday morning sermon, he held Bible study meetings on Sunday afternoons and other religious meetings here and there in the parish during the week. He had the reputation of being a very earnest "revivalist preacher," and was a zealous temperance advocate, often appearing on the same platform with that warm-hearted temperance agitator Pehr Wieselgren.

In 1845, after serving there for three years, he became curate under old Rector Nordström of Önnestad, after whose death he became temporary rector of the church. The arrival of Hasselquist to Önnestad marked the beginning of a period of spiritual revival for that locality. He labored assiduously, sowing the seed of truth, and was gratified to notice that it bore rich fruit. Toward the end of the forties, Hasselquist was assigned as curate to Åkarp and Wittsjö, in northern Skåne, where he labored for several years. His time of service as assistant pastor was thirteen years in all. His frequent transfers from place to place gave him the advantage of an extensive personal acquaintance throughout a large part of northern Skåne. He thus became widely known for his Christian zeal and sincerity, his ability as a preacher and his earnest efforts to substitute good morals for the prevalent license of the times.

Had he remained in Sweden, Hasselquist would doubtless very soon have occupied a prominent place among the clergy. But providence had decreed that he was to serve, not the state church of Sweden, but the Lutheran Church at large by becoming a pioneer of Lutheranism and of general culture in a foreign land. It was a trifling circumstance that primarily brought about Hasselquist's emigration. Rev. Esbjörn greatly needed an assistant in his work among the Swedes of Illinois, and was casting about for a suitable man. The outlook was not encouraging, and for a time it seemed as though these people were to be left to the choice between joining American churches and living without any church connections whatever. At this juncture, a settler named Ola Nilsson, hailing from Önnestad, came to the assistance of Rev. Esbjörn. He knew Hasselquist well and suggested that he would undoubtedly come, provided he were fully convinced of the urgent need of spiritual workers among his fellow countrymen here.

Rev. Esbjörn promptly followed his friend's advice. He arranged to have the newly organized congregation in Galesburg call Hasselquist as pastor, with the promise of a small salary. In addition, Esbjörn obtained a small appropriation from the American Board of Home Missions. Rev. Hasselquist received the call in the early part of the year 1852. Looking upon it as a call not only from the Swedes of Galesburg, but directly from God, he accepted it without hesitation, although his chances for promotion in the state church were the best.

Before starting on his long and significant voyage, he was united

in marriage to his heart's choice, Miss Eva Helena Cervin of Kristianstad, a woman of exceptional strength of character, who was to be of
inestimable assistance to him in the great work he was about to under-
take in the new country.

Accompanied by his bride and a party of sixty emigrants from
northern Skåne, Hasselquist left for America late in the summer of
1852. The party arrived in New York Sept. 28th, thence taking the
usual route to Chicago. The Synod of Northern Illinois was just in
session in the latter city, and there Hasselquist and Esbjörn now met
for the first time. We can readily imagine the cordiality of this meeting. Hasselquist was at once admitted to the synod and soon thereafter
preached his first sermon in this country. After adjournment of the
synod, he left for Andover, whence Esbjörn took him and his wife
across country to Galesburg, a twenty-five mile ride over the worst
kind of country roads.

The reception accorded the new pastor by his church was rather
discouraging. It was a raw and drizzly autumn day. Everything
about the place had a poverty-stricken appearance. There was no
delegation of church members to bid him welcome, and no home in
readiness to receive him. Just outside the town, Esbjörn with his
guests met a Swedish settler, and, thinking to please the man, introduced Hasselquist as the new Swedish pastor. Instead of politely
bidding him welcome, the Swede rudely inquired, "What business has
he got to come here?"

The congregation in Galesburg was a very small one. Organized
in 1851, just a year before, it had only a few members, all poor, and
neither a church nor a parsonage. All this might have been ignored,
however, had it only been what it purported to be, a Lutheran church,
but such was not the case. It was more Congregationalist than anything else, being under the influence of the American Congregationalists, with students from Knox College, a Congregationalist institution, conducting its Sunday school.

Rev. Hasselquist and his bride were assigned quarters in a little
shanty, half of which was occupied by a former Erik Janssonist,
addicted to drink. The man was comparatively peaceable, but his wife
was a veritable virago who kept lecturing and cursing her liege lord
from morning till night. Here, indeed, extremes met under one roof:
on one side of the partition there was quarreling and cursing, on the
other, praying and singing. The Hasselquists occupied two rooms, the
one fair-sized, the other a mere closet. The first was made to serve as
sitting-room, study, parlor, kitchen and bedchamber combined. The
furniture was in keeping with some of these functions, while most of
the things making for home comfort were lacking. At first they had

no bed, but slept on the floor; the trunk in which Hasselquist had brought his books had to do duty as a dining table. The roof of this primitive dwelling leaked so badly that the floor was flooded every time it rained.

Hasselquist's First Home in Galesburg

Thus Rev. Hasselquist began his labors in Galesburg under anything but favorable auspices. Not only was the congregation a small and poor one, and split up by divergences in religious beliefs, but worse still, there was a general opinion decidedly antagonistic to Swedish

Lutheran church work in this locality. From the neighboring Bishop Hill colony many persons who had tired of the Prophet Erik Jansson and now were indifferent to religion in any form had moved into Galesburg. On the other hand, there was the Swedish Methodist stronghold at Victoria which had extended its operations to Galesburg and there made many converts. And after the year 1852 the Baptists added a third element of opposition. To all these people a Swedish Lutheran clergyman, in the garb of the state church and following its prescribed ritual, was not much better than a Catholic. The Methodists, in particular, made Esbjörn and Hasselquist out to be spiritually dead, although in the old country these same men had been looked upon as altogether too zealous and devout in their Christianity to suit the free and easy church members.

By his preaching and his living, Hasselquist, however, soon disproved the statements of his antagonists. But he found greater difficulty in overcoming the prejudices entertained against him by the professors at Knox College. These men evidently held a poor opinion of the Swedish clergy to whom they considered themselves far superior in every respect. Eventually, they learned to know him as a man of erudition, zeal and earnestness in his calling, qualities which compelled their respect.

Among the very first cares that fell upon Hasselquist's shoulders was the task of raising funds for a church building. With much difficulty the means were procured and a church erected, which not long after was found inadequate and had to be enlarged. The field was constantly being extended, so that at the synodical meeting of 1853 Hasselquist could report that his pastorate consisted of no less than four congregations, with a total of 191 communicants. The four congregations referred to were those of Galesburg and Knoxville and, supposedly, Wataga and Altona. The Sunday school of the Galesburg congregation, which up to that time had been in the hands of the Congregationalists, was reorganized in August, 1853, and at that time consisted of five teachers and 27 pupils.

Rev. Hasselquist remained at Galesburg for eleven years. During this period, besides his pastoral work in the local field, he carried on an extensive missionary work both in Illinois and in adjacent states. Numberless were his journeys during these eleven years, and beset with the hardships that attended travel in those days, when railroads were still unknown in this territory. A number of new congregations were founded by him, among which the Immanuel Church of Chicago. His missionary field extended eastward all the way to New York and to the north as far as Minnesota. In the new country Hasselquist evinced the same qualities that distinguished him in Sweden, only in

a more potent degree. His zeal was increased and his love of his
fellow countrymen grew in warmth when he saw what was their condition, spiritually and materially.

Rev. Tuve Nilsson Hasselquist

In the intense opposition he encountered, even within his own
church, he had ample cause for not strictly adhering to the ritualism
of the state church of Sweden. Within and without his congregation
there were many who cherished not the slightest respect for the re-

ligious usages of their forefathers, but had the greatest admiration for everything that they knew or supposed to be American.

Among the growing number of Swedish Lutheran churches of America Hasselquist early came to be recognized as a very efficient man. · And when the Augustana Synod was organized he was chosen its first president. To this responsible position he was subsequently re-elected each year for a decade. This was the patriarchal period in the history of the synod. Hasselquist was no stickler on parliamentary law, the main thing with him being to get a clear and many-sided view of the subject in hand for the purpose of arriving at a good, sensible decision. Whether or not such decision was in accord with the intricate rules of debate caused him no worry. Nevertheless, he could not be accused of despotism or arbitrariness. He was simply a father among the brethren. Though not in name, yet in fact he was the bishop of the widely scattered congregations of the synod, among which he made frequent official visits, learning to know his people and becoming known by them.

The life work of Hasselquist, however, was neither that of a pastor nor of a synodical president; it was to be performed in the capacity of president of the Augustana Theological Seminary, to which was subsequently added a complete college. In 1863 Hasselquist was elected the successor of Rev. Esbjörn as president of that institution, a position in which he was destined to exert a far-reaching influence.

Previous reference has been made to Hasselquist as the founder of the Swedish press of the United States. He earned that title in the autumn of 1854 when he began preparations for publishing from Galesburg "Gamla och Nya Hemlandet," the first Swedish-American newspaper, whose first issue appeared on Jan.3, the following year. Hasselquist held the position of editor for four years, until 1858. In 1856 he also founded a religious paper, "Det Rätta Hemlandet," from which sprung "Augustana," the present organ of the Augustana Synod. From 1868 to 1889 this paper was published under the name of "Augustana och Missionären," Hasselquist continuing these twenty-one years as its editor. He is also author of several books of a religious character.

In 1881 Rev. Hasselquist lost his wife through death, their daughter Hanna having died four years before; and ten years after his wife's death the venerable patriarch himself passed away. He died Feb. 4, 1891, and at his funeral both the speakers and the great silent assemblage bore testimony to the great loss sustained by the Swedish-American nationality. Hasselquist left two sons, Nathanael and Joshua, and a daughter, Esther.

Among the marks of distinction conferred upon Hasselquist may mentioned the title of Doctor of Divinity by Muhlenberg College and the order of the Polar Star by King Oscar of Sweden.

Lutheran Work in Galesburg

The foundation for Swedish Lutheran church work in Galesburg was laid in November, 1849, by Rev. L. P. Esbjörn. In the early part of 1850, the building of a small meeting-house was begun at his suggestion and with his coöperation. The sum of $550 was subscribed as early as Feb. 28th. Although many Americans interested themselves in the undertaking, the work was delayed, and not until the latter part of May the foundation, outer walls and steeple were constructed. The foundation was of brick, the superstructure of frame and the dimensions of the building were, length, 40 feet, width, 30 feet, and height, 18 feet. As yet, the congregation had not been organized, owing to the opposition of the Methodists.

Aug. 24, 1851, Rev. Esbjörn, on request, held communion services at Galesburg and after services the names of those wishing to become members of a Swedish Lutheran congregation were asked to give their names. Forty persons responded and these constituted the first Swedish Lutheran congregation of that city. In the fall of the same year, Rev. Esbjörn designated Gustaf Palmquist, a former school-teacher from Sweden, as pastor of the church. He gained the confidence of the people, but being a Baptist at heart, although not a confessed one, his work was not calculated to strengthen, but rather to disrupt and weaken the church, whose members were already wavering between the Methodist and the Congregational faith. In June, 1852, Palmquist joined the Baptists and celebrated the event by calling a jubilee meeting in the Lutheran meeting-house, at which he declared that not until now had he obeyed the will of God in receiving the Christian baptism. To show the nature of the Methodist opposition to Lutheran work in Galesburg it may be stated that Rev. Jonas Hedström, by spreading the report that the Swedish Lutherans in the place were a mere handful, that they differed very little from the Catholics, succeeded in dampening the interest of the Americans in the Lutheran meeting-house to the extent that many of them repudiated their subscriptions toward its erection. By intrigue, the building, before completion, fell into the hands of the American Methodists, the Lutherans, however, being privileged to use it. After the arrival of Rev. Hasselquist, the Swedish Lutheran congregation purchased the building for the sum of $1,600, and shortly afterward had it enlarged. This first church edifice stood on the same spot where the present church is located. Having now a house of worship of their own, the Swedish Lutherans were in a better position to avoid undue influence from the other denominations. The

church was neither lighted nor provided with seats, making it necessary for the churchgoers to bring their own chairs and tallow candles.
In spite of the latter, the gloom that pervaded the edifice of a Sunday
night was so dense that the preacher was scarcely able to distinguish
his hearers.

In the cholera epidemic of 1854, the church suffered the loss of a
number of members. The scourge, however, had the effect of causing a
spiritual revival among the survivors, and Hasselquist seized this favorable opportunity to work upon the hearts of his flock by holding meetings every evening for one week during the month of August. He was

The First Swedish Lutheran Church of Galesburg, Erected in 1852

assisted by Rev. M. F. Hokanson of New Sweden, Ia. The result of
the week's work was that about one hundred persons applied for membership in the churches at Galesburg and Knoxville. In the latter
place the ravages of the pest were greater than at Galesburg, craving
no less than forty victims among the Swedes.

In the fall of 1855, Rev. Hasselquist obtained an assistant in the
person of P. A. Cederstam, a theological student from Chicago who was
licensed to preach the following March. Owing to the great lack of
ministers, he was not long permitted to remain here, but was sent to
Minnesota the following May. A year later Hasselquist received a new
assistant in his brother-in-law, A. R. Cervin, a teacher from the old
country, who aided him in the work for more than a year.

There was much ungodliness to contend with during this period, necessitating a very strict application of church discipline. The warnings and admonitions of these men being left unheeded, excommunication was resorted to. Drunkenness and licentiousness were the vices most prevalent. Dancing, improper conduct in church and negligence in attending divine services were also causes for disciplinary measures.

Surrounded on all sides by those who hated everything savoring of the cult and practices of the Swedish state church, Rev. Hasselquist was driven too far in his concessions to the customs and usages of the American Reformed churches. Thus, it was no uncommon thing for him to make his appearance in church of a Sunday morning dressed in a white linen duster in place of the black clerical coat, and walk down the aisle singing one of Ahnfelt's songs in which the congregation would join. He would then go directly to the pulpit, read a text, offer a prayer and then commence preaching. Suddenly he would interrupt himself by singing another familiar song, subsequently picking up the thread of his discourse where he had dropped it. The services would end as unceremoniously as they began. These concessions to arbitrary usage were not without effect on the congregation. A faction was formed that held it to be wrong for the minister to wear a coat of clerical cut, read the confession or follow the ritual. These persons also considered it wrong to remain standing during the reading of the gospel and epistle text before the altar, and consequently remained seated when the congregation arose. They demanded that the pastor should sit, and not stand, before the altar, and insisted that he discard the clerical neck-band. They made so much of this that when Håkan Olsson, one of Hasselquist's pupils, after ordination appeared with that mark of the ecclesiastical office, one of the deacons stepped up to him with the evident intention of tearing that innocent little article of apparel from his neck. This movement, which at first seemed insignificant, developed to such an extent that even before Hasselquist left Galesburg lists were circulated for the purpose of soliciting members for a free church. Such a one was established in 1869 under the name of the Second Lutheran Church of Galesburg. Such was the result of Hasselquist's thoughtless departure from a strict conformity to orthodox usage in the church of his native land.

When Rev. Esbjörn returned to Sweden, Rev. Hasselquist became his successor as president of the Augustana Theological Seminary, taking his new position in 1863. In the fall of the same year Rev. A. W. Dahlsten assumed charge of the Galesburg church, preaching there once a month until New Year's, 1864, when he removed to Galesburg. The influence of the saloons and the dance halls at this time was a great source of worry to the pastor and the church council. The

disturbing element from the time of Hasselquist was still active and
had acquired added strength. Certain persons worked with might and
main against the pastor and to have the existing order of services
abolished, demanding that any clergyman, no matter of what denomination, should have the right to preach in their church. When this was
refused, they sent a petition to the synod, setting forth these demands,
adding the request that part of the liturgical service be abolished.

The synod positively refused to grant the petition, whereupon the
petitioners set to work on a plan to secede from the synod. They failed
again. At a special meeting of the church, a large majority of the
congregation resolved to abide by the decision of the synod.

The First Swedish Lutheran Church of Galesburg, Erected in 1870

In 1868 the old church, which had been enlarged by an addition
during Hasselquist's time, was found to be too small and a new edifice
was planned. At first it was decided to build a second addition at one
end of the old structure, but as this would involve a considerable expense without affording the space needed either for the present or for
the future, this plan was given up. Next it was resolved to widen the
church by moving the side walls, but this plan also fell through.
Finally, the congregation resolved to erect an entire new edifice, to be
100x60 feet, but only $400 being subscribed, the whole enterprise was
abandoned for the time being. The following year the matter was
again taken up and on the 4th of April a resolution was passed to begin
building as soon as $2,000 had been subscribed.

Rev. Dahlsten having resigned after serving the church for six
years, the congregation, a few days after deciding to build a new
church, extended a call to Rev. A. Andreen to succeed Dahlsten. Fif-

teen members left the church and, together with a few others, organized
the proposed free church. During the ensuing vacancy, several others
deserted. This had the effect of cleansing the church from that unwholesome and pernicious element which for some time past had
created disturbances and stunted the growth of the congregation. Rev.
Andreen declined the call, and the church again called Rev. Hasselquist only to receive a negative answer. Next a call was extended to
Rev. N. Th. Winquist of DeKalb, who accepted and remained in charge
for somewhat over three years. During his term, the new church was
finished and the final report of the work was rendered March 4, 1870.
The edifice was found to have cost $13,371.75, of which amount $6,784
had been raised by subscription, the balance representing debt. This
church, which for many years was the largest in the city, is still used
as a house of worship. Its dimensions are: length, 100 feet; width, 60
feet; height of side walls, 22 feet; height of steeple, 165 feet. The task
of reducing the church debt was next taken up, and much was accomplished, partly by subscription, partly by the collection of pew rents.
At this juncture, the members living at Henderson left and organized a
congregation of their own. The schoolhouse was moved and provided
with new seats, and new life was injected into the work of construction; a church bell was purchased; the parsonage was renovated, and
about this time the new constitution for the churches, revised by the
synod, was adopted.

Rev. Winquist left in 1873 and was succeeded in the fall of the
same year by Rev. S. P. A. Lindahl. The peace and harmony that had
prevailed during the time of Rev. Winquist was disturbed by one F.
Lagerman, who filled the pulpit in the interval, sharply criticising in
his sermons everything that fell below his exalted standard of Lutheranism. By coolheadedness and a conciliatory policy, the new pastor
succeeded in restoring peace, the work progressing smoothly thereafter. In 1878 the church purchased an organ at a cost of $2,350 and
built a new parsonage. A house and lot was bought, the old house was
sold and a new one erected, the total outlay for the new property stopping at $3,000. During Rev. Lindahl's time in Galesburg, the church
carried on a vigorous campaign against the secret societies, but in
spite of this and other disturbing influences the church, on the whole,
made steady progress.

In November, 1884, Rev. Lindahl resigned his .charge. He was
succeeded by Rev. C. A. Bäckman of Ishpeming, Mich., who moved to
his new field July 1st, the following year. In the summer of 1885 a
large and commodious schoolhouse was erected. A year later, the
church was renovated at an outlay of $1,300, and in 1887 a hall was
provided for the young people by raising the schoolhouse, the total

expense amounting to $1,300. Societies were organized and several new lines of endeavor were taken up.

Rev. Bäckman, however, was not permitted long to labor in this field, death cutting short his promising career on March 6, 1888, before he had completed his thirty-fifth year. The vacancy was temporarily supplied by a student who by his personal conduct created the most serious disruption in the stormy history of the congregation, resulting a couple of years later in the expulsion of no less than 236 communicant members. The effects of this schism were felt for years afterward.

This movement was headed by C. A. Nybladh, who subsequently became a minister of the Episcopal Church. From his following the Swedish Episcopal Church of Galesburg was organized.

The permanent successor of Rev. Bäckman was Rev. C. J. E. Haterius whose installation took place April 11, 1889. His first years at Galesburg were made disagreeable by the effects of the foregoing dissension. In 1891, an addition was built to the church affording space for the organ and the choir, besides a pastor's study. The cost of these improvements amounted to $1,276.

The question of starting English work within the church now began to be much ventilated, resulting in the calling of an English assistant April 18, 1896. Having received a negative answer, the congregation, at a second business meeting, called for the same purpose June 19th, was advised to permit those especially interested in the English work to take up such work under the auspices of the church council with a view to organizing an independent English Lutheran church. The young people's hall was set aside for the English services. This plan was not carried out, but the English question in this instance was solved by arranging for the holding of divine services in the English language at certain intervals during the year.

In the summer of 1898, Rev. Haterius resigned and was succeeded Nov. 1st by Rev. Peter Peterson of Essex, Ia. The next summer, the church edifice underwent a thorough renovation at a cost of $1,894, and besides a number of old debts were paid. From this time on the work has progressed without friction.

Rev. Peterson left the charge in 1905, removing to St. Paul. His successor is Rev. F. A. Johnsson, one of the abler young pastors of the Illinois Conference. At New Year's, 1907, the church had a membership of 1,672, including 1,198 communicants. The church property was valued at $36,450.

The Lutheran Congregation in Moline

As previous pages will show, Rev. Esbjörn at an early day took up mission work at Moline and Rock Island. When visiting Moline, he generally stopped at the home of Carl Johansson, a tailor, the second Swedish settler in the place. Johansson occupied a 14 by 16 room in a brick house belonging to one Mrs. Bell, and here the first Swedish Lutheran services were held. Johansson later became a very zealous Baptist and a bitter antagonist of the Lutherans.

At first the Swedish Lutherans of Moline were enrolled in the Andover church. This arrangement being found impracticable, a separate congregation was organized in Moline Dec. 1, 1850, with fifty charter members. This number soon increased. There being as yet no book of record for the church, the names of applicants were recorded on loose slips of paper.

The first question arising after the organization of the congregation was how to get a church edifice. A lot was purchased for the sum of $100, and the next summer they began to build, having received for this purpose $340 out of the $2,200 solicited by Esbjörn in the East. The balance was raised among the Americans and the Swedish settlers of Moline. This little church, a frame structure 36 by 24 and 15 feet high, was situated on the same spot where stands the present one, and was built at a cost of $646. The building was not finished for many years, yet served its purpose. On Sunday, Jan. 11, 1857, it was ultimately dedicated as a house of worship, the steeple having been finished just the day before and provided with a bell purchased at a cost of $50. This was the first church bell of any Swedish Lutheran church in America since the days of the Delaware Swedes. It is now the property of the Swedish Lutheran church of Port Byron, Ill. The year after the dedication, a fourteen foot addition to the church was built, and in 1866 a 12 by 14 addition was made. The structure was finally sold to the plow manufacturing firm of Deere and Company and moved across the street, where it is used as a storehouse for agricultural implements.

The first parsonage owned by the congregation consisted of a small house and lot, donated in 1854 by a bachelor, Abraham Andersson from Gnarp, Helsingland, on condition that it be used as the home of the Swedish Lutheran pastor. This property was located in the northeast corner of the block lying just north of the block in which the church is situated. This modest little parsonage was rebuilt in 1856. In 1858 the church property was valued as follows, church, $14,000; parsonage, $850.

Rev. Esbjörn was himself in charge of this field for the first five years, but was obliged to leave part of the work to others. In the summer of 1852, he formed the acquaintance of a young man by the name of C. J. Valentin, from Stockholm, a former salesman, possessing very little schooling but much religious fervor and great zeal in behalf of the Lutheran Church. In October, 1852, at a time of great lack of ministerial timber, Valentin was examined before the Synod of Northern Illinois and given a license to preach and administer the sacraments in Moline and Rock Island. Valentin almost immediately clashed with the Baptists in Rock Island, the conflict growing so bitter during the early part of 1853 that Valentin had to leave the community.

From Moline Valentin went to Princeton, where he served the Swedish Lutherans for a short time. At the synodical convention in

The First Swedish Lutheran House of Worship in Moline

Galesburg in the fall he was absent but appears nevertheless to have had his license renewed. At the subsequent synod in Peru, his license was again renewed, on condition that he take up studies under the direction of Esbjörn. Instead of so doing, he returned to Sweden without leave of absence, remaining there for a few years. At the synod of 1855 he was suspended and deprived of his license until he should return to the synod, provided, however, that the license would be renewed, should he be found worthy of reinstatement into the ministerial office. Nothing was now heard of him for several years. During the Civil War, he reappeared in this country and enlisted as a volunteer in Company D, of the 57th Illinois Infantry. He proved, however, no better a soldier in the ranks of the Union army than in those of the church. As he had deserted his little flock in Princeton, so he now deserted his regiment, fleeing to Sweden, whence he sent a written statement declaring that his conscience would not permit him to fight for the Union cause, his sympathies being on the side of the confederates. After the close of the war, he is believed to have again returned to this country.

After Valentin left Moline, the services were conducted by one of the deacons, named Carl Lindman, a native of Jersnäs parish, in Småland. This man, who was a mason by trade, was exceptionally gifted mentally and spiritually, was well informed and ready of speech, and was uncompromising in matters of right and wrong. In his capacity of deacon he did a great deal of good for the church.

The congregation, nevertheless, was greatly in need of a pastor, surrounded as it was by Methodists and Baptists, who made every effort to gain proselytes among its members. In 1854, Rev. P. A. Ahlberg of Sweden was called and promised to come, but subsequently declined. Through the medium of Dr. Peter Fjellstedt a call was then extended in 1855 to O. C. T. Andrén, curate of Carlshamn, who accepted and came over on July 3¼, 1856, to take charge.

Rev. Andrén remained in Moline only four years, but in that short time accomplished much for the good of the church, the fruits of his efforts being apparent for a long time to follow. When he came there, the congregation was small and its members poor, giving him much to do and meager recompense for his work. Moline and Rock Island at that time, and for many years after, were included in one pastorate; besides, he was in charge of churches at Geneseo and other places. One year after his arrival, the church had 172 members. Rev. Andrén was more strict than his predecessors in the exercise of church discipline and was no respecter of persons. He fostered a greater interest in the common affairs of the church body. When the question was put to each of the congregations whether they would be willing to contribute $25 each toward the salary of a Scandinavian professor at the seminary in Springfield, provided such professorship were established, and the matter was presented by Rev. Andrén to his church, the request was at once granted, the amount to be raised by collection. This resolution was passed Sept. 18, 1857. On the 15th of April, 1860, the congregation resolved to withdraw from the Synod of Northern Illinois and declared in favor of organizing an independent Scandinavian synod. The revenues of the church at this time were quite modest. At the annual meeting in May, 1858, the income was reported at $114.14, while the outlay footed up to $124.75, not including the salary of the pastor. The next year the resources had grown to $284.49 and the expenditures to $277.70, but in 1860 the figures dropped to $109.29 and $129.45, respectively, while the church had a debt of $70.15.

Having been chosen by the newly organized Augustana Synod as its representative to solicit funds in Sweden and Norway for the seminary to be established, Rev. Andrén with his family left Moline early in September, 1860, with the intention of returning after accomplishing his mission. This plan was later given up, and on Aug. 11, 1861, he sent in his resignation. Rev. Peters, who had been called to fill the temporary vacancy, was called as regular pastor on the 21st of the same month. Rev. Peters was also in charge of the missions in Rock Island, Geneseo and Fulton. He removed from Moline to Rockford Dec. 29, 1863, leaving the place vacant for two years, during which time the parsonage was rented out and the neighboring pastors, Jonas Swensson, John Johnson and A. W. Dahlsten, took turns in preaching and officiating at ecclesiastical acts. Elections were held time and again, but no call was accepted. Finally, J. S. Benson, a student of the theological seminary at Paxton, was called as preacher and school teacher in 1865. On petition by the church, Benson was ordained the following year and then became its regular pastor. He inspired his congregation to renewed efforts; the church was enlarged and in 1868 a schoolhouse was erected on the vacant portion of the church lot. The members living in Rock Island in 1870 were authorized to organize their own congregation which up to May 1, 1873, remained a part of the same pastorate. In the fall of 1872, Rev. Benson resigned his charge, remaining, however, until August of the following year. He passed away in Marathon, Ia., March 13, 1889.

After several fruitless attempts, the church finally, in the spring of 1874, obtained a new pastor, Rev. A. G. Setterdahl. With him came a period of renewed activity and extensive external improvements were made at considerable cost. All the old buildings were razed to give room for new ones. The old parsonage was sold for $210 and moved to the other side of the street and in its place a more commodious house was erected. On Dec. 8, 1875, the congregation resolved to build a new church, and now, more than ever before, harmony and unity of action was needed. But quite the contrary occurred. That very decision caused a dissension, and a number of dissatisfied ones withdrew to form a new congregation, named the Gustaf Adolf Church, and built their own house of worship in the western part of the village. This congregation later joined the Mission Friends. The old church building was sold and moved off the lot. The cornerstone for the new edifice was laid June 15, 1876. The new building, a brick structure, was 116 feet in length and 62 feet in width, and was provided with a tall, imposing steeple. The building, costing $19,551, was enclosed before Dec. 1st of that year. The following summer Rev. Setterdahl visited Sweden on a leave of absence, with Prof. O. Olsson in charge. The first high mass in the new edifice was preached by him Oct. 13, 1878. In 1879

Rev. Setterdahl resigned and removed to Sweden, where he has been rector of a parish in the province of Östergötland for many years.

In the fall of 1879, Rev. H. O. Lindeblad assumed charge. His was the onerous task of getting the church building completed and furnished. Being a man of business acumen, he proved equal to the occasion, successfully piloting the church through its financial straits. Weary of the burden, he resigned in the fall of 1887, but was prevailed upon to stay, and subsequently completed the work, making it possible

The Present Swedish Lutheran Church in Moline

to dedicate the edifice free of debt June 9, 1889. Besides the financial ones, Rev. Lindeblad had numerous other problems to solve. At the annual meeting of the church in 1887, the faculty of Augustana College in the adjacent city of Rock Island petitioned for permission to organize an English Lutheran congregation at the institution. The petition being denied, the church was nevertheless established and is known as the Grace Lutheran Church, with its house of worship situated in the east end of the city of Rock Island. In 1890 members of the Moline church who resided at or near the college and in the neighborhood lying between the institution and the church in Moline petitioned the annual meeting for permission to organize a new Swedish Lutheran congregation in that same territory. This plan also was realized, the new congregation, named the Zion Church, building a small church near the boundary line between the cities of Rock Island and Moline.

In the spring of 1892, two lots were purchased, one in the east, another in the south part of Moline and chapels were erected where regular weekly services were conducted for the benefit of members residing in those localities.

Rev. Lindeblad again resigned in the spring of 1892 and left the charge Oct. 16th, following. Just one week later, he was succeeded by Rev. C. A. Hemborg. The enlarged field and consequent increase of work necessitated the engagement of theological students from the nearby seminary to assist the pastor. The new minister also had his share of extra work. Both the church and the parsonage were renovated and an addition was built to one of the chapels. A new parsonage was purchased July 1, 1895, at a cost of $5.000, and in 1899 the old one was sold for $4,000. During Rev. Hemborg's term of service the church records were collected and properly arranged in an archive by Mr. G. Lindahl. The church celebrated its fiftieth anniversary Dec. 1, 1900, with appropriate festivities and in connection therewith published an attractive and interesting historical memorial.

In 1904 Rev. Hemborg gave place to Dr. L. A. Johnston of St. Paul, Minn., who still remains in charge. At New Year's, 1907, this church had a total of 1,529 members, 1,110 being communicants. The value of the church property is estimated at $55,000.

Olof Christian Telemak Andrén

Rev. O. C. T. Andrén, although remaining only a few years in this country, by his successful achievements earned an honorable place among the Swedish Lutheran pioneers in the state of Illinois. Olof Christian Telemak Andrén was born in Malmö Sept. 21, 1824, the son of a merchant named Christian Andersson and his wife Johanna, nee Malmquist. After his father's death in 1828, his mother endeavored to make a living for herself and her two children by teaching school, By hard work and great privations she incurred consumption and died in 1830, two years after the death of her husband.

A near relative who had taken the widow and her children into his home sent Olof to the Latin school of Malmö three years later, providing meals for him in a number of families in rotation. He continued his studies under the same arrangement until 1841 when he entered the university of Lund. During these eight years, he had been the laughing-stock of the rich men's sons at the school on account of his poverty and wretched appearance. Mortified by their taunts, the poor orphan repeatedly laid plans for flight, which circumstances, however, prevented him from carrying out.

Leaving the school in his home city about midsummer, he went to Lund and there passed the collegiate examination the following spring.

Not having the means to continue his studies at the university, he gladly accepted a proffered position as private tutor in the province of Småland, where he remained for three years, meanwhile preaching his first sermon in the Hestra parish church. In the autumn of 1845, he returned to Lund entering upon his theological studies. Again he faced a financial struggle during which he often had to go without the common necessaries of life. But his strenuous industry and unflinching energy carried him through, enabling him in the short time of two years to complete his courses and passing his examinations both in theoretical and practical theology in 1847, the former in the spring,

Rev. Olof Christian Telemak Andrén

the latter on Dec. 17th of that year. On the 19th of the same month he was ordained at the early age of twenty-three, by the venerable Bishop Faxe.

During the first three or four years in the ministry, Andrén served as assistant pastor under four elderly clergymen. The last was Rector C. M. Westdahl of Carlshamn, where Andrén remained from February, 1851, to the summer of 1856, when he left for America. At Carlshamn his spiritual life and experience attained to greater fullness, the home of Rector Westdahl, pervaded as it was by taste, tact and refinement, ennobled by Christian culture, furnishing a splendid school for a young clergyman. Andrén also had an extensive field for his pastoral labors, the charge comprising, besides the city of Carlshamn, the large parish of Asarum.

Oct. 3, 1855, Andrén through Dr. Peter Fjellstedt received a call to become pastor of the Swedish Lutheran Church in Moline. After much reflection and hesitation, he finally accepted and left for America the following summer with leave of absence for six years. On May 26, 1856, just before emigrating, he was married to Miss Mathilda Pihl, daughter of Henrik Pihl, adjunct pastor of Ousby parish. The couple traveled by way of Lübeck and Hamburg, landing in New York July 18th and reaching Moline the 31st. An account of his four years' service there having been given in previous pages, it may be added that Andrén also gathered the Swedes of Geneseo into a small congregation of 32 members who built a church at a cost of $1,300.

On Aug. 21, 1860, Rev. Andrén left his charge in Moline never to return. He went back to the old country, arriving in the middle of September. There he immediately set to work soliciting funds for the theological seminary just founded by the Swedish Lutherans of America. He made stirring appeals in Lund, Stockholm, Upsala and other cities, setting forth the need of an educational institution in so convincing a manner that the response came in the form of a fund of no less than 36,000 riksdaler. In order to present the matter to the king in person, he was granted an audience before Charles XV. who listened with favor to his request and tendered as a personal gift to the new institution 5,000 volumes out of his own private library, leaving the choice of books to Rev. Andrén himself. This liberal contribution of money and books from Sweden was of the greatest value to the young Swedish-American institution.

Andrén worked constantly in behalf of Augustana Theological Seminary till the fall of 1861 when he was appointed pastor of Billinge and Röstånga parishes in Skåne to fill a vacancy. While there, Rev. Andrén became involved in a long and disagreeable feud with the organist, Nils Lilja, doctor of philosophy and an author of note, who was finally discharged on the ground of immorality. Lilja appealed from the parish to the Lund chapter which rescinded the action of the congregation and reinstated Dr. Lilja in his former position where he remained until his death.

After having taken the pastoral examination at Lund Jan. 31, 1863, Andrén was elected minister of Asarum, now separated from Carlshamn and made a distinct pastorate, taking charge in the fall of 1866 and laboring with signal success for nearly four years. While visiting typhus patients in several families in May, 1870, Rev. Andrén was smitten with the disease and died on the 11th of the following month. His demise was deeply felt both in Sweden and in this country, Rev. Andrén having everywhere left the impression of a faithful, pious and self-sacrificing pastor.

The Immanuel Church of Chicago

The Swedish Evangelical Lutheran Immanuel Church of Chicago had a peculiar origin. A small party of emigrants from Vestergötland arrived in Chicago in the summer of 1852, and from here they left by boat for Sheboygan, Wis., where they were left helpless, finding no one who was able to understand them and willing to help them. Men, women and children were in hopeless distress. They spent a couple of days among their bags and baggage on the boat landing, and when the boat returned from Chicago, they piled on board again bound for the city whence they had just come. Here they succeeded in obtaining lodging with certain Norwegian families belonging to the Lutheran church organized as early as 1848, and served by Rev. Paul Andersen. Cholera was raging at this time, reaping its greatest harvest among the newly arrived immigrants. One night when several members of the party were attacked by the pest, one of the victims expressed a desire to see a Lutheran minister. Rev. Paul Andersen was sent for at once and did what he could to cheer and comfort the sick and dying, as well as to speak words of encouragement to those in good health and giving them advice and aid.

A firm and fast friendship was thus established between these strangers and the benevolent divine, resulting in most of them, including a few earnest Christians, joining the Norwegian church. Rev. Andersen, however, at once began to lay plans for the organizing of a Swedish Lutheran church, whose first members were to be the Swedish members of the Norwegian church.

When T. N. Hasselquist came to this country in October, 1852, he passed through Chicago and was the guest of Rev. Andersen for a few days. When he left, his host exacted a promise that Hasselquist should return at his first opportunity to preach to his fellow countrymen here and to organize a church among them. After having attended a conference meeting at Moline early in January, 1853, Hasselquist started on his way to Chicago, crowded into a stage coach packed with travelers. He now preached several times to the Swedes in Rev. Andersen's church, and on Sunday, Jan. 16th, he organized the Swedish Lutheran Immanuel Church.

Eighty persons applied for membership at the time. The plan was to call as pastor Rev. J. P. Dahlstedt, of Hofmantorp, Vexiö chapter, in Sweden, but the call was sent through Dr. P. Fjellstedt of Lund, authorizing him to call another man in the event that Rev. Dahlstedt, whose health was poor, should not see fit to accept. Dr. Fjellstedt was obliged to extend the call to Rev. Erland Carlsson, who had served for four years in the chapter of Vexiö. After obtaining his passports from the government, he started on his way to America on the 3rd day of

June, 1853, from Kalmar, via Lübeck, Hamburg, Hull and Liverpool, in a company of 176 emigrants. The ship anchored in New York harbor on Saturday, Aug. 13th, and the party reached Chicago on the 22nd of the same month. Rev. Carlsson was met at the railway station and was given a cordial welcome by members of the church he was to serve. On the following Sunday, being the 14th after Trinity Sunday, he preached his first sermon to his countrymen in Chicago.

The Immanuel Church—Edifice on Superior Street

While the joy over the new pastor was intense, yet the outlook was far from bright. Of the eighty people who had joined the congregation at the outset, there were only thirty-six left, including eight families and twenty single persons. The others had either moved away from the city or joined other churches. Those remaining were all newcomers in poor circumstances. There was not a family among them capable of housing the new pastor, who for that reason was subjected to additional discomfort. In October, 1853, the church joined the Synod of Northern Illinois to which Paul Andersen, L. P. Esbjörn and T. N. Hasselquist, with their churches, already belonged.

The congregation held its first annual business meeting Jan. 27, 1854. At the time of the organization, no minutes had been kept, no church council elected and no constitution adopted. There was no record whatever, beyond the mere list of names of the persons who pledged themselves as members. At this meeting, therefore, it was decided to enter, first of all, in the newly procured record-book, a brief account of the origin of the church. Also a constitution was adopted, which afterward was used as a model for the constitution drawn up for adoption by the congregations of the Augustana Synod. It may be said that the church was legally organized now for the first time, by the election of the following officers: deacons, C. J. Anderson, John Nilson and Isak Peterson; trustees, Johan Björkholm, Göran Svenson and Gisel Trulson.

The same week that Rev. Carlsson arrived, and before he had preached his first sermon, several leading members of the church visited him to consult with regard to the order of services. The question was very guardedly put whether he intended to don the ecclesiastical garb of the Swedish state church, and when he stated that to be his purpose his visitors expressed great satisfaction, explaining that because neither Esbjörn nor Hasselquist had done so when they appeared in Chicago, many had openly declared that they were certainly no Lutheran clergymen, and that if they ever were they had doubtless deserted Lutheranism and its established order.

But these men had had their reasons for departing from established usage. In Andover and Galesburg, at this time, certain groups of church members claiming to correspond to the so-called "readers" of the old country, made much ado about ritualism, attacking Esbjörn and Hasselquist as being spiritually dead, on the ground that they recited prayers out of the churchbook, and characterizing them as superstitious and papistical, believing, as was alleged, that the word and the sacraments would not be efficacious without the use of ecclesiastical garb. For these reasons the pastors in question deemed it a duty to use their liberty as Lutherans in discarding both the ministerial garb and the churchbook. Rev. Carlsson, on the contrary, used both when officiating at high mass, as well as at all ministerial acts. A couple of years later, however, a compromise was agreed on, Rev. Carlsson discarding the gown while the other two pastors returned to the use of the churchbook and the ecclesiastical neck-piece. Such has since been the custom in the Augustana Synod until in recent years the gown has been readopted to a great extent in the East, as also by many clergymen in the West.

The Immanuel Church had great financial and other difficulties to contend with from its inception. The year 1854 was especially fraught with trials and terrors for this church and for the Swedish immigrants in general. The cholera epidemic was then at its height in this country, and the newcomers more than any other class were subject to its ravages. About one-tenth of the communicant members of the church died of the pest and among the children the death rate was very much higher. Next, the congregation was seriously affected by the financial panic of 1857, many of its members being compelled to leave the city in order to look for employment elsewhere. But common afflictions brought the people closer together, and the pastor gladly shared the poverty and sufferings of his flock. During the first three years he had no fixed salary, being dependent on free-will offerings, amounting in 1854 to $116, in 1855 to $180, and in 1856 to $240, as shown by the records of an annual meeting held on the "Thirteenth day of Christmas," 1857, when the salary was fixed at $350 for the coming year. That year the church numbered 204 communicant members.

In 1860, with an adult membership of 220, the church entered upon a new era of its existence. The same year the Augustana Synod was organized, and the Augustana Theological Seminary was established in Chicago and located within the confines of this church. These important steps in advance naturally stimulated the people to increased activity. The times improved. The outbreak of the Civil War caused a great advance in the prices of all commodities. In all lines of employment work became more plentiful, and as a natural result immigration increased. All these things tended to promote the growth and prosperity of the church, which in 1865 had no less than 525 communicant members.

The church edifice which had been purchased of the Norwegian Lutherans in 1854 for the sum of $1,500, had grown too small, although enlarged in the latter year. Mission work was therefore begun on the south side, where services were held every Sunday morning and one evening a week, in a schoolhouse at 21st st. and Arnold avenue. In connection herewith, Rev. Peter Erikson was called as assistant pastor. In 1868 the Salem Church was organized on the south side. At the time the Immanuel Church lost to it a considerable number of its members, yet numbered 1,020 communicants. A new church edifice was needed and in 1869 steps were taken to build one. An imposing structure was built at Sedgwick and Hobbie streets, at a total cost of $34,400. It was dedicated Nov. 7th, that year, but was not completed until 1870. That winter a great revival took place, giving joy to the heart of the pastor and to all faithful Christians within the church. But new trials and difficulties were in store. The great fire destroyed both church buildings, and the majority of the members were made homeless, some being reduced to penury. Many of them left the city and for a time it looked as though the congregation was to be entirely wiped out. But the very first Sunday after the fire, quite a number gathered for worship in a Norwegian church on the west side, and a few days later the church authorities resolved that the church should continue to exist under its legal name, constitution and charter and that, with the help of God, every cent of its debt would be paid. This was a heroic step,

The Immanuel Church—Second Edifice

considering that the debts amounted to $22,600 after deducting the insurance received on the old church building. On the new structure no insurance could be collected.

Not long afterward, the work of clearing away the ruins of the newly built temple was begun. A large number of members volunteered to aid in this work, women and children vying with men and boys. On New Year's Day, 1872, the congregation at its annual meeting appointed a building committee with authority to erect a church similar to the one destroyed in the fire. Work on the new building was not to be begun until at least $10,000 had been raised. When Rev. Carlsson returned home after having visited a number of Swedish churches in the West and both Swedish and other Lutherans in the East for the purpose of soliciting funds, he brought back a little more than the stipulated amount, making it possible to go ahead with the work at once. On Christmas morning following, the congregation was enabled to worship in the basement of the new church, fitted up as a temporary meeting hall. The edifice was not completed until the spring of 1875. It was dedicated on April 4th, and on the same day Rev. C. A. Evald, its new pastor, was inducted into office to succeed Rev. Carlsson, who had resigned by reason of ill health, after serving the church for a period of 22 years. The new church, with steeple, bells and organ still lacking, represented a cost of $31,845. At the annual meeting that year the church debt amounted to $21,558. This was a pressing burden for a long term of years, retarding progress and weighing down the spirits of the members. Subscriptions were taken from time to time in an effort to reduce the obligation. At the annual meeting, Jan. 1, 1885, the trustees were pleased to report that the last remnant of the debt, amounting to $6,700, together with the interest thereon, being $534.33, had been paid off. To commemorate the joyous event, a thanksgiving festival was arranged which took place on the 18th of January. Since that time extra funds have been raised for the church from time to time for various purposes, such as renovating, erecting a steeple and providing it with a clock and church bells, and purchasing a new pipe organ. The steeple was built in 1886 at a cost of $2,579; at the same time a tower clock was procured for $600 and three church bells weighing 5,900 lbs. and costing $1,174.35. A new pipe organ was installed in 1892 at a cost of nearly $6,000.

In 1897 the house at 218 Sedgwick street was purchased for a parsonage at a cost of $8,500. The basement of the building was turned into a library and reading room for the use of the young people's society. From March, 1890, the church has published a monthly paper, named "Församlings-Vännen," edited by the pastor.

This has been a mission church in more than one sense. In the course of years, its leaders have begun Sunday schools and other forms of mission work in various parts of the city, thereby laying the foundation for new Swedish Lutheran churches. The Salem Church on the south side is the first example. The second in order was the Gethsemane Church on the west side, organized two years later, or 1870. Several other churches in the city sustain the same filial relation to the Immanuel Church. Members who have removed to other places during these fifty years, and they have not been few, have been taking an active interest in the organizing of churches wherever they have come, and by reason of their training have become valuable members of these churches.

From its organization to the present time, the church has had only two regular pastors, Erland Carlsson from 1853 to 1875 and C. A. Evald from that year to the present time, but the assistant pastors have been not a few and besides a large number of students have assisted in the pulpit and in the Sunday and parochial schools.

From its earliest years the Immanuel Church has made great sacrifices for the Christian education and training of the young. Short-

The Immanuel Church—Interior of Third Edifice

ly after Rev. Carlsson's arrival, a Christian school was started. The first teacher was Eric Norelius, then a student of the university at Columbus, Ohio, later pastor of the Augustana Synod and at present its president. The need of a schoolhouse soon was felt, and in 1853 funds were gathered for the building, which was finished shortly. It was a two story structure, 24 by 32 feet, only the lower part being used for school purposes, while the upper story was rented out to raise revenue for the payment of the debt on the building.

This insignificant little schoolhouse attained historical importance not only for this church but for the Augustana Synod as well. It was the first business office of the Swedish Lutheran Publication Society. The printing office of "Hemlandet," a paper then published by that association, was for a time located in the schoolroom itself, the bookstore being located in a room above. Moreover, this same building was the first home of Augustana College and Theological Seminary, the principal institution of learning among the Swedish-Americans. When Prof. Esbjörn in the latter part of March, 1860, with seventeen Scandinavian Lutheran students, left the seminary at Springfield and came to Chicago, this schoolhouse was placed at their disposal. The lower story was used as a lecture hall, while the upper one was pressed into service as a dormitory for the students. The building was used thus for nearly three years, or until the fall of 1863 when the institution was removed to Paxton.

At first the parochial school, conducted by some student, was kept up only in summer, and the subjects taught were confined to religion and the Swedish language, but during various periods since 1870 other branches have been taught, including the English language, history and geography, natural history and music, necessitating the engagement of three or four teachers simultaneously. Of late years, however, the original plan is followed. Either students from synodical institutions or other teachers have been permanently engaged and thousands of Swedish-American children have here received their first instruction in the language and religion of their fathers.

The Sunday school of the Immanuel Church is, no doubt, the largest and the best organized in the Augustana Synod. The latter attributive properly applies also to the congregation as such. A large number of societies are at work, each for its specific purpose, but without losing sight of their common interests and those of the church at large. In his great work, and more particularly in this phase of it, Dr. Evald has a most energetic and valuable assistant in his wife, Mrs. Emmy Evald, a daughter of Rev. Carlsson, the first pastor of the church.

From the 16th to the 18th of January, 1903, the fiftieth anniversary of the Immanuel Church was celebrated with great festivity. At the time a comprehensive and attractive historical memorial was published, containing, together with a wealth of other facts and data, the following totals for the years 1854-1901, to-wit: income and outlay, $426,977.-21; communicant members, 51,959 and total number of members, 64,680.

At the beginning of the year 1907 the church numbered 1,212 communicants and 1,971 members all told. The Sunday school had an attendance of 1,469 pupils. The property value, including church and parsonage, was estimated at $60,000.

Rev. Erland Carlsson

One of the most noted clergymen who came over from Sweden to take up work in Illinois was Rev. Erland Carlsson. He was born Aug. 24, 1822, in the village of Suletorp, in Elghult parish, Småland. His parents, who were godfearing country folk, desired to give him a good Christian training. When the boy was but ten years of age, his father died, throwing the whole responsibility on the shoulders of the mother, who did as much as any pious mother could do for her son. The thought of becoming a minister arose early in the mind of the boy, but poverty placed what seemed insurmountable obstacles in the way. After a conversation with Sellergren, a noted evangelist, young Carlsson's mind took a more serious turn and he resolved to realize his youthful ambition, whatever the cost. At seventeen he began his theological studies under the direction of clergymen of the district, who kindly lent their aid to the earnest young seeker after knowledge. The services rendered by these men were never forgotten by him. A connection seems to be traceable between these kind offices and the readiness which Carlsson in after years spoke words of encouragement and extended a helping hand to young men who sought his advice and aid.

In 1843, Carlsson went to the university of Lund, completing his collegiate courses the following spring. Shortly thereafter, Bishop Esaias Tegnér of Vexiö licensed him to preach, a privilege which he availed himself of during the following summer. In the fall of 1844, he returned to Lund to study for the ministry. He was obliged to work under the most trying circumstances, his health failing and his funds giving out. But these difficulties seemed to spur him on to greater exertion, and his courage never failed him. In 1848, he passed his theological examination with high honors, but was not ordained until June 10, 1849, after having served in the interval as pastor at the watering place of Ramlösa and at the Lessebo paper mills.

Of Carlsson's career in the Swedish state church we know that he had the reputation of being a gifted and earnest preacher, the fruits of whose labors soon became evident. His sermons were full of power and spirituality and this, together with his simple and popular manner of expounding the Scriptures at religious gatherings and his private conversations with troubled souls, had the effect of attracting large audiences to the little factory church. While he was still pastor at Lessebo, there were signs of spiritual revival in that and adjoining congregations. While this was a source of joy to the young pastor, it aroused apprehension in the minds of the bishop and the consistory.

The so-called Conventicle Placard designed to arrest the free church movement in Sweden was still in force. All efforts at taking religion seriously the authorities characterized as "pietism" and fanaticism. So when Carlsson sounded the alarm to those reposing in the sleep of the self-righteous, he aroused the enmity of those who saw danger in "too much religion."

But the young pastor, holding that the prime object of all preaching was the salvation of men's souls, was not to be frightened by protests. He continued to preach the full gospel and the fire of revival continued to spread. When he also began to lecture on temperance, the authorities decided that the Lessebo pastor must be made harmless at any cost. They were not particular about the means to this end. Although the pastorate at the mills was a fixed position, the consistory sent him from one place to another. Carlsson, with true Christian meekness, bowed to its wishes, and submitted to an injustice calculated to injure him, but which, on the contrary, endeared him all the more to the people. The unjust acts of the consistory also had a great deal to do with his decision to emigrate in order to preach the gospel to his countrymen in the New World, unhampered by governmental restrictions.

When Carlsson, through the medium of Dr. Fjellstedt, received the call to become the pastor of the Immanuel Church in Chicago, he was favorably impressed with the opportunity therein implied, yet he was not blind to the difficulties and acts of self-sacrifice which it would impose. This was a work in full harmony with his innermost desire, and he felt it his duty to go, still he was not over-hasty in reaching a decision. He received the call to America early in 1853, and on the third of June the same year, after having obtained leave of absence for six years, he left Sweden.

The Immanuel Church in Carlsson obtained just such a pastor as it needed, and his labors soon showed results. The Swedes of Chicago felt that Rev. Carlsson had their interest at heart and worked unselfishly in their behalf. For this reason they gathered about him like sheep about the shepherd or children around their father. He not only became their pastor but also their confidential adviser on all vital matters. His sound judgment and practical mind was at first placed at the service of the poor and often totally helpless newcomers, later to become a useful factor in the working out of the plans and destinies of the entire Swedish Lutheran Church in the United States. From the very first, he became one of the leaders and most respected men in the Swedish colony in Chicago.

The call extended to Rev. Carlsson also provided that he should have charge of the congregation organized in Geneva in 1853. For a number of years, he served that church too, but this was not the extent of his field of usefulness. Immigration in the early fifties was very large, and Swedish settlements sprang up in a number of localities round about Chicago. Swedes settled in small groups in eastern Illinois, western Indiana and southern Michigan, and to each of these settlements extended Rev. Carlsson's solicitations for their spiritual welfare. He paved the way for many Swedish Lutheran churches in these states and saw a number of them safely through the storm and stress of the first few years. His sound judgment, practical wisdom and unflinching energy often were of invaluable service to the newcomers in their perplexity and helplessness. By his sympathetic personality he won well-nigh unbounded respect and confidence.

The terrible experience of the Swedish immigrants during the cholera epidemic of 1854 form the dark background which gives vivid relief to the portrayal of Carlsson as pastor, man and Christian. The situation was appalling; sickness and death visited almost every home and so numerous were the victims of the pest that it was only with the greatest difficulty that the bodies could be promptly interred. From morning till night, Carlsson would spend his time with the sick, lending aid and comfort, while his own vitality was almost spent, and even when he was himself physically ill. He constantly exposed himself to the contagion, evidently without any thought of his own safety. There were those who did not like him, but none could say that he was afraid or that he spared himself. Where there was greatest need of help, there you would find the Swedish Lutheran pastor, giving aid and succor, without distinction between friend and foe, members or enemies of his church; they were all fellow mortals in distress, that was enough for him.

In 1855 Carlsson was married to Miss Eva Charlotta Anderson, daughter of a well-known settler. From now on, he had at his side a faithful helpmeet who, in the estimation of many, was the ideal of a Lutheran pastor's wife. With her arrival as the presiding spirit of the parsonage of the Immanuel Church, that became the headquarters of a mission of great importance to the church and to the Swedish colony of Chicago at large. The home of Rev. Carlsson was, as some one has expressed it, "a miniature Castle Garden." Here helpless newcomers were sheltered and fed, however scarce the room and however low the supplies of the larder. On Sunday he would preach to his countrymen; on Monday, he had to scurry about town trying to find work for them; on Tuesday, he would be called upon to help some one disentangle an intricate business affair; on Wednesday, there would be a party of immigrants arriving, whom he had to meet and assist; on Thursday, he might be in court, acting as the interpreter of some newcomer in trouble; on Friday, people might call on him to act as private secretary, with the duty of reading and writing their letters, and on Saturday there would generally be any amount of similar private commissions for him to perform. This strenuous work was appreciated by many, while others gave him no thanks for his endeavors. The discomforts and privations the Carlssons brought upon themselves in their efforts to assist others were often made light of, and Rev. Carlsson was not

Rev. Erland Carlsson

spared the grief of seeing many whom he had rendered valuable services afterward turning against him in bitter enmity.

To recount the labors of Rev. Carlsson in Chicago at this period would be to repeat the history of the Immanuel Church, for he was the moving spirit in every enterprise in the church and to his splendid leadership and capacity for organization is due in great measure the credit for everything then accomplished by that church.

Having lent his best efforts to the work of restoration after the destruction and disintegration caused by the Chicago fire, Rev. Carls-, son did not long remain in charge of the Immanuel Church. In 1875 he received and accepted a call to Andover, to take the place of Rev. Jonas Swensson, deceased, as pastor of that church. Carlsson left the Immanuel Church, not from choice, but because he hoped that the quiet country would afford him that rest for mind and body which was not to be had in the turbulent metropolis. In leaving Chicago, however, he did not cease to follow the work there with great interest. When Carlsson came to Chicago, the Immanuel Church consisted of a handful of poor immigrants, but when he left, after laboring there for twenty-two years, it was the largest congregation in the synod.

From 1875 to 1887, Carlsson served as pastor of the Andover church. He obtained the desired rest in this respect that he was no longer required to have charge of missions and organize new congregations, but could devote his entire time to the upbuilding of his own congregation. The pastoral duties, so dear to his heart, he was now left to perform without having other work constantly interposed, but a pastorate of the size of Andover does not afford rest in the ordinary sense of the term. Besides, he took an active interest in the general affairs of the church at all times. He was president of the Illinois Conference up to 1882, and in 1881 he was elected president of the Augustana Synod, serving until 1887. Membership in a number of committees imposed on him many extra duties. Under the burden of all this work, Carlsson's health began to fail. In 1884 he had an attack of apoplexy which made it difficult for him to attend to his ministerial duties. Nevertheless, he continued his pastoral work until June, 1887, when he removed to Rock Island, having accepted the position of business manager of Augustana College and Theological Seminary.

This office, far from lightening his burden, added new cares and responsibilities. Industrious, energetic and practical as he was, he still found himself unequal to the task. His health steadily failed and soon it was apparent to him that he could not long hold out in the service of the institution he so dearly loved and in the upbuilding of which he had always taken an active part.

At the advice of his physician to seek a milder climate, Carlsson removed to Kansas, purchasing a large farm near Lindsborg and building for himself a comfortable home which he named Rostad, after a cherished place in his fatherland. Here, together with his loving wife, he spent the last few years of his life, surrounded by relatives and friends.

To know Rev. Carlsson was to love and esteem him. For the young people in particular he had a peculiar attraction. Socially, he was free and natural, and a fine conversationalist. That his independence was distasteful to some is not to be wondered at. He was deferent to others, but not in matters of principle; from what he held to be right, he was never known to deviate a hair's-breadth. His whole-souled Christianity impressed everyone who came in contact with him. But to ascribe to him a perfection which was not his would not be honoring his memory. He had his faults, which he could not conceal and which we cannot here overlook. Among these was a hot and excitable temper which would often get the better of his judgment in the course of public deliberations. He was himself fully conscious of his shortcoming, which caused him the keenest regret, and he was not too proud to apologize to any one whom he felt guilty of having done an injustice or injury.

His sympathetic personality and vivid presentation made him a truly popular preacher. He did not overlook the essential requirement of thorough preparation. His sermons were logical and to the point. He laid much stress on the form of the sermon but not at the expense of the contents. He always appeared with a dignity becoming a minister of the church of God.

In 1892 the directors of Augustana College and Theological Seminary conferred upon Carlsson the degree of Doctor of Divinity, in well-deserved recognition of his theological learning as well as of his long and tireless work toward the upbuilding of that institution of learning and of the Augustana Synod as a whole.

Carlsson was an energetic promoter of every branch of benevolent work. While in Andover he was the chairman of the board of the orphanage at that place. He was one of the incorporators of the Augustana Hospital of Chicago and was intensely interested in the development of that institution.

To the very last he labored in the interest of the home mission work. On a visit to Sister Bay, Wis., where he had a relative living, his real purpose was to seek health and rest in its invigorating northern climate, but he could not refrain from preaching the gospel to the Swedish settlers there, and thus it happened that his last sermon was preached in that locality. A slight apoplectic attack soon compelled his return to Chicago, to the home of his daughter and son-in-law, Mrs. and Dr. C. A. Evald. A second attack followed shortly after his return, and on the 19th of October, 1893, Erland Carlsson peacefully passed away, with his wife, children and grand-children at his bedside.

On the 25th of the same month, after impressive funeral services in the Immanuel Church, where Carlsson had preached for more than a score of years, his remains were laid to rest in Graceland cemetery, where a fine monument, erected by the Immanuel congregation, marks the resting-place of this eminent pioneer.

The Swedish Lutherans of Geneva

This church was organized in the first week of January, 1853, by Rev. Hasselquist and the Norwegian clergyman, Rev. Paul Andersen, of Chicago. Its membership, starting with forty, rapidly increased with the arrival of new immigrants. The organization did not take place in Geneva, but in the neighboring settlement of St. Charles, where the Swedes were more numerous. In the fall Rev. Erland Carlsson arrived from the old country, taking charge of this congregation, together with that in Chicago, and making regular visits to St. Charles the first Sunday of each month.

The first house of worship was the little church mentioned in the sketch of the St. Charles congregation, which was erected in 1852, at the initiative of the adventurous Nils Jansson. For two reasons the Geneva people, however, soon determined to provide their own church edifice. One was that the church at St. Charles was too small to accommodate the people, so that in the summer of 1854 a large part of the audience had to remain outside of the church during Sunday morning services. The second reason was a more peculiar one. There was a debt of $150 on the church building, for which the trustees had given a note with the proviso that receipts for all work and building material were to be submitted, together with a deed to the lot, before the money would be paid. This was never done. The trustees refused to pay the debt until the conditions should be fulfilled. On the other hand the creditor was unable to carry out his part of the agreement for the simple reason that the lot on which the church was built had been sold to a railway company.

In the meantime the Swedes in Geneva had materially increased in number. This fact, together with the tangle regarding the St. Charles church property, gave added impetus to the movement toward the erection of a church in the first named place. In the center of the village stood a large stone building begun five years before, intended for a hotel, but never completed. It occurred to the church members that this might easily be altered so as to serve the purpose of a church edifice. After having looked over the structure and ascertained that it was for sale together with the surrounding premises, comprising one entire block, the Swedish Lutherans of Geneva and St. Charles, at a meeting held in St. Charles Nov. 22, 1854, resolved to purchase the property at a price not exceeding $2,000 and reconstruct the building for their purpose. The church members, no matter in which place they lived, all pledged themselves to do their utmost to raise the money, promising, as a rule, to contribute one month's wages. A subscription was started at once and during the evening a total of $400 was pledged. Later it reached the final amount of $1,200. Two days after the meeting, the bargain was made and work was at once begun. In the latter part of December, the building was under cover and so far completed that services could be held there. The edifice was 36 by 47 feet and 18 feet in height. There were thirty benches on the main floor, which with the gallery seated 300 people. On Sunday, the 11th of May, 1856, the church was dedicated, having been finished at a total outlay of $1,420. This amount, together with the purchase price and interest, ran the total expenditure on the property up to $3,540. At the time of the dedication an even $1,000 remained unpaid.

After the St. Charles church had been lost in a litigation the members worshiped with their brethren in Geneva, belonging to that congregation until 1882 when they organized a church of their own.

As early as 1857, Rev. Erland Carlsson found his field too extensive and accordingly engaged assistants for the work in Geneva. Several pastors, including A. Andreen, E. Norelius and G. Peters, took turns with him in preaching there. When no pastor was to be had, the services were conducted by Deacons Karl Samuelsson or P. Carlsson. Rev. Carlsson, however, had pastoral charge of the congregation until August, 1863. During the first decade of its existence, the church prospered greatly both spiritually and materially. It had its finances so well in hand that at the tenth anniversary the debt amounted to only $40.

The second pastor of this church was Rev. P. A. Cederstam, who took charge Aug. 3, 1863, meanwhile serving the DeKalb church by preaching there every third Sunday. Rev. Cederstam aroused the congregation to great activity during the short period of three years that he was permitted to serve. Broken down in health, he resigned July 16, 1866, when Rev. Erland Carlsson again took charge of the pastorate.

In the early part of the year 1869, Rev. C. O. Lindell succeeded to this charge. During Cederstam's time, mission work had been begun in Aurora, and at the next annual meeting the members living there asked permission to withdraw and organize a distinct church. Their request was granted, but for some time both congregations were served by the pastor in Geneva. Rev. Lindell resigned his post in January, 1875.

The following March a call was extended to Rev. C. H. Södergren, who accepted and labored in Geneva for nine years, or until 1884. In 1879 the congregation celebrated its 25th anniversary, when the speakers were the founder and the subsequent pastors of the church. It was during Rev. Södergren's time that the members in St. Charles withdrew and, in January, 1882, organized themselves as a separate congregation. Thereby the membership of Södergren's church was materially decreased, carrying with it a reduction of his salary from

$800 to $500. In spite of its reduced circumstances, the congregation incurred a heavy expense for new church furniture and repairs.

After Rev. Södergren's removal to Bertrand, Neb., in 1884, the pastorate was left vacant for one year. Nov. 9, 1886, the St. Charles and Geneva churches agreed to call Rev. C. E. Cesander as their common

The Swedish Lutheran Church of Geneva

pastor, whose time was to be equally divided between them. The year after, a new organ was purchased, and in 1893 it was resolved to build a new church, $2,000 being subscribed for the purpose. The enterprise was postponed, however, owing partly to several disasters in Geneva but principally to the financial panic of 1893 and successive years.

He was succeeded by Rev. J. A. Axelson in September, 1895. During the intervening vacancy, a comfortable parsonage was erected on the church lot at a cost of $1,894. Rev. Södergren and Cesander had lived in a parsonage situated halfway between the two cities and owned by the pastors themselves. After serving the church for four years, Rev. Axelson resigned and soon afterward returned to Sweden.

In August, 1899, the congregation called Rev. Carl Christenson of Lincoln, Neb., who took up his duties at the beginning of the next year. In March of that year the congregation resolved to build a new church, to cost $9,000, the work to begin as soon as $6,000 had been subscribed. In June, the bid of C. A. Anderson, of St. Charles, to erect the structure for the sum of $10,837, was accepted, and on Sept. 9th, the cornerstone was laid. Services were held in the new edifice for the first time on the first Sunday of the year 1901, but the formal dedication did not take place until March 24th. This temple is built in the Gothic style, the material being stone for the basement and pressed brick for the superstructure. Its dimensions are: length, 94 feet; width, 40 and 49 feet; height of steeple, 117 feet. The interior finish is in oak throughout. It has an organ worth $1,400, placed to one side of the chancel. The total cost of the church, completely furnished, exclusive of the organ, was $13,866.

The fiftieth anniversary of the church was celebrated on the fifth, sixth and seventh of June, 1903, a historical memorial being published in connection therewith. Rev. Christenson left in 1905, and his successor is Rev. F. A. Linder, president of the Illinois Conference for several years past. At New Year's, 1907, the congregation numbered 332 communicants and 559 members all told. Its property was valued at $20,000.

The Knoxville Church

This congregation also was organized by Rev. Hasselquist, in the year 1853. The founder was its pastor up to 1863, simultaneously with his pastorate in Galesburg, the church afterward receiving it own minister.

A small frame church was built in 1854 and dedicated Dec. 2nd, the following year, while still unfinished. The Americans in Knoxville had lent some aid toward its erection, but the bulk of the expense fell on the impecunious members themselves, who scraped together the needed funds in various ways, ending by a voluntary assessment of one dollar for each hundred dollars worth of property, the valuation to be made by the owner. The little church, which they considered light and lofty, cost about $1,700, of which sum $800 had been paid.

The church in 1860 numbered 173 communicants and its current annual expenses amounted to $250. In after years the congregation has had but a modest growth, the Swedes in this locality not being very numerous. At the beginning of 1907, the membership had reached 285, of whom 183 were communicants. Its church property, including church building, parsonage and the lots appertaining, was valued at $5,000.

There lived in Knoxville from 1852 to 1855 a blacksmith by the

THE LUTHERANS

name of Håkan Olson who, in view of the lack of clergymen, was induced by Rev. Hasselquist to study for the ministry. He was ordained in June 1860, when the Augustana Synod was organized, and labored in the ministry for more than forty years, including ten years in Illinois. Rev. Håkan Olson died in Port Wing, Wis., June 1, 1904.

Another of the laymen of the Knoxville church during the fifties who entered the ministry at the instance of Rev. Hasselquist, was a farmer named Johannes Jönsson, afterwards known as John Johnson, who became minister of the churches in Moline and in Princeton.

The First Lutheran Church of Rockford

Rev. Erland Carlsson of Chicago in October, 1853, visited Rockford for the first time, forming the acquaintance of its Swedish settlers. To them his visit suggested the need of a Swedish Lutheran minister, and they accordingly sent a delegate to the united Chicago and Mississippi conferences, which met in Chicago Jan. 4-9, 1854, to present a request for a pastor. The conference replied that as Rev. Carlsson would again visit Rockford on the following Sunday all Swedes and Norwegians in and around the city ought to meet then and advise with him as to the organization of a church.

In accordance herewith, Rev. Carlsson came to Rockford Sunday, Jan. 15th, and, after conducting divine services and administering the Holy Communion, organized a congregation under the name of the Scandinavian Evangelical Lutheran Church of Rockford. Those joining at the time were 77 in number, including 32 children. The first deacons were Jonas Larsson and Johan Pettersson and the first trustees Johan Lundbeck and Josef Lindgren. Rev. Carlsson and his assistant A. Andreen subsequently visited the congregation four Sundays every year and the first Monday of each month.

On the 5th of March, 1855, the first annual meeting of the church was held, when the accounts submitted showed a total income of $10.49 and a total expenditure of $4.56. These modest figures, however, did not include the amount paid out to the pastors, which was raised by subscription and by occasional collections.

A special business meeting was held June 30, 1855, to devise ways and means of procuring a house of worship, the rapid growth of the Swedish population and their affiliation with the church making such a step imperative. It was decided to start a subscription and solicit funds among both Swedes and Americans for the purchase of a lot to build on, it being pointed out that the longer the delay, the higher the price. By the end of July Andreen, who seems to have had charge of the soliciting, had $300 subscribed by Swedes and $700 by Americans. In the meantime a committee composed of two men, John Larsson and

John Nelson, had purchased a lot at the corner of North First and Rock streets for the sum of $325, this transaction being ratified by the congregation Aug. 20th. The contract for building the church was let Sept. 12th to Lars Grönlund and G. P. Johnson for $725. The plans had been prepared under Rev. Carlsson's supervision and the contract specified that the building was to be completed by Dec. 1st; but only the basement was ready when the time expired.

In the spring of 1855, Andreen obtained ad interim license to preach and perform ministerial acts, but spent the following fall and spring at the seminary at Springfield. During vacation he assisted Rev. Carlsson and often preached to his countrymen in Rockford. Oct. 10th he was called as regular pastor of that church, but was not ordained until Sept. 12, 1856, having removed to Rockford and ·taken charge the month before.

Under the supervision of the pastor, the work of completing the church building progressed so that the edifice was finished in the fall and could be dedicated Nov. 23rd, Rev. T. N. Hasselquist officiating. It was a frame building, 45 by 28 feet and 28 feet high. In the basement was a schoolroom extending half the length of the structure. The interior was neatly painted and the aisles were laid with carpets, a luxury not common in the early Swedish-American churches. The edifice, which had a capacity of 300, was in use until the early part of 1870, when a new brick structure was ready for occupancy.

A parsonage was simultaneously erected, Rev. Andreen having made an agreement with the congregation by which he was to build a house on a part of the church lot, which the church would buy on the installment plan at actual cost, or else sell to him the ground it occupied.

In 1856 a parochial school was opened, with instruction in the Swedish language and Christianity. Magnus Munter was the first schoolmaster here as in Geneva. This parochial school has been kept up ever since. Sunday school was also begun in the early years of the church. Nov. 4, 1858, the name of the church was changed by the substitution of the word "Swedish" for "Scandinavian," its membership now being exclusively Swedish. In May, 1860, it was resolved to withdraw from the Synod of Northern Illinois and, together with other Swedish Lutheran churches, form the Augustana Synod. Harmony and unanimity reigned and the congregation contributed much to mission work, temperance work, the synodical school and other Christian endeavor.

Rev. Andreen at first had a salary of $150 and two free-will offerings a year. Not until 1859 was this amount increased, and then by only $50. At the annual meeting in 1860, no salary was fixed but instead a subscription was to be taken, the pastor to receive the whole amount raised, whether more or less than $200. The membership was 213, 122, being communicants, and the current expenses for the year 1859 amounted to $300.

Aside from his arduous work in Rockford, Andreen found time to serve the congregation in the neighboring settlement of Pecatonica. There he organized a Swedish Lutheran church in 1857, which built a little frame church, 36 by 24 feet, the same year, at a cost of $600. It was dedicated Oct. 11th. For a number of years this church continued a part of the Rockford pastorate.

Laboring under great difficulties, Rev. Andreen nevertheless performed telling work in Rockford. Under his guidance the church made sure, if slow, progress and was given an orthodox training which proved a safe and sound foundation for future upbuilding.

He was not long to remain in Rockford, however. In 1860 he left the charge, removing to Attica, Ind., Jan. 3, 1861, the church held a meeting for the election of a new pastor, the candidates being Revs. G. Peters, J. F. Duwell and A. W. Dahlsten, a student. Twice Peters and Dahlsten received almost the same number of votes and when the election was decided by the drawing of lots, the choice fell on Dahlsten. His salary was fixed at $250. During the three years he served the church, work progressed quietly and in the right direction. The economic condition of the church improved year by year. Toward the close of 1863, Rev. Dahlsten removed to Galesburg, necessitating the calling of a pastor for the third time.

At the special meeting held for this purpose, Rev. Peters was called. This event inaugurated the most important period in the first half century of this church. Rev. Peters was destined to do the principal work of his life in the capacity of pastor of this congregation. Seldom is any pastor permitted to remain so long as he, or almost a quarter of a century, at the head of any one church, leading it through so many changes and vicissitudes, yet ever on from one triumph to another. Rev. Peters had the joy of seeing his church grow to be the largest in the Augustana Synod.

At the church meeting held upon the arrival of Rev. Peters on Jan. 1, 1864, many important questions were up for discussion. Among other things, it was decided to purchase from Rev. Andreen the parsonage erected by him, $318 being immediately subscribed for that purpose. In March the house was bought for the sum of $725 cash, several church members advancing the difference.

At the annual business meeting in 1865 the trustees submitted a very encouraging report, showing receipts amounting to $2,000 for the past year, a handsome result for those days. The audiences at divine services had outgrown the capacity of the church and a remedy had been sought in an addition to the gallery. Nevertheless, it was plain that the old church soon would have to be abandoned by the rapidly growing congregation and on that account it was decided to proceed with the work of raising a church building fund for future needs.

At the annual meeting two years later a committee was appointed to solicit subscriptions for a new edifice. Later a building committee was appointed, consisting of four persons, who on Feb. 22, 1869, proposed plans for a church edifice seating 600 persons and costing $9,500. The dimensions were 85 by 55 feet. A couple of church members had on their own responsibility bought two desirable lots which they now tendered to the congregation. The cornerstone was laid Aug. 28, 1868, and the work was pushed to completion with such vigor that early mass could be celebrated in the new temple on Christmas morning, 1869. On New Year's day, 1870, it was dedicated by Rev. T. N. Hasselquist, president of the Augustana Synod. Although very heavy expenditures had been incurred, there was a debt of only $5,502. In 1873 a subscription toward paying off the debt was taken, amounting to $3,085.

The following year the balance of the debt was lifted. The congregation now numbered 720 communicants and 1,240 members in all, the result of only twenty years of labor, and to all appearances the future promised unimpeded progress. But in 1877 an interruption seemed imminent. From seemingly trifling causes arose dissensions which grew so serious as to theaten the church with disruption. But just then something happened which left a lasting impression in the minds of the members. On all sides they stood prepared for strife and were only awaiting the moment when the storm should break. But the storm did not come. Instead there came a gentle breeze in the form of a spiritual revival before which the storm-clouds soon disappeared. Rather than judge one another, the members now began to bring themselves to trial. For a period of two months meetings were held in the church daily, all crowding the edifice to the doors.

Having received this added impetus to further growth, the church returned to normal conditions and uniform progress. On Jan. 15, 1879, it celebrated its twenty-fifth anniversary, when Rev. Erland Carlsson, the founder of the church, was present and preached an impressive sermon. Not long afterward, it began to appear that the church edifice, although but ten years old, was inadequate to hold the crowds that came there to worship. In 1881 a committee was appointed to devise a remedy and the next year it was decided that the only way was to build a new church. A great deal of preliminary work was done that year, no less than nine general business meetings and thirty-seven council and committee meetings being held. Much discussion and investigation finally led to the conclusion that it would be impracticable to enlarge the old edifice, and after all efforts to satisfy everybody had failed, it was resolved at a general church meeting Jan. 31, 1883, to erect a new edifice on the site of the old one. The dimensions of the new house of worship were to be 80 by 126 feet, with a seating capacity of 1,950. The last services in the old sanctuary took place on Midsummer day. In two weeks from that day it was torn down, and on the 17th of July work was begun on the new structure. The cornerstone was laid Aug. 21st, by Rev. J. Wikstrand, then president of the Illinois Conference.

The First Swedish Lutheran Church of Rockford

On Aug. 27th, less than a week after the laying of the cornerstone, the malcontents withdrew from the church and organized a new congregation, styled the Zion Swedish Lutheran Church. In time the old differences were forgotten and cordial relations were established between the mother and the daughter church. The year prior a small number of dissatisfied ones had withdrawn and organized the Emanuel Church, which for a time belonged to the General Synod and subsequently joined the Augustana Synod, being for many years one of its English congregations.

The work on the new church edifice progressed rapidly and the temple was ready for occupancy on the first Sunday in Advent. About one year later, or Dec. 7, 1884, the completed edifice was dedicated by President J. Wikstrand. The cost of this spacious and handsome church was $48,716, exclusive of three hundred days' work done by members without pay and material used out of the old structure. A debt of $28,129 was incurred. An excellent pipe organ was installed at a cost of $3,100. Improvements and alterations to the value of five hundred dollars were subsequently made by Mr. A. T. Lindgren, the present organist, who defrayed the expenses out of his own pocket.

Rev. Peters resigned his charge in 1882, but his resignation was rejected by unanimous vote at the annual meeting in 1884, after having lain on the table for two years. At the subsequent annual meeting Rev. Peters again resigned, but was not released from service until June, 1886, when the church secured an acceptance of its call. The new pastor was Rev. L. A. Johnston, of Des Moines, Ia., who entered upon his duties in Rockford that fall. The congregation left by Rev. Peters to his successor was quite different from the one he himself began to serve in 1864, being now a large church, requiring the full time and all the energy of its pastor. It now remained for him to build on the foundations already laid. The history of the church at this stage forms a chapter remarkable in many respects. About that time the city of Rockford enjoyed a period of exceptional prosperity, which was not without its influence on the church. The congregation grew so rapidly that in January, 1894, its membership reached 3,205, of whom 2,066 were communicants. In the meantime the daughter church also grew apace. In the winter of 1889 there was within the church a marked spiritual movement, exercising a wholesome influence on the inner life of the members and also aiding in its outward growth. The need of a pastor's assistant was felt, and as such was chosen Rev. E. C. Jessup of Peoria, who accepted the call and served from March, 1893, to May, 1895.

During Rev. Johnston's incumbency the congregation erected two new buildings, namely, a chapel in the south part of the city and a large schoolhouse and young people's hall on Kishwaukee st. These entailed an expenditure of about $10,000 and retarded in a measure the reduction of the church debt. At the annual meeting in 1892, a subscription was decided upon for the purpose of effacing that debt, then amounting to $21,000. Rev. Johnston, who undertook the task of soliciting, succeeded in obtaining subscriptions covering the entire amount, but just as the debt was about to be lifted, there came the great financial panic,

during which Rockford suffered as much as any city in the land, and
thus nearly the whole result of the subscription was lost. Such was the
financial stringency in the city that it was only with great difficulty
this large and populous church was able to meet current expenses.

The eight years that Rev. Johnston had pastoral charge of the
church formed the period of its most rapid growth. The charge was
such as to tax the capacity of the most energetic worker. In the summer of 1894 Johnston was called to the First Swedish Lutheran Church
of St. Paul, Minn., and removed to that field in the fall. To succeed
him, Rev. Joel L. Haff of Stillwater, Minn., was called, and took up his
new duties in April, 1895. His labors in Rockford were cut short within
one year, sickness and death overtaking him during a visit to his former
church in Stillwater, in February, 1896.

Rev. Haff in September, 1896, was succeeded by Rev. J. F. Seedoff,
who took up the work under unfavorable auspices, lack of employment
compelling hundreds of members not owning homes to leave the city.
Adding to this the fact of a debt of $20,000 and the further circum-
stance that a large number of members neglected to pay their membership dues, the seriousness of the situation may be readily comprehended.
The first act of Rev. Seedoff was to ascertain, with the aid of the
church council, the exact number of actual members; the second, an
effort to reduce the church debt. These things involved a vast amount
of work and worry both for the pastor and his council. The church
records were carefully searched, and the deacons visited all those, whose
relations to the church were not entirely clear. In this manner the
membership figure was reduced in 1901 to 1,434, the smallest number
recorded since 1888. But the dues paid in by members that year
amounted to $4,026, one of the largest totals for any one year. This
work completed, the records of the congregation were rewritten in
1902, when the total membership was found to be 2,143, 1,493 being
communicants.

For the purpose of reducing the debt, monthly meetings were
arranged, when each member was expected to contribute whatever he
or she was able toward the general fund. The contributions were
gradually increased, making quite considerable amounts in the end.
Thus the necessity of arranging bazaars and other entertainments was
obviated. On Midsummer night, 1902, the congregation assembled in
church, and then and there a collection was taken up, amounting to
$700, with which sum the remainder of the debt was paid. From that
time work has progressed without financial stress, although a costly
parsonage has been purchased and about $2,000 has been expended in
repairs on the church property.

The fiftieth anniversary of the founding of the church was celebrated with fitting festivities Jan. 15-18, 1904. At the time an illustrated souvenir album was published at the expense of the young people of the church. In that publication Rev. Seedoff gives a historical sketch from which the following data are taken: during the past half century 3,659 baptisms had been performed by the various pastors of the church, 1,483 persons had been confirmed, 942 couples had been united in holy matrimony and 1,032 burials had taken place. The sum total of money raised by the congregation during the same period amounted to $321,125.52.

At the end of the year 1906 the church numbered 2,191 members, 1,541 of whom were communicants. The property of the church was valued at $83,340.

Rev. Andreas Andreen

Rev. A. Andreen was born in Grenna parish, Småland, Sept. 10, 1827. His father, who was a poor land tenant, died while the son was but a child. About the age of twelve or thirteen, Andreen was apprenticed to a country tailor, who went from house to house plying his trade. The boy, who worked for his board alone, was badly clothed and worse shod, but despite all privations he was cheerful of mood and kind of heart. Having learned his trade and begun to work on his own account, he soon improved his circumstances.

About the age of twenty-one, he experienced a significant change of heart. His one desire was to devote his life to the service of God, but he realized the lack of the education required for the performance of fruitful work in that field. At the instance of friends he entered the teachers' seminary at Vexiö, from which he was graduated in 1851, at the age of twenty-four. He then was engaged as school-teacher at the Gripenberg estate, owned by Baron Hermelin, a son-in-law of Dr Peter Fjellstedt. In the meantime he conducted religious meetings at intervals in various parts of the district, and as he had a natural talent for public speaking, the people gladly went to hear him.

His longing for a field of greater opportunity and a chance of further development soon cut short his labors in his native locality. In the fall af 1853 we find him in New York, where he came in contact with Rev. O. G. Hedström and the Swedish Methodists, without knowing at first that they had left the Lutheran Church.

He spent the winter there, in what he thought to be a stifling spiritual atmosphere. In the spring of 1854 Rev. Erland Carlsson, having learned of the young schoolmaster and preacher, called him as his assistant in pastoral work. Highly gratified, Andreen left for Chicago late in April. During that terrible year of the cholera plague he was of great help to Rev. Carlsson. Upon recommendation of the

united Chicago and Mississippi conferences he obtained from the president of the Synod of Northern Illinois a license to labor as missionary
among the Swedish and Norwegian immigrants in Chicago. This work
he is said to have prosecuted with greater zeal and self-sacrifice than
any other immigrant missionary that ever trod the streets of Chicago.
He also labored in the Immanuel Church, especially during the absence
or illness of Rev. Carlsson.

In September, 1854, Andreen went to Springfield, entering the
theological department of the Illinois State University. He spent four

Rev. Andreas Andreen

terms there, continuing as Carlsson's assistant during vacations. In
April, 1855, at the recommendation of the conference, he obtained a
license ad interim as clergyman and was called to the church at Rockford in the fall of the same year. Sept. 12, 1856, at the synodical
meeting in Dixon, Ill., he was ordained to the ministry and continued
his pastoral work in Rockford till the close of 1860, when he removed
to Attica, Ind., taking charge of the churches at that place, together
with those of LaPorte and Baileytown, the three forming one pastorate
up to 1863. About the close of 1862 or early the following year, he
resigned from the church at Attica and removed to Baileytown, continuing to serve that and the LaPorte church to the end of 1865. Then

he accepted a call to Berlin, Ill., but did not assume permanent charge until fall, having been placed by the Augustana Synod in charge of the. Gustaf Adolf Church in New York for five months of the year 1866.

At Berlin he labored for a term of years with noteworthy success. The unexpected loss of his wife, Hilda, daughter of Julius Esping, a pioneer settler of Geneva, broke his health and gave to his mind a brooding and pensive turn. Somewhat over a year later he was married to Gustava A. Esbjörn, née Magnusson, the widowed third wife of Rev. L. P. Esbjörn. In assuming the care of the younger of his nine children, she lifted a great burden from his mind. Nevertheless his mental state grew worse, and when his condition gave cause for alarm he was finally consigned to the Passavant Hospital at Jacksonville, in the hope of possible recovery. On the way there a visit was paid to friends in Rock Island, where, on Feb. 14, 1880, Andreen took his own life, presumably in a fit of complete insanity. He was then 52½ years old and had served in the ministry for 23 years. His death caused sincere regret wherever the zealous and sympathetic churchman was known.

Andreen was physically a good specimen of manhood and possessed a graceful and captivating manner. Naturally gifted as a speaker, with proper training he might have become an orator of note. There was that in his voice which set the chords of one's soul vibrating. Under a calm surface he concealed great depth of feeling, but rarely did he show evidence of a lack of balance in his mental equipment. Taking him all in all, Andreen holds a place alongside of Esbjörn, Hasselquist, Carlsson and Swensson in the memory of the Swedish Lutheran pioneers.

Rev. Gustaf Peters

G. Peters, who is also entitled to be classed with the pioneer pastors, was born Jan. 4, 1832, at Stödsboda, in the parish of Åsheda, Småland, where his parents, Peter Emanuel and Eva Andersson, were poor cottagers. In his childhood he suffered great hardships owing to extreme poverty. When he grew old enough to be useful, he hired out as shepherd boy during summer, and having attained the age of twelve he took a trade apprenticeship for four years.

Having had his mind directed to spiritual things in the confirmation school, and become a true Christian, he was advised by friends to become a schoolmaster. In September, 1848, he accordingly began preliminary studies under S. M. Wirsén, the schoolmaster at Elghult. He was soon given an opportunity to take part in the instruction of the younger pupils, and a couple of years later he was engaged as

assistant teacher, first at Åsheda, then at Elghult. The salary, though
meager, sufficed for his urgent needs, such as clothing and books,
leaving a pittance over for his parents. In January, 1854, he entered
the teachers' seminary at Kalmar, remaining one term. After having
taught during the following summer and fall, he returned to the
seminary for the spring term of 1855, being graduated, June 15th, with
fair standing.

Rev. Gustaf Peters

The goal of his ambition, as he supposed, had now been attained,
but the future had other things in store for him. Through Erland
Carlsson he received a call to go to the United States, which he
declined, going instead to Stockholm, where he studied at the divinity
school of Dr. Fjellstedt and Rev. Ahlberg in 1857-8, and when in the
spring of the latter year Ahlberg returned to Småland, Peters accepted
a position as assistant instructor in his newly founded school for the
training of lay preachers and remained there for one year. In response
to a repeated call from America, he emigrated, leaving Kalmar July

27, 1859, arriving in New York Aug. 17th and in Chicago Aug. 24th. Having obtained a preacher's licence Sept. 12th, he became assistant to Rev. Carlsson in his arduous labors in Chicago.

Peters attended the conference meeting held in Chicago April 23-27 of the following year, when the organization of the Augustana Synod was resolved upon. He was also present in Clinton, Wis., the following June, when the resolution was carried out, being one of eight candidates who at the time were ordained for pastoral service in the new synod. Rev. O. C. T. Andrén of Moline being at the time commissioned to go to Sweden to work in the interest of the newly founded Augustana Theological Seminary, Rev. Peters was called to fill the temporary vacancy, and later, when Andrén failed to return, became permanent pastor of the Moline church. In the latter part of August, 1861, Peters was united in wedlock to Ida Helena Ström, from Kristdala, Småland. She died May 18, 1863, leaving a daughter ten months old. After that, Rev. Peters no longer felt at home in Moline. The following August he resigned the charge, and having been elected pastor of the church in Rockford the same week without his knowledge, he removed to the new field the following December.

Under another head is given an account of the work performed by him in Rockford, where he was stationed for twenty-two and one-half years. In 1886 he removed to Lincoln, Neb., and after remaining there for a year and a half went to York, Neb., for a term of years, subsequently returning to Illinois, where he labored in the ministry at various points so long as his powers permitted. Of late he has resided in Rockford, a place dear to him for having been the principal field of his labors.

In 1864 Rev. Peters was remarried, the issue of this union being eight children, four of whom are now living.

The Church in Princeton.

The first Swedish Lutheran minister to visit the Swedish settlers in Princeton was T. N. Hasselquist, who made a brief stop there in the fall of 1852, en route from Sweden to his new pastorate in Galesburg. He then officiated at a baptism, but made no effort in the direction of founding a church. In the summer of 1853, C. J. Valentin, whose acquaintance we formed in the sketch of the Moline church, began preaching at this place. The meetings were held either in the Smith schoolhouse or in the city hall. A certain Johan Anderson, who was said to have been foreman of the printing shop of "Stockholms Dagblad" and who came to Princeton in 1852, also pretended to be a minister and sometimes conducted divine services. He also went so far as to perform marriage ceremonies, and not a few couples were united by the imposter. Neither Anderson nor Valentin long remained in this field, the former dying of cholera in 1853, the latter returning to the old country in the fall of 1854.

The need of organized church work, however, soon made itself felt in Princeton. On June 16, 1854, a handful of Swedish settlers gathered in the Smith schoolhouse, located at Smith and Fourth streets, intent on organizing a congregation, Rev. L. P. Esbjörn of Andover, presiding. The total number of original members was 68, including 52 adults and 16 minors. At the annual meeting of the Synod of Northern Illinois, held in Peru, Ill., the following autumn, the new church was joined to the synod.

During the summer following its organization, the church had visits from Erland Carlsson of Chicago, T. N. Hasselquist of Galesburg and L. P. Esbjörn of Andover. To the conference meeting held in Andover in the fall, the church sent as its representative Per Pihlström with a request that the conference provide a regular minister or see to it that more frequent pastoral visits were made. Hasselquist was accordingly appointed to have pastoral charge of the church, also to provide for divine service every other Sunday. Having been licensed to preach, P. A. Cederstam, a divinity student, in March, 1855, was sent to Princeton in charge of the church. After a short time he was transferred to Minnesota, where the need of ministers was still more pressing than in Illinois, leaving Princeton in May, when the church was again left in Hasselquist's charge.

As yet the congregation had no house of worship. At a business meeting held May 27, 1856, it was decided to purchase two building lots located at the northwest corner of Randolph and Putnam streets, and to begin at once collecting funds for the erection of a church edifice. At this occasion the first board of trustees was elected, the members being, E. Wester, S. Frid, W. P. Lind, Carl M. Sköld and Jacob Nyman. The church extended a pastoral call to Rev. L. P. Esbjörn, who accepted and took up his new duties in Princeton June 1st, removing his family there in the fall. Early that summer he began soliciting for the church building fund, raising $540 among the American and $340 among the Swedish residents. On November 23rd the first services were held in the partially completed edifice, which was not dedicated until Sept. 12, 1858, in connection with the annual meeting of the conference. The structure, 42 by 30 feet, cost, inclusive of furniture, $1,600, of which sum $400 remained unpaid.

Sept. 20, 1857, the congregation adopted, with certain amendments, the church constitution proposed by the joint conferences. All were deeply impressed with the solemnity of the step taken, and when, at the close of the meeting, the congregation rose and all joined in singing: "Praise be to Thee, O, God," tears came to the eyes of many, who in that moment probably realized that a tree had now been planted, in the shadow of which many generations yet unborn were to dwell. Esbjörn presided at the meeting and P. Fagercrantz acted as secretary.

The Swedish Lutheran Church of Princeton

During a great part of his term of service in Princeton Esbjörn was troubled with sickness. On occasions when he was unable to serve, the meetings were conducted by Deacon A. P. Larson. But despite ill health, Esbjörn served as the leader of his countrymen even in worldly affairs. For a time he was a member of the municipal council. He did not remain long as pastor of the Princeton church. Sept. 1, 1858, he entered upon his duties as professor of the Scandinavian department of the seminary at Springfield, leaving his pulpit vacant.

During the ensuing vacancy the church was visited as often as practicable by neighboring clergymen, but under such insufficient care it was losing ground. Repeated efforts to obtain a pastor were made in vain. In 1859 a son of the well known Swedish preacher, Per Nyman, came to Princeton, where he succeeded in inspiring such confidence that he was practically made pastor of the church, although without any commission or recommendation from the conference. After a brief period of popularity, he lost the confidence of the people, whereupon his services were dispensed with.

This same year, 1859, a clergyman from Sweden named C. J. Vossner tried to get himself elected pastor of the church at Princeton. The incident forms a rather ludicrous story of pioneer life.

Vossner, who hailed from the vicinity of Eksjö, Sweden, was a regularly ordained minister of the state church and had been connected with some technological institute or other in the old country. He seems to have come to America about 1855, stopping in Michigan, where he purchased from a Norwegian named Hansen a hut and a four acre lot at White River, in Oceana county. Here he went to raising corn and potatoes on a small scale. On Sundays he held religious services in his little hut, provided any of his "parishioners," the Swedish and Norwegian settlers, put in an appearance. It frequently happened that services had to be postponed in the absence of auditors. These settlers were all single men like Vossner himself, and were employed in a sawmill near by. There was no semblance of church organization, aside from a tacit understanding that a collection for the preacher was to be taken every time the sacrament of the Lord's Supper was administered. The preacher's resources being extremely meager, the communion services grew rather frequent and the attendance fell off in consequence, until the pastor and his unpretentious meetinghouse were entirely deserted. Poor Vossner, left to provide for himself, is said to have subsisted entirely on corn and molasses.

Learning that the Princeton church pulpit was vacant, Vossner opened correspondence with the notorious Erik Wester, who was at the time a member of the church, offering his services as pastor. The answer seems to have been encouraging, for Vossner forthwith loaded his few belongings, consisting of wearing apparel, earthenware, a washtub, a wooden shovel, a gun and sundry other things, into a wheelbarrow and started on his way southward. He went by boat across Lake Michigan and then by rail to Princeton, where he arrived safe and sound. Wester, who was greatly pleased with the man, did everything in his power to bring about his election to the pastorate. When Vossner began to read off his old, well-worn manuscripts, Wester turned around in his pew, well to the front, in order to study the effect on the listeners. A deep sigh escaped him, when he noted with what total lack of interest the exhortations of the new preacher were received. So one day, when Vossner called on his friend Wester to inquire about the outlook for his election, he received the crushing reply that he "stood no show at all." Pacing up and down the room, clad in a sort of housecoat, Wester went on in outspoken fashion: "I am very sorry for you, Pastor, but the fact is, the people don't like you. They say your sermons are sheer rot."

Completely disheartened, Vossner had to leave as he had come, taking his wheelbarrow with him to Chicago. The people in Princeton, however, raised about $18 for him as a recompense for his trouble in coming. Vossner subsequently took up the practice of medicine in Chicago and, possibly, in other localities until his final return to the old country.

In the summer of 1860 the Princeton church again obtained a permanent pastor in the person of Rev. John Johnson, who was ordained at the occasion of the organization of the Augustana Synod the same year. Early in the following year the congregation purchased for $225 a house and lot for a parsonage. In the spring of the same year efforts were made to procure a pipe organ. A certain sum for that purpose was raised and sent home by those Swedes of Princeton who had enlisted in the Union army and were now serving in the field. Toward the close of 1864 Rev. Johnson was incapacitated by illness and other ministers had to be called in. He remained, however, until March, 1866, enjoying meanwhile the greater part of his salary in evidence of the esteem in which he was held by the congregation. The communicant membership during his term of service grew from 149 to 226.

Rev. Johnson was succeeded in the spring of 1866 by Rev. A. Lindholm. In 1868 the church edifice, which had grown too small, was enlarged by an addition of 36 feet, and the same year the parsonage was sold, Rev. Lindholm having purchased a home of his own north of the city. The Swedish Lutherans in Wyanet and vicinity at this time belonged to the church in Princeton, and Rev. Lindholm preached in their locality one Sunday each month. July 3, 1871, he resigned from his labors, which had brought the membership up to 450 communicants.

His successor, Rev. J. Wikstrand, was called Jan. 14, 1872. The following year the erection of a new parsonage was resolved upon and two lots at First and Mechanic streets were purchased for the sum of $750. By New Year's the building committee reported that the work had been completed at a total outlay of $2,808. Before the parsonage was built, the question of erecting a parish schoolhouse had been ventilated, but the matter was postponed until 1874, when a schoolhouse was put up at a cost of $593. This structure still stands. At the annual business meeting at New Year's, 1875, the members living at Wyanet upon their own request were granted permission to withdraw and organize a separate congregation.

. The Swedish Lutherans of Putnam, who also were members of the Princeton church, at the annual meeting in 1878 asked permission to build a chapel which was to become the property of the whole congregation, and they were aided in carrying out the enterprise. For a number of years the church had been illuminated with an altar-piece, representing Jesus blessing the little children, in which the artist had carelessly put wings on the shoulders of the mothers who brought the children to the Savior. At the aforesaid meeting the congregation resolved to have the wings removed from the picture, which was done.

After a year Rev. Wikstrand resigned, the date being March 26, 1880. He had been in charge also of the church at Kewanee, visiting there a certain number of Sundays in the year, and had served the church at Wyanet in a similar manner from its organization. At a meeting held May 3, 1880, S. A. Sandahl, a theological student, was elected to take pastoral charge at Princeton following his ordination a year later. The call was accepted with the proviso that the constitution of the church at the next annual meeting be altered to conform to the one drafted and recommended by the Augustana Synod at Andover in 1870. This was done in 1882, but with the result that 56 members withdrew at once, followed later by many others, making a total loss of 80 communicant members. Shortly after this split a new church building was proposed and a soliciting committee appointed, which reported to the annual meeting in 1885 that $2,046 had been subscribed.

In the spring of 1886 Rev. Sandahl removed to Chicago, taking charge of the Trinity Church. He was succeeded in Princeton by Rev. E. Edman, who remained only two years, or until 1888. His successor was O. A. Nelson, a theological student who, after being ordained the following spring, became the regular pastor of the church. In the fall of the same year, it was resolved to erect a new church edifice of brick, built in the form of a cross, with a steeple to one side. The dimensions were to be 82 by 40 feet, in the widest section 54 feet, and height of steeple 110 feet. There was an available building fund of $5,900, to which was added by subscription $2,615. The cost of the church furnished complete, with the exception of the organ, was $10,000. In the fall of 1891 the new sanctuary was dedicated by Rev. L. G. Abrahamson, president of the Illinois Conference. The old structure was sold and moved away, its site being occupied by a schoolhouse.

In the spring of 1894 the pulpit again became vacant, Rev. Nelson removing to the Emmanuel Church in Minneapolis. During the term of vacancy Rev. E. Edman, who had served as missionary to India, had temporary charge. The next permanent pastor was Rev. J. A. Carlström, who assumed the pastorate in April, 1895, and served until the fall of 1898, when he went back to Sweden and entered the service of the state church, returning to America after a few years.

In September, 1899, G. E. Hemdahl, a theological student at Rock Island, was called to supply the pulpit for the ensuing school year, and after a few weeks he was chosen the regular pastor of the church, his election to take effect immediately after his ordination the following spring.

In the year 1900 the sum of $1,000 was raised by subscription to be used partly in wiping out the congregation's debt to Augustana College, partly for repairs on the parsonage. The following year the interior of the church was frescoed, and at the annual business meeting in 1902 it was resolved to purchase a new pipe organ, which cost $1,500. In 1903 a mortgage of $2,000, placed on the church property when the new edifice was erected, was lifted by general subscription. The fiftieth anniversary of the founding of the church was celebrated June 17-19, 1904, with customary festivities and by the publication of an illustrated historical memorial. In 1906 Rev. Hemdahl accepted a call to Paxton. The present pastor is Rev. John A. Berg.

The Princeton church at New Year's, 1907, had 534 communicants, 761 members all told, and property to the value of $19,000.

Rev. John Johnson

Among the Swedish Lutheran clergymen of Illinois during the pioneer period, John Johnson was one of the most interesting characters. While not eccentric in the ordinary sense, he was a man of very distinct individuality, practical views and strong personal convictions. To his credit it must be said that he was fearlessly outspoken on all questions of right and wrong.

John Johnson, whose name was originally written Johannes Jönsson, was born July 21, 1822, in Åkarp, in the Swedish province of Skåne. Beyond learning to read and write, he obtained no schooling. Being naturally bright, he endeavored to quench his thirst for knowledge by omnivorous reading. His favorite reading was books on history, law, political science and civic reform. He owned and cultivated a farm near the village of Slätteryd, and frequently acted, not without success, as legal counsel for his neighbors at the district court.

While T. N. Hasselquist was assistant pastor at Åkarp and Witt-sjö, Johnson seems to have formed such an attachment for him that from that time on he was never so happy as when in his company, and he seemed to have taken the greatest delight in reasoning and debating over religious topics with Hasselquist whenever opportunity offered.

In 1851, at the age of 29, he emigrated to America, following his brother, who had left Sweden the year before. Purchasing a farm at Knoxville, Ill., and settling there, he appears to have familiarized himself with the political and religious conditions in that locality in a very short time. During the first few years he also rented land from others, and took contracts for harvesting broomcorn, employing numbers of newly arrived Swedish laborers. He apparently was a leader among the Swedish settlers in the locality, and after the arrival of Rev. Hasselquist he took a live interest in the affairs of the local congregation and was especially active in promoting the building of a church.

During the cholera epidemic of 1854 and a resultant spiritual awakening in the community Johnson seems to have experienced a complete change of heart. From that time he, as deacon of the church, used to conduct services in the absence of Rev. Hasselquist, besides leading weekly meetings in private homes conjointly with one Nils Randau. Johnson, who was a man of fluent tongue, spoke logically and with effect. Taking all this into account, and realizing the great need of ministers, Rev. Hasselquist urged him to devote himself entirely to the service of the church. He then took up private studies with Hasselquist and made occasional trips to other points to preach. In 1856 he made a preaching tour of Minnesota. Time and again he served as delegate to conference and synod meetings, always taking an active interest in the proceedings.

During the vacancy in the Princeton church, Johnson had preached there repeatedly, making himself favorably known. The congregation having tried in vain to obtain a pastor, he was finally called. Hesitating at first, Johnson, after consulting with the older ministers, decided to accept the call on condition that he would be ordained. Accordingly he went before the ministerium at the meeting in June, 1860, and was then ordained, together with seven other candidates, immediately afterward taking charge of the Princeton congregation.

Johnson, however, seems to have inclined more to a political than an ecclesiastical career. While a gifted preacher, he was still more successful as a political speaker. True, he was actuated with a live interest in church work, but still greater was the enthusiasm with which he partook in the discussion of the great civic issues which stirred the nation at this time and which were finally solved by an appeal to arms. Johnson was bitterly opposed to slavery; to Lincoln's platform he gave his most hearty support and threw himself into his campaign with might and main. Neglecting pastoral work, he campaigned with great energy, advocating not without success the cause of the Republican party in the press and on the platform. There was a poetical vein in Johnson's makeup, and he sometimes engaged in versemaking. His lyre was attuned to the praise of liberty, justice

Rev. John Johnson

and truth. In his campaign songs he displayed great zeal for human liberty and civic rights, as applicable to conditions in the United States. His verses fired many Swedish-Americans to participation in the great campaign for the preservation of the Union. There was none among them who realized the significance of the strife more deeply than did this simple and unpretentious country parson, who also knew how to kindle the fire of enthusiasm in the hearts of his fellowmen. And when a number of the Swedes of Princeton, at the call of the great Lincoln, joined the colors and left for the field of conflict, Rev. John Johnson accompanied them to the train and handed to each and every man a copy of the New Testament—the best gift that could be bestowed.

In his last years of service at Princeton Rev. Johnson's mental powers began to fail, leaving him a sufferer for the remainder of his life. In 1866 he lived in Paxton, not, however, in active service as pastor. The following year he was so far restored as to be able to serve the church at Attica, Ind., but in 1868 he returned to Paxton, where he lived in retirement until 1871. Subsequently he had pastoral charge of the church at Farmersville, Ill., 1872-3, returning to Paxton for two years, 1874-5, and then removed to Moline, where he lived as a mental wreck until his death, Oct. 9, 1882. He left a wife, Johanna, née Bengtson, to whom he was wedded in Sweden, in 1846, and two daughters, Mrs. Rev. H. P. Quist and Mrs. C. G. Thulin of Moline.

Eric Norelius, Historian of the Augustana Synod

Eric Norelius, though young at the time of founding the Swedish-American Lutheran Church, yet must be counted among its veterans for the eminent part he took in the work of organization. His career was begun in Illinois, where he rendered valuable service to the church before removing to the state of Minnesota, his principal field of usefulness. Norelius drafted the constitution for the early churches, which underlies that of the Augustana Synod, suggested the name of the synod, has served as its president for two lengthy periods, still retaining that office, and is the historian of the Swedish Lutheran Church of America.

Eric Norelius was born Oct. 26, 1833, in the parish of Hassela, Helsingland, Sweden, and pursued elementary studies in the city of Hudiksvall prior to his emigration to America in 1850. He came over with a party of a hundred emigrants, including also an elder brother of his, Anders Norelius, who subsequently affiliated with the Swedish Baptists. At the suggestion of Esbjörn, whom he met at Andover, Norelius in the spring of 1851 entered the Capital University at Columbus, Ohio, a Lutheran institution, where he spent four years.

While a student, he received some aid from a Lutheran education society, but spent his vacations earning his living as best he might as a book colporteur and by teaching and preaching. Part of this time he conducted the parochial school of the Immanuel Church of Chicago. His studies completed, Norelius received his preacher's license from the Synod of Northern Illinois in 1855 upon recommendation of the joint Chicago and Mississippi conferences and was ordained in September of the following year. Since 1855 he has served as follows: in LaFayette, Ind., 1855; Vasa and Red Wing, Minn., churches founded by him, 1855-8; Attica, Ind., 1859-60; mission field of Minnesota, 1860-61; Vasa and Red Wing, 1861-8; Vasa, 1868-78, and continued to serve as pastor of the Vasa church, with intervals, until a few years ago.

In the fall of 1857 Norelius and Jonas Engberg began to publish from Red Wing the first Swedish newspaper in Minnesota, entitled "Minnesota-Posten." In October, the year after, this paper was consolidated with "Hemlandet" of Galesburg, Ill. Chicago became the place of publication and there Norelius for the first nine months of 1859 edited this paper, besides the religious monthly, "Det Rätta Hemlandet," both under the supervision of Hasselquist. Frequent appointments to preach in neighboring churches added to his duties. His health failing, the task became too burdensome, and he resigned the editorship to resume exclusive pastoral work.

After having taken an active part in the building up of the Illinois and Minnesota conferences and the organizing of the Augustana Synod, Norelius has continued to this day one of the foremost workers of the church. In 1862 he started a private school at Red Wing. This was removed to East Union and from there to St. Peter and formed the foundation for the present Gustavus Adolphus College. Three years later he founded the orphans' home at Vasa and himself managed the institution for eleven years. In 1872 he began publishing "Luthersk Kyrkotidning," which was merged with "Augustana" the following year, and in 1877 he and Rev. P. Sjöblom founded the present "Minnesota Stats Tidning," which was first known as "Evangelisk Luthersk Tidskrift" and then for many years as "Skaffaren." When in 1889 Hasselquist's paper, "Augustana och Missionären," was increased in size and scope and made the official paper of the Augustana Synod, Norelius was chosen editor. The condition of his health compelled him to resign the editor's chair after a seven months occupancy. In 1898-9 he published "Tidskrift för svensk evangelisk luthersk kyrkohistoria," and is one of the editors of the religious quarterly "Tidskrift för teologi och kyrkliga frågor," published since the year 1900 as a continuation of the historical magazine. To "Korsbaneret," the synodical yearbook, which he edited in 1891-6, Norelius before, during and after that period contributed a number of historical and personal sketches dealing with the early period of the Swedish Lutheran Church in this country. Almost from the time he set foot on American soil Norelius has been a systematic collector of materials bearing on the Swedes of America, and this historical treasury is thought to be the most valuable of its kind. Much of it has been embodied in his principal work, a history of the Swedes and Swedish Lutheran congregations of America, not yet completed. Part I, a large volume of 870 pages, embracing the period from the beginning of wholesale immigration in the forties up to 1860, was published in 1890 by authority of the Augustana Synod. Next in importance of the seven works by Norelius, published separately, is a biography of Dr. T. N. Hasselquist.

In 1874 Norelius was elected president of the Augustana Synod and served upon successive re-elections for seven years. Again in 1899 he was chosen to the same office, and still presides over the church of

Rev. Eric Norelius

which he is now the only surviving patriarch. In 1892 the directors of Augustana College and Theological Seminary conferred upon him the honorary degree of D. D., and in 1903 King Oscar II. made him a Knight of the Order of the Polar Star in recognition of meritorious achievement in behalf of Swedish-American culture.

In 1855 Norelius was united in marriage to Inga Charlotta Peterson and in 1905 at their home in Vasa was celebrated the joint golden anniversary of the aged pair and of the church Dr. Norelius founded and with which he has been connected for the better part of the half-century.

Norelius tells us that he came to this country as one of the so-called Luther Readers, a group of devotionalists of the Old Lutheran type, who saw in Rev. Hedberg, a Finnish divine, their spiritual leader. These believers adhered to the old books, suspecting depart-ures from the faith in the newer ones, frowned on synergism and had misgivings about any presentation of the word of God that did not have the true Lutheran ring. Methodism did not appeal to these earnest people, but shortly after their coming to this country many of them became Baptists. In fact, Wiberg and Palmquist enjoyed the full confidence of this entire group before they changed their convictions and became pioneers of the Swedish Baptist Church in the two countries. With those who went over was his brother, Anders Norelius, but he himself stood firm. We quote this to show the stanch Lutheranism of Norelius at this early period in his life. He was among those who fought the movement for ''New'' or ''American'' Lutheranism in the fifties, and the uncompromising stand for the unaltered Augsburg Confession taken by the Augustana Synod is due in great measure to him. By one of his brethren Norelius has been characterized as a strictly logical thinker, whose apparent speculative tendency is held within proper bounds by his firm and childlike faith in the revealed Word; a positive Lutheran theologian; an objective preacher, who commands attention and interest by the soundness, depth and dignity of his presentation of gospel truths, without playing upon the feelings of his hearers.

As a historian, Dr. Norelius has accomplished a task deserving of the gratitude of the whole Swedish nationality in this country, principally for the wealth of historical material from the fifth and sixth decades of the past century embodied in his historical work. While purporting to be in the main a history of the Lutherans, it is by no means limited to them, but throws much light on the origin of other Swedish church denominations and gives many graphic first-hand sketches from pioneer days. The religious movements among the immigrants are here described by one who knew the leaders personally and stood near to many of them. Dealing, as he does, pre-eminently with his own church, Norelius could not escape the charge of bias and partiality. Inaccuracy in details is another charge urged against his work, which seems less justified in view of the fact that for many data of the pioneer period the historian was bound to trust the memory of others. Taken all in all, the Norelius history is easily superior to any of a number of works in the same field.

Augustana College and Theological Seminary

Augustana College and Theological Seminary at Rock Island, Ill., is a general institution of learning owned, controlled and maintained by the Evangelical Lutheran Augustana Synod of North America. While it is, therefore, a denominational school, and as such aims to serve, primarily, the interests of the Swedish Lutheran Church, it is open to all who desire a liberal education. Its original scope, which was that of a divinity school, has been broadened from time to time, until now the institution, while retaining the theological seminary as a university department, aims to prepare, directly or indirectly, for every vocation in life by giving the general culture or special training which modern conditions require. Its courses of instruction are patterned after the most modern and approved models, and qualitatively, at least, Augustana aims to be in the front rank of American educational institutions.

The English language is used as a medium of instruction in all subjects, except the Swedish language and literature and partly in the theological branches. The subject of Swedish naturally occupies a prominent position in the curriculum, and the institution, not forgetful of its origin, nor of present day practical needs, nor of its future mission as the exponent of Swedish culture in America, provides ample facilities for instruction in the language, literature and history of the northern fatherland. It is the object of the institution to throw about the student all the influences which make for a healthy and harmonious physical, mental and moral growth.

Augustana College is situated in the eastern part of the city of Rock Island, on the slope of a prominent bluff, reverently named Zion Hill, from which the view is striking and picturesque. To the northwest, on the opposite banks of the Mississippi, lies the city of Davenport, commandingly located on the bluffs which rise almost directly from the river. To the east the eye rests on the tall chimneys of the busy city of Moline, rendered famous by her manufactures. To the north, directly in front of the college grounds, stretches Rock Island, from which the city took its name, comprising over nine hundred acres of ground upon which is built the largest of the government arsenals together with extensive federal manufacturing plants. At the lower end of the island the two branches of the river are spanned by bridges for railroad and general traffic.

The college grounds consist of about 36 acres of land. On this tract are located the following buildings belonging to the institution: the new main building, a handsome stone structure built in the pure Renaissance style, occupied since 1888, and containing in its three stories and basement the principal recitation rooms and lecture halls and the chapel; the old main building, occupied since 1875, used chiefly as a dormitory and refectory, with its class rooms and chapel now given over to the use of the business college; the gymnasium, the ladies' dormitory, Ericson Hall, and two buildings used as residences.

When about the year 1845 a stream of immigration from the Scandinavian countries to the United States began, the earliest settlements, as shown in the foregoing, were made in Illinois, Wisconsin,

Immanuel Parish School-house, Erected 1856, First Home of
Augustana College and Theological Seminary

Iowa and Minnesota. These immigrants had been members of the Lutheran state church in their mother countries and were, as a class, religious and churchly people. Earnest and pious men came over to serve as their pastors, and Lutheran congregations were early established among both Swedes and Norwegians. At the organization of the Evangelical Lutheran Synod of Northern Illinois in 1851 several Scandinavian clergymen were present and took part in the organization. The scattered Scandinavian and American Lutherans in this section of the country thus were united in one common synod. The constant stream of immigration rapidly added to the numbers of the Scandinavians who before 1860 constituted about one-half of the synod, then made up of three separate conferences, the American and German Rock River Conference, the Norwegian Chicago Conference and the Swedish Mississippi Conference. This synod, in co-operation with other Lutheran bodies in the West, established a school, known as the Illinois State University, at Springfield, for the special purpose of educating Lutheran ministers.

In the two Scandinavian conferences the need of pastors was very pressing. At their common meeting in Waverly (Leland), Ill., Oct. 3, 1855, they resolved to send a representative to Sweden and Norway with a view to inducing ministers and students of earnest and irreproachable character to come over and aid in the work. The Synod of Northern Illinois, in session at the same place for the next few days, amended this resolution by voting to found a Scandinavian professorship at the seminary in Springfield. In January, 1856, Rev. L. P. Esbjörn began to solicit funds for the maintenance of the new chair. At the next joint annual meeting of the Chicago and Mississippi conferences, held in Rockford Sept. 26-27, 1857, Rev. Esbjörn was unanimously chosen for the Scandinavian chair, the election being ratified by the synod, sitting at Cedarville Sept. 27th to Oct. 4th. Rev. Esbjörn assumed his new duties at Springfield in the fall of 1858 and served for two years. Owing to doctrinal differences between the Scandinavian and the other members of the synod, Esbjörn resigned his position in March, 1860, and early in April removed with his family to Chicago, where shortly afterward he resumed instruction, seventeen of the twenty Scandinavian students at the Springfield seminary having followed their teacher. This action brought matters to a crisis. On April 23-28 the Swedes and Norwegians met in convention at Chicago and after thorough deliberation unanimously resolved to withdraw from the synod, to organize a synod for themselves and to establish a theological seminary of their own. The result was the organization of the Scandinavian Evangelical Lutheran Augustana Synod at a subsequent convention, held at Jefferson Prairie, near Clinton, Wis., June 5-11, 1860.

The Chicago Period

It is to this meeting that Augustana College and Theological Seminary traces its origin as a synodical institution. The seminary had already been established at Chicago by Esbjörn's act af removing to that city with the Scandinavian students and continuing their instruction. By resolution at the first synodical meeting, it was officially recognized and accepted by the synod, and Rev. Esbjörn was expressly declared the synod's choice as "Scandinavian and theological professor at the Augustana Seminary in Chicago." But the first article in the constitution for the school adopted at the same meeting read: "The Augustana Synod shall establish and maintain a theological seminary now (or, for the present) located in Chicago and known as Augustana Seminary." It was an oddly worded article, which foreshadowed the strife over the location of Augustana that has agitated the synod more or less down to recent years. Esbjörn and others favored the permanent retention of the school in Chicago, while Erland Carlsson, Hasselquist and others were for locating it in the country. The article in question could be interpreted to favor either side. Carlsson at this same meeting moved, and it was resolved, to draw up plans for purchasing land and starting farming for the benefit of the seminary. Thereby the door was opened for experiment and we find its promoters and sponsors again and again in quest of land where the institution might be located in the heart of some populous Swedish agricultural section. The institution was removed first to Paxton, then to Rock Island, but in neither place quite successful realty investments were made, the farming project was never carried out, and the advantages obtained by the removal from Chicago are still a matter of opinion.

The first president of the new institution was Rev. Esbjörn and the following constituted the first board of directors: Rev. T. N. Hasselquist and Mr. F. Langeland, elected for four years, Rev. Erland Carlsson and Mr. S. Gabrielson, for three years, Rev. O. Andrewson and Mr. C. Strömberg, for two years, Rev. O. J. Hatlestad and Mr. C. J. Anderson, for one year. Mr. Andrew Nelson Braekke of Chicago was elected treasurer. Rev. Carlsson was the first president of the board, but Rev. Hasselquist soon succeeded to the presidency of the directorate and made the annual report to the synod on the first year's progress. The Immanuel Church is credited with having furnished the students with room, board and washing for the first two weeks of the fall term, and of the $737 in cash donations received during the first year $576 came from Swedish and $161 from Norwegian churches.

The urgent need of means for the maintenance of the school and the prosecution of its work prompted a resolution by the board to send a representative to Sweden to petition the king for a collection to be taken in all the churches of the realm for the benefit of the new seminary. The emissary was also to solicit donations of money and books by direct personal effort.

Prof. Esbjörn was appointed to solicit funds in the United States and to go on a special mission to Columbus, Ohio, to secure the transfer to the seminary of $1,500 given by Jenny Lind-Goldschmidt to the Capital University as a foundation for a Scandinavian chair.

King Charles XV. granted the privilege of soliciting and receiving collections from the churches in Sweden during a period of two years. Rev. O. C. T. Andrén, who was the emissary, resigned his commission Sept. 1, 1861, to settle down in Sweden, but the work was subsequently taken up by Esbjörn and so successfully pushed that a total sum of $10,846 was realized from that source. In addition thereto, King Charles XV. himself donated 5,000 volumes from his private library.

As to the Jenny Lind donation Dr. Norelius, who was at the time the only Swedish student at Capital University, gives this account: Dr. Reynolds, then president of the institution, arbitrarily used the money without rendering any account of it to the board of regents, and upon inquiry into the matter no trace of the fund was found, either in the treasury or in the records. It may be added that Dr. Reynolds left his position after putting the school into serious straits by bad financial management. Later he became president of the Springfield seminary, named the Illinois State University, and it was his peculiar tactics that forced Esbjörn's sudden resignation and removal, although doctrinal differences in the Synod of Northern Illinois had paved the way for that step.

How to secure capable instructors was another vexed question. During the first year Prof. Esbjörn, the only regular professor, was assisted by Rev. Abraham Jacobson and several students, while Rev. C. J. P. Peterson, recently from Norway, gave instruction without charge to the Norwegian students, but declined an offer of a professorship. The attendance during the first year was 21.

The synod in 1861 instructed the board to extend a call to P. P. Waldenström of Upsala, who years afterward dissented from the state church and became the leading spirit in the Mission Covenant of Sweden. It was decided to send A. J. Lindström, a student, to Upsala University to prepare for teaching at the seminary. Lindström earned the degree of Ph. D., was ordained to the ministry and then assumed the designated position, serving 1870-71. Despite appeals to the Norwegian constituency of the synod, a suitable man to give instruction in that language had not been found up to 1863. An English tutor was not secured until the following year, when Rev. William Kopp of the Pennsylvania Synod was called.

While in Sweden in the interest of the seminary in 1862, Prof. Esbjörn resigned his position and accepted an appointment by the crown to become pastor of the parish of Öster-Våhla.

The chief motive for this step doubtless was his love of the fatherland, but he had other reasons. On many points he and Rev. Hasselquist held different views. The latter had opposed his election to the Scandinavian professorship in Springfield, having negotiated with Peter Fjellstedt of Sweden to take the place, and now they took issue with one another on the removal of the seminary to Paxton. Several months prior to Esbjörn's resignation the board of directors had urged Hasselquist to remove to Paxton and use his influence as president of the synod in promoting the colonization plan in behalf of the school. He thus became the pastor of the new congregation there and as one of the prime movers in the enterprise naturally would have a decisive voice in affairs. Disliking to stand in the way of either the financial plan or the personal ambitions of his brother churchman, Esbjörn chose to yield, when so favorable an opportunity was given.

Both Waldenström and Andrén having declined calls to become his successor, Rev. Hasselquist was chosen temporary professor to fill the vacancy. In 1863 the synod authorized the board to secure Rev. Sven L. Bring, or some other capable man from Sweden. Failing in this, the synod at its next annual meeting made Hasselquist the incumbent of the theological chair until further action should be taken. No change was ever made, and Hasselquist remained as professor and president of the institution until his death, Feb. 4, 1891.

The Paxton Period

The permanent location of the seminary had not been determined. In 1860 a tract of land in Grundy county, Iowa, was offered on condition that the institution be located there. Of this tract 700 acres was to be a gift to the school and 2,640 acres to be sold, partially for its benefit. The land being found unsuitable for the purpose, the offer was rejected, but other tracts in the same locality so appealed to the investigators that they recommended the founding of a colony in Butler, Grundy or Black Hawk county, Iowa, and the removal of the seminary to the locality that should be selected. A detailed colonization plan was formulated, a site was selected at Applington, Butler county, and purchasers were invited, but none responded. The failure of the plan was charged to the uncertain business conditions incident to the Civil War.

Subsequently the directors received from the Illinois Central Ry. Co. an offer of 5,000 acres of land at $6 per acre, and a commission of one dollar per acre on a tract of 20,000 acres and 50 cents on an additional 40,000 acres to be sold through their efforts, all on condition that the institution be located at some station along the Illinois Central line.

At the synodical meeting held in Chicago June 23-29, 1863, the removal of the seminary to Paxton, Ill., was decided upon, an agreement with the Illinois Central people being simultaneously ratified. Pursuant to this agreement 1,000 acres of land had already been purchased from the company at $6 per acre, and the directors had been given the agency for the sale of 30,000 acres at a commission of one dollar per acre and an additional 30,000 at a commission of 50 cents per acre. The board bound itself to dispose of 10,000 acres within one year from the signing of the contract. By June 1st four thousand acres had been sold and $2,350 in commissions had been received. A congregation had been organized at Paxton and a schoolhouse costing $750

Augustana College—"Valhalla," First School Building at Paxton

had been purchased for the use of the seminary, which was to open there in the fall. About the middle of September the fall term opened. Owing to the unfinished condition of the new quarters, Rev. Hasselquist had to accommodate the students for the first two months in his private residence. During the first year at Paxton the seminary was attended by ten students, of whom seven were Swedes and three Norwegians.

In 1865 the institution was granted a special charter stipulating that Augustana Seminary was to have its location in Paxton or its vicinity and might own $50,000 worth of property free of taxation. In 1869 the charter was amended, changing the name to Augustana College and Theological Seminary, requiring merely that its location be within the boundaries of the state, and raising the limit on non-assessable property to $100,000.

Instruction was given in college classes as early as 1866, but it was not till ten years later, in 1876, that a senior class was formed. From 1863 to 1870 the average number of students in attendance was about 35.

In 1870, following the friendly separation of the Norwegians from the synod, new by-laws for the institution were adopted, providing for both a preparatory and a complete college course of instruction in addition to the theological course comprising two years. At their withdrawal the Norwegians received the sum of $10,000, which had been collected as a fund for the establishment of a Norwegian professorship at the common institution.

The Rock Island Period

In the meantime the stream of Swedish immigration bore mainly westward and northwest from Chicago. The plan to surround the institution with populous Swedish settlements about Paxton miscarried and the desirability of a more central location became more apparent year by year. The matter was first broached publicly at the synodical meeting in 1868, an offer of $40,000 in cash and 10 acres of ground having been made on condition that the school be located in Geneseo. Later the would-be donors went back on their promise, and the authorities looked about for some other acceptable location. Five years passed before any definite step was taken. Then Rock Island was settled upon as the most favorable location available, and in 1873 a tract of 19 acres in the eastern part of the city was purchased for $10,000.

On this site the first main building, a brick structure with three stories and basement, was erected with all possible expedition. It was completed for occupancy in the summer of 1875; the removal of the institution took place at that time and instruction was begun in the new college building at the opening of the fall term in September of that year. In addition, two frame dwellings were built, also a two-story and basement brick structure for the use of the president and the theological classes. The cost of the first four buildings was $53,000.

By a synodical resolution in 1873 every adult member of the synod was required to pay 25 cents annually toward the support of the institution.

Augustana College—Main Building, Dormitory and Gymnasium

From 1868 to 1873 there had been two classes in the preparatory department, two in the college and one in the seminary. The latter year a third college class was added and the year after a third preparatory class. Two years later the fourth or senior class was formed in college and was graduated in 1877. The first college class graduated from Augustana consisted of: Carl Aaron Swensson, C. J. Petri, Matthias Wahlström, Constantine M. Esbjörn, Joshua Hasselquist and J. H. Randahl.

In the year 1879 Augustana College was placed on the same level with the colleges in Sweden by act of the Swedish department of ecclesiastics granting its graduates admittance to the universities of Upsala and Lund without examination.

A scientific course in college was established in 1880, but efficient instruction in the natural sciences had been previously given, especially since 1878, when Josua Lindahl, a well-known scientist of Sweden, was engaged to teach that branch. He occupied the chair of science for ten years, until his appointment in 1888 as state geologist and curator of the museum at Springfield.

Gradually the institution attracted students of other than Swedish descent, and to meet their needs a special classical course without Swedish was introduced in 1882.

Prior to 1885-6 female students were rare at Augustana and were not matriculated. During the next few years their number rapidly increased and co-education became an established fact. The principal impetus was the establishment of the conservatory of music in January, 1886. Two years later there was added a commercial department, named Augustana Business College. A normal department followed in 1891 and an art department in 1895.

The original plan of the theological seminary, to have at least three professors, one for each of the leading languages used—Swedish, Norwegian and English—was not fully realized until 1868, when Rev. S. L. Harkey was elected to the chair of the English language and Rev. A. Wenaas to that of the Norwegian. When the synod was split in 1870 the plan had to be completely recast. The courses were gradually made to embrace two years, and from 1874 there were two regular classes in the seminary up to 1890, when the university plan was adopted, substituting courses for classes. The number of courses, at first fourteen, has since been increased to twenty.

In the college proper ten departments have gradually been established, viz., Swedish, English and philosophy, Latin, Greek, modern languages, Christianity, history and political science, biology and geology, physics and chemistry, and mathematics and astronomy. Swedish and English were provided for in the original plan. Around the Swedish chair clustered Christianity, German and the classics, and around the English chair, history, philosophy, mathematics and the sciences. As a rule these subjects were taught in the language around

which they were grouped. Post-graduate courses were introduced in
the college in 1891 and in the seminary a year later.

Within ten years of its erection the first college building became
inadequate. The synod in 1883 resolved to erect a new main building
of brick at an estimated cost of $55,000. The cornerstone was laid
in 1884, on November 6th, a date memorable in the history of the
Reformation. A total of $30,000 had been subscribed and the next
year Mr. P. L. Cable of Rock Island came to the assistance of the
synod by donating the sum of $25,000 to the building fund.
The building plans were then changed so as to provide for stone

Augustana College Chapel

instead of brick as building material, thereby adding about $30,000
to the estimated cost. The outer shell of the structure having
been erected, the building stood thus for some time before the additional funds necessary for its completion could be raised. This was
finally accomplished, and early in 1888 the interior of the new building
was so far finished that the class rooms could be occupied. The dedication took place June 12, 1889. In 1891 the finishing touches were put
to the building by the erection of the cupola and the portico.

The institution has always been open to students without regard
to language, race, nationality or creed. Of the students in the
theological seminary about 650 have been ordained to the holy ministry
in the Augustana Synod. From the college department about 425 have

been graduated with the degree of A. B. or B. S. The commercial college numbers some 650 graduates, the conservatory of music over 40 and the normal department about the same number. During the academic year ending in 1907 the total attendance was 570.

As recorded, Prof. L. P. Esbjörn was the president of the institution during the first three school years, his term ending by resignation in 1863. He was succeeded by Dr. T. N. Hasselquist, who served for several years as temporary president and then as permanent head of the institution until his death in February, 1891. His successor was Dr. Olof Olsson, whose services were determined by death in May, 1900. That year the synod called to the presidency Dr. Carl A. Swensson, head of Bethany College, upon whose declination Dr. C. W. Foss, the vice president, became acting president for the year 1900-1901. In June, 1901, the synod elected as president Dr. Gustav A. Andreen of Yale University, who is the present incumbent of the office.

Following are the men of other than Swedish descent who have been connected with Augustana as professors for various periods: Rev. W. Kopp, 1864-7; Rev. A. Wenaas, 1868-70; S. L. Harkey, D. D., 1868-70; Rev. Henry Reck, A. M., 1873-81; W. F. Eyster, A. M., 1875-82; R. F. Weidner, D. D., 1882-94; Rev. G. W. Sandt, A. M., 1884-88; A. W. Williamson, Ph. D., 1880-1905; Rev. E. F. Bartholomew, D. D., Ph. D., 1888—.

During the school year that ended in the spring of 1908 the teaching force of the institution in its entirety consisted of a faculty of twenty-two regular professors, besides sixteen instructors, teachers, and assistants. The regular professors are here given: Rev. Conrad Emil Lindberg, D. D., R. N. O., vice president, professor of systematic theology, hermeneutics, liturgics, apologetics and church polity; Rev. Carl August Blomgren, Ph. D., secretary, professor of Hebrew, Old Testament introduction, propaedeutics and English homiletics; Claude W. Foss, Ph., D., professor of history and political science; Charles Linus Eugene Esbjörn, A. M., professor of modern languages; Rev. Edward Fry Bartholomew, D. D., Ph. D., professor of English literature and philosophy; John August Udden, Ph. D., F. G. S. A., F. A. A. A. S., Oscar II. professor of natural history; Rev. Nils Forsander, D. D., R. N. O., professor of historical theology and Swedish homiletics; Rev. Sven Gustaf Youngert, D. D., Ph. D., professor of philosophy, Greek New Testament exegesis, New Testament introduction and catechetics; Isaac Morene Anderson, A. M., professor of the Greek language and literature; Linus Warner Kling, A. M., professor of the Latin language and literature; Rev. Jules Göthe Ultimus Mauritzson, B. D., professor of the Swedish language and literature; Emil Larson, professor of organ, piano and theory, director of conservatory; Rev.

August William Kjellstrand, A. M., professor of English in the academy and assistant professor of Latin; John Peter Magnusson, Ph. D., professor of physics and chemistry; William Emanuel Cederberg,

Augustana College—Gustav Andreen, President

B. S., Ph. B., professor of mathematics and mechanical drawing; Mrs. Edla Lund, professor of voice, sight singing and ear training; Olof Grafström, professor of painting and drawing; Caleb Larson

Krantz, M. Accts., professor of bookkeeping, penmanship, spelling, correspondence and grammar; Andrew Kempe, A. B., M. Accts., LL. B., professor of banking, commercial law, bookkeeping, civics and mathematics; Sigfrid Laurin, professor of piano; Iva Carrie Pearce, B. E., professor of elocution and physical culture; Gertrude Housel, professor of violin and piano and director of orchestra. The total enrollment for the school-year of 1907-8 was 462, the number of male students being 306 and the female, 156.

Olof Olsson, Pastor, Educator and Author

Dr. Olof Olsson's chief service to the Swedish-Americans was rendered during the twenty-one years he was connected with Augustana College and Theological Seminary. His pastoral work in this country was performed mostly during the years he was in charge of the church at Lindsborg, Kansas, but he continued to be an influential preacher in the Augustana Synod until his death. Before coming to America he had labored fruitfully as a minister of the state church for more than five years. His authorship, which consists of devotional works or books of travel written in a religious vein, is mostly the leisure work done during his last twenty years, yet rank with the best Swedish literary products in the United States.

Olof Olsson was a native of Vermland, Sweden, born at Björntorp, Karlskoga parish, March 31, 1841. Being the son of a common workman in the iron range, the boy was early put to hard work. His parents were Pietists of the strictest sort, who brought up their children according to Christian precepts. The father was extremely stern, but the mother's milder aspect of religion enabled her to make it attractive to her sons, and Olof at an early age became imbued with her spiritual ardor. He was studious and showed decided musical talent, wherefore he was placed under the tutorship of Svante Sedström, organist and cantor of Fredsberg parish, Vestergötland, who, being a man of liberal education, took his apt pupil quite a little way in his studies. Returning home after one year, he much preferred his books to manual labor. About this time Dr. Fjellstedt sent out ringing appeals for pious young men to dedicate their lives to work in the foreign missionary field, and after a talk with the pious divine on one of his visits to Vermland, Olsson entered the Fjellstedt missionary institute, determined to devote himself to work among the heathen. Friends of the family and brethren in the faith in the circle of evangelical Pietists in Karlskoga promised the needed support. He entered the school in 1858. After a year the authorities of the institution concluded to send the able and devout young student to the missionary institute in Leipsic to complete his course. But the stale formalism and high-church orthodoxy pervading that school was repulsive to him and he soon returned home disheartened and with shattered ideals. He was engaged for a short time as teacher at an orphanage in Wall, then went to Upsala, determined to study for the ministry and enter the service of the state church of Sweden. He completed the college course in January, 1861, and the divinity studies in 1863, whereupon

Rev. Olof Olsson

he was ordained in December, in the Upsala Cathedral. He now served in turn as adjunct pastor in Brunskog, vice pastor in Elgå, pastor at the Persberg mines and mills near Filipstad and curate in Sunnemo. Olsson proved a stirring preacher, whose work resulted in notable revivals, wherever he was stationed. By his affiliation with the evangelistic movement promoted by the Readers, or Devotionalists, he won the favor and confidence of his earnest brethren in the clergy, but incurred also the odium of the worldly class, and notwithstanding perceptible pastoral successes, he finally became discouraged and concluded that true gospel work could hardly be carried on under the trammels of the state church.

To escape the religious restraint, Olsson resolved to emigrate, and soon headed a party of people who shared his sentiments on the voyage to the New World. They came over in 1869 and founded a settlement in McPherson county, Kansas, now known as Lindsborg. Olsson became their pastor and served as their spiritual and temporal adviser for seven years. Prior to his coming to this country, he had familiarized himself with the work and status of the Augustana Synod, but the question of joining that body was left open for the time being. It was not long, however, until he and his church joined the synod. While at Lindsborg, Olsson was elected superintendent of schools of the county and for a term represented the district in the Kansas legislature.

After a few years Rev. Olsson enjoyed the confidence of the synod to the extent that he was in 1875 called to a chair in its theological seminary at Rock Island. Accepting the proffered position he entered upon his duties as an educator the following year. He taught there for twelve years. After resigning his professorship he worked for a short time in behalf of Bethany College, at Lindsborg, then spent one year abroad with his family, consisting of three daughters and one son. His wife, Anna Lovisa Johnson, whom he married in 1864, had died in 1887. Upon his return Olsson assumed charge of the church in Woodhull, Ill., but a position of greater responsibility was soon to be his. When in 1891 death removed Dr. Hasselquist from the presidency of Augustana College and Theological Seminary, Olsson was the logical successor. He was called by the board as acting president and was unanimously elected president of the institution at the synodical meeting the same year. In this capacity he served until his death, which occurred May 12, 1900.

Without a great deal of schooling, Olsson was a man of profound scholarship, attained by constant private study, travel and research, and of wide knowledge and experience, gained in the great school of life. Consequently, when in 1892 the Augustana College board conferred on him the degree of D. D. and Upsala University the following year that of Ph. D., these were no empty honors. Aside from his services to Augustana, as teacher and president, Dr. Olsson rendered this institution valuable services in soliciting many thousands of dollars for its maintenance. Upon his return from a European trip in 1879 he presented several new ideas applicable to the work of the Augustana Synod, and the great oratorio festivals at Rock Island and Lindsborg, the Augustana Conservatory of Music, as also the Augustana Hospital in Chicago, were realized at his initiative. During the prevalent defection from Lutheranism to Socinianism in the seventies, Dr. Olsson, although favoring free evangelism, took a determined stand in opposition to this movement on doctrinal grounds, and but for him the synod's loss to Waldenström's following and the Mission Friends in general would unquestionably have been much greater.

In the character of Dr. Olsson the qualities of the heart were predominant. He was a man of intense feeling, a warm sentimentalist, with a temperament oscillating between the extremes of joviality and melancholy. He knew the art of popularizing his learning. His sermons and writings were on a level with the intelligence of the common people and appealed strongly to them. His books were published in comparatively large editions, enjoyed great popularity when first published, and they are still extensively read.

The following are the published works of Dr. Olsson: "Vid korset," devotional; "Det kristna hoppet," being meditations upon the death of his beloved wife, dedicated to her memory; "Helsningar från fjerran," his first book of travel, dealing with his trip in 1879; "Något om känslans bildning"; "Reformationen och socinianismen"; "Vi bekänna Kristus"; "Till Rom och hem igen," 1890, an arraignment of Romanism in the form of a book of travel, containing also snatches of philosophy, church and profane history, descriptions and meditations in pleasing profusion; lastly, a posthumous volume of sermons and lectures, 1903. Dr. Olsson possessed a fascinating literary style, and his writings, like his public addresses, abound in wit, epigram, delicate sentiment and profound thought.

The Illinois Conference

The Synod of Northern Illinois was composed of Lutherans of various nationalities—Americans, Germans, Norwegians and Swedes. It was early subdivided into two districts, the Rock River and the Chicago conferences. These divisions were not strictly geographical but based largely on nationality, the Americans and Germans being counted with the former and the Scandinavians, or rather, the Norwegians, with the latter; for the district comprised, when organized in 1851, no Swedish minister or congregation. Where Rev. Esbjörn and his churches in western Illinois should belong was not definitely stated, but at the second synodical convention, held in 1852, a third conference district was formed, to be known as the Mississippi Conference. The pastors Esbjörn and Hasselquist and the licensed preachers Valentin and Hokanson, with the churches in their charge, constituted its first membership. The Swedish churches which soon came into existence in the Chicago Conference were added to the Mississippi Conference. Thus the former came to be all Norwegian and the latter all Swedish. But the two held point conferences annually, wherein the younger Minnesota Conference soon joined.

Swedish Lutheran Church at Paxton—First Edifice

The meeting of the Mississippi Conference held at Moline, Jan. 6-9, 1853, was the first Swedish Lutheran church convention in America. The delegates in attendance were: ministers, Esbjörn, Hasselquist and Valentin; laymen, Samuel Jönsson of Andover, Johannes Jönsson of Knoxville and Carl Lindman of Moline. Of two other meetings held the same year, at Andover and Galesburg, respectively, no minutes

were preserved.   The joint meeting held in Chicago Jan. 4-9, 1854, by
the Mississippi and Chicago conferences, was the first of its kind and
one of the most important conventions held prior to 1860.   The lack
of ministers being one of the most pressing needs of the time, a remedy
was sought in two ways—licensing devout and able lay preachers and
calling ministers from the fatherland.   Before going abroad for
teachers it was thought best, however, to organize regular congregations.   Many and widely scattered as the Swedish settlements were,
this work could not be accomplished at once by the mere handful of
Swedish pastors in the field, but the plan was imparted to the various
communities in a circular letter.   At this stage the idea of the conference calling ministers for the individual churches, as set forth in
the plan, was probably the only practicable method, and this was
the practice for a number of years.   Later the choice was vested in
the congregations themselves.   The license system, though a temporary
expedient, did not meet the needs, and was gradually abandoned.   In
all other essentials, this meeting committed itself to the principles and
practices ever since generally followed among the Scandinavian Lutherans of America.

When the Mississippi Conference met in Andover in December of
the same year, Dr. Peter Fjellstedt of Sweden was commissioned to
select and call pastors who were thought willing to leave their country
to preach the gospel to their scattered countrymen in the United States.
At this meeting the Andover church was dedicated.   When, at a joint
conference meeting in Waverly (Leland), Ill., in October, 1855, calls
extended to ministers in the old country were found to have elicited
no favorable responses, the plan to educate men to supply the need
was first suggested, and resolutions were passed looking to the establishment of a Scandinavian professorship at the theological school
maintained at Springfield by the Synod of Northern Illinois.

At a joint meeting of the two conferences in Chicago March 18-23,
1857, it was decided to ask the churches to contribute $25 each per
annum toward the maintenance of the proposed professorship and to
call a professor as soon as $500 had been raised.   The other important
thing done at this time was the adoption of a proposed constitution
to be accepted in its essential parts by the congregations as a condition
of membership in the conferences.   This document, submitted by L. P.
Esbjörn, E. Norelius, Erland Carlsson and O. C. T. Andrén, and chiefly
the work of Norelius, committed the churches to the unaltered Augsburg Confession and laid down the law for church government, which,
with certain alterations, has been followed by the Swedish Lutherans
generally to the present time.   In September of the same year, while
assembled at Rockford, the conferences elected a candidate for the

Gethsemane Swedish Lutheran Church, Chicago

professorship, subject to the action of the next synodical convention. Esbjörn was the choice, with all but two votes cast in his favor. The lack of ministers was a standing topic for discussion at the meetings. Calls extended to clergymen in Sweden were continually declined, and the education of its own pastors had become an imperative condition for the progress of the young church.

The lack of unanimity between the orthodox and the New Lutherans of the synod and difficulties which hampered the work of Esbjörn at the seminary in Springfield, prompted the organization in 1860 of an independent Scandinavian Lutheran church body named the Augustana Synod. Prior thereto the northern part of the Mississippi Conference had been formed into a separate organization named the Minnesota Conference. With this exception the Mississippi Conference comprised the entire Swedish Lutheran field in the United States, mainly the settlements in Illinois, Indiana and Iowa. The Swedes and the Norwegians remained one synodical body until 1870, when their ways parted. The separation was amicable and the Norwegian brethren withdrew to form a distinct synod. At the subsequent subdivision of the Augustana Synod into the New York, Illinois, Minnesota, Iowa and Kansas conferences, the Illinois Conference, whose territory comprised Illinois, Indiana, Michigan and the southern part of Wisconsin, became the natural continuation of the old Mississippi Conference, wherefore the origin of the Illinois Conference is dated back to 1853.

At the first meeting of the conference under its new name in August, 1870, the field was divided into two districts corresponding to the respective territories of the former Chicago and Mississippi conferences. In 1877 there were seven districts in all, and after further growth and subdivision thirteen districts now compose the conference.

Augustana College and Theological Seminary was founded in the territory of this conference, which has always contributed the greatest share toward the support of the school. The other conferences, having each established one or more colleges or schools of their own, look to the Illinois and Iowa conferences to furnish the main support of the synodical institution.

This conference maintains four charitable institutions exclusively its own, namely, the Augustana Hospital in Chicago, orphans' homes at Andover and Joliet and the Salem Home for the Aged, also at Joliet.

At the organization meeting of the Mississippi Conference divine services were held once in the English language, but aside from the English classes in the Sunday schools the work has been conducted almost exclusively in the Swedish language until in recent years several congregations worshiping exclusively in the language of the land have been established. Many others are using the two languages interchangeably, as a concession to the needs of the younger generation.

Trinity Swedish Lutheran Church, Chicago

For the first few years of the conference there are no statistics. The first report of the condition of the treasury is found in the minutes of the meeting held in 1867, showing $173.67 in receipts and $76.10 in disbursements. In 1871 there were 41 congregations with a total membership of 15,292, the result of about 20 years of work. During the next period of 18 years there was an increase to 132 churches and 40,702 members, as shown by the statistics of 1889. These also show

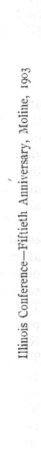

Illinois Conference—Fiftieth Anniversary, Moline, 1903

the value of church property, less debts, to be $642,500. The expenses and contributions for all purposes aggregated $200,000. From the statistics of 1906·for the entire conference we derive, by excluding the six conference districts lying wholly outside the state, the following data relative to the Swedish Lutherans in Illinois: number of congregations, 117; members, 46,239; value of church property, exclusive of the charitable institutions, $1,373,622; debt on same, $186,862; local church expenditures, $285,568; contributions of local churches to general funds, of the Augustana Synod, $16,318, of the Illinois Conference, $18,170; expenditures for all church purposes for the year, $320,057.

The Augustana Hospital

The need of a Swedish hospital was early felt in Chicago, especially among the Swedish Lutherans. Rev. Erland Carlsson had not labored long in this field, when, realizing this need, he established a private hospital in rented quarters. This institution, especially designed for sick and ailing immigrants, later was merged with the hospital established by Dr. Passavant. The great fire put an end to this work for many years, but the idea of a Swedish Lutheran hospital was still kept alive, and in 1880 the first step toward its realization was taken.

That year Dr. O. Olsson in a newspaper article suggested the establishment of a deaconess institute in connection with a hospital after the pattern of benevolent institutions in Germany, which country he had visited the year before. At Dr. Olsson's initiative a meeting to discuss the matter was held at Moline Nov. 6th of the same year. Then and there a committee was chosen to pave the way for the enterprise. Its members were, Revs. O. Olsson, G. Peters, C. A. Evald, C. P. Rydholm, H. O. Lindeblad and Messrs. Peter Colseth and C. G. Thulin. They were instructed to make inquiries whether one or two deaconesses could be had from Stockholm, also to advise with Dr. Passavant and to negotiate with him for the use of part of certain grounds in Lake View given him for hospital purposes. Letters containing much encouragement and some cash, the latter amounting all in all to $161, were received, but nothing further was accomplished up to February, 1881, when the question was taken up at the meeting of the Illinois Conference in Chicago. There Rev. C. B. L. Boman was added to the committee and the cause was recommended to the congregations as worthy of their hearty support. In October the committee recommended Lake View as the location of the future institution and the conference at its next meeting authorized the purchase of property in that part of Chicago for a sum not to exceed $10,000. But up to that time little more than $600 had been received. The committee was, therefore, given the alternative of starting hospital and deaconess work in rented quarters. Dr. Passavant, while warmly favoring the project, was constrained to decline the committee's request for the purchase of any part of the ground controlled by him, but he offered

Augustana Hospital

to erect thereon a building for $5,000 that might be used for the purpose in question almost gratuitously for a period of five or ten years.

At this same conference meeting, held in February, 1882, the first hospital board was elected, consisting of the following: ministers,

Erland Carlsson, O. Olsson, C. B. L. Boman, M. C. Ranseen; laymen, C. P. Holmberg, G. A. Bohman, John Erlander. At its first meeting, Feb. 13th, incorporation papers were made out and the following officers chosen: Erland Carlsson, president; O. Olsson, vice president; C. B. L. Boman, secretary, and C. P. Holmberg, treasurer. An executive committee was made up of the president, the treasurer and M. C. Ranseen, as the third member.

By New Year's, 1884, the hospital fund amounted to about $1,200. With this money at their disposal the board had instructions to open the institution shortly after the following conference meeting in February. On Feb. 20th, the board accepted an offer from Dr. Passavant to the effect that four acres of the hospital grounds in Lake View would be leased to them for twenty years and a building for $5,000 to $10,000 erected for their use, on condition that the new hospital would care for a reasonable proportion of the patients for whom Dr. Passavant had assumed responsibility. This agreement was sanctioned by the conference then in session. The constitution adopted at this same meeting named the new hospital The Deaconess Institution of the Swedish Evangelical Lutheran Church, and defined its aim and purpose as follows: to care for the sick according to the Lord's command and to educate and train Christian nurses of the evangelical Lutheran faith.

In March, 1884, the homestead of Rev. Carlsson, located at Lincoln and Cleveland avenues, was secured as a temporary hospital, at a rental of $50 per month, Dr. Truman W. Miller was selected as chief physician, with two assistants, and on May 28th the institution was dedicated and formally opened, its first patient being a Miss Nibelius, who broke her leg in stepping off the street car which brought her to attend the dedication.

The Deaconess Institute of Stockholm having declined to send trained deaconesses, Mrs. Hilda Carlsson was appointed matron and Miss Lottie Freid assistant, the latter being in reality the first nurse at the institution. The new hospital had fifteen beds, which were soon occupied. All went well until Oct. 29th, when a disastrous fire occurred, stopping operations until the beginning of the year 1885, when the building was again occupied, repairs having been made and one story added to the building.

In September, 1884, the conference rescinded its action with respect to Dr. Passavant's offer, which had been found unsatisfactory. At the next meeting the corporate name was changed to The Augustana Hospital and Deaconess Institution.

During its first year of activity the hospital had a total of 35

patients, 18 being charity cases. Up to February, 1885, the totals of
income and expenditure for the hospital balanced at about $3,500.

The Carlsson residence had been leased for three years from
February, 1885, but the conference was desirous that property should
be purchased for the growing institution. In October, 1886, in response
to inquiries, Rev. Carlsson offered his property, consisting of the house
and several lots at Lincoln and Cleveland avenues, for $35,000, agree-
ing to donate $1,000 of the amount. The offer was declined for the
time being, and later four lots at Larrabee street and Belden avenue
were purchased from a real estate agent for $12,000. By a singular
coincidence the owner had simultaneously sold the same lots for $12,500
to another party, who came into possession. After several other futile
attempts to acquire a suitable site, Rev. Carlsson's offer was accepted
in February, 1887. He demanded payment in full by Feb. 23, 1889,
and, after having raised $9,600 by means of a bazaar and other sub-
stantial amounts through subscriptions, and taken a loan of $20,000,
the directors in May, 1890, paid off $14,176, thereby settling in full
with Rev. Erland Carlsson.

In the spring of 1890, Drs. Miller and his assistants, Chew and
Woodworth, having resigned, Dr. Charles T. Parkes was chosen physician and surgeon in chief and Dr. A. J. Ochsner attending physician
and surgeon. Upon the death of Dr. Parkes one year later, Dr. Ochsner
became chief of the medical staff.

About this time a donation of $5,000 was received from Henry
Melohn, a Dane, the gift being in memory of his Swedish wife, for
whom a ward in the hospital has been gratefully named. In 1890
115 patients were cared for and the accounts for the year showed an
income of $8,326, exclusive of the $20,000 loan, and an expenditure of
$31,072, including the last payment of the debt to Rev. Carlsson, $6,500
on redeemed notes and $5,400 to the bank.

In view of the urgent need of increasing the capacity of the institution the conference in 1891 empowered the board to erect a new
building and called upon the members of the churches to provide the
means by liberal subscriptions. The result was a disappointment, only
a few thousand dollars coming in through that channel.

The interest of the women of the conference had been enlisted in
this enterprise from the start, and about 1890 a ladies' board was
organized in order to do more systematic and telling work in behalf
of the institution and to superintend its household affairs. This board
consisted of the following named ladies: Mrs. Emmy Evald, Mrs. M. C.
Ranseen, Mrs. L. G. Abrahamson, Mrs. J. Blomgren, Mrs. E. Olson and
Mrs. P. Johnson. Another agency doing efficient service for the

hospital was "The Good Samaritan," a Swedish quarterly, published in its behalf.

Undismayed by the lack of means, the board through its building committee proceeded to have a new building erected. Ground was broken Oct. 22, 1892, and on Feb. 12th the following winter the corner-stone was laid. The building, designed as a part of the future hospital structure, was to be 62 by 84 feet, 6 stories high, with basement, built of iron, brick and stone, at a cost of $85,000, and to provide room for 125 beds. A loan of $50,000 was taken and through a bazaar held in April, 1893, an additional $5,749 was realized. In the early fall the building was finished and its dedication took place Sept. 17th. At the end of the year the total resources were $122,390 and the liabilities $65,825.

The records for 1893 show 267 patients, providing an income of $5,668, but at this point, after the completion of the new building, a period of greater prosperity ensued. In 1895 the corresponding figures were 721 and $21,170, and the institution again began to be crowded for room. By housing the nurses in the old building and—in rented quarters and by adding several wards, the capacity of the hospital was substantially increased. In 1897 the number of patients passed the thousand mark and three years later it reached 1,500.

In 1902 the board, being pressed for room to accommodate the ever increasing number of patients, recommended the completion of the hospital building according to the original plan. With the sanction of the conference the directors took the necessary steps but a bitter fight waged on those in control intervened, delaying building operations until late in the following year.

This fight ensued when in July, 1902, Dr. M. C. Ranseen was called as superintendent of the institution and Rev. Henry O. Lindeblad, who had acted as chaplain and solicitor since January, 1898, resigned, protesting that he had been called to that position and had in fact served as superintendent. To his grievance was added that of Dr. C. O. Young, since January, 1898, attending physician, who raised a variety of complaints. In December a special conference meeting was held, at which these grievances were aired for days in heated and acrimonious debate. The outcome was that Rev. Lindeblad obtained a nominal vindication, but without reinstatement, Dr. Young's connection with the hospital was severed by the board and Dr. Ranseen resigned the superintendency before having fully entered upon his new duties. The struggle seemed to accentuate the fact that capable management on the part of the board and the efficient service of Dr. Ochsner, a surgeon of high repute, have been the chief factors in the upbuilding and maintenance of the institution.

The storm over, building operations were begun in August, 1903, and about Dec. 1, 1904, the annexed structure was ready for occupancy, giving the hospital a total capacity of 220 beds. The additional structure, completing the building as originally planned, was finished at a cost of about $100,000.

In 1902 the debt on the old structure was wiped out, but on the new building a debt of $100,000 was incurred. This is being gradually reduced.

In 1894 a training school for nurses was opened, comprising a two years' course, and in 1896 the first class of trained nurses, eight in number, was graduated. This school heretofore has taken the place of the deaconess institute originally contemplated and implied in the corporate name.

In the natural course of development the Augustana Hospital has ceased to be an exclusive retreat for patients of a particular faith or nationality and become, as it is today, a hospital for the general public, pervaded, however, by the religious influences of the Swedish Lutheran Church.

The men who have remained longest on the board and given the institution the most efficient and faithful service in that capacity are: Dr. M. C. Ranseen, who has been on the board since 1882, with the exception of three years, 1902-5; Dr. C. A. Evald, from 1884 to the present; Dr. L. G. Abrahamson, from 1886 to the present; Samuel Anderson, 1890-94 and from 1898 to the present; Theodore Freeman, from 1892 to the present, and Rev. M. Frykman, from 1895 to the present.

The training school for nurses at present has an enrollment of 75. It is in charge of Miss Lila P. Pickhardt, the head nurse, and her assistant, Miss Johanna Nelson. The course now covers a period of three years and since the first graduation in 1896 177 nurses have received diplomas. A number of these hold positions of trust and responsibility in various hospitals.

In 1904 Rev. Dr. M. Wahlstrom, president of Gustavus Adolphus College, was called as superintendent. Having resigned his former position, he assumed his new office in September. With the duties of superintendent are combined those of chaplain of the institution.

The present hospital staff numbers sixteen physicians and surgeons, all of whom are either specialists or medical men of large experience. Besides these, seven internes and ten externes serve as assistants to the doctors in charge.

The growth of the institution in the last few years is indicated by these figures:

In 1904 1,739 patients were cared for and the income from paying patients was $57,699. In 1905, after the completion of the building, the number of patients grew to 2,205 and the income from that source to $80,394. The corresponding figures for the year 1906 were, 2,353 patients and cash from patients, $96,752.

Since the founding of the hospital its principal support, aside from current income, has been derived from the following sources: church bazaars, more than $35,000; donations and legacies about $80,000, the largest amount willed to the institution being $20,000 from Thomas D. Lowther. In the first quarter century of its existence, the total earnings of the hospital through the treatment and care of patients foot up to about half a million dollars.

The Orphans' Home at Andover

Three years after its organization the Augustana Synod took up the question of founding a home where poor orphans might be cared for and given a Christian bringing up. The decision to establish such an institution was reached at the Chicago convention of the synod in 1863. A committee of five was appointed to solicit funds, purchase land near Paxton and carry out the plan. Within the next two years $3,000 were raised and a 160 acre farm was purchased for $3,520. Cultivation of the land had begun when in 1867 the orphanage committee was instructed to sell this farm, secure a more favorable location for the proposed home near Andover or Swedona and open the institution, if practicable, in the fall of the same year. As a temporary arrangement a two story house, 18 by 28 feet, was erected on an acre lot near Swedona and the home was opened at the time designated, with S. P. Lindell and wife in charge. During the first year they had three wards under their care. In 1870 a farm two miles from Andover was purchased for $5,150. Here the orphanage was permanently located shortly afterward. Additional land purchases were made until the farm comprised 440 acres, valued at over $40,000. In 1902 the total property value was $47,930, but the institution was burdened with a debt of $11,000.

At its Jamestown convention in 1876 the Augustana Synod turned the establishment over to the Illinois Conference, which from that time has been responsible for its administration. When the exigencies required the building of a schoolhouse the Sunday schools were appealed to for the funds needed. The response was generous, and from that time the home has had a substantial annual income from the mites contributed by and through the Sunday school pupils in a similar manner. By 1880 the number of children at the home had reached 40, overtaxing the house first erected, wherefore a new building was put up the following year, costing $3,364. In 1902 an annex was added at a cost of $7,746, a building strictly modern in construction and equipment.

Mr. Lindell served as superintendent of the home until his death in 1881. His successor was J. S. Swenson, who served for eight years. Thereafter frequent changes in the management have taken place. The

Orphans' Home, Andover

control of the institution is vested in a board of nine directors chosen by the Illinois Conference. The number of orphans in the care of the home is about seventy, and its present superintendent is Rev. A. G. Ander. The annual disbursements for the home, according to a late report, aggregate $8,000 and the net present worth exceeds $43,000.

The Orphans' Home and Industrial School at Joliet

In 1887 the Illinois Conference, after having found the Andover orphans' home inadequate to the growing needs, took preliminary steps toward increasing its facilities for taking care of the helpless young. A committee then appointed reported at the following annual meeting, submitting a plan, whereupon the conference resolved to found a second orphanage and instructed the committee to select a suitable site. In 1889, at the annual conference in Joliet, it was proposed to locate the new orphans' home within the territory of either the Chicago or the

Orphans' Home, Joliet

Rockford district, whose respective churches were asked to submit offers for securing the institution in their immediate neighborhood. No definite offers were submitted until 1891, when an advantageous bid was reported from Joliet. It was then resolved to locate the home at Joliet and put up a $15,000 building, $8,000 having been pledged by the city, the remainder to be raised within the conference.

A set of seven directors now elected reported progress at the annual meeting of 1892. Work on the new building had been begun, and on the 9th of August following, the corner-stone was laid by Dr. L. G. Abrahamson, president of the conference. On May 26, 1896, the building having been completed by slow stages, according as the means could be raised, the institution was dedicated to its purpose under the corporate name of The Orphan Home and Industrial School of the

Illinois Conference of the Swedish Evangelical Lutheran Augustana Synod. On Feb. 11th, a few months prior, it had been opened for the reception of wards. Sister Frida Schelander, who had been trained at the Swedish Lutheran Deaconess Institute in Omaha, was secured as superintendent of the home. During the first year she had 22 orphans under her care. The number has since grown to nearly one hundred. The full capacity being already taxed, the directors are constrained to refuse a large number of applications for admission every year.

The home is pleasantly situated in a parklike spot a short distance outside the city of Joliet, with which it has excellent connections by means of a street-railway line and a good driveway.

The treasurer's report of 1907 shows disbursements for current expenses for the year last past aggregating $8,000. From partly paying inmates the home had an income of $2,000. The grounds of the institution are valued at $25,000 and the total net worth is about $30,000.

The Salem Home for the Aged at Joliet

The Salem Home, at Joliet, Ill., which is an old age retreat for the worthy poor among the Swedish Lutherans, is the most recent charitable institution established by the Illinois Conference. In 1903 the need of such a home was officially recognized by the conference in the appointment of a committee to solicit funds and prepare tentative plans, and to report to the conference at the subsequent meeting. Certain property was offered by parties in Chicago on condition that the institution be located in that city, and other conditional donations were promised. As locations were suggested Joliet and West Irving Park, Chicago. This being reported, the conference in 1904 definitely decided that an old people's home should be established, but left it with another committee to propose the location and continue the preparatory work. The following year it was resolved to locate the new institution adjacent to the orphans' home in Joliet, on ground belonging thereto. By February, 1906, some three thousand dollars had been raised and the committee in charge accepted plans for the proposed building, a two-story building with basement, 30 by 86 feet, to contain thirty rooms. The corner-stone was laid on May 6, 1906, during the conference meeting held that year at Joliet. A permanent board of directors was elected, with instructions to complete the building at an added cost not to exceed $12,000, and to prosecute the work of soliciting funds so that the institution should, if possible, be completed without debt. In the fall of 1906, the exterior of the building was completed, the total cost so far being $9,500. In May, 1907, the conference authorized the board to take a loan of $5,000 in order to complete the interior and put the building in condition for occupancy without further delay, and early in the present year the Salem Home welcomed its first inmates. By resolution of the conference in May, 1908, the home for the aged and the orphanage were placed under one board of management. The object of the institution is to provide and maintain a Christian home for worthy old people, with preference given to members of the Illinois Conference.

The Augustana Synod

The relation existing between the Illinois (Mississippi) Conference and the Augustana Synod, of which it is now but a part, reminds one of the adage, "The child is father of the man," for the greater of these bodies is virtually the product of the smaller.

Pursuant to a resolution passed at the common convention of the Chicago and Mississippi Conferences in Chicago, the Scandinavian Evangelical Lutheran Augustana Synod of North America was organized June 5, 1860, at a meeting held in the Norwegian Lutheran Church of Jefferson Prairie, Rock county, Wisconsin. Delegates were present from the aforesaid conferences and from the Minnesota Conference, forty all told. The numerical strength of the new organization at the time is shown by the following figures: Swedish—36 congregations, 3,753 communicants, 17 ministers; Norwegian—13 congregations, 1,220 communicants, 10 ministers, making a total of 49 congregations, 4,967 communicants and 27 ministers. There were 21 Swedish and 8 Norwegian church edifices.

The next synodical convention of great importance was that of 1870, at Andover. After having worked together in harmony for a decade, the Swedish and Norwegian brethren now decided upon a friendly separation. The growth of the synod and the complexity of work seemed to both sides to demand such a step, while all were agreed that the union had lent strength to the synod in its early stages. In the official name of the Augustana Synod the word "Swedish" was substituted for "Scandinavian," and the new body was named the Norwegian-Danish Augustana Synod. To preserve amicable relations between the sister synods it was resolved that each send representatives to the conventions of the other; that neither should admit ministers or congregations to membership except by mutual agreement, and that in places where the Scandinavians were few in number all be recommended to join one local church, be it Swedish or Norwegian. At this convention also was adopted a constitution for the congregations in all its essentials corresponding to the one adopted by the Chicago and Mississippi conferences in 1857.

The progress made during the past ten years was shown in figures, as follows: congregations—Swedish, 99, Norwegian, 30, mixed, 13, tutal, 152; communicants—Swedish, 16,376, Norwegian, 1,784, total, 18,160; general membership—Swedish, 26,322, Norwegian, 2,880, total, 30,555; church edifices, 76 in all; ministers—Swedish, 46, Norwegian 27, total, 73.

In 1870 three new conferences were organized as integral parts of the synod. This meant a decentralization of power and entailed a change in the plan of operation, so much of the authority of the synod being vested in the subordinate bodies as almost to make them co-ordinated district synods. Prior to this,' all mission work was in the hands of a central mission board, and the various institutions were under synodical control, but after the change in the direction of Congre-gationalism the bulk of the mission work was left to the conferences, as were also existing educational and charitable institutions, except Augustana College and Theological Seminary, together with authority to establish and maintain new ones, and sole responsibility for the same; the power of exercising church discipline as well as the duty of installing pastors and dedicating churches was transferred from the synodical to the conference officials, the right of ordination alone being reserved by the synod. The real or apparent need of these constitutional changes lay in the growth of the synod far beyond the bounds of expectation and the local needs arising from changing conditions. The loss by the separation in 1870 was more than made up by the organization of the three new subdivisions, the Iowa, Kansas and New York conferences.

The growth and activity of the synod will appear from the following concentrated statistics, exclusive of the Norwegian element of the first decade:

Statistics of the Augustana Synod, 1860—1906

Year	Minis-ters	Congre-gations	Church B'ld'gs	Commu-nicants	Total Membe ship	General Contri-butions	Local Ex-penditures	Total Dis-bursements
1860	17	36	21	3,753	Not Known	$ 622	$ 8,549	$ 9,171
1870	46	99	51	16,376	26,322	7,381	124,707	132,088
1880	147	332	226	41,976	74,716	36,757	217,155	253,912
1890	325	637	499	84,583	145,503	75,467	552,986	628,453
1900	449	921	781	121,446	201,100	154,887	794,977	949,864
1906	558	1,049	903	154,390	243,705	212,190	1,338,193	1,550,383

The synod has sixteen benevolent institutions worth, less debts, $570,000, and nine educational institutions whose net present worth aggregates $825,000. Two schools have been discontinued, namely,

Hope Academy, located at Moorhead, Minn., and Martin Luther College, at Chicago. The total value of church property, according to the statistics for 1906, was $7,290,162, and debt on same was $849,682, showing a net worth of $6,440,480.

The Augustana Synod now comprises eight conferences, the Nebraska Conference having been organized in 1886, and the Columbia and California conferences in 1893. In addition, mission work is carried on in three large districts, known as the Utah, Montana and Alabama mission districts. Rounding out the figures, we find that in a period of fifty years the Swedish Lutheran Church of America grew to one thousand congregations, served by five hundred ministers, and that this church body now contributes annually more than one and one-half million dollars to Christian work.

CHAPTER IX

The Swedish Baptist Church

Earliest Known Swedish Baptists

 NDIVIDUAL Swedish Baptists are known to have lived and labored in the United States long before any Baptist church of the Swedish nationality was organized here or in the old country. As they were affiliated with the general Baptist congregations in the localities where they happened to live, there is no special record of them, except as they asserted themselves through religious activity. The first of whom we have any record was one Robert Nordin. In their writings on Swedish Baptist history A. G. Hall and G. W. Schroeder make no reference to him, but from other sources we learn that he came over from England to West Virginia as early as 1714 and there preached the gospel until his death in 1735. The second of these isolated Swedish Baptists to be historically traced is John Asplund. A Swede by birth, he went to England in 1775 and served in the British navy, deserting which he came over to North Carolina. There he joined the church at Ballard's Bridge, and soon afterward removed to Southampton county, where he was ordained. More than a century ago, when Washington served his first term as president of the United States, Asplund traveled seven thousand miles in eighteen months, mostly on foot, through all the states and territories of the newly formed Union, collecting facts and statistics of the American Baptist churches, which he first published in a yearbook in 1790. This work, entitled the "Baptist Register," and forming an invaluable record of the Baptist denomination for that period, was afterwards issued in revised editions for several years in succession, up to and including 1794. Of his first published register or yearbook only two copies are known to be in existence, and copies of those for the following years are very rare. The two original copies are preserved in the archives of Colgate University. John Asplund lived for many years in the city of New York, where he labored assiduously in behalf of the church. He settled lastly in Maryland, and met his death in Virginia in 1807, being accidentally drowned in attempting to cross Fish Creek.

For almost forty years following the death of John Asplund, we have no record of any Swedish Baptist, until Gustavus W. Schroeder, then a sailor before the mast and later a sea-captain, was baptized in New York City. "When I became a Baptist," says Captain Schroeder in his memoirs, "I did not know of the existence of another Swedish Baptist in the whole world." The erroneous supposition that he was the first Swedish Baptist known, Schroeder himself corrects by reference to the aforementioned John Asplund.

Gustavus W. Schroeder, while on a voyage from New York to New Orleans, was converted in April, 1844, through Methodist agencies, in the latter city. His purpose was to join a Methodist church in New York after his return from a subsequent voyage to England. In the meantime, the articles of faith and practice issued from the Baptist Seamen's Bethel in New York won him over to the views therein expressed, and on Nov. 3, 1844, he was baptized in East River, near Corlear's Hook, and became a member of the Seamen's Bethel, subsequently known as the First Baptist Mariners' Church, and its house of worship as the Mariners' Temple. In 1894, fifty years later, the Swedish Baptist Church of New York celebrated the third of November as a day of jubilee, in commemoration of the event. Schroeder, although brought in touch quite extensively with the Swedish Baptists, both in this country and in Sweden, has remained almost continuously a member of the American Baptist Church.

Prior to 1853, probably for a number of years, one John Åkerblom, a well to do Swede, was a deacon and an influential member of the First Baptist Church of Detroit, Michigan. A Swedish nobleman, one Count Piper, and a daughter of Katharina Broberg, one of Sweden's pioneer Baptists, both were members of American Baptist churches in New York at an early date. Captain Schroeder states that, having become a Christian, his first desire was to go to Sweden to make known his new religious views among relatives and friends; but heretofore no one of these pioneer Swedish Baptists, as far as known, had undertaken to labor especially among their own countrymen.

The founder of the first Swedish Baptist church in America was still to come. This was Gustaf Palmquist, a former schoolmaster, who came over in 1851 and joined the American Baptist Church in Galesburg the year following. He was soon after engaged by the American Baptist Home Missionary Society to missionate among his fellow-countrymen and was instrumental in organizing at Rock Island, Ill., the first Swedish Baptist church in the United States. The first Baptist church on Swedish soil had been organized just four years prior, and Palmquist had inclined to Baptist views before emigrating. Five days after the organization of the Rock Island church Rev. Anders Wiberg, who had left the ministry of the Lutheran state church of Sweden and embraced the Baptist faith, landed in New York and there labored among his countrymen for eight months, but without building up a separate congregation, the converts being brought into the fold of the Mariners' Church. This church is notable in the history of the Swedish Baptists for having mothered two of their eminent pioneers and leaders, namely Capt. Schroeder and Dr. J. A. Edgren, while Col. Broady, prominent in the work in Sweden, was originally a member of the Tabernacle church in the same city.

Pioneer Work in Sweden

In most cases the Swedish-American religious denominations have been transplanted from Sweden to America, but in the case of the Baptists the order was reversed, inasmuch as the seed from which sprung the Baptist Church in Sweden was sown first by Schroeder, followed by a number of other workers, who had embraced the Baptist faith in this country or had labored here for greater or less periods.

Schroeder's desire to preach Baptism in Sweden was soon realized. In May, 1845, a few months after his conversion and baptism in the United States, he started for Sweden and arrived a month later in Göteborg. After the home salutations were over, his first call was on Fredrik Olaus Nilson, the American Seamen's Friend Society's missionary in that city, to whom, in their first interview, he related how he had become a Baptist. The following Sunday Nilson and his wife were invited to Schroeder's old home, four miles from the city, for private worship. Nilson preached to a small gathering of friends and neighbors, and after the close of the services proper, Schroeder spoke to the gathering about the doctrines and practices of the Baptists. Thus, in his childhood home, Schroeder was the first to expound Baptist doctrines publicly in Sweden. Schroeder also visited Stockholm and northern Sweden, meeting with groups of Pietists and dissenters, but refraining, according to his own statement, from proselyting among them.

In 1843, two years prior to Schroeder's visit, a Danish Baptist preacher named Ryding had visited the village of Mala in southern Sweden, where lived a single Baptist who had been converted and baptized in Copenhagen. Ryding had come intent on preaching, but encountering bitter public prejudice he confined himself to operations strictly private. He was soon compelled to return home, and the lone convert emigrated to America to escape persecution.

Schroeder left for Hamburg without any direct attempt to win Nilson over from Methodism, which he professed, but his conversations and certain tracts sent from that city convinced Nilson on the subject of baptism so that he himself went to Hamburg where he obtained further instruction by J. G. Oncken, a pioneer German Baptist preacher, and was baptized by him in the river Elbe Aug. 1, 1847. As between emigrating to America, where he might worship and preach according to the dictates of his own conscience, and remaining in Sweden to propagate Baptism in the face of persecution, Nilson chose the latter. After one year the Hamburg church sent A. P. Förster, a Danish preacher, to assist him, and by united effort they organized the first Baptist church in Sweden. This took place in the house of Bernt Nikolaus Nilson in Landa parish, province of Halland, Sept. 21, 1848. The members were six in number, including Nilson, five other persons having been baptized in the sea, near Göteborg, by Rev. Förster, under cover of darkness the night before. The ceremony took place at Ullervik, and those baptized where Nilson's wife Sofia, his brothers Sven Christian and Bernt Nikolaus, Andreas Wrång and Abraham Anderson. Sven Christian Nilson, who was the first to be immersed, like his brother Fredrik had been in the United States, where both were converted among the Methodists. He emigrated and in 1898 was still living in Wastedo, Minn. His was the first baptism by immersion that took place in Sweden, the foregoing adherents of the movement having been baptized in Copenhagen or Hamburg.

The Swedish Baptist Church of Rock Island

Of the origin of the Swedish Baptist Church of Rock Island, the mother church of the Swedish-American Baptists, there is but meager information available. It appears that a few members of a party of so-called "Hedbergians," who came over from Sweden in 1850, located in Rock Island and Moline. Among these people Gustaf Palmquist was in good repute in Sweden and he came to America for the specific purpose of serving as their pastor. Upon his arrival he found his intended parishioners widely scattered, and when, after joining the American Baptist Church in Galesburg, he was made missionary to the Swedish settlements, it was most natural for him to turn first to this little group. He soon won them over to his views, and Rock Island thus became in the summer of 1852 the starting-point for the propagation of the Baptist doctrine among the Swedish people. He brought in his first sheaves from the new harvest field on the 8th day of August, when three persons were baptized by him, one of whom, Peter Söderström, had been a member of the Swedish Lutheran Church of Moline. On the thirteenth of the same month* a church was formally organized. Its first members are said to have been six in number, to-wit: A.

* The date, also given as Sept. 13th and Sept. 26th, cannot be definitely fixed owing to the absence of church records.

Theodor Mankee (also written Mankie), A. Boberg, Fredrika Boberg, Peter Söderström, Karl Johanson (Charles Johnson) and Anders Norelius. The organizer and first pastor of this flock was Palmquist, who, from the absence of his name on the list, appears to have retained his membership of the Galesburg church. After eight months the new church was officially recognized by a council of delegates from American churches, who met in Rock Island May 5, 1853, when Rev. Anders Wiberg of Sweden also was present, having came on a visit to this country shortly before. The church now numbered thirteen members, all of whom are said to have been baptized by Palmquist. The additional members as recorded were: Charles Håkanson, John Asp, G. H. Peterson, Hans Smith, formerly of the Moline Lutheran church, Hans Mattson, Margreta Peterson and Maria Johnson. A number of the members lived in Moline. In his published memoirs Col. Hans Mattson makes incidental mention of his connection with these people early in the year 1853.* But that he was one of the original members of the church would nevertheless seem uncertain in view of the fact that he became one of the first members of the Lutheran church organized at Vasa, Minn., in 1855, and that there was among the earliest Swedish Baptists another person of the same name, who is said to have preached in Altona about 1858.

A revival followed, bringing the membership up to fifty, and in the summer of 1853 Fredrik Olaus Nilson, a pioneer Baptist preacher of Sweden, arrived with a small number of followers of whom three families from Berghem parish located in Moline and joined the Rock Island church.

With the support of the American Baptist Home Missionary Society, Rev. Palmquist was pastor of the church up to August, 1857, but divided his time between his pastoral duties and mission work in Iowa and Minnesota, also in Chicago and New York during the last two years.

Rev. Palmquist was succeeded by Anders Norelius, who had pastoral charge until April, 1858. The pulpit was now vacant until the fall of 1859, when F. O. Nilson became pastor in Rock Island, remaining for six months, until his return to Sweden. After that the church had no regular pastor till the fall of 1862, when L. L. Frisk was stationed there. Owing to lack of pastors and consequent neglect of

---

* As forming a bit of the history of this church, Mattson's reference is here quoted:
"Dr. and Mrs. Ober (who had befriended Mattson) were deeply religious people and members of the Baptist Church; and as I was now under their influence and soon came in contact with Gustaf Palmquist, the Swedish Baptist preacher, and the handful of people who formed the core of the first Swedish Baptist Church in America, I became one of their circle before spring and doubtless would have remained one of them to this day, but for the fact that circumstances over which I had no control brought me into different environments and another field of activity. That same winter Rev. Wiberg of Stockholm visited Moline, when I likewise formed his acquaintance." (Minnen, p. 36.)

its interests this first church did not attain noteworthy growth, its membership remaining at a standstill for many years. In 1864 the total was but 72, showing little increase since 1853.

A period of prosperity for the church came in the seventies, while Rev. Olof Lindh was in charge. Lindh came there in the winter of 1870 on a preaching tour and in July located in Moline, intent on leaving the ministry to engage in ordinary employment. He was requested to put this off until the local church had held its monthly meeting, when he was elected its pastor. The Rock Island-Moline church was at this time the largest in the denomination, numbering as it did about 125

The Rock Island Church—First Swedish Baptist House of Worship in America

members. Lindh preached here for several years with but indifferent success. But early in 1873 a revival was inaugurated which brought large numbers into the fold. The church grew to a membership of 200, notwithstanding many removals, and a hundred or more converts should be credited to Rev. Lindh's efforts.

After six years of service Lindh contemplated leaving to return to Sweden. His ultimate determination so to do led indirectly to an amicable division of the flock and the organization of the Moline contingent into a distinct church. For many years past they had had a house of worship in Moline, where meetings were regularly held. The increase had been greatest among the Moline members, and they now felt able to support their own pastor. When the Moline church was organized, some seventy-five persons joined at once, depleting the ranks of the mother church, and leaving it with a membership about the same as in 1870. The younger church wished to retain Lindh as pastor, but he was fixed in his resolve to leave for the old country and at his suggestion Rev. Olaus Ockerson was called. During the six years Lindh was in charge the Rock Island church flourished more than at any time before or afterwards. While the daughter has grown ever stronger, the mother has been on the decline, and according to the statistics of 1907 the Rock Island church numbered but 36 members.

The church was without a house of worship during the first five years of its existence. In 1857 a small edifice was erected, seating 70 persons. It was a very ordinary frame building, remarkable in no other respect than this that it was the first house of worship erected by Swedish Baptists in the United States. The present church property is valued at $5,000.

The Moline church is in a flourishing condition, with 234 members at the last accounting and owning a church edifice valued at $15,875, seating 500, and a parsonage worth $3,000. Rev. Detlof Löfström is the present pastor, having served since 1905.

The Swedish Baptists of Galesburg

The Baptist movement in Galesburg in 1852 was not without effect upon the Swedish people there, but those among them who, like Palmquist, embraced that faith, apparently joined the American church, and no Swedish church was organized at the time. Not until five years later was such a step taken, when, in 1857, seven persons met and organized a Swedish Baptist church. Among them was one Ahnberg. In the fall of the same year all but Ahnberg removed to Altona, whereby the original church organization in Galesburg was dissolved. L. L. Frisk served as their pastor in both places. Galesburg, however, was for a time the headquarters of the Baptist propaganda, inasmuch as from that city were published two newspapers in the interest of the church, first, ''Frihetsvännen,'' then ''Evangelisten,'' both engaged in hot controversy with the Lutheran paper ''Hemlandet.'' Of the status of local church work during this period little is positively known. The fact is that a small group there continued without an organization until 1869, when Rev. Lindh, then traveling missionary, and Rev. Rundquist, then stationed in Altona, met in Galesburg and organized a church, the second in order in that place. A young preacher named Hamilton was chosen pastor, superseding Rev. Lidén, who had preached in Galesburg and vicinity for a long time. They held their initial public services in the American Baptist church, when two persons were baptized, making ten or twelve members all told. This church organization went the way of the first, being broken up after some time.

A third organization was formed in 1879 or 1880 by Rev. C. Silene, from new material and possibly the remnants of the former church. Even this did not attain permanence, and in 1888, for the fourth time, the Swedish Baptists in Galesburg went through the forms of organizing. The church then formed has endured to the present day. Rev. P. E. Sörbom has served this church during the past five years. The latest statistics give it a membership of 89. The Altona church, which sprung from the first one in Galesburg, is still on the records of the denomination and was credited with 13 members in the year 1907.

General Organization of Early Churches

During the period of 1852 to 1864 there were organized in Illinois, Iowa and Minnesota fourteen churches, three of which had been disrupted prior to the latter year. The oldest churches outside of Illinois which still survive are: Village Creek, Ia., organized 1853; Stratford, Ia., 1856; Scandia, Minn., 1855.

In 1856 the first step toward organic union of the Swedish Baptist churches was taken through the holding of a conference, June 20th to 25th, at Rock Island. Gustaf Palmquist presided and A. Norelius acted as secretary. Nine churches were represented, those of Rock Island and Chicago, Allamakee and New Sweden, Ia., Root River (or Houston), St. Paul, Clear Water Lake and Chisago Lake, Minn., and New York City. There were reports on the work in the various fields, but this and several successive conferences met and adjourned without effecting a permanent organization. Little interest was shown in these meetings. Of the first six, all but two were held at Rock Island, and at the sixth conference but one church besides the local one was represented. No conferences took place in 1861 and 1863. At a meeting, the seventh in order, held at Village Creek, Ia., June 16-18, 1864, the Illinois-Iowa Conference was formally organized.

With those of his followers who did not remain in Moline and Rock Island F. O. Nilson proceeded to Iowa and thence to Minnesota, where they formed the nucleus of a church in Houston. Nilson preached in various localities between Houston and St. Paul and three other congregations sprung up which on Sept. 18, 1858, were organized into a conference of their own. The churches were at Houston, Scandia, Wastedo and Chisago Lake and their pastors were Nilson and Norelius. In July, 1860, the Rock Island congregation in a circular letter to the sister churches submitted the question whether the general conference should be continued and how, indicating that, although Nilson had been present at the preceding annual conference at Rock Island, the brethren there were still ignorant of the existence of the Minnesota Conference.

Swedish Baptist Founders and Leaders—Rev. Gustaf Palmquist

Gustaf Palmquist, the pioneer Swedish Baptist preacher in the state of Illinois and the West, was born in Solberga parish, Småland, May 26, 1812. At the age of six he lost his father through death. His mother, who was converted at the deathbed of one of her sons, gave the remaining six children a Christian training, resulting in their conversion, Gustaf last of all. In 1839 he obtained a situation as school-teacher in Filipstad and later held a like position at Gustafsberg, near Stockholm. After his conversion he began evangelizing among his pupils and in the tenements and prison cells of the capital.

Gustaf Palmquist.

Rev. Gustaf Palmquist

In 1850 a group of Pietists in Norrland, known variously as "Luther-Readers" and "Hedbergians," prepared to emigrate in order to secure greater liberty of worship than was accorded them in the state church, with which they were dissatisfied also on doctrinal grounds. In the United States they intended to form a genuine Lutheran congregation. They wished to secure a minister on whose doctrinal soundness they could depend and asked Rev. Anders Wiberg, then a clergyman of the state church, to accompany them to America as their spiritual teacher. Himself unable to accept the call, Wiberg suggested Palmquist, who agreed to come over the following year. Upon their arrival, these people were scattered to the four winds, and when Palmquist came, in August, 1851, he did not meet one of their number for several months. Some had located in Princeton, others in Rock Island and Moline, still others in Andover and vicinity, and some time after a few went to McGregor, Ia. The only one of the party who stuck to the original plan was Per Anderson from Hassela, Helsingland, who in the spring of 1851 went to Minnesota and founded the Chisago Lake settlement.

According to his own statement Palmquist in 1845 and thereafter had his belief in infant baptism shaken by the study of the Bible, church history and the writings of Luther, Martensen, Pengilly, Hinton and others, and by conversations with Nilson of Göteborg and Johans-

The Present Swedish Baptist Church of Galesburg

son of Hull. On all other doctrinal points he considered himself a sound Lutheran, and his new position did not ripen into full conviction and open profession until 1852.

Palmquist came to Andover in the fall of 1851 and remained there a short time. His situation was rather cheerless, and while he was debating with himself whether to join the Swedish Lutherans or not, Rev. Esbjörn suggested that he go to Galesburg to preach to the people under his spiritual care, which he did, remaining in charge over winter. In the spring he made a trip north, visiting Lansing, Ia., St. Paul, Stillwater and other points in Minnesota with a view to locating somewhere as a preacher, but finding his countrymen few and living far apart, he returned to Illinois. During a Baptist revival at Galesburg he now took the decisive step, and was baptized June 27th, joining the American Baptist Church. He severed his connection with the Lutherans of Galesburg in rather dramatic fashion by calling his former flock together as if to rejoice over the step he had taken. In July he was assigned as Baptist missionary among the Swedish settlers in the surrounding territory. Work was taken up at Rock Island, resulting in the organization of a small church there in the late summer. Palmquist became its pastor. During his six years of service he spent much time in the mission field in Illinois, Iowa and Minnesota, planting new churches wherever practicable.

In August, 1857, Rev. Palmquist went back to Sweden to aid in the work started there under American auspices by Rev. Anders Wiberg in the fall of 1855. Before leaving, he gave the following statement of the number of Swedish Baptists in the United States: Rock Island, 45; Chicago, 25; New Sweden, Ia., 13; Boone county, Ia., 25; Allamakee county, Ia., 45; Scandia, Minn., 45; Chisago Lake, Minn., 20; Houston county, Minn., 17; Red Wing, Minn., 11; besides, there were 26 Swedish Baptists affiliated with American churches, viz., in New York City, 14, in Galesburg, 8, and in Keokuk, Ia., 4, making a total of 272. The predominance of the figure 5 in Palmquist's statement indicates an estimate. It should be noted that Palmquist visited and labored in most, if not all, of the places named, and that a goodly share of the result must be credited to his endeavors.

In Sweden he found a large field. The cities of Stockholm, Örebro and Sundsvall were given into his charge and, besides, he made extensive missionary trips throughout the country. In both Stockholm and Örebro he conducted private schools for the training of lay preachers. After ten years of faithful labor in Sweden, where his success was greater and the growth of the denomination more rapid than in its early stages in this country, Rev. Palmquist passed away Sept. 18, 1867, at 55 years of age. Of Palmquist's sermons, which are said to have been of the old-fashioned, pithy and powerful variety, none have been preserved, but as a writer of religious verse he has left a rich heritage to his church. He combined poetic genius with musical talent, and wrote many of the gospel hymns found in a collection entitled "Pilgrimssånger," first published in 1859.

Rev. Anders Wiberg

Rev. Wiberg is one of the fathers of the Baptist movement among the Swedish people on both sides of the Atlantic. His biography contains much interesting history.

Anders Wiberg was born in Tuna parish, near the city of Hudiksvall, Sweden, July 17, 1816. His parents were farmers. In his childhood he had some religious impressions. In his early youth he attended a so-called Lancaster school. When about fourteen years old, he was near being drowned, but was saved as by a miracle. In consequence he became anxious for the salvation of his soul and began to read the Bible and other religious books, among which was "The Holy War," by Bunyan. He was at that time a shopkeeper's clerk in Hudiksvall, but had an ardent desire to study and become useful in God's kingdom. For a year he was under the guidance of a pious country clergyman in the home of the latter, then pursued his studies at the Hudiksvall elementary school under a more learned, but ungodly teacher, and now yielded to worldly influences. In 1833-5 he attended the Gefle gym-

Rev. Anders Wiberg

nasium, from which, after his college graduation, he entered Upsala University. There he maintained himself by private tutorship in the homes of the gentry. During his four years at the seat of learning he became, from associations and from the nature of his studies, an infidel. At the end of this period, however, he reached the turning-point in his life and became a devout believer.

In 1843 he became a minister of the state church, after a course in theology, during which he made diligent research of religious writings, particularly those of the German mystics. He was now stationed at different places as assistant to aged clergymen, and was permitted to see the fruitage of his preaching. Scruples soon arose in his mind about admitting the ungodly to communion. Having obtained from the Upsala consistory leave of absence from duty, he was occupied for two years translating and publishing certain works of Luther and in editing a church paper, called "Evangelisten."

In the spring of 1851 Wiberg went from Stockholm, where he then resided, to Hamburg in company with a friend, to act as his interpreter. At Hamburg he visited the Baptist church and formed the acquaintance of Oncken and Köbner and other Baptist preachers. The constitution, discipline and the pious spiritual life which he discovered in this church appealed to him and he thought he saw in them the true apostolic order. To their doctrine of baptism, however, he could not assent. After warm disputes with the pastors named, he left them without being convinced of the error of infant baptism. On his way home, he read Pengilly's treatise on baptism, by which his faith in the Lutheran tenets was somewhat shaken. Later he eagerly studied Hinton's "History of Baptism," but it was long before he could be fully persuaded.

Before he visited Germany, a number of Christians in northern Sweden, who had conscientious scruples against the state church, but put confidence in Wiberg as an evangelical minister, had requested him to sever his connection with the state church and become their pastor. He was about to comply with their request when he became acquainted with the Baptists and their teachings. After that he sent them word about his change of views, stating that as he was about to become a Baptist, he could not sprinkle their children and minister to them in the way they had thought. Shocked and amazed, they knew not what to make of the matter, but wrote to Rev. Hedberg of Finland, a man of learning and highly esteemed among them, for advice. He replied by drawing a very dark picture of the Anabaptists, and making Wiberg out as a noxious heretic and an apostate. Wiberg endeavored to convince his friends of his biblical position, but without success. At length, he promised them that he would write a book on the subject. Not being as yet fully persuaded, but believing the truth to lie on the side of the Baptists, he set to work on the book. Needing help and advice on many points, he wrote F. O. Nilson, who sent him Dr. Carson's work, "Baptism in Its Mode and Subjects," and also several tracts. Having studied these and compared the arguments with passages in the Greek New Testament, he finally became fully satisfied on all matters pertaining to the question of baptism. His own work on the subject was completed before he left Sweden for America, and was left in the hands of the printer.

Soon after his return from Hamburg, Wiberg lay dangerously ill for about three months. During his convalescence he wrote to the consistory requesting his dismission from the state church. Before that tribunal he had been twice summoned to answer to the charge of affiliating with the separatists in Northern Sweden. The first time, after long and heated disputes with several members of the consistory, he was suspended from the ministry for three months for non-conformity. The second time, his accuser, a dean in the city of Hudiksvall, urged that Wiberg should be banished. The latter appealed from the ecclesiastical to the civil power, but in the meantime his accuser and persecutor, a man of learning and ripe age, put an end to his own life by hanging.

Having regained strength, Wiberg began to preach in public, but the clergy sought to prevent these assemblages, and twice the lord mayor of Stockholm forbade the meetings.

Still infirm, Wiberg was advised by his physician to take a sea voyage as the best means of regaining strength. Several of his friends in Stockholm were just then building a vessel for carrying emigrants to the United States. He applied for and obtained free passage, much to his satisfaction, as he greatly desired to go anywhere out of Sweden to be baptized, but lacked the means. The vessel sailed from Stockholm July 17th. At Copenhagen the vessel was delayed by head winds for two days. Here he met Rev. F. O. Nilson, who was in exile, and by him was immersed in the sea at 11 o'clock in the evening of July 23rd, in the presence of many brethren and sisters.

The ship arrived in New York harbor on Sept. 18th. With a letter from Nilson recommending that Wiberg be employed by the American Baptists as a missionary in Sweden, he sought Rev. Steward of the Mariners' Church. Shortly afterward he gave an account of himself, substantially as here narrated, in the Olive Street Church, before an audience met to hear the annual report of the New York Baptist Female Bethel Union. Having been given a cordial public welcome, Wiberg was soon employed by the Mariners' Church as colporteur and missionary among the Scandinavian immigrants and seamen. He was the first Swedish Baptist home missionary in New York and the East. Having united with the church, he was ordained March 3, 1853, as a regular Baptist minister. In the summer of the same year the American Baptist Publication Society of Philadelphia invited him to come there and prepare his work on baptism, and when ready a large number of copies were sent over to Sweden and there distributed.

This work, entitled, "Det kristliga dopet," was published in Philadelphia in 1854. It is a duodecimo volume of 288 pages. A pamphlet of 36 pages by Wiberg, entitled "Är du döpt?" was published the following year by the same society. These are the first known Baptist publications in the Swedish language in this country.

Next to the banishment of Nilson, the fact that Wiberg, a devout man and a scholar, had left the established church with all its allurements of comfortable living, promotion and honors, to cast his lot with the despised and persecuted sect of Baptists, had great moral effect on the advancement of their cause in Sweden. Calls for Wiberg to return to the old country were both frequent and urgent. He remained three years in America and became intimately acquainted with the ways and means of operation in the American Baptist Church. After being married in Philadelphia Aug. 23, 1855, to Miss Caroline Lintemuth, he started on his mission to his native land, arriving at Stockholm in October. From now on the work in Sweden took a more organized form, and under his able direction the Baptist propaganda attracted widespread attention.

While in the United States, Wiberg solicited means for the erection of a Baptist church edifice in Stockholm, and for a long time he received from the American Baptists support for his work in Sweden.

Wiberg's work on baptism had commanded attention and aroused vigorous opposition. During his three years' sojourn in the United States no less than fourteen pamphlets against the Baptists had been published, and these were but the beginning of a "watery war of words" waged by a host of clerical writers. Wiberg ably defended his position with tongue and pen. He took part in two public debates with representatives of the state church, held a few weeks after his return, the latter of which broke up in a riot. Wiberg and his associates narrowly escaping bodily violence by fleeing through a side door.

From the moment Wiberg set foot on Swedish soil, he was strenuously at work. It is said that he went directly from the docks to preach in a hall where an expectant crowd had assembled. The little bands of Baptists everywhere requested his aid and advice, and it devolved upon him not only to give counsel in temporal matters, but also to make the doctrines and principles which they professed more clearly understood. It is said of Rev. George Scott, the pioneer Methodist missionary to Sweden, that he admittedly questioned the right of any church to carry on mission work in an evangelical land and laid himself open to the charge of hypocrisy by pretending that he did not seek to win over members of the state church. Wiberg, on the other hand, worked in the open and made no attempt to dissemble or compromise. With him at the head of the movement, persecution of the Baptists soon ceased in the capital, but still continued in several provinces.

The day after Wiberg's arrival, the congregation at Stockholm, organized in the spring of 1854 and numbering now eleven souls, decided to rent a larger meeting hall and reorganized, choosing as elders Wiberg and one Möllersvärd, an ardent promoter of the cause.

At Wiberg's initiative the first general conference of Baptists in

Sweden was opened at Stockholm June 13, 1857. At that time he estimated their number at 1,400, and the number of delegates present was 20, besides Wiberg, who presided. He was also one of the prime movers in the establishment of a Bible institute at Stockholm, named the Bethel Seminary. The matter was discussed at several annual conferences up to 1861, when on Wiberg's motion it was resolved to take action. Yet the plan was not realized for several years to come. In 1866, while Wiberg was in the United States, he induced two influential brethren, Broady and Edgren, to accompany him to Sweden and take charge of the instruction in the proposed school. With financial aid pledged by the American Baptist Missionary Union, through Wiberg's efforts, the annual conference of 1866, held in Stockholm Aug. 27-28, finally took the decisive step, founding the institution and electing a board of directors and a corps of instructors, K. O. Broady being made the head of the school and J. A. Edgren, Gustaf Palmquist and A. Drake associate teachers.

In 1864 Wiberg spent some time in the West, visiting the struggling little churches in Illinois, Iowa and Minnesota. Here his genius for organization was again in evidence. At the conference held in Village Creek, Ia., in June, 1864, he presided and took part in the formal organization of the Illinois-Iowa Conference. He was the soul of the meeting, the proceedings of which were printed and form the first yearbook of the Swedish-American churches.

During the thirty-two years that Rev. Wiberg labored so effectually in Sweden, he had the pleasure of seeing the Baptist Church in that country grow in membership from 1,000 to 30,000.

We have indicated the extent of Wiberg's literary labors. His principal works are: translations of works by Johan Arndt and Luther; "Hvilken bör döpas?" — a work on baptism, published in 1852; "De kristnas enhet"; a reply to P. Waldenström's book, "Barndopets historia"; a tract entitled, "Är du döpt?" and "Det christliga dopet." For various periods he edited "Missionstidningen," published "Evangelisk Luthersk Tidskrift," edited and published "Evangelisten," and contributed to "Kristianen." He assisted in editing a hymnal, "Psalmisten," and began a translation of the New Testament which was never completed.

Rev. Wiberg passed away Nov. 5, 1887, in his seventy-second year.

Rev. Fredrik Olaus Nilson

A sketch of the career of Fredrik Olaus Nilson, Sweden's first regular Baptist preacher, who subsequently lived and labored in the United States, will more fully illustrate the hampered yet successful progress of the Baptist movement in its early days.

He was born on Vändelsö on the coast of Halland, Sweden, July 28, 1809. His parents, who were of the middle class, gave their children the religious education imparted in the common schools. At ten years the boy awoke to his spiritual needs and seems to have earnestly sought salvation until his eighteenth year, when he went to sea, leaving Göteborg in 1827. Spiritual indifference followed until 1835, when a terrific storm off Cape Hatteras, threatening with destruction the vessel on which Nilson was employed, deeply stirred the mind of the young sailor. Fearing death, he took the works of Thomas Paine, which he had been studying at leisure moments, and threw them into the sea,

Rev. Fredrik Olaus Nilson

with a solemn promise that, should his life be spared, he would become a Christian. Upon his return to New York safe and sound, he attended the Mariners' Temple, and there found peace with God.

During the summer af 1836 Nilson was employed by the New York Tract Society to distribute tracts among the immigrants, but he continued seafaring until 1839, when he shipped in a Swedish vessel and returned home. Several souls were won by his preaching on board the ship, a fact that strengthened his desire to proclaim the gospel among his relatives and friends at home.

During the next few years Nilson worked as an independent evangelist in a number of parishes on the west coast. In 1842 he was engaged by the American Seamen's Friend Society, a Methodist organization, as a missionary among the seamen in the harbor of Göteborg. During the sailing season he was stationed in the city, but in winter

made missionary trips inland to the provinces of Halland, Vestergötland and Bohuslän. In 1844 he married Ulrika Sofia Olson.

When he became a Baptist, Nilson was deserted by many of his
former followers. The little Baptist congregation organized at Landa
in 1848 was the result of Nilson's efforts, but not until May 8, 1849, was
he ordained as a regular Baptist preacher. His ordination took place
at the Baptist meetinghouse in Hamburg. After that Nilson received
the support of the Baptist Mariners' Church in New York.

The Baptists, who openly attacked the doctrines of the state
church, could not hope to escape molestation. At first they worked
privately and in secret, seeking thereby to avoid giving offense and to
escape persecution. Nilson for a time pursued the same tactics, but
shortly after the organization of the first church opposition to the
Baptist "proselyters" appears to have grown more bitter than before.

At Christmas, 1848, while a little group of Baptists were gathered
in Nilson's home in Göteborg to worship and break bread behind closed
doors, a crowd collected outside and began to bombard the house with
stones. The windows were shattered and the candles extinguished by
the wind. In the darkness the worshipers escaped and hid in the
attic while their assailants stormed the house and destroyed everything
they could lay their hands on. Many instances of similar outrages
have been recorded. Nilson's followers were frequently accosted in
the streets with vile epithets or bodily assaulted, and the saying was,
that "it costs but eighteen shillings to kill a Baptist." These outrages
were committed by the lawless element, but with the connivance of the
clergy. The Baptists were persecuted in other ways, by being discharged from work, boycotted by shopkeepers, ostracized from the
society in which they were wont to move, and in some instances
expelled from their own families. By the pastors they were repri-
manded and disciplined, and Nilson himself was summoned before the
consistory of Göteborg. After a hearing on July 4, 1849, he was declared an apostate and charged with teaching heresy. He escaped with a
severe reprimand and an order to cease spreading dangerous doctrines
at the peril of punishment to the full extent of the law. Nilson, however, continued preaching unmolested by the civil authorities the
remainder of the year.

On New Year's day, 1850, Nilson was conducting divine worship
in the house of one Abraham Anderson in Berghem parish of Elfsborg
län. In the day they had set watch to guard against surprise, but
in the evening, reassured by the absence of any show of molestation,
the watchmen had left their posts to join the brethren inside. About
to celebrate communion, the worshipers were alarmed by a loud rap
at the door. When it was opened, they found the house surrounded

by men armed with sticks, clubs, rusty old sabers, pistols and muskets. Led by a fjerdingsman, the men made a rush for Nilson, who was violently kicked and beaten. The constable, after demanding Nilson's name, had him bound hand and foot, dragged from the house, placed in a sleigh and driven first to another village, where he was confronted with the länsman, or sheriff, thence to the Skened jail. After six days spent in a cold, dark cell, he was taken to the prison in Göteborg to await trial, but was released in two hours, through the intercession of his wife with the governor of the province.

A month later Nilson was summoned before the high court at Jönköping to answer to the charge of preaching false doctrine. He was

The First Edifice of the Swedish Baptist Church of Rockford

on trial March 8th and 11th, resulting April 26th in a verdict of banishment from the realm. Through the publicity given the trial Baptist teachings were made known generally throughout Sweden.

Nilson went to Stockholm and made a personal appeal for pardon before the king, who denied the petition. Sixteen petitions in his behalf, addressed to the leading men in the state church, and signed by one thousand Baptist churches in Great Britain and Ireland, were ignored. Availing himself of every recourse, including the court of last appeal, Nilson was able to remain in Sweden for more than a year from the time the verdict was pronounced. He left the country on July 4, 1851, and came to the United States after one year spent in Copenhagen.

He arrived in New York in June, 1853, at the head of a party of 23 of his followers from Sweden. They proceeded westward via Chicago to join their brethren in the faith in Rock Island and Moline. Only a few of the party located there, while Nilson with others of the party seems to have proceeded shortly afterwards to Burlington, Ia., and in 1855 to Minnesota. There he labored practically alone for several years, organizing a number of the earliest Swedish Baptist churches in the state. While in Burlington he converted and baptized John Erickson and John Anderson, both prominent workers in the early days of the church.

In the fall of 1859 Nilson assumed charge of the church in Rock Island, remaining as its pastor for six months. In December, 1860, the Swedish law punishing dissenters with banishment was rescinded and Nilson forthwith returned to his native country. During his absence, the handfuls of Baptists in various localities had been scattered, not a few of them having left for the New World. The remnants of the church in Göteborg now rallied and reorganized, electing Nilson pastor, with Captain Schroeder as his right hand and chief backer.

In 1862 Nilson returned to the United States and continued to preach for many years. Ultimately he wavered in the faith, and is registered in Baptist history as a "backslider." He spent his last years at his home in Houston, Minn., where he died Oct. 21, 1881, at 72 years of age.

Rev. Johan Alexis Edgren

An event af prime importance to the Swedish Baptist Church of America was the founding of its first institution of learning by Rev. J. A. Edgren, in 1871, at Chicago. His work in behalf of the Swedish Baptists on this side of the Atlantic probably was of broader scope than that of any other man.

Johan Alexis Edgren was born at Östanå, Vermland, Sweden, Feb. 20, 1839, being the eldest child of Axel Edgren, superintendent of the Östanå steel works. A younger son was Hjalmar Edgren, deceased, who fought in the Civil War, and afterward became renowned as an educator, author, scholar and linguist, who during his last years was connected with the Nobel Institute of Stockholm. Johan Alexis entered the Karlstad elementary school in 1849, but abandoned his studies after three years to go to sea, following his boyish penchant for adventure. In Göteborg he attended a school for intending sailors for a short time, then hired out to a Norwegian sea-captain and made his first trip on board a rotten old brig destined for a French port with a cargo of lumber. With a few needful hints the captain put the boy to work in the kitchen, and his first maritime experience consisted in an attempt to cook peas, porridge and coffee for the crew, while the first attack of seasickness was playing havoc with his own stomach. When he returned home the following Christmas the lad had had his thirst for adventure quenched to a considerable extent, having been almost shipwrecked in a severe storm while outward bound and robbed of all his savings by a Norwegian stage driver on his way home. Undismayed by these reverses, he returned on shipboard at the opening of the next season, but being disabled by over-exertion he spent almost a year at home and subsequently entered the school of navigation in Stockholm, graduating after a year's studies as captain's mate. The next fall he went to sea as ship's constable, a position which proved so distasteful to him that, contrary to his sense of duty, he deserted on reaching England, and went with the English clipper "Wild Wave,"

Rev. Johan Alexis Edgren

bound for Malta with a cargo of powder for the British forces then engaged in the Crimean War. At Valetta Edgren, not quite restored from his former injuries, was again prostrated by illness and when dismissed from the hospital found himself a penniless stranger in a strange city. To raise money for his next meal he sold his blouse to a Maltese laborer. He was fortunate, however, in finding in the harbor a Swedish bark, with which he shipped to Alexandria and thence back to Sweden.

At London Edgren joined the crew of an American vessel, bound for New York. Reaching that port he learned accidentally that there was a letter for him at the Methodist Bethel ship in East River. This brought him in contact with the Methodist seamen's missionaries, whose ardent prayers for his soul so impressed the young sailor that he himself from that moment began to seek the way of salvation.

Edgren next shipped with a brig bound for the West Indies. Returning to New York the following year, he again sought the society of Christians, visiting various churches. On his next voyage, to the coast of Virginia, he gave his heart to God and during a terrible storm pledged himself to the Lord's service as a missionary, whenever called, provided his life was spared. Back in New York, he again sought the brethren and brought them the joyful news of his regeneration. His intention now to visit his old home was changed when he was offered a place on a large frigate bound for Valparaiso. With this long voyage he planned to finish his practical course in common seamanship before eventually adopting another vocation.

Touching at New York again on returning from the South American trip, Edgren, while at a loss to determine what denomination of Christians to affiliate with, chanced to visit a Baptist seamen's mission chapel, where he was partially convinced that baptism should follow, not precede, conversion. He reasoned with his Methodist friends, but found their arguments unconvincing, and after inner struggles and earnest scriptural study, was baptized by Rev. I. R. Steward in the spring of 1858, just before starting for his home in Sweden.

With a two years' course ahead of him, Edgren again entered the Stockholm school of navigation, but succeeded in completing his studies in one year, and the following spring gave his parents a pleasant surprise by showing a captain's diploma, with the highest honors of the class and a first prize besides.

On a subsequent voyage to American ports as second mate on a Swedish brig, Edgren visited Charleston, S. C., and there received his first direct impressions of the curse of slavery, impressions that later prompted him to lend a hand in blotting it out. His plan to enter the Swedish navy having miscarried, Edgren was still in the service of the merchant marine when the Civil War broke out. He chanced to be on board a vessel off Charleston at the time and became an eye-witness to the first shots exchanged in that great conflict.

In the fall of 1861 a friend in Sweden proposed to Edgren that they open a navigation school in the United States, but he had planned to fit himself further by taking an advanced course at Stockholm and, unable to choose, cast lots, which fell in favor of the latter plan. In the capital he came in contact with Rev. Wiberg and preached now and then. Some two years prior, he had preached his first sermon on Christmas Day, 1859, to a ship's crew on the Atlantic Ocean. Though urged by Wiberg to forsake the sea, Edgren did not yet see his future mission clear. In the spring of 1862 he came over to the United States as a passenger, to visit his brother Hjalmar, who was in the Union army and had just been through the memorable battle of Hampton Roads. He found him at Fort Rip Raps, and returning to New York at once applied for service in the navy as a non-commissioned officer, but was given a commission upon passing examination. He first served as navigator on board a bark participating in the blockade of the Atlantic ports. When his brother, now an officer of staff, resigned from the army on account of illness and left for Sweden, he also left the service and took up theological studies at Princeton University. Still undecided about entering the ministry, he resumed his commission in the navy at the end of the school year. He was now given command of the small armored steamer "Catalpa" and ordered to report to Admiral Dahlgren at Port Royal. Disliking the inactivity on board the blockading ships, he applied for service in a battery at Cumming's Point. From now until the fall of Charleston he was almost constantly on the firing line, and was present when on that memorable 15th of April, amid the thunder of guns and deafening cheers, General Anderson again hoisted the selfsame Union flag he had been compelled to haul down at the opening of the war, over the shattered ramparts of Fort Sumter.

The close of the war was at hand, and after commanding for a time a confederate vessel taken as a prize, Edgren resigned from the navy and was engaged by the American Baptist Publication Society as a colporteur and seamen's missionary in New York. In the fall of 1865 he entered Madison University. After one year's study he was appointed missionary by the Baptist Missionary Union, accompanied Rev. Wiberg to Stockholm, and became professor of mathematics and natural science at the Bethel Seminary at the opening of the institution. He was accompanied to Sweden by his wife, formerly Miss Annie Abbott Chapman of Becket, Mass., whom he married at Hamburg, March 10, 1866.

When Dr. Warren, secretary of the Missionary Union, on a visit to Stockholm, found too many missionaries stationed there, Edgren resigned, and removed to Upsala to devote himself to preaching and theological study. Of the local church there was but a remnant left, almost all the members having become adherents of one Helge Åkesson, who taught Christian perfectionism. The church, after being reorganized, again had begun to grow when Edgren was compelled to leave, his wife being unable to endure the climate. The following winter he labored as a missionary at Göteborg and in the spring the pair returned to America. Edgren now accepted a call to the Chicago church and served until its chapel was destroyed in the great fire.

The need of missionary forces in the West was apparent, and Edgren soon conceived the idea of meeting this want by means of a Bible school. In the fall of 1871 he was about to begin instruction in the rooms of the Baptist chapel, when the Union Theological Seminary, in Morgan Park, which planned to open a Scandinavian department, invited him to establish his school in conjunction with it. Edgren accordingly made arrangements to move and his library was saved from destruction by being removed just a few days before the fire.

At first the students of Edgren's department were very few, and he gave part of his time to study at the seminary, preaching and editing a religious monthly. Failing health soon forced his complete retirement for one year. Almost destitute, he was enabled by a friendly donation to go back to his old home for a rest. The vessel on which he returned was almost battered to pieces in a storm and he was in greater peril of his life than ever before in his seafaring career. In New York he met—and left—his wife, who without informing him, had hired out as wetnurse in order to earn a living for herself and children.

He resumed his professorship in Chicago, which was in no sense a sinecure, the incumbent being required to raise the means of maintaining himself and the school. Before long his family could rejoin him at Morgan Park. For fifteen years Edgren remained at the head of the Swedish department of the seminary, which meanwhile reached a maximum attendance of 40. Owing to failing health, Edgren in 1887 withdrew from his various activities and since lived in retirement in California until his death, which occurred on Jan. 26, 1908.

Prof. Edgren, who in 1880 received from the Chicago University the honorary degree of D. D., was a noted biblical scholar and commentator, and has written interesting memoirs of his life. His literary work, aside from newspaper editing, comprises these published volumes: "Bibeln en gudomlig uppenbarelse" (1867); "Minnen från hafvet och kriget" (1872); "Efter döden;" "Den öppna kommunionen i skriftens ljus;" "Sabbaten och Herrens dag," the last three revised and re-published under the common title, "Brännande frågor;" "Minnen från hafvet, kriget och missionsfältet" (1878), a revised reprint; "Bibeln Guds bok" (1878); "Försoningen," a lecture (1880); "Epiphanea: A Study in Prophecy" (1881); "Bibeltolkningens lagar;" "Kristlig troslära för barn;" "Biblisk troslära;" "Öfversättning och utläggning af Mattei evangelium," and "På lifvets haf" (1898). The church papers edited by Dr. Edgren were, "Zions Vakt," started in 1873 and continued for a brief period, and "Evangelisk Tidskrift," established in 1877 and continued by him until 1880.

Capt. Gustavus W. Schroeder

Gustavus W. Schroeder was born near Göteborg April 9, 1821. At sixteen he became a sailor and followed the sea for the next thirty years. He was twenty-three years of age when baptized by Rev. Ira R. Steward in New York and continued for 29 years a member of the Mariners' Church. While in Sweden in 1845 he learned that his two brothers, one master, the other second officer of a Chilian bark, were in

Capt. Gustavus W. Schroeder

Hamburg. He met them there, and being tendered the chief officer's place, shipped for Valparaiso, where, at the age of twenty-five, he was made captain of a vessel. Four years later he married Miss Mary Steward, daughter of his pastor, and in 1861 located in Göteborg to champion the cause of the little flock of Baptists in that city. After two years he returned to the United States, and lived first in Illinois, then in California until he again located in Göteborg about 1883 and joined the church in which he had formerly labored. In 1891 he came back to this country and is now a member of the Memorial Baptist Church of Brooklyn.

The Baptist congregation in Göteborg had just been organized, when Captain Schroeder came there in 1861. He built a house, in which a large room was fitted up as a meeting hall. Here, as elsewhere in Sweden, the state church resisted the movement as heretical. The local consistory appealed to the police to have the hall closed and brought suit against F. O. Nilson, pastor of the church, and Captain Schroeder, charging the former with holding religious meetings illegally, and the latter with aiding and abetting the crime. After a vigorous fight by Nilson and Schroeder, the case was decided against them and a fine of 100 crowns was imposed on the latter. The course of the clergy was at the time publicly criticised as unwise, to say the least, as the persecution of the leaders, instead of serving to suppress the movement, had the opposite effect and proved a moral victory for the Baptists.

The Chicago Field

The earliest Swedish Baptist church in Chicago existed from 1853 to 1864. It was organized by some thirty persons, formerly members of the American First Baptist Church. These are known to have been among the organizers, viz., Peter Peterson, Peter Modine, Andrew Anderson, John Uberg, Matthew Matson, Fred Blomquist, William

The First Swedish Baptist Church of Chicago, Second Edifice

Wigland, Ira J. Collings, F. M. Winterset, one Mr. Mullen, all with their wives. L. L. Frisk was ordained to become their first pastor. Meetings were held in the homes of members until November, 1854, when the American church raised $900, for which sum a small edifice situated at La Salle avenue and Erie street was purchased from the German Lutherans for the use of the Swedish brethren. It was removed to Bremer street in 1858 and there used as a house of worship until destroyed by fire in 1860 or 1861. A schoolhouse was then rented, in which the meetings were held for an indefinite period. Rev. Frisk remained as pastor until 1857, when he was succeeded by Rev. Palmquist, who served for six months. After him the church appears to have had no permanent pastor, but the congregation continued in existence until 1864, when the unsettled conditions incident to the Civil War caused the members to scatter, which resulted in the disintegration of the church.

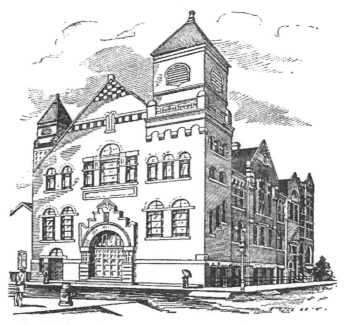

The First Swedish Baptist Church of Chicago, Present Edifice

The present First Swedish Baptist Church of Chicago, therefore, is not the original one. It was not called into existence until 1866. On Jan. 16th of that year a little group of persons who had belonged to Baptist churches in Sweden met at the house of J. C. Fasten to talk over the outlook for a local church. The meeting, over which Captain R. E. Jeanson of New York presided, was barren of results. After six months a second meeting was held at the same place, when it was unanimously resolved to organize a church. Nine preliminary meetings were held before action was taken.

In the meantime a party of Baptists from Hudiksvall, Sweden, arrived. With them were two preachers, Olof Lindh and N. E. Axling, and their presence in Chicago hastened action in the matter. The newcomers first joined their brethren at a meeting in the house of one Nylund, at 185 Townsend street, held on the 19th of July, when the plan to organize a church was further matured. Some were members of the Danish Baptist Church, which opposed the plan; others carried their letters of membership in their pockets. A couple of weeks later came John Ring and J. H. Ullmark, also Baptist preachers from Sweden. Finally, on Aug. 19, 1866, the formal organization took place in the edifice of the North Star Baptist Church, which had been opened for the use of the Swedish brethren. On this occasion Lindh, Axling and Ring officiated. John Ring, who had been called as pastor at a

The Englewood Swedish Baptist Church

salary of $150 a year, was installed by the laying on of hands and the invocation of the blessing.

The church numbered from the outset 38 members. That same fall the new church was recognized by a council held in the Danish church. The services were held there and in the North Star Church on Division street until November, when a Presbyterian schoolhouse on Bremer street was rented for the purpose.

Rev. Lindh remained a member of this church until the following spring, when he accepted a call from Altona. He assisted Rev. Ring in the work, taught the Bible class and served at Ring's request as chairman of the church council. Ring resigned in the spring of 1869,

whereupon Lindh stepped in and filled the pulpit temporarily, until
Rev. C. W. Segerblom, a Baptist preacher from Sweden, arrived
and was at once claimed by this church as their pastor. Segerblom
was an erratic character and proved untrustworthy as a leader. He
did not last long in Chicago. Subsequently he went over to Methodism
and became pastor of the Swedish Methodist Church in Jamestown,
N. Y., where he operated to the detriment of that church. He next
flopped to Lutheranism and changed his name to Sidger. This clerical
turncoat died in Missouri, time unknown.

The Lake View Swedish Baptist Church

In 1868 the congregation built its own edifice, on Oak street,
between Sedgwick and Townsend streets. This church, which was
dedicated May 14th, had a seating capacity of 700 and cost $5,000,
inclusive of the lot. When it was destroyed in the great fire the
congregation was on the point of disbanding, but its scattered members
rallied and built a new edifice, seating 300 persons and costing $2,500.
This was dedicated Feb. 15, 1873. An addition was built in 1876.
Having far outgrown its capacity, the congregation in 1889 erected a
$37,000 edifice at Milton avenue and Elm street, which was dedicated
the first Sunday in March, 1890. This structure, which is one of the

costliest owned by the Swedish Baptists, accommodates an audience of one thousand people.

The pastors of this church, permanent or temporary, have been:

The Humboldt Park Swedish Baptist Church

John Ring, Olof Lindh, C. W. Segerblom, J. A. Edgren, E. Wingren, E. Lundin, John Ongman, P. A. Hjelm, G. A. Hagström and Thorsten Clafford, the present incumbent.

Rev. John Ongman who served the church as its pastor from 1875 to 1881 and again from 1885 to 1886, making a total of eight years, came to Chicago from Sweden in 1868, but soon left for Minnesota, where he labored for the church in various localities for about thirteen

The Berwyn Swedish Baptist Church

years, including the pastorate of the First church in St. Paul, which he served during three different periods, aggregating ten years. Since 1890 he has been active in the Baptist Church of Sweden. Rev. Ongman's labors in this country were very fruitful. He was chosen president of the Swedish Baptist General Conference at the organization of that body in 1879 and served for three consecutive years.

During Rev. P. A. Hjelm's term of service, from August, 1888, until October, 1896, the church made remarkable progress. It was his privilege to welcome no less than 711 new members, 240 of whom were baptized by him. In the same period there was a loss of 644 through death, removals and expulsion, leaving a net increase of 67. The principal drain on the membership was caused by the organization of four daughter churches, each of them claiming members directly from the First church and indirectly impeding its growth.

Succeeding Hjelm, Rev. G. A. Hagström served this pastorate for ten years. In 1902 the fiftieth anniversary of the Swedish Baptist Church of America was celebrated in this church, with a jubilee held in connection with the General Conference sessions.

The fortieth anniversary of the founding of the church was

Rev. John Ongman

Rev. P. A. Hjelm

celebrated Oct. 18-21, 1906. At that time a historical review was published, giving many data and figures.

Five daughter churches have been organized from the membership of the First church, viz., the Evanston church, in 1886, with 26 members, to which have been added 59, total gain from the First church, 85; the Lake View church, in 1889, members, 30, total gain from First church, 96; the Salem church, in 1890, members, 9, total gain from First church, 20; the Austin church, in 1891, members 9, total gain from First church, 27; the Humboldt Park church, in 1891, members, 16, total gain from First church, 64. Beyond this, the First church has lost to other Chicago churches a large number of members, including 56 to the Second church, 81 to Englewood and 34 to American churches.

Up to 1880 this church had gained 549 members and lost 316, retaining a net total of 233; in 1890 it had 515, in 1898, 695 and in 1907, 657 members. It is the largest of the Swedish Baptist churches in this country, leading the largest in Minneapolis and St.

Paul by about 70 and those of New York and Brooklyn by about 200 members. The church property is valued at $43,000.

Rev. John Ring

John Ring, who became pastor of the Chicago church at its organization in 1866, had just come over from Sweden, where he had preached for five or six years. He was born in Delsbo parish, Helsingland, Feb. 16, 1829. After his conversion and baptism in 1859 he began to preach the Baptist doctrine in his home locality and shared the persecution then contingent on teaching at variance with the state church. For holding services during the hours of 10-12 a. m. on Sundays, reserved

Rev. John Ring

by law for the state church, he was arrested and convicted, and served a sentence of one month in the Hernösand jail in the winter of 1862-3.

He was pastor of the Chicago church from its inception in August, 1866, until May, 1869, when he located as a farmer at Trade Lake, Wis. He became instrumental in organizing a church there and later laid the foundation for the First Swedish Baptist Church of Minneapolis. Subsequently Ring removed to Omaha, where he lived for many years, at various periods in charge of the local Swedish Baptist church. For three years, 1877-80, he was in pastoral charge at Kiron, Ia., then for five years conducted a jewelry store in Oakland, Neb., and removed the business to Omaha, where he died Oct. 6, 1896, from injuries received in a bicycle accident. Ring was twice married and had three children.

Rev. Olof Lindh

Among the successful Swedish Baptist workers in Illinois, as well as in the Eastern states and in Sweden, Rev. Olof Lindh holds an eminent place. He was born in Helsingtuna, Sweden, Sept. 24, 1835. His father, a prominent farmer and a trusted man in the community, was a lay preacher among the religionists styled Readers. The son Olof was deeply influenced from childhood by his father's pious precept and right living, but did not experience regeneration of the heart until his twenty-fifth year. He was baptized in the sea near Hudiksvall on May 8, 1860, by his brother, Per Lindh, and began preaching after much trepidation some two years later, meanwhile supporting himself by his trade as shoemaker. For four years he was pastor of the Baptist church in Hudiksvall, then emigrated and located in Chicago. There he helped to organize the church in August, 1866, and was elected elder at the time. Prior thereto he preached his first sermon here

Rev. Olof Lindh

on July 22nd, a week after his arrival. He took turns with Ring in preaching in Chicago, then was stationed for a time at Altona in 1867-8, and next became traveling missionary in Illinois and Iowa. In 1869, during the vacancy after Rev. Ring, and before the arrival of Seger-blom, his successor, Lindh supplied the pulpit of the Chicago church for a brief period. Segerblom made things so disagreeable for him that he left Chicago, determined to give up preaching. Going to Moline to work at his trade, he was by the Swedish Baptists there and in Rock Island induced to become their pastor and served them for the next six years. In that period no less than 139 members joined the church at Rock Island.

Lindh returned to Sweden in 1876 and labored there for three years, serving as pastor in Sundsvall and Hässjö. In that time he was instrumental in bringing a large number of new members into the Baptist churches.

Returning to the United States, Lindh had a call to preach in Boston, but owing to the burning of Tremont Temple, where the Swedish Baptists met, just after his arrival, he left in discouragement. After a brief stay in Moline, he accepted a call to the church in New York, which was about to go to pieces, but under his leadership began to flourish and has thrived greatly ever after. During his eight years in New York Lindh began mission work in a number of places, including Brooklyn and Jamestown, N. Y.; Bridgeport, New Haven, Meriden and New Britain, Conn., and Antrim and McKeesport, Pa., and organized churches in the places named. In 1887 he became pastor of the Boston church, but left the following year to become traveling missionary of the Eastern Conference. As such he labored until 1891, whereupon he was stationed at Bridgeport, Conn., until 1893, when he went again to Sweden, returning in 1895. He withdrew from pastoral work in 1900, after serving in Cambridge, Mass., Concord, N. H., and New Haven, Conn.

Rev. Lindh's work as a pastor and preacher during thirty-eight years has been blessed in more than ordinary measure. He has organized a score of churches in this country, including three in Illinois, and baptized 500 converts in the United States and 300 in Sweden. Among those converted through his instrumentality several have become prominent Baptist preachers. Lindh has lived a life rich in experience, and these he recounts in a goodnatured and entertaining manner in a volume of reminiscences, entitled, "Minnen och iakttagelser från en förfluten lefnad," published in 1907.

The Swedish Theological Seminary of the University of Chicago

The founder of this the theological seminary of the Swedish Baptists of America was Dr. J. A. Edgren. He returned in 1870 from Sweden, where he had taught in the Bethel Seminary at Stockholm, with a live sense of the importance to the Swedish Baptists in this country of educating their own preachers and pastors, as their brethren in Sweden were doing. After the decision had been reached to begin instruction in the Oak Street church, the Baptist Union Theological Seminary invited Edgren to take up this work at that institution, an offer thankfully accepted. In the fall of 1871 the course was opened with an attendance of one student—Christopher Silene. Later a few others were added.

In 1873, after an interruption in his work, caused by ill health, Edgren was officially called to conduct a Scandinavian department at the seminary, with the added burden of providing for the support and maintenance of himself and the department. Undismayed by such a prospect, he accepted the position and worked under the same disheartening conditions for the next five years. The opening attendance in 1873 was four, and among the first graduates were N. Hayland, A. A. Linné, C. Silene and A. B. Orgren. In 1877 the seminary was removed from Chicago to the suburb of Morgan Park, where the Scandinavian

Morgan Hall, Present Home of the Swedish Baptist Theological Seminary, Morgan Park, Ill.

department was conducted by Edgren until 1884. A desire on the part of the Swedish brethren to have a school distinctly their own then ripened into action, after a resolution to that effect had been passed by the General Conference three years before, designating Minneapolis as its location. During the following year instruction was given at St. Paul, pending a definite location of the institution. That year ample means for its support were contributed, while no less than $20,000 were subscribed to a building fund and a site between the twin cities was offered.

A year later, however, the school was removed to Stromsburg, Neb., where it had been given 10 acres of land and a bonus of $10,500. Apparently the desired end had now been attained, yet it has been intimated that this move probably did more than anything else to cross the purpose of the Swedish Baptists to build up their own school. Its location there seems to have been dictated by private interests, and the name now given to the institution—The Central Bible Seminary—was a misnomer from the church point of view. As early as 1888 it was generally realized that a mistake had been made, and a majority of the directors favored a more central location. Negotiations were taken up for moving the institution back to Minneapolis-St. Paul, or Chicago. Rev. Eric Sandell, having secured acceptable terms from the Baptist Theological Union, the question of reuniting with the Chicago institution was taken up the same year by the General Conference, when the proposition was carried by a vote of 42 to 7.

In 1887 Edgren's impaired health had compelled his withdrawal from the teacher's chair occupied by him for fifteen years, and now Rev. C. G. Lagergren was called from Sweden to take his place. The other teachers, Eric Sandell and N. N. Morten, were continued in the service. At the opening of the school year we find the school again at Morgan Park, after having received pledges for the maintenance of the department and aid for its students from the Baptist Theological Union and the Baptist Education Society. The former organization agreed to provide lecture halls and lodgings for the students in Walker Hall at Morgan Park and to pay the salaries of two of the Swedish professors, while the entire department was to be under the supervision of the Divinity School of the University of Chicago. In 1895 Sandell and Morten were succeeded by Profs. W. A. Peterson and O. Hedeen, and Prof. Lagergren, who accepted the call in 1888, remains at the head of the Swedish instruction. Others who have taught for longer or shorter periods are: E. Wingren, N. P. Jensen, Frank Peterson, John Ongman and A. B. Orgren.

At the celebration of the tenth anniversary of the seminary it was reported that instruction had been received by 87 students, of whom 63 were Swedes, 17 Danes and 9 Norwegians.

The Home of Rest at Morgan Park

A donation of $25 received from a benevolent lady in the spring of 1898, by Rev. Eric Rosén, started the fund through which the Swedish Baptist home for the aged has been realized. Rev. Rosén, who had cherished the idea for some time, continued to speak for the cause, presenting the matter at various conferences, yet without calling forth definite action. Four years passed without any advancing step. Then a devout couple promised to donate $1,000 to the cause, as a memorial to their deceased son, and this gave the impulse to a definite movement among the Swedish Baptists toward establishing an old people's home. At a private meeting of interested persons, held Nov. 26, 1902, it was resolved to accept the gift and proceed to incorporate an association whose object should be to found such an institution. The date of incorporation was Jan. 14, 1903, and the object of the association was thus stated: "to provide a home and place of rest for aged and destitute Swedish Baptists and other worthy persons in need of a temporary or permanent home."

During 1904 the cause did not advance beyond the drawing up of plans for a building to be erected in sections according to the future needs. It being deemed advisable to open the home without further delay, a private house at 236 Sunnyside Ave., Chicago, was leased from Dec. 12, 1904, to May 1, 1906, and opened as an old age retreat. Its first inmate was Johan Gunnarson, aged 80 years, who arrived on Jan. 28, 1905. The dedication of the temporary home took place Feb. 19th following. During the year ten other inmates were accepted. Rev. C. J. Almquist was employed as traveling solicitor for the institution and in six months raised $7,000 in cash and subscriptions.

A permanent location for the home having been selected in Morgan Park, in the neighborhood of the Swedish Baptist theological seminary, building operations were begun, and the central section of the proposed structure was completed and occupied in 1906. This the permanent building of the Swedish Baptist home for the aged was formally dedicated in connection with the holding of the General Conference in September of the same year. The present valuation of $24,000, less a debt of $7,000, shows the net present worth of the institution to be $17,000, while outstanding subscriptions amount to $14,000.

Prior to the eighties the work of the Swedish Baptists showed no great results in Illinois, there being but four or five small, struggling churches in the state up to that time, the youngest of which was that of Princeton, organized in 1877. During the last twenty-five years greater success has attended their efforts. In Chicago and vicinity thirteen congregations have been added, nine of them being among the most populous ones in the state. The church in Rockford, organized in 1880, now has a membership of 270, and is the largest in the state, outside of Chicago.

The statistics of 1907-8 showed that the state conference comprised 35 churches, with a total membership of 4,392. The number of ministers was 22; the total value of church property, $297,157. The total disbursements for the year were $70,614, including $36,708 for local current expenses and $33,906 for all other purposes.

From Illinois the Swedish Baptist Church has been extended to every section of the country populated by Swedish people. Its greatest gains have been made in the state of Minnesota, where work was begun almost as early as in Illinois. Today the church is subdivided into 21

"Fridhem," The Swedish Baptist Home for the Aged, Morgan Park

conferences, each embracing one or several states, in addition to which there are a number of scattered congregations in other states and in Canada. A General Conference is held annually since 1879, when it was organized at Village Creek, Ia.

The statistics published in 1908 give the following figures: Congregations, 357; ordained ministers, 208; preachers and woman missionaries, 135; church buildings, 305; net increase in membership for the year last past, 902; total membership, 26,645; value of church property, $1,837,830; debt on same, $327,514; local disbursements, $400,075; contributions to missions and benevolent purposes, $88,375.

Besides the theological school, there are two educational institutions, Adelphia College, in Seattle, Wash., and Bethel Academy, in Minneapolis, Minn., also an orphans' asylum, located at New Britain, Conn., all of which receive their main support from the Swedish Baptist Church.

CHAPTER X

The Swedish Mission Church

The Movement Defined

HE denomination of believers known as the Mission Friends is one of the outgrowths of a movement within the state church of Sweden toward deeper spirituality, greater freedom from dogmatism and set forms of worship and church practice, the exclusion of all but true Christians from participation in the holy communion and ultimately the reorganization of the church on the basis of admitting as members true believers only. Many of the adherents of this movement, known by the common and reproachful name of Readers, remained loyal to the Lutheran state church, but about the middle of the last century numbers of them became Methodists, Baptists and Erik Janssonists. In the sixties and seventies another part of this same church element, organized into local "communion societies" and more general mission societies, began to crystallize into a new denomination of dissenters, who became known as Mission Friends and in 1878 established a free church, named the Mission Covenant of Sweden. Its counterpart in this country is the Swedish Evangelical Mission Covenant of America, organized in 1885. This is the only well-defined body of the Mission Friends in the United States, who are otherwise divided into three groups, the Mission Covenant, the Swedish Congregationalists and the Swedish Free Mission. The lines of demarkation between these cannot be distinctly drawn. Owing to a peculiar looseness in organization, these groups overlap and run into one another. Thus, by way of illustration, a pastor who is duly registered as a member of the Mission Covenant may be in charge of a church not organically connected with the Covenant, but either independent of all church denominations or allied with the Congregational Church, and vice versa. The so-called Free Mission Friends are the ultras, who at first frowned upon all forms of denominational organization as unbiblical and, therefore, unchristian. In later years they have formed an organization of their own, differing from the Mission Covenant chiefly in the higher degree of looseness in construction.

Beginning of the Movement in Chicago

In the year 1867, a number of Mission Friends from the city of Jönköping and vicinity emigrated and came to Chicago. Here they joined the Immanuel Swedish Lutheran Church, but did not feel at home in the Augustana Synod, which to their mind was no great improvement on the state church of the old country. As a consequence they soon formed a group by themselves and began to hold meetings in the various homes. One Martin Sundin was in the habit of reading to them from the religious periodical "Pietisten," but as yet they had no recognized leader. In 1868, John Peterson and several others from Jönköping came over and joined the group. Peterson, who had been a lay preacher in Sweden, naturally took a leading part in the private meetings, which for a time were held in his own rooms. Another of the earliest preachers was C. J. Lindahl, who took a prominent part in the work in 1869. The arrival of J. M. Sanngren, and a powerful evangelical sermon preached by him, is said to have given the real impetus toward a distinct organization, and on December 26, 1868, at a meeting held in the home of Martin Sundin, 134 E. Superior street, the preliminary steps were taken in the organization of a Mission Association on the order of those in Sweden. This was the nucleus of the North Side Lutheran Mission Church subsequently established independently of the Immanuel Church. The growing attendance at these meetings necessitating a larger meeting-place, a little old school-house on Bremer street (now Milton avenue) was procured and adapted for the purpose. This was soon taxed to its full capacity and, although put in fairly good condition, threatened to fall from overcrowding. The need of a better hall was apparent and work to that end was begun, the building fund starting with the sum of 18 cents. A sewing society was formed for the purpose of increasing the fund and at its first auction sale the sum of $117 was realized. One of the brethren, A. W. Hedenschoug by name, a prominent member of the group, suggested the purchase of a certain property on Franklin street, comprising three building lots. The price, $5,300, looked prohibitive, but one Samuelson, a leading member of the Immanuel Church, where many of them still were enrolled, came to their assistance by mortgaging his own home for the amount needed. The purchase was made May 21, 1869. As soon as the new mission house, a structure 80 by 42 feet, had been enclosed, in October, a meeting was held there, Brother Peterson preaching to a jubilant audience seated on planks.

Having attained such proportions, the movement began to attract the attention of the synodical pastors, who endeavored to prevent a separation by assuming a friendly attitude. The dedicatory services were attended by Rev. Erland Carlsson and J. G. Princell, an Augustana student, then continuing his studies at the Chicago University. Rev. Hasselquist and other ministers showed their interest by preaching in the new mission house. They offered the suggestion that this be made a "week-day church," while all should attend the Sunday services at the Immanuel Church, as formerly, or that it be turned into a refuge for the needy. Neither suggestion was agreed to. The breach widened, and the trend was in the direction of a separate church, with or without any such intention on the part of those involved. The primary purpose had been to hold evangelistic meetings in the spirit of the "Readers' meetings" in the old country; to this was added the secondary one of missionating and building up a society or congregation of true believers only, patterned after the mission societies in Sweden. At this juncture a certain lawyer inquired whether any legal organization had been affected. Being instructed by him as to the necessity and advantage of such organization, the adherents of the movement proceeded to organize, adopting the name of The Swedish Evangelical Lutheran Missionary Association of Chicago. The next question raised was that of "recording" or incorporating the association, which was also done. A Swedish newspaper now propounded the question, what was the spirit and tendency of the so-called Mission Friends, and in its next issue answered by stating categorically that they were "un-Lutheran, unchurchly and unchristian." At a meeting of Mission Friends held in Princeton in the fall of 1869 two brethren, Peterson and Hedenschoug, were selected to call upon the ministerium of the Augustana Synod for a correction of that uncharitable statement. The onus was then thrown upon a certain editor employed on the newspaper who, in resigning his position shortly afterward, gave it out that certain clergymen were responsible for the article in question.

The association thus formed for a time existed as an organization within the Immanuel Church. It had a board of ten or twelve directors, its first set of officers being Martin Sundin, president; Olof Anderson, secretary, and S. Samuelson, treasurer, and the total membership in the association during the first month of its existence probably did not exceed a score. C. J. Lindahl, the first preacher engaged by the association, was a brother of Rev. S. P. A. Lindahl of the Augustana Synod, and had previously been in the service of the Swedish Lutherans of Chicago as city missionary, but was discharged on the ground of "hyper-evangelical" tendencies. Lindahl, who was engaged by the association in February, 1869, remained only a few months in its service, subsequently going over to the Lutheran General Synod to serve as its missionary among the Swedish people. Lindahl was succeeded in the summer of 1869 by J. M. Sanngren, the first regular pastor of this flock.

When the mission society had taken the decisive step, separating from the church and founding an independent congregation, one of its first cares was how to obtain a regularly ordained pastor. After some trepidation as to the propriety of celebrating the holy communion without the services of a minister, the society had accepted the Eucharist at the hands of Sanngren, but while they held him competent as a layman to administer the sacraments, there was still a difference of opinion among the members as to whether ordination by a clergyman of the church was a prerequisite for exercising the functions of the apostolic ministry. At its incorporation the society was invested with authority to license preachers, and the first four to be licensed were its own preachers, Sanngren and J. Peterson, and, at the request of other societies, C. A. Björk and H. Blom. Others who shortly after were given their licenses were: C. P. Mellgren, P. Wedin and C. J. Magnuson. But that a mere license, granted by the civil authorities, was quite different from the biblical consecration for the holy ministry, was clearly realized, and soon all were agreed that to come into the full exercise of ministerial functions the preacher should be consecrated by prayers and the laying on of hands, without agreeing, however, as to who was the proper person to perform this act.

For light on this mooted question the New Testament as well as the writings of Luther and Rosenius were consulted. The latter authorities were found to support the position that the consecration of men to the ministry is the function of ordained ministers. These writers being held in high esteem by all the brethren, no one ventured to oppose them, although several differed with them on this point. The outcome was, that the Mission Society of Chicago through C. Anderson, a Danish pastor belonging to the Lutheran Synod of Northern Illinois, petitioned for J. M. Sanngren's ordination by that body. The request was granted, and accordingly, at a special meeting of the society, Sanngren was by the said synod ordained to the ministry of the gospel.* The question of "apostolic succession" having been thus settled, so far as the society was concerned, C. A. Björk was ordained by Sanngren in 1870 and the same order has been subsequently followed.

Traveling missionaries, supported by this church, were sent out to different parts of the country to preach, including the aforesaid John Peterson, and through their efforts or independently little

* Bowman: Missionsvännerna i Amerika.

groups of Mission Friends sprung up in various localities, such as Princeton and Galesburg, Ill., Swede Bend, Keokuk and Des Moines, Ia., St. Paul and Minneapolis, Minn., and elsewhere.

The Mission Church on the north side, which dates its independent existence from the early part of 1869, prospered and finished its house of worship in a short time, but hardly had this been done when the great fire of 1871 swept it away. The members were now scattered in all directions, the majority taking refuge on the west side. There they were sheltered in a schoolhouse, together with other refugees of all nationalities. John Peterson was appointed quartermaster for this aggregation of hungry and ill-clad fire sufferers, who were furnished food and clothing by the relief committee. Scrupulously avoiding every suspicion of selfishness or mismanagement, Peterson would not appropriate a single thread of clothing for his own use, but turned to his personal friend D. L. Moody, who had charge of a relief station near by, for what he needed for himself. Moody regretted to say that he came too late, all his supplies having been exhausted the day before. "But," said he, "I have here an old coat from a Catholic priest, if you care to take it." Grateful for any favor, Peterson donned the garment and returned to his party. There he was at once surrounded by Catholic women who called him "Father" and implored him to administer the sacraments to them. He refused them on the ground of not being a priest, but they were insistent in their prayers, and as against the silent testimony of that coat no arguments could convince them of their mistake. When Peterson shortly afterward was sent to preach in Des Moines that long, black, ecclesiastical garment so shocked the free church friends there that they ushered him post haste to a clothier's shop and bought him a coat of more "evangelical" cut.

After the fire, the Mission Friends at first held their meetings in a rented church on the south side, but bent their efforts toward rebuilding the mission house on the north side. When, after a few months spent in Des Moines, Peterson returned to Chicago, he was engaged to solicit funds for a new edifice. In the short period of six weeks he raised $2,600. C. A. Björk, who had begun preaching in Swede Bend, Ia., came to his assistance and succeeded in raising $4,000 more. With these funds a new and more commodious mission house was reared on the site of the first. Rev. Sanngren continued in charge of the church from 1869 till 1877, when he was succeeded by Rev. Björk. He served the church for a period of seventeen years, until February, 1895, when he was required to devote his entire time to his duties as president of the Covenant. His successor was Rev. August Pohl, who resigned in 1899. The next permanent pastor was Rev. K. F. Ohlson, who was in charge from May, 1900, till the end of

the year 1903. Rev. F. M. Johnson, the present pastor, succeeded to
the pastorate Jan. 1, 1904.

The splendid edifice in which the congregation now worships was
dedicated in December, 1887. The lots which it occupies were purchased in 1886 for $10,000 and the same year ground was broken for
the new structure, which was completed and furnished at a cost of

The Swedish Mission Church, Orleans and Whiting Streets

$35,000. A parsonage also was built, and the property of the congre-
gation is valued at $60,000.

Simultaneously with that on the north side, the Mission Friends
started a movement on the south side. Meetings were held in a hall
on Archer avenue until after Rev. E. A. Skogsbergh had been called
from Sweden to labor in this field, when the attendance reached a
point where it was found necessary to make other arrangements.
Funds were secured through Skogsbergh's efforts and in the summer
of 1878 a tabernacle measuring 90 by 70 feet was erected on a piece
of ground comprising three ordinary building lots.

Rev. Johan Magnus Sanngren.

Johan Magnus Sanngren was born in Alsheda parish, Småland, Sweden, July 4, 1837. He remained on his father's farm until the age of twenty, when after his conversion he entered Rev. Ahlberg's seminary at Ahlsborg, Småland. He preached while a student, and after having finished the course of instruction, he labored fruitfully for five years as a preacher in his native province. In 1868 he emigrated, reaching Chicago in September. Appearing in the pulpit of the Immanuel Church, he impressed favorably those not contented with the average Augustana minister. After having lived for a short period in Altona, and preached in the Lutheran churches roundabout, Sanngren was called to the newly organized mission society in Chicago, which, upon its subsequent organization as the North Side Mission

Rev. Johan Magnus Sanngren

Church, retained him as its pastor until the year 1877. Seeking to improve his impaired health by a change of climate, he removed to Red Wing, Minn., in the fall of that year, upon a call to the local Mission Church. Here his condition grew worse, and after a period of confinement to the sick-bed Rev. Sanngren passed from this life Sept. 26, 1878, survived by his wife and son.

Sanngren was a pioneer of the Mission church movement in this country and the first regular pastor of the first organized church of that denomination. When the Mission Synod was organized in 1873, Sanngren was chosen its head, and held the presidency until his death. At the synodical meeting in Bethesda, Saunders county, Neb., in May,

1878, he preach what proved to be his farewell sermon to the church body he had so faithfully served.

Sanngren has been described as a man of rich gifts but of peculiar temperament and odd manners in the pulpit. He often spiced his sermons with a dash of humor and punctuated them with violent gesticulation. Some would take offense at his manner and reject the course on account of the dish in which it was served. Far from defending his eccentricities, he regretted them, but as they were temperamental, he strived in vain to overcome these faults. But he was sincere and free from affectation, and those who knew him best lost sight of his shortcomings in their appreciation of his worth. If the pulpit humorist drew smiles from his hearers, it was apparently without intent, for the next moment he would hurl a thunderbolt of divine truth with a vigor that bespoke intense seriousness.

Rev. John A. Peterson

John A. Peterson, one of the first preachers among the Mission Friends in this country, was born March 24, 1838, in Ljunga parish, Småland, Sweden. In his infancy he lost his mother by death. After

Rev. John A. Peterson

attending common school, he was apprenticed to a shoemaker at fourteen years of age and at nineteen began to ply that trade on his own account. He was converted at the age of twenty-one. In 1862 he removed to Svenarum, where he was married to Anna Sofia Asp. After two years they moved to Jönköping where Peterson opened a shoe-shop. He was now called by the Mission Society of Jönköping to aid in its work through preaching and colportage of religious books and tracts.

In April, 1868, Peterson emigrated with his family, and reached Chicago May 20th. Here he took a prominent part in the work of the Mission Friends, then recently begun, and he holds an honored place among the early preachers of the Mission Church in Chicago. Responding to a call from Des Moines, Ia., Peterson removed from Chicago in the fall of 1871, shortly after the fire. He served as pastor of the Mission Church of Des Moines for a period of eight years with unqualified success. His next removal was to the Salem Church, a country congregation in Burt county, Nebraska, which remained in his charge for twenty-four years. With his wife he is now living in the city of Oakland, while his sons are cultivating a farm owned by him in the same county. He resigned the pastorate several years ago, but continues to preach occasionally. Rev. Peterson is revered as one of the fathers of the Mission Church, to which he has given the best efforts of a long and useful life. He has been a member of the directors of the Mission Covenant and was often called to offices of honor and trust in the various branches of its activity.

Rev. Erik August Skogsbergh

In 1876 the Mission Friends of Chicago and elsewhere were stirred to religious activity as never before, chiefly by the virile evangelistic work of one man—Rev. Erik August Skogsbergh. He had just come over from Sweden to assist Rev. Sanngren, but soon became the leading factor in a notable revival. Skogsbergh, who was born at Elgå, Vermland, June 30, 1850, and was pursuing studies at Jönköping when called to Chicago, took up the work here with a will and energy remarkable in so young a man. His first sermon in Chicago was preached on the day of his arrival, Oct. 10, 1876. With a burning zeal for the salvation of men's souls, he at once kindled his hearers, and people went to hear this "Swedish Moody" in ever growing numbers. Skogsbergh proved both a preaching and a singing evangelist, who wielded a twofold influence over his audiences.

He was assigned a field on the south side, where the north side church had conducted a mission since 1871. From there the revival resulting from Skogsbergh's sermons and songs spread to the north side. From the mission a separate congregation was soon formed, named the Tabernacle Church, and Skogsbergh became its pastor. The mission-house having become inadequate, a large structure, known as the Mission Tabernacle, was erected in 1877, where Skogsbergh continued to preach to large audiences for upwards of eight years. His reputation meanwhile spread to the other mission churches, and during the same period he was in constant demand for evangelistic work in other fields. In January, 1884, he removed to Minneapolis and his labors there as pastor of the Tabernacle Church for almost a quarter century have been richly blessed. He there founded a school of which

Swedish Mission Tabernacle, Chicago

North Park College in Chicago is a continuation, and subsequent to the removal of this institution he has been engaged in educational work at Minneapolis. As a preacher and religious leader Skogsbergh for thirty years has held a pre-eminent position in the Mission Church of the United States.

The Mission Movement in Galesburg

The Swedish Lutheran Church of Galesburg had been organized with some difficulty, and formed from rather heterogeneous elements. Part of the membership consisted of persons of free church tendencies from Sweden, who had been fostered among the Readers and mission societies in the old country. Hasselquist, its first permanent pastor, made concessions to this element. This church did not as a whole sanction the act of the Swedish Lutherans in leaving the Synod of Northern Illinois to form the Augustana Synod. When Hasselquist was succeeded by Dahlsten in 1863, the services became too ritualistic to suit the liberalists, who now began to gather in private for devotional services led by laymen. Among the initiators was S. W. Sundberg. Warnings against the separatists did not have the desired effect, and the active opposition of the pastor seemed rather to hasten actual separation. The feud continued for several years, not without uncharitable bitterness on both sides. To the annual convention of the Augustana Synod in 1868 the congregation sent through its lay delegate a protest against the ritualistic order of services prescribed by the synod and certain other regulations not conforming to the ideas of this church. One of its demands was that the lay delegate should be admitted to the closed session of the ministerium. Rev. Hasselquist and one or two other pastors were sent to Galesburg to reprimand the rebellious' church and admonish it to remain true to Lutheran doctrines and usages. All but about 40 members submitted, and no further action was taken at the time.

About this time a lay preacher named Bergensköld, who had been educated at the Fjellstedt school in Upsala and served as preacher at Count Stackelberg's factory in Öfverum, came to Galesburg. His friends asked that he might be allowed to preach occasionally in the church, but when the pastor refused him his pulpit, Bergensköld's friends, several of whom were on the board of deacons, arranged private devotional services, led by Bergensköld. Alarmed by the spread of the "New Evangelism" in his church, the pastor called in Hasselquist, Carlsson of Chicago and Swensson of Andover, who administered a second reprimand.

In August five deacons and several other members met for counsel in the home of Olof Johnson, the Sunday school superintendent, Bergensköld being absent. Johnson declared the situation intolerable and announced his decision to leave the church. Others shared his views, and then and there it was resolved to form a mission society modeled on those in Sweden. The organization took place at a subsequent meeting, when about forty persons signed for membership. A hall was procured, where Bergensköld now preached regularly.

The need of a legally incorporated church and a regularly ordained minister was soon felt. Bergensköld was only a lay preacher, who had no inclination to join any particular denomination. Many of the new society still felt kindly toward the Synod of Northern Illinois,

Rev. S. W. Sundberg

and favored joining that body and calling the aforementioned Rev. Carl Anderson as their pastor. · The proposition and call were submitted in November, at the synodical convention, and after the society had adopted the confession and constitution of the synod it joined that body under the name of the Second Evangelical Lutheran Church of Galesburg. Rev. Anderson, after having been duly elected, succeeded to the pastorate upon Bergensköld's departure for Iowa in April, 1869.

At first the church held strictly to the purity rule, but after joining the synod it became more lax in the admission of members. Years of contention on this point.followed and not until after the year 1876, when Rev. J. G. Sjöquist assumed pastoral charge, was any effective attempt made to weed out the worldly-minded members. This process was completed by his successor, Rev. E. G. Hjerpe, whose efforts resulted in the expulsion of many. This church, now known as the Mission Church of Galesburg, is the second oldest in the denomination. Shortly after Rev. Anderson's succession to the pastorate in 1869, a building lot was purchased for $1,200, on which a church edifice was erected at a cost of about $10,000. This building is the one still in use.

Rev. Carl Anderson

Rev. Anderson was a man af more than ordinary ability. His American education and his familiarity with conditions in this country placed him in the forefront of the Scandinavian churchmen of his period. In 1871, while pastor in Galesburg, he started a church paper, "Zions Banér," which for a time was the mouthpiece of the Mission Friends and did much to advance their interests. Later it changed its tone and became an advocate of the plans and interests of the General Synod and more especially the Synod of Northern Illinois anent the Scandinavians. Prior thereto, Anderson's paper had, however, earned the thanks of the Mission Friends as the first to champion their cause.

The proposal to organize the mission societies or churches into a general body originated with Anderson. His secondary purpose was to make the new organization a part of the General Synod, but finding this idea unpopular among the brethren, he declared his willingness to aid in forming an independent synod of the Mission Friends. When some such measure was proposed at a meeting in Princeton in July, 1871, action was deferred for fear that it would lead to a worldly church.

In 1873, after having lost part of his prestige among the Mission Friends, Anderson left Galesburg for Keokuk, Ia., where a Swedish church of the Synod of Northern Illinois had been established in 1870. Here he started a school for the training of preachers, which was the forerunner of Ansgarius College in Knoxville.

The Mission Church of Princeton

The beginning of the mission church at Princeton was a family named Lundholm, man and wife, who arrived there in 1867. They began missionating among their countrymen after the manner of the Readers of Sweden, to whom they had belonged, thereby gathering a little group of persons who later united into a mission society. In the fall of the next year, C. P. Mellgren, a lay preacher, arrived. He was born at Torpa, Småland, March 7, 1836. Converted at the age of twenty-one, he began to testify in intimate circles of the faithful and was a few years later assigned as colporteur by the Sunnerbo Mission Society. He labored as such for six years prior to his emigration. After his coming to Princeton, where he was dependent on the labor of his own hands for his support, he continued preaching, meetings being usually conducted in a schoolhouse outside the city. On the

14th of December, 1868, there was organized a mission society of 30 members, which in 1871 was incorporated as a church. The second general meeting of the various mission societies was held in Princeton in the fall of 1869, the first having taken place in Chicago in July of the same year.

While in Princeton, Mellgren extended his labors to other places in Illinois, including Altona, Geneseo, Galesburg and others. He often undertook long missionary journeys to Minnesota, Iowa, Missouri and Kansas. In 1873 he removed to Osage City, Kans., where he has ever since resided. His successor was P. Wedin, born at Agunnaryd, Småland, March 1, 1835, died in Aurora, Neb., April 11, 1907. Wedin came to Princeton direct from Sweden in 1870, and at first obtained work on the railroad. He preached on occasion, prior to Mellgren's leaving, and subsequently filled his place for seven years, during which time the Mission church flourished, and became one of the strongest of the early ones of the denomination. Wedin was engaged for several years as traveling missionary of the Mission Synod, and during that period preached the gospel throughout the country from coast to coast.

Wedin opposed the organization of the Mission Covenant in 1885, demanding a strict and clearly defined confession in place of the one proposed. Yet, when the Mission Synod to which he belonged virtually joined the Covenant in a body, Wedin automatically became a member, but withdrew from his former brethren and for a short time was a member of the Augustana Synod. During his last years he belonged to no church body, but continued to preach to little bands of followers at places in Texas, Kansas and Nebraska, where he lived.

The Rockford Field

A little group of Mission Friends in Rockford were wont to hold private meetings there as early as 1868. The same year P. Undeen came there from Sweden and went to work for a neighboring farmer, meanwhile forming the acquaintance of these people and eventually becoming their preacher. While working as a painter in the city, he acted as pastor of the little flock, which was not formally organized as a church until 1875. The first man to devote himself exclusively to the charge of this church was Rev. P. J. Lindell.

Undeen, who was in a way the founder of this church, was born at Undenäs, Vestergötland, Aug. 13, 1835. He is known to have attended Rev. Ahlberg's seminary prior to 1865, whereupon he worked in Vermland and elsewhere as a Bible colporteur and lay preacher in the service of Evangeliska Fosterlandsstiftelsen. After the loss of his wife, whom he married in 1866, he pursued studies at the same school for another year prior to his emigration. Engaged as a traveling missionary by the first conference of Mission Friends, Undeen soon after entered the service of the General Synod of the American Lutherans, and was ordained by that body in 1870. The change is thought to have been prompted by lack of support from the Mission Church. He removed to Swift county, Minnesota, and his labors in the northwest bore rich fruit. The founding of the Mission churches in Red Wing and Minneapolis, as also in Lund, Wis., is credited to his efforts. Undeen joined in organizing the Mission Synod in 1873, and devoted his last years to the service of that body. He passed away at Lund, Wis., Feb. 9, 1876.

The Swedish Lutheran Mission Synod

As the movement grew and groups of Mission Friends were formed in various Swedish localities, the need of union and co-operation became apparent, and at a meeting held at Princeton in 1871, it was proposed to unite all Mission Friends in a synod, the initiative being taken by the North Side Mission Church. Acting on the suggestion, a little group of preachers and laymen met at Keokuk, Iowa, and on May 22, 1873, organized the Swedish Evangelical Lutheran Mission Synod. On the same day the synod was incorporated under the laws of the state of Iowa, the incorporators being the following five persons: Peter Englund, Charles Anderson, C. G. Svenson, S. W. Sundberg and C. A. Björk. Of these, Englund, Svenson and Björk were elected trustees for the first year. In the articles of incorporation the object and business of the organization was stated to be: "To organize and govern churches, to educate and ordain ministers of the Gospel, to promote the cause of home and foreign missions, to hold synodical meetings in the state of Iowa and elsewhere in the United States, and to promote the preaching of the Gospel therein." In all matters specified in the articles of incorporation the synod was to be governed by the constitution adopted. In Art. II of said constitution, the synod proclaimed its adherence not only to the three oldest Symbola, the Apostolic, the Nicene and the Athanasian, but also to the Augsburg Confession, thereby affirming allegiance to the Lutheran Church in principle. By way of reassurance, the last article stipulated that said Art. II was to stand unaltered forever. The representation at the synodical meetings was to be by delegations of three, the minister and two lay members, from each and every congregation having adopted the synod's constitution.

Subsequent events in the Mission Synod may be briefly summarized. In 1874 the synod began publishing a religious monthly, called "Missions-Wännen," patterned after "Pietisten," published

in Sweden by C. O. Rosenius, a paper extensively read by the Devotionalists in the old country.   Later a songbook, entitled "Samlings-
sånger," was published, which was in general use throughout the
synod for a number of years.   At the synodical meeting of 1879, held
in Chicago May 27th to June 2nd, it was recommended that the individual congregations adopt the plans and practices of church government prevailing in the Mission Covenant of Sweden.   At this same

Rev. Carl A. Björk

meeting the council of the Ansgarius Synod, a Swedish church organization similar to the Mission Synod, the chief difference being
the latter's greater freedom in receiving members, proposed a union of
the two synods.   A plan of union, based on the constitution and by-laws
of the Mission Covenant in Sweden and conditioned on the dissolution
of both synods, was laid on the table after some discussion, the matter
being postponed on the ground that the time was not yet ripe for such
a step.

In 1881 the Tabernacle Church on the south side in Chicago
withdrew from the Mission Synod.   This action was the result of
agitation against all forms of organization or federation of local

congregations or societies into larger church bodies, those holding this view maintaining that such organizations are contrary to biblical precept and endanger and hamper Christian life and liberty. Agitation on this point for years finally divided the Mission Friends into two camps, the anti-organization people being thenceforth known as the Free Mission Friends.

In the late fall of 1884, a circular authorized by the Tabernacle Church was issued to the ministers of the Ansgarius and Mission synods, inquiring whether they desired a general meeting in Chicago for the purpose of devising plans of unification. The proposition was discussed at the subsequent meeting of the directors of the Mission Synod, held at Randolph, Kans., Dec. 4—8, and a resolution was passed fixing Feb. 18, 1885, as the date of the proposed meeting, also stipulating that the sessions be equally divided between the Tabernacle and the North Side Mission Church. At this meeting the proposition carried and a new church body, entitled the Swedish Evangelical Mission Covenant of America, came into existence. The two synods were not thereby dissolved, the question of joining the new organization being left to the individual congregations.

The Ansgarius Synod

The Swedish Evangelical Lutheran Ansgarius Synod of the United States was organized at Galesburg, Ill., May 18, 1874. The Mission Church in that city, organized in 1868 as an independent Lutheran congregation under the name of the Second Swedish Lutheran Church, had called as its minister Rev. C. Anderson. He was of Danish descent but was educated in this country and had worked as a Scandinavian missionary under the auspices of the Synod of Northern Illinois.

In 1873 he started a theological school in Keokuk, Ia., and was one of the men who organized the Mission Synod in that city the same year. He had expected this synod to become a Scandinavian department or district of the Synod of Northern Illinois, but finding the brethren unwilling to affiliate with that body, he withdrew before the close of the meeting. Several mission churches already belonging to the Synod of Northern Illinois did not join the Mission Synod. Rev. Anderson, desirous of obtaining funds for a school building, issued a circular in English setting forth the purposes and plans of his institute. A copy fell into the hands of James Knox, a wealthy banker of Knoxville, Ill., who summoned Anderson to his home and offered to donate $12,000 toward a Swedish institution of learning to be located in the city of Knoxville. The donor stipulated that the teaching was to conform to the professed doctrines of the church under whose auspices the school was to be established, otherwise it should become the property of the city. His offer was accepted, and the city subscribed $5,000 more, while the sum of $3,000 was raised among the Swedish people. Anderson, realizing the need of an organization to back him and the institution, became the prime mover in organizing the Ansgarius Synod. This was done at a conference of the Swedish churches of the Synod of Northern Illinois, held in Galesburg May 16—20. Anderson and C. J. Lindahl from Brantford, Kans., seem to have been the only ministers present. Among the laymen was J. Anjou, a teacher in Anderson's school at Keokuk, who was chosen president of the new organization. The synod affirmed its adherence to the Augsburg Con-

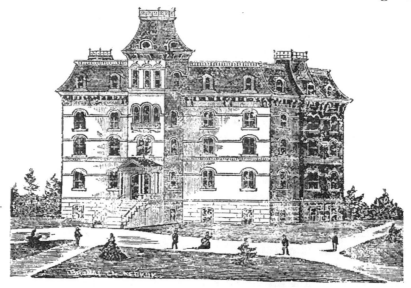

Ansgarius College, Knoxville

fession and adopted a constitution very similar in other respects to that of the Mission Synod. But Anderson's arbitrary action aroused suspicion among the Mission Friends. A misunderstanding between the two synods existed for a time, and petty quarrels among the leaders and ministers on either side forced the two organizations farther and farther apart. The breach was still further widened when the Ansgarius Synod officially joined the Lutheran General Synod.

In the course of a few years, however, the differences were so far obliterated that the Ansgarius Synod, at its fourth annual meeting, held in Galesburg June 5-12, 1878, resolved to invite the co-operation of the Mission Synod with especial reference to the educational work carried on by the Ansgarius College at Knoxville.

The religious revival in Sweden was intensified in the seventies by the great agitation against the Lutheran doctrine of atonement and justification, led by P. Waldenström, a prominent free church man, whose views of the atonement have been briefly stated by himself as follows: "The Scriptures teach that no change took place in God's disposition towards man in consequence of his sin; that, therefore, it was not God who needed to be reconciled to man, but it was man who needed to be reconciled to God; and that, consequently, reconciliation is a work which proceeds from God and is directed towards man, and aims not to appease God, but to cleanse man from sin, and to restore him to a right relation with God."

The movement had a similar effect on this side of the water, the powerful preaching of Skogsbergh, Björk, and others, together with the defection of Waldenströmians from the regular Lutheran congregations, combining to bring large numbers of converts into the Mission churches. Waldenström's views were very generally accepted by the Missions Friends. His rejection of dogmas, confessions, and "man-made rules," as being needless, unauthorized and prejudicial to a correct interpretation of the Holy Scriptures and to the Christian life, caused both the Ansgarius and the Mission synod to amend their constitutions by inserting in the respective articles dealing with the creed the specification that the Augsburg Confession was to be "interpreted in accordance with the Bible." The revival movement had a tendency to unify the Mission Friends spiritually, and thus paved the way for organic union. At the annual meeting in Moline, May 30, 1879, the Ansgarius Synod had reached a new point of contact with the Mission Synod, according to the statement of the president that true Christianity was now a requisite both for membership and participation in the breaking of bread. At the same occasion the result of the overtures for consolidation was reported. The answer of the Mission Synod was favorable in sentiment but pointed out that, in the absence of hearty sympathy and true harmony on which the outward union should be based, a consolidation had better be postponed until the members of the Mission Synod churches themselves should ask for such a move. In its records the Ansgarius Synod made note of the fact that many churches in both synods favored a union based on the constitution and by-laws of the Mission Covenant of Sweden, and urged the remainder to join in the movement, whereby all cause for further strife would be eliminated.

In 1880 the synod adopted a new constitution essentially different from the one in force. The article affirming adherence to the Augsburg Confession was practically annulled by an amendment, in disregard of a specific constitutional provision that said article should never be changed. To get around this legal obstacle, the amendment was made a separate article.

The control and management of the Ansgarius College was now entrusted to an association of individuals within and without the synod, for a term of three years, Anderson and his associate teacher, K. Erixon, having disagreed and in turn left the institution. The association engaged J. G. Princell as head professor and carried on the work until the spring of 1884, when it resigned its stewardship for lack of encouragement and financial support. Two years before, the Ansgarius Synod had severed its connection with the General Synod.

The constitutional changes proved unsatisfactory and led to further difficulties. The regular Lutherans pointed out the falsity of the synod's position in not living up to its professed creed, the Augsburg Confession, while the Free Mission people attacked it on account of its alleged adherence to that creed. Still the Ansgarius people dared not summarily dispose of the troublesome Art. II for fear of invalidating the incorporation and losing its property, consisting chiefly of the college at Knoxville. At the annual convention in 1883, in Jamestown, N. Y., a committee was appointed to ascertain the legal status of the case. In the event that desired changes could not be made without jeopardizing the corporation, the Synod was to be dissolved at its next meeting. When the synod convened in Galesburg the following year, the committee reported, on the authority of the secretary of state at Springfield, that everything in the constitution, except Art. II, might be altered without hazard, but that any change in said article would annul the charter. In its dilemma the synod tentatively adopted an entirely new constitution, drawn up by J. G. Princell and A. Larson, changing the name to "The Swedish Mission Covenant of America" and adopting the Bible as the only perfect guide in matters of faith and living. Princell himself, who had previously withdrawn from the synod, agreed to abide by the drafted constitution at the sacrifice of certain personal convictions, he being opposed to any denominational organization whatsoever.

The synod re-assembled at Worcester, Mass., in August the same year to take final action on the constitution. Further disintegration had set in, aided by doctrinal dissensions and personal differences between Princell and J. Hagström, the former leading the ultra free-church, or anti-organization, forces, the latter belonging to the party that favored organization. No agreement could be reached, and for the second time it was decided to dissolve the synod at its next annual meeting. It was voted to turn the school property over to the city of Knoxville on the first day of September, shortly after adjournment. The synod met at Moline the following May, to wind up its affairs, and on the second day of June, 1885, the Swedish Evangelical Lutheran

Ansgarius Synod passed out of existence. At the synodical meeting in Worcester, Princell had again proposed the forming of some sort of a general body, but the suggestion found little favor with the delegates, who by this time were tired of the strife and dissension that had characterized the synod throughout its existence.

The Swedish Evangelical Mission Covenant

The convention that gave birth to the Mission Covenant was not devoid of travail and partisan bitterness. At the opening of the meeting 55 ministers and lay delegates were present, seven more arriving later. Rev. C. A. Björk was elected chairman. The first question raised was who should be entitled to vote. The call having been understood to include all Mission Friends interested in the question of union one way or another, several anti-organization men came to the meeting, chief among whom were Rev. J. G. Princell, leader of the Free Mission Friends, and John Martenson, publisher of "Chicago-Bladet," the organ of that movement. By raising the question whether he, as a pastor and elder, although not a member of either synod nor a duly elected delegate from any independent Mission church, would be entitled to a seat in the convention, Princell precipitated a warm debate, resulting in a resolution seating all members of the respective synods, but only such ministers and delegates of independent churches as favored the proposed union. Princell declared himself in favor of the unification of all Christians on a biblical basis, meaning thereby unity in faith and good works, without any organic connection, but the convention held that this did not bring him within the terms of the call and, putting the question to a vote, unseated him by a vote of 18 to 6, less than half of the delegates voting. Later, by a vote af 11 ayes to 17 noes, the convention refused to reconsider its action. Princell then withdrew, explaining that he knew very well he could not be seated according to the letter, but only according to the spirit, of the call issued for the meeting. The principal, though not the technical, objection to seating Princell was his determined effort to set at naught the proposed union by relentless agitation against it for months before the meeting. In a series of articles in "Chicago-Bladet," of which paper he was then the assistant editor, he denounced the organization movement in unmeasured terms, going so far as to characterize the combining of congregations into a synod, union or federation of any kind whatever as "lawlessness from a scriptural point of view; rebellion against the church of God and its local authorities; ecclesiastical communism; an unchaste relation to sister congregations, and faithlessness and harlotry in relation to the betrothed bridegroom of the church, Jesus Christ." These words were quoted from his own paper in support of the position taken by the convention, which, however, stood ready to reverse its action on condition that Princell would withdraw his charges against the brethren supporting the movement. This he refused to do; on the contrary, he persevered in his antagonism and it was largely due to his stand and the treatment he received at the hands of the convention that quite a number of free churches refused to join the Covenant and have remained independent to this day. In justice to the Covenant, it should be added that at a sub-

Rev. John G. Princell

sequent meeting it admitted its mistake by apologizing to Princell for its action.

Having determined the basis of representation, the convention proceeded to discuss the main issue. Owing to the difference in opinion as to church organizations, a preliminary discussion was held on the significant subject: "Is it right or wrong for Christian congregations and societies to combine in their endeavor to further the kingdom of God, and on what basis can such union be effected?" The meeting answered the question as follows: "A union of Christian congregations ought to be accomplished on a scriptural basis, among such Christian believers as have confidence in and true love for one another and are actuated by a desire for peace and harmony." At the third session, the question of organizing was put to a formal vote.

By a rising vote the proposition was almost unanimously carried, only two or three persons remaining seated when the ayes were called for.

A constitution was adopted, closely corresponding to that of the Mission Covenant in Sweden. Its striking resemblance to that proposed for the Ansgarius Synod by Princell less than a year before bears evidence to the fact that the dissension between the Free Mission Friends and those forming the Covenant was based not so much on principles as on quibbles and personal differences.

The Swedish Evangelical Mission Covenant of America, now organized, recognizes no creed or confession beyond the words of the Bible itself; it consists of congregations and associations, whose members are required to be converts as a condition of admittance. In most other respects, the Covenant is not different from other bodies or synods, except in its lack of solidity and compactness, owing to the fact that it officially includes independent churches and mission societies as well as those having joined the Covenant in the prescribed order.

The Mission Synod, after ascertaining the wishes of the individual churches at a meeting in Des Moines, Ia., in May, 1885, joined the Covenant in a body, while those of the dissolved Ansgarius Synod and independent congregations were required to make individual application. Many of the latter stood aloof, as did the majority of the Free Mission churches. The Mission Synod not having been formally dissolved before joining the Covenant, a number of its ministers resolved to maintain the old organization by holding a legal meeting each year. They assembled in Phelps Centre, Neb., in 1886, and there decided to meet only when it would be found necessary. The attempt to keep the synod alive was apparently due to dissent from the opinion of the majority and doubt as to the future of the Covenant, but the precaution proved needless. No meeting has been held since 1886, and the synod is considered legally dead.

The Covenant held its first annual meeting in Princeton, Sept. 25-30, 1885, the delegates being the same as at the organization meeting in Chicago. John Martenson, who appeared with credentials from the Swedish Christian Church of North Star Hall, Chicago, signed by Princell, was refused a vote on the ground that the church he represented had not applied, and did not wish to apply for membership in the Covenant. Martenson was, however, made advisory member. At the meeting 46 congregations were admitted, and the Christian Association of the Northwest, organized in 1884, was given two delegates, its congregations being required to seek admittance singly. Ministers of independent congregations known to be well disposed toward the Covenant were admitted at their own request and registered in the roll of ministers. A total of 38 ministers were matriculated

at this time, several newcomers being licensed to preached for one year.
In order to further the mission work it was recommended that the
churches within a certain state or geographical division be organized
into conferences and these be subdivided into mission districts. Such
conferences, called associations, have since been formed in several
states, but only those of Minnesota and of Illinois have been subdivided into districts.

The Swedish Mission Church of Moline

One of the most important questions dealt with was that of co-
operation with the Swedish Congregationalists in the control and
support of a theological seminary. The Chicago Theological Seminary
having promised to open a Swedish department and to support a
teacher to be selected by the Covenant, Prof. F. Risberg from Sweden
had been called at the suggestion of the Covenant's school committe and
had already accepted the position, and this arrangement was now
sanctioned by the Covenant. The Covenant also decided to incorporate
and selected the following seven men to carry out the decision, viz.,
C. A. Björk, J. O. Heggen, A. Hallner, Swen Youngqvist, A. Larson,

C. R. Carlson and F. G. Häggqvist. It was resolved to establish a home for orphans, poor widows and invalids, and H. Palmblad was appointed to solicit funds in Chicago for the proposed institution. At the following annual meeting, held in Rockford, it was reported that a charity home had been established at Bowmanville, Chicago, with twelve inmates.

At the annual meeting held in Chicago in September, 1888, Rev. Princell, claiming to represent the general opinion among the Free Mission Friends, proposed a constitutional change, permitting three classes of members in the Covenant, which change, he alleged, would open the door for himself and his followers. While maintaining his views on church organization, he admitted that even the Free Mission Friends now recognized the need of some form of organization. The Covenant respectfully declined to adopt the change, at the same time apologizing for the treatment accorded Princell three years before.

Owing to a desire on the part of many Mission Friends in each of the three groups, the Covenant in 1905 took action looking to the unification of the Covenant, the Free Mission and the Swedish Congregational churches. It was recommended that a committee of seven peacemakers be appointed to confer on the matter and plan the proposed union. Of these, two were to be appointed by each of the three interested parties, the seventh to be chosen by these six and to act as chairman of the committee. Representatives were appointed to act for each of the three groups, and at the call of this committee a union conference was held in Chicago in the fall of 1906. This conference recommended the establishment of a common divinity school in place of the three existing ones, and suggested as additional factors for the promotion of union, frequent interchange of pulpits and union revival meetings, common evangelists for the home and foreign mission fields, common district conferences for the discussion of questions of faith and doctrine, and common religious textbooks and hymnals. The recommendations of the committee have subsequently been discussed at the various annual conventions, but no decision has been reached, and the main question of unification still remains open.

North Park College

The idea of establishing an institution of learning within the Swedish Mission Covenant is as old as the Covenant itself. In its articles of incorporation the founding and maintenance of schools is specifically mentioned as one of its prime objects. The first opportunity to realize this purpose was offered the same year that the Covenant was formed, when the Congregational theological seminary in Chicago agreed to establish a Swedish department to be partly

North Park College
President's Residence—Dormitory—Main Building

under the control of the Covenant. This was done, but the arrangement did not prove entirely satisfactory, and the idea of founding a school distinctly its own was never abandoned by the Covenant.

The first step leading to the establishment of such an institution was taken in 1891, at the annual meeting in Phelps, Neb., the Covenant resolving to take over a school conducted by Rev. E. A. Skogsbergh and David Nyvall in Minneapolis, combining theological courses with instruction in general subjects and business training. For the next two years the Covenant maintained this school at its old location, with comparative success. In 1894, at the end of the second year, the total

North Park College—General View

attendance was 125, including 31 in the theological department, a number not again reached until very recently. The school was in a sound condition financially, with a small surplus in the treasury.

These advantages were outweighed, however, by the difficulty in obtaining the necessary buildings in Minneapolis and the offer of substantial aid from people in Chicago, on condition that the institution be removed to this city. Accordingly the removal was brought about, and the school was located in North Park, Chicago, in the year 1894, and named North Park College. A tract of land was secured and subdivided to be sold in building lots for the benefit of the institution.

The inner growth of the school did not keep pace with the material development during the next few years. Year by year the attendance fell off, until in 1899 the lowest mark was reached, namely, a total of 51 students in all departments and but fourteen in the divinity school. But from that time on there has been a uniform increase, to 62 in 1900, 83 in 1901, 107 in 1902, about 150 in 1903, and 204 in 1907, followed by a decrease to a figure below 190 in the last year.

The institution now comprises, besides the theological department, a complete academy, a business school and a conservatory of music, the collegiate department to be completed by the adding of college classes as fast as the growth of the institution warrants.

There are three buildings on the college premises, a main building, a dormitory, and the president's residence. The grounds comprise 8½ acres. The present value of the school property is $56,800.

The number of teachers, which was six at the time of the removal to Chicago, has since reached as high as fourteen, and is at present twelve. These, with the subjects taught respectively, are: A. W. Fredrickson, A. M., English language and literature, and mathematics; A. Mellander, Old Testament, church history and systematic theology; Rev. Carl Hanson, New Testament, homiletics and mental science; C. J. Wilson, A. M., Latin and natural science; Alfred N. Ahnfeldt, Greek, German, Swedish and history; Lena Sahlstrom, English and arithmetic; Mrs. Blanche Waldenstrom, piano; Esther Wallgren, piano; C. F. Fredrickson, violin; F. J. Hollenbeck, English language and literature; A. E. Anderson, mandolin and guitar.

Prof. David Nyvall was president of North Park College up to the close of the school year in 1904. After having served as acting president in the interval, Prof. A. W. Fredrickson was regularly elected to the position by the Covenant in 1905. The school is under the control of a board of twenty-three directors, elected by the Covenant, and Rev. John Hagstrom serves as business manager and treasurer. An organization named the Auxiliary Society has lent material aid in raising funds for the institution in years past.

The Swedish Covenant Hospital and Home of Mercy

It was not included in the original plans and purposes of the institution now known as the Swedish Covenant Hospital and Home of Mercy to make it a regular hospital to which the public in general might have access, but rather a home for the aged and destitute. The idea of founding such a home must be credited to Mr. Henry Palmblad, for several years city missionary under the auspices of the North Side Mission Church. In his missionary work he met with many of his countrymen and brethren in the faith who were homeless, destitute and sick. Moved by compassion for these, he went before the Swedish Mission Covenant at its annual meeting at Princeton, in September, 1885, and presented his cause. His project met with decided approval, and a committee to select and purchase a site for the proposed home of mercy was at once appointed, consisting of the following Chicago gentlemen, Revs. C. A. Björk, F. M. Johnson, J. P. Eagle, and Messrs. H. Palmblad, S. Youngquist and C. G. Peterson.

This committee at once began its work with the result that the property of one Mr. Becker, situated on West Foster ave., in Bowmanville, within the city limits of Chicago, was purchased. This property consisted of three acres of ground, a two story brick house and a

The Swedish Covenant Hospital and Home of Mercy, Bowmanville

stable. The price was $5,500, of which $2,500 was to be paid May 1, 1886, and the balance in annual installments of $1,000. So well did the committee succeed in raising funds that on the following May first the entire balance of the purchase money was paid. Additional contributions proved adequate for repairing and remodeling the buildings at a cost of $1,400, and the purchase of furnishings and chattels for $1,200.

In the early part of May, 1886, the home was opened for the acceptance of wards and patients. Shortly afterward everything was in readiness for the public opening, and in the presence of a large number of its friends and supporters the institution was solemnly dedicated on the 27th of June, Rev. C. A. Björk delivering the dedicatory address.

It did not take a great while until the Home was filled and unable to accept all who sought admission. The committee went to the annual meeting at Galesburg, in 1890, with a proposition to enlarge it, and the Covenant authorized such enlargement as the treasury and additional funds received for the purpose might warrant, and a loan in addition thereto not to exceed $2,000. At the next annual meeting of the Covenant, held in Septembr, 1891, the president of the home was able to report that a large two-story addition had been erected and improvements made in the other buildings, all at a cost of some-what over $7,000.

From the Swedish Home of Mercy has developed the Swedish Covenant Hospital. Many of the inmates of the former soon after their arrival were found to be in need of medical treatment or surgical operations. The home had enlisted the services of several able physicians, including Dr. C. W. Johnson and Dr. F. I. Brown, and these men soon attracted patients from Chicago and elsewhere. Although the home was enlarged in 1891, yet the many applications for admission to the hospital department created a demand for a hospital building, well equipped and modern in all its appointments.

In the meantime the question of raising funds for such a building was much pondered, but several years passed before anything could be done. Two financially able persons had held out promises of sub-stantial aid toward the erection of such a building, one preferring that it be located in Lake View. At the Covenant's annual meeting in Duluth in 1901 this matter was taken up, resulting in definite action. A committee was appointed to select a site and confer with the would-be donors. It developed, however, that these parties withdrew their offers because of the decision of the committee to build the hospital adjacent to the Home of Mercy. Prior to their decision, however, the committee had issued a general appeal to the people of the Mission Covenant for means wherewith to purchase a new site, but the lack of response caused them to decide in favor of the old one. A definite decision to erect a hospital building on the grounds of the Home of Mercy was reached at the annual meeting of the Covenant at Galesburg, in 1902. Ground was broken for the new building early in October that year, and the cornerstone was laid on the nineteenth of the same month, Rev. K. F. Ohlson officiating and Prof. David Nyvall delivering the address. The building was completed during the ensuing winter, and was dedicated on May 31, 1903. The hospital is open not only to the people of the Swedish Mission Covenant, but it invites patronage from all denominations and nationalities.

The first superintendent or manager of the institution was Mr. Edward Johnson, and the first trained nurse, Miss Annie Anderson. Mr. Palmblad for many years was the president of the board of directors and general superintendent of the institution he had fathered. Dr. C. W. Johnson served as chief of the medical department for a long period.

The present personnel of the institution is as follows: medical staff, Drs. O. Th. Roberg, F. I. Brown and K. L. Thorsgaard; superintendent of nurses, Miss Ida C. L. Isaaeson; manager, Albin Johnson, successor of Rev. A. Lydell, who served for a number of years.

A training school for nurses is conducted, from which a class of trained nurses has been graduated each year since 1900.

The only large donation received by the institution was one of $2,500 from the late Louis Sand of Manistee, Michigan.

The hospital has accommodations for about 60 persons, besides the force of attendants, and an average of 40 to 50 wards are being cared for at the home. The institution during the last fiscal year had resources amounting to $21,310, including an income of $10,691 from paying patients. The present worth of the property is $46,350.

The Swedish Evangelical Free Church

Those Mission Friends who are opposed to a hard and fast general organization, whether it be local or general, have maintained local groups or societies in a number of localities ever since the beginning of the Mission Church as a specific Christian denomination in the United States. Many of them having been subjected to disciplinary measures and even persecution by the state church of Sweden, they had formed an aversion to everything savoring of established church authority and for that reason they were suspicious of every form of church organization, however liberal in scope. As they had held aloof from the Mission and the Ansgarius synods, so they shrank from affiliating with the Mission Covenant formed to take the place of the other two. Besides, there was a great deal of agitation on the subject, in which the very defenders of organization feared to commit themselves to too rigid a system, having but recently left the regular Lutheran Church as a protest against formalism, while the opposition went to extremes both in their denunciations of order and system and in their demand for liberty and a literal return to the customs and usages of the earliest Christians. Some even went so far as to frown on the very idea of binding the members of a local church by registering their names. Had they wished to join the Covenant, no creeds or dogmas stood in the way, for it pledged allegiance to no special creed or confession. And in matters of faith the Mission Friends were all one, being guided in the main by Waldenström's interpretation of the Bible on the subjects of atonement, justification, sanctification, baptism, eternal punishment and other essential teachings. It appears, therefore, that the main difference of opinion was not on doctrines and tenets, but on methods and practices. The Free Mission Friends, in maintaining that the local churches shall govern themselves and be independent of others, really favor Congregationalism, while the Covenant Mission Friends combine Presbyterianism with Congregationalism.

The first sign of co-operation among the Free Mission Friends was a meeting held in Boone, Ia., Oct. 14-19, 1884, when a number of pastors gathered for Bible study and discussion of common interests. Six articles relating to the church, local and general, its functions, membership, etc., were agreed upon, printed and circulated among the congregations, who seem to have adopted the article without a vote, by tacit consent. A committee was appointed to arrange for a similar meeting the following year, its members being J. G. Princell, L. Lindquist, K. Erixon and John Martenson. For several years, Princell was the chairman of this committee, to which three members were added at the second annual meeting held in Minneapolis, in March, 1885. There Martenson was elected treasurer, an office subsequently held by him for more than fifteen years. The committee, elected each year, was merely to serve as an agency for the carrying on of mission work in home and foreign fields. After a couple of years, meetings were held semi-annually. In 1890, the Swedish-American Mission Society was organized, all men and women being admitted as members upon pledging themselves to give one dollar a year to the mission fund. The society existed only for a short time. In 1894, the sense of union had developed to the extent that a common name and title was adopted, the federation being thereafter known as The Swedish Evangelical Free Mission. At a pastoral conference, held May 24-27 of that year, a decisive step toward ordinary church organization was taken by the adoption of a set of by-laws, defining the doctrinal tenets, laying down rules for membership, providing for a set of officers and even going so far as to stipulate disciplinary measures. In several essential features, these by-laws are identical with corresponding provisions in the constitution of the Covenant, and as if to carry out the parallel, the meeting held at Chicago in October, 1896, adopted "Rules," which are practically a constitution, completing the organization of the federation of the churches, as the aforesaid by-laws had that of the ministerial association. Grown wise by experience, the Free Mission Friends have abandoned the theories of Princell as to organization and changed their attitude in various other respects. Indeed, they have faced about completely, turning their back on some of the principles held most sacred during the controversy preceding the forming of the Mission Covenant. At that time, the leaders, as also the public organ of the Free Mission Friends, were gratified to find that the Covenant did not give every pastor a vote at the meetings, but only those elected as representatives of congregations, thereby avoiding the creation of "a privileged class of ministers"; but the rules of the Free Mission now gave a vote to every preacher in good standing. Again, when its ministerial association assumed the right to discipline and expel ministers whose teachings and acts are not in accord with the beliefs and objects of the association, it arrogated unto itself an authority which Princell denied to any organization but the local congregation itself and which is not even granted in the constitution of the Mission Covenant. It is especially worthy of remark that the congregations themselves were not given a vote in the disciplining of their ministers.

At its annual meeting in June, 1908, at Minneapolis, the Free Mission took another step toward better organization. It was there decided to incorporate as a church body under the name of the Swedish Evangelical Free Church, thereby practically rejecting the original theory underlying the movement. The organization is, however, so liberal as to give representation to all independent congregations who desire to co-operate. Each local church of fifty members or less is allowed one lay delegate, two delegates for one hundred members, and one delegate for each additional hundred. Moreover, a vote is granted every pastor, preacher, evangelist and missionary affiliated with the church. These are empowered to vote and act on all matters coming before the annual meetings, while the corporate affairs are placed in the hands of a board of trustees, nine in number. By this last act the Free Mission Friends have formed a church organization nominally distinct and tending toward greater solidity.

The Free Church supports missionary work in Utah and southern China. It maintains an orphanage with a capacity of 50 to 60 children, founded at Phelps Centre, Neb., in 1888, by Rev. A. Nordin. In Chicago, Rev. Princell for a number of years has conducted a Bible institute for the education of pastors and missionaries.

The Oak Street Swedish Mission

As the educational and publishing center of the Swedish Free Church of the United States the Oak Street Mission in Chicago holds a pre-eminent place in the denomination, aside from the fact that its age and size lend it prominence.

This church dates its origin from the autumn of 1880, when some seventeen brethren met at 90 Milton avenue, then known as Bremer street, and decided to hold regular devotional meetings thenceforth. When this meeting-place would no longer accommodate the worshipers, they were given the use of a basement in the building occupied by John Martenson's newspaper, "Chicago-Bladet," at 308 Wells street. From

May, 1881, week-day meetings also were held in the Chicago Avenue Church. In the fall of that year, Freja Hall, at 155 Chicago avenue, was secured for the holding of meetings, and the brethren met there for the first time on Oct. 30, 1881. As yet they had no regular preacher, the most gifted among their number taking turns in speaking at the meetings. At intervals visiting preachers appeared, chiefly Rev. Sahlström. During the two years the Sunday services were held at Freja Hall, the flock increased rapidly, and in October, 1883, the church secured larger quarters, at 243-5 Chicago avenue, where an old shop was remodeled as a meeting hall, with a capacity of about 750. It was named for the owner of the building, Bush Hall. From now on all the meetings, including the week-day meetings continued at 90 Milton avenue and the Chicago Avenue Church, were held here. About this time a Sunday school was started, comprising six or seven classes. Such was the enthusiasm among those who desired to teach that if there were no pupils for them, they went out in the streets and picked up material for a class wherever they could find it.

After occupying Bush Hall for two years, at an annual rental of $900, which proved too heavy a burden, the congregation removed to North Star Hall, on Division street, near Sedgwick street, which was secured for $500 per year. For the next two years Rev. J. G. Princell preached regularly here. His successor was Rev. J. W. Strömberg, who served for one year.

Driven from North Star Hall (now Phoenix Hall) by a raise of $300 in the annual rental in 1886, the congregation in January of the following year decided to purchase the old church on Oak street, owned by the Swedish Baptists. By its failure to complete the deal after paying down $200, the congregation lost that amount. In anticipation of the purchase, the church was incorporated under the name of the Oak Street Mission.

In Sept., 1888, two lots, 205 and 207 Oak street, and a frame building, were purchased for $10,660. Here a building was erected in 1889, at a cost of about $16,000, the total debt incurred for the property being $24,000. The structure is 54½ by 109 feet, two stories and basement, and contains, besides a large hall, seating about 800 people, two apartments and two stores for renting purposes. One of the latter has been occupied for a number of years as the office of "Chicago-Bladet"; the other was until recently used as a smaller meeting-hall and also served as quarters for a Bible school. The new structure was formally dedicated in July, 1889, when addresses were made by Rev. Princell and Prof. P. Waldenström of Sweden.

The need of a permanent preacher was not supplied until August, 1891, when Rev. Axel Nordin took charge, serving until July, 1901.

During this decade the membership was doubled, reaching 180, while many participated in the work of this church without being registered members.

In the fall of 1898 the congregation opened the lower hall for a divinity school, named the Swedish Bible Institute, which was conducted by Rev. Princell, assisted by the pastor of the church. When in July, 1901, Rev. G. A. Young succeeded to the pastorate, he entered energetically into the work both as a preacher and a teacher in the institute. After three years' work his flock exceeded 250 in number. In 1903 a constitution for the government of the church went into effect. In 1907 Rev. Young was succeeded by Rev. Victor Swift, the present pastor of the Oak Street Mission. The membership of the church now approaches 250.

The Swedish Congregationalists

A number of Mission Friends have associated themselves with the American Congregational Church, the first step being taken in 1881 by the Mission Church of Worcester, Mass. The cause for this defection is twofold: first, the education of Mission ministers at the Chicago Theological Seminary, a Congregational institution; second, the chance of obtaining financial aid from the American Congregationalists for the Swedish Mission churches. Doctrinally, the Swedish Congregationalists do not differ from other Mission Friends, and if they did, that could not cause a separation on their part, holding, as they do, that all true believers may unite with their churches while still remaining Lutherans, Methodists, Baptists or whatever they may be.*

The fountain-head of Swedish Congregationalism is located in Chicago, at the Swedish Institute of the Chicago Theological Seminary, but the main stream has run eastward. In the New England and other eastern states, that group has the bulk of its membership, and it is freely admitted that the mission funds of the American Congregational Church are largely responsible for the general transition of the Mission churches in the East to Congregationalism.

There were no Mission Friends, in the specific sense of the term, in the East until the year 1879, when a number of followers of Rev. Princell, then a Lutheran pastor of the Augustana Synod, seceded from the Lutheran congregations in New York City and Campello, Mass., and went over with him to the Mission Friends. The movement spread successively to Brooklyn, Boston, Worcester, Quincy and other cities, Mission churches being formed in each of these places. The men who carried on the work were, besides Princell, C. W. Holm, Emil Holmblad, A. Lidman, A. G. Nelson and George Wiberg. On the

* Nelson: Missionsvännernas historia, p. 678.

principle of pure churches, it was not possible to build up large congregations, especially in places where the Swedes were few in number. It was, therefore, very difficult to maintain pastoral work in the different localities, and when the Congregationalists profferred pecuniary aid, this was gratefully accepted. The example of the Worcester church was followed within five years by the Mission churches of Boston, Campello, Lowell, Brooklyn and New Britain, and after that the movement became general. When in the '80s Swedish emigrants began to settle in the East in greater numbers than before, a large mission field was opened up, which the Swedish churches themselves were not prepared to care for. The Congregational home mission board came to the aid of the Mission Friends and resolved to maintain a Swedish missionary in the field, Rev. C. J. Erikson being engaged for that work. To supply the need of more traveling missionaries, the Massachusetts Free Mission was organized in 1886. It engaged Eric Östergren, who served until 1892. In the meantime the Congregational mission board supported Rev. Holmblad and others on the mission field in Massachusetts.

The aid rendered by the American Congregationalists mostly took the form af salaries for the Mission pastors and liberal contributions to the church building funds of the Mission churches. The church edifice at Worcester dedicated in 1885 was erected at a cost of $8,395, of which amount $7,800 was contributed by the Americans. In 1896 this edifice was sold for $8,000 and another purchased from the American Congregationalists for $40,000. What part of this sum was advanced by the Congregational mission board has not been published. The Worcester congregation is the largest of the Swedish Congregational churches, numbering at the present time somewhat over 500 members.

The Lowell church, which had joined the Congregationalists in 1885, was among the first to experience trouble in the effort to live up to the principle of tolerating doctrinal differences among its members. Almost from the start it was torn by dissensions which came to a head in 1891, when 26 members left in a body and formed a Methodist church. They were followed by others, and shortly afterward a second group seceded to start a Baptist church.

The ministers of the Swedish Congregational churches in the East are united in a ministerial association, known as The Swedish Pastoral Conference of the East, organized Feb. 8, 1888, at New Britain, Conn. Its by-laws, adopted the following year, under which the Conference was incorporated in 1891, admit all ministers, but provide discipline and expulsion for false teaching and unchristian living, from which it appears that while all Christian beliefs are tolerated among the members of the church, the Conference does not sanction every interpretation of the Scriptures. The Conference now numbers about 70 members.

Congregationalism was almost unknown to the Mission Friends of the West up to the year 1885, when at the organization of the Mission Covenant the Chicago Theological Seminary generously offered to defray the expenses for the education of its ministers. A denominational historian is authority for the statement that with very few exceptions the clergy and laity of the Mission churches were unacquainted with the Congregational church organism. From subsequent events it is apparent that the Covenant's acceptance of the offer did not imply organic connection with that denomination, nor did the Covenant suspect any hidden motive in the offer or foresee the subsequent developments.

While refraining from open antagonism, the Covenant has looked with disfavor on the trend toward Congregationalism. In the East its influence has been insufficient to outweigh the financial inducements held out to the Mission churches, but in the western and northwestern states the movement has been discouraged and its progress has been correspondingly slow.

In 1889, the church papers "Missions-Vännen" and "Minneapolis Veckoblad," both speaking for the Covenant, took a stand against going over to the Congregationalists. The answer was a unanimous resolution passed at the Pastoral Conference of the East, held in Boston in December of that year, protesting against the view expressed that the movement was derogatory to the Mission church and testifying to its great usefulness to the churches in the eastern states.

The question again came up for discussion in connection with the establishment of the Covenant's own theological school. The brethren in the East pronounced the new school not only unnecessary but dangerous, inasmuch as it would create a rivalry with the Swedish department of the Chicago Theological Seminary, which might lead to unwholesome competition in soliciting students and breed partisanship among the graduates of the respective institutions.

In 1890 the question was raised of making the Covenant a conference, i. e., an integral part of the Congregational church. The plan was to give it representation at the triennial Congregational General Council and allot to it a suitable appropriation for home and foreign missions, and leave it in full control of its own mission work. Leading men of the American Congregational Church and of the Covenant met in Chicago to discuss the proposed union. At that meeting the Swedish ministers emphasized that they differed from the Congregationalists in regard to condition of membership in the churches, and also in regard to wordly amusements. Almost to a man the Covenant opposed the union, and the plan fell through. It seems to be a fact that until recently discussion looking to the establishment of closer relations among the three groups of Mission Friends has only served to embitter the feelings on all sides and caused further estrangement. The last of the series of heated debates on the question of uniting the three groups was carried on in the respective newspaper organs in 1903. After lasting for some six months, the discussion grew so acrimonious and personal that it had to be shut off in the public prints, proving, naturally, worse than fruitless. The results of the overtures for unification made in 1905 by the Covenant are yet to come.

The foreign mission work of the Swedish Congregationalists is carried on principally through the medium of the Scandinavian Alliance Mission, with headquarters in Chicago. A mission association of that name was organized there in 1890, by F. Franson, a missionary. This mission is independent of the Congregationalists, but is favored by the Swedish Congregational churches and also the Free churches. It has an elective board of seven directors, and Rev. Franson was general director until his death in 1908. All persons paying at least $10 a year to its mission fund are counted members of the association. Its function is that of an agency or connecting link between the congregations and the missionaries in the field. The latter are about 100 in number, half of whom are engaged in China, the remainder in India, Mongolia and Africa. The majority of them are sent out and supported by individual churches of the Congregational group in the East and the Free Mission and independent Covenant churches in the West, their contributions merely passing through the hands of the Alliance Mission. In sixteen years the Scandinavian Alliance Mission handled mission funds amounting to upwards of $400,000, aggregating $25,000 per year.

To date the Swedish Congregational churches in Illinois have been twelve in number, two of them being now almost extinct and a third having severed its connection.

The oldest of these is the Bethlehem church in Chicago. In the autumn of 1886, Prof. Fridolf Risberg, assisted by students of the Chicago Theological Seminary, rented a vacant store in West Lake street and began to conduct religious services for the Swedish people in that neighborhood. The mission was kept up for three years, and in 1889, Sept. 21st, a congregation was organized under the name of the Swedish Christian Bethlehem Church. Its meetings were held successively in an old Baptist church at Washington boulevard and Paulina street, Castle Hall, in Lake street, a Unitarian church at

Monroe and Laughlin streets, and again in Castle Hall up to November, 1900, when it moved into its own church edifice, a remodeled residence in Fulton street, representing an outlay of $2,500. The church has never had a permanent pastor, the services being conducted in turn by Prof. Risberg's pupils during the school year and by students or teachers during each vacation. Since 1891 the church has supported one of its members, Miss Alma Svenson, as a missionary in China. It joined the Congregational denomination in 1897, but has enjoyed no financial aid from that source.

Up to the year 1900, the Swedish Congregational churches had received $365,000 from the American Congregational Church. A historical work on Swedish Congregationalism, published in 1906, accounts for 112 churches of that denomination.

The Swedish Institute of the Chicago Theological Seminary

The Chicago Theological Seminary is one of eight similar institutions owned and maintained by the Congregational Church. The Chicago institution was founded in 1854. A German department was instituted in 1882, followed by a Scandinavian department in 1884. The following year this latter was divided in two, a Danish-Norwegian and a Swedish department. The institution is located at 81 Ashland boulevard.

Rev. Fridolf Risberg of Sweden was called to assume charge of instruction in the Swedish department in 1885. During the prior year of its existence the department had fourteen students in attendance. For three years Prof. Risberg was alone in the work. Then Rev. David Nyvall was called as his associate. After two years of teaching Rev. Nyvall resigned, and his successor, Rev. M. E. Peterson, has been connected with the school up to the present time. During the first six years the department was in connection with the Swedish Evangelical Mission Covenant of America, which for three years had the authority to select the associate teachers and also contributed the greater part of their salaries.

After the department had been fully developed the average number of students was 40, until the Covenant in 1891 secured a school of its own, when that number was materially reduced, the present attendance being about 25.

Tuition is given free of cost, and gifted and deserving students are granted a stipend of $50 per year.

The Swedish students pursue partly general elementary studies, such as the Swedish and English languages, history and other subjects, partly theological studies, including the Old and New Testament, church history, dogmatics, pastoral theology, and kindred subjects.

The Swedish language is the medium of instruction in most churches, certain subjects, however, being taught in English.

The students are comfortably housed in the dormitories of the institution, and have access to Swedish and general libraries and a well equipped gymnasium.

One hour every week is set aside for addresses and discourses in English by missionaries or eminent preachers on topics of especial interest to divinity students. Aside from the regular class practice

Fisk Hall, home of the Swedish Institute of the Chicago Theological Seminary

in preaching, the students are frequently assigned to pulpits in Chicago and vicinity. In the neighborhood of the seminary is the Bethlehem Church, organized by the department and constituting the spiritual home of the students and teachers.

In the year 1903 the foreign departments of the Chicago Theological Seminary acquired a status of greater independence by being placed partially under the control of the churches for which they were called into existence, and who now contribute regularly toward the salaries of the assistant teachers. To accentuate their position they were named institutes. The name of the Swedish department was thus changed to the Swedish Institute of the Chicago Theological Seminary.

From its inception as a department the Swedish Institute has been attended by a total of over 250 young men, no women having as yet availed themselves of the instruction for teaching or missionary work. Twenty have engaged in missionary work among the heathen in Alaska, Japan, Mongolia, and China proper, India, West and South Africa and South America. Three of these missionaries were murdered in the Boxer riots of 1900. About 150 of the graduates are engaged in pastoral work in America, Sweden and Norway.

Denominational Estimate

The Mission Friends publish hardly any statistics worthy of the name, and only a rough estimate can be made of their numbers, expenditures for religious purposes and the extent of other activities. A work on the Mission Church of America published in 1907 gives a summary from which we quote, adding certain figures found in recent reports.

The Mission Covenant comprises 190 churches with a combined membership of about 16.000. Of these there are 28 churches in Illinois. Co-operating with the Covenant, although not organically united with it, are a number of congregations with an aggregate membership of 4,000, making a total of 20,000. The Congregationa· churches, including only a few small ones in this state, are about one hundred in number, with a total membership of about 8.000. The Free Mission in 1907, according to Rev. Princell, claimed some 200 churches, with a total membership of 12,000, the 20 churches in Illinois having about 1.500 members. Bowman, however, gives an estimate far below these figures, allowing at most 5,000 members. Other figures, based on Princell's estimate, are: numbers of pastors, not including student preachers, 130, 14 of whom labored in this state. There were 13 churches in this state and 100 throughout the country. Those in Illinois were valued at $123,000, and the total value of church property was $840,000. The largest and most influential Free Mission churches in Illinois are the Chicago churches at Oak street, Lake View, West Twenty-second street and Pullman-Roseland; and those of Rockford and Moline.

It is with respect to mission work in heathen lands that the Mission Friends especially earn their name.

The Free Mission group was the first to go into foreign fields. Its first heathen missionary, H. J. von Qvalen, was sent to Canton in 1887. Two years later the Covenant began work in Alaska. The Free Mission in 1907 supported five missionaries of its own in Canton and besides contributed generously to the Alliance Mission. The Covenant had 13 missionaries and 3 native assistants in Alaska and 14 missionaries in China. The Swedish Congregationalists maintain no foreign missions of their own, but contribute considerable amounts to the

Alliance Mission and somewhat to the missions carried on by the Covenant, the Free Mission and the American Congregational Church. In foreign mission work the Mission Friends rank second only to the German Brethren, who are said to have one foreign missionary to every 52 members. According to the statistics of 1906 the American Congregationalists, who lead the larger denominations in mission work, maintained a foreign missionary to every 1,184 members, and the per capita contribution was $1.10. The ratio among the Mission Friends of Sweden was for the same year 1 to 943 and $3.39 per capita, and among those in the United States, 1 to 252, with $2.08 per member paid into the foreign mission treasury.

CHAPTER XI

The Swedes in the Civil War

Early Swedish Patriots

MEN of Norse blood have helped to make American history from the first chapter to the last. Swedes have played a part in shaping the destinies of our country at every important epoch. By early settlement they became a component part of the population of at least two of the thirteen original colonies. In the framing of a nation by a union of these fragments, two conspicuous Swedish-Americans had a hand—John Morton, who, as chairman, had the casting vote which determined Pennsylvania's stand for American independence, and John Hanson, Maryland's most noted representative during the revolutionary period and at one time president of the congress. Two noted Swedish commanders. Hans Axel von Fersen and Curt Bogislaus von Stedingk, fought in the war for independence, both receiving the Order of Cincinnati for heroism, while many less renowned patriots of Swedish descent. their number unknown, took part in the great struggle for liberty. Again, in the peaceable conquest of the great West, the Swedes participated by colonizing great areas in the central states—a movement vastly more far-reaching in its consequences than that of founding the colony on the Delaware.

In the year 1860 this influx from Sweden had but fairly begun, yet, when the great national crisis came, there were Swedes in every rank and station fighting and working for the cause of freedom and union, and the Civil War marks the beginning of their general participation in public affairs. Among the Swedes who rendered eminent services to the nation in this conflict were men of the old Delaware stock, like Admiral Dahlgren, naval commander and inventor of the Dahlgren gun, and Gen. Robert Anderson of Fort Sumter fame; men who came over directly from Sweden to aid the Union, like Gen. Ernst von Vegesack; that isolated genius, Captain John Ericsson, inventor of the Monitor; and last, but not least, the thousands of Swedish-Americans of the West, who fought in the volunteer ranks of the Union army, and the scores of brave and skilled commanders of companies, regiments and brigades, foremost of whom were Stolbrand and Malmborg.

A Study of Swedish Enlistments

When President Abraham Lincoln on April 15, 1861, in reply to the rebel attack on Fort Sumter, issued a proclamation calling for 75,000 volunteers to serve three months for the purpose of putting down the rebellion in the South, many times that number in the loyal states offered their services. The Swedish-Americans, then less than 20,000 in number and mostly new arrivals from their native land, hastened to respond to the call for defenders of the Union and enlisted in the service of their adopted country as eagerly as the most patriotic of her native-born citizens. On the first call an entire Swedish company was organized at Galesburg, and Stolbrand raised a company of artillery in Chicago, both of which were at first rejected as supernumerary, and individual Swedes enlisted in all the various localities in which they lived. To subsequent calls for troops they responded in increasing numbers, and the estimate which has been made that one Swede out of every six in the central West and Northwest joined the colors cannot be far wrong, even if applied to all Swedish-Americans. In the latter part of the year 1861 an all Swedish company was raised by Major Forsse in and around Bishop Hill, Ill., the Galesburg company was reorganized and accepted, Capt. Silfversparre recruited a battery, largely Swedish, in this state; Col. Hans Mattson organized a Scandinavian company in Minnesota; some Swedes joined a Norwegian regiment, the 15th, of Wisconsin, and the muster rolls of the northwestern states show a goodly number of Swedish names.

The general census of 1860 records a total of 18,625 Swedes in the United States. Of these, 11,800 were living in the four states of Illinois, Iowa, Minnesota and Wisconsin. The immigration from Sweden in the next two years was 2,300. Allowing two-thirds, for these four states, their combined Swedish population during the main period of enlistment would approximate 13,500. The best estimates made of Swedish enlistments in the four states gives a total of 2,250, or exactly one-sixth of their Swedish population. Illinois, with a

Swedish population, in 1860, of 6,470, and approximately 7,000 at the end of the year 1861, contributed not less than 1,300 Swedish volunteers, indicating that in this state one Swede out of every five volunteered for military service, while out of the whole population one to every seven persons enlisted. Army statistics compiled in 1863 show that among immigrants and the foreign element the able-bodied males of military age, 18 to 45 years, constituted one-third of the total number. Thus, it will be seen, more than half of the Swedes of Illinois fit for military service actually served—all of which speaks volumes for the loyalty of the liberty-loving Swedish nationality.

No figures to show the total number of Swedes engaged in the war can be given, however, with any claim to accuracy. In the government army statistics the English, the Irish and the Germans were accounted for, but all others were entered under the head of "other foreigners." O. N. Nelson, who has endeavored to ascertain the number of Swedish soldiers mustered in the states of Minnesota, Iowa and Wisconsin, gives an estimated total of 950, but he shrunk from the task of an actual canvass of the reports of the adjutant generals of those states for Swedish names. That being the only method yielding anything like reliable information on this point, the laborious search through nine volumes of names of Illinois volunteers has been undertaken, with the result stated.

The Swedish organizations, Co. C of the 43rd regiment, and Co. D of the 57th, and the largely Swedish Silfversparre battery gives us 335 to start with. The remaining thousand Swedish names are scattered among the 255,000 on the Illinois muster rolls. The enumeration has been made with conservatism and due care. Names characteristically Swedish have been counted without question; Andersons, Johnsons, Nelsons and like surnames, rarely, except when preceded by a Swedish given name or known to have been borne by Swedes or men from Swedish settlements. Names like Smith, Young, Hall, Holt. Freeman, Newman, Swan. Stark, Berg, Beck, Holmes, Benson, Gibson. etc., although borne by many Swedes, have been counted only in known cases, a loss which doubtless is not outbalanced by those erroneously credited to the Swedish nationality. We have, furthermore, guarded against claiming as Swedes the several hundreds of other Scandinavians who fought in the Illinois regiments. Again, the tendency of the Swedes to Americanize their names or adopt new ones that completely mask their nationality must necessarily cause a number of omissions in the count. Other difficulties have been encountered in the attempt to pick out the Swedish soldiers from among the promiscuous mass. Their names were often distorted by the clerks of the recruiting stations, who spelled them phonetically. or they have been rendered almost unrecognizable by the state printer. Thus for instance. Carlson is frequently written Colson, Hedenskog has been found in the two forms Hadenscogg and Aadenskoy, Person is anglicized into Parson and even such a typical Swedish name as Åkerblom in the reports takes the Celtic form of O'Kerblom. Common Swedish given names, like Nils, or Nels, August and Jonas are usually changed to Nelson, Augustus and Jones.

With these remarks we submit the result of our struggle with the problem of enumeration in the following tabulated form:

Swedes in the Illinois Volunteer Regiments

Three Months Service

INFANTRY

Regiment	Number of Swedes
Seventh	3
Ninth	2
Tenth	3
Eleventh	1
Twelfth	17
Total	26

It should be borne in mind, however, that one whole company of Swedish volunteers at the first call for troops, and one battery, recruited by Stolbrand, were not accepted. Most of these volunteers undoubtedly enlisted again and would then figure in the report next following.

Three Years Service

INFANTRY

Regt.	No. Swedes	Regt.	No. Swedes	Regt.	No. Swedes	Regt.	No. Swedes
7	15	43	161	71	6	107	4
8	10	44	6	72	12	108	5
9	5	45	11	78	1	109	1
10	14	46	8	82	8	110	1
11	10	47	4	83	16	111	2
12	43	48	6	84	5	112	33
13	9	49	4	88	1	113	12
15	5	50	7	89	14	114	3
16	6	51	20	91	15	115	1
17	12	52	15	93	11	116	2
19	6	53	9	95	8	118	3
20	2	54	2	96	1	119	5
23	3	55	19	97	2	120	3
32	1	56	1	98	1	122	3
33	7	57	151	99	1	123	2
36	17	58	1	102	26	124	14
37	11	59	6	103	2	125	2
38	5	65	2	104	13	126	9
39	7	66	6	105	9	127	9
40	2	67	1	106	3	129	1
42	21	69	4				

Total...925

CAVALRY

Regt.	No. Swedes
1	13
2	11
3	3
4	10
5	4
6	2
7	10
8	5
9	9
14	1
15	3
16	2
17	8
Total	81

ARTILLERY

	No. Swedes
First Regiment	93
Second Regiment	34
Henshaw's Battery	3
Total	130

One Hundred Days Service
INFANTRY

Regt.	No. Swedes	Regt.	No. Swedes
132	53	141	12
134	7	142	3
136	1	143	3
137	5	144	2
138	17	145	2
139	17	Alton Battalion	2
140	2		
		Total	126

One Year Service
INFANTRY

Regt.	No. Swedes	Regt.	No. Swedes
146	10	151	10
147	11	152	3
148	22	153	5
149	3	155	1
150	1	156	14
		Total	80

Summary

Infantry, three years service	925
Cavalry, three years service	81
Artillery, three years service	130
Infantry, one hundred days service	126
Infantry, one year service	80
Grand total	1,342

Some allowance should be made for repetitions, caused by transfers from one regiment to another, yet these ought not to outnumber the probable omissions. The great majority of the Swedish soldiers enlisted for three years and, judged by the two wholly Swedish companies, they very generally re-enlisted in the veteran regiments, so that even when reduced to a basis of three years' service their number will not be greatly lessened. Some Swedish Illinoisans doubtless went elsewhere to enlist, but probably more Swedes came from other states into Illinois for the same purpose. The spirit of sympathy with a republic struggling for the maintenance of free institutions brought many volunteers to our army from continental Europe. Not a few came over from Sweden. Illinois being the state then preeminently settled by their countrymen, they were most likely to come here before enlisting. All things considered, we would probably be warranted in claiming at least fifteen hundred Swedes in the Illinois regiments. Any skepticism then arising as to the resultant high ratio of Swedish volunteers to the Swedish population of the state would be disposed of by two unquestioned facts—that the census and immigration figures as to foreign nationalities are commonly too low and that these volunteers were not all residents of the state.

The sense of patriotism and the justice of the Union cause was the chief incentive to enlistment on the part of the Swedish-Americans. Among the Norwegians there arose a controversy as to the moral justification of slavery and the Norwegian Synod split on that question. Not so among the Swedes: they were abolitionists practically to a man. When conscription had to be resorted to, there was hardly a Swede left to be drafted. nearly all able to fight having taken the field. Nor were they lured by bounties to any great extent. for by the time these were held out, most of the Swedes willing and able to fight at all, were already trained soldiers. inured to hardships and cheered on by assurance of ultimate triumph.

There were Swedes also in the South in those days, some 750, according to the census. Presumably a few of them took up arms for the Confederacy, others probably went north to fight or to live in peace among their fellow countrymen—the problem is as yet new to inquiry. This much has been learned, that a genuine Swedish name was borne by at least one Confederate commander—August Forsberg. mentioned in the reports as lieutenant in the corps of engineers and as colonel of the 51st Virginia, at times in command of a brigade.

The fighting qualities of the Swedish soldiery were tried on many a hotly contested battlefield. With other Europeans. many of them had an advantage over their American-born comrades in having undergone a course of compulsory military instruction in their native land. Generally, they submitted more readily to military discipline than the Americans and took greater pride than they in developing tactical skill, order and precision. The Bishop Hill company of the 57th Illinois proved itself the best drilled company in that regiment; the Scandinavian Co. D of the 3rd Minnesota, Col. Hans Mattson's regiment, was the crack company of the model regiment of that state, and Col. Malmborg made the 55th what it was—the best all-round regiment from Illinois.

From good soldiers naturally sprung able commanders. It is complained, and not without justice, that American history is chary in giving credit to the foreign elements which rendered so material aid in putting down the rebellion, freeing the slaves and saving the Union. While the Swedes were fairly well rewarded in the way of minor promotions, it is but the plain truth to say that they earned well every advancement accorded them and in sundry cases they did the hard work for which others took the honors. The history of the 55th Illinois regiment is convincing proof that Col. Stuart received his ill-fated appointment to a brigadier-generalship on the merits of the fighting done under the direction of his Swedish lieutenant-colonel. Stolbrand did duty as brigadier-general a year or two before commissioned to that rank, and even then he was promoted only after he had resigned in mild protest against official ingratitude. And many an officer has attained the same rank for less brilliant services than the parts played by Malmborg and Silfversparre on the first day at Shiloh in staying the enemy's last onslaught and saving the day for Grant's army.

In order to convey, otherwise than by empty boast, some idea of the high grade of military service rendered by the men of Swedish extraction, bare mention of the known Swedish officers in the Union army and navy is here made, down to and including first lieutenants: Rear Admiral Dahlgren; Brigadier-Generals Robert Anderson. Ernst von Vegesack. Stolbrand; Colonels Ulric Dahlgren, Malmborg. Mattson. Steelhammar, Elfving, Brydolf, Broady, Burg; Lieutenant-Colonel Gustafson; Majors Forsse. Holmberg, Bergland; Adjutant Youngberg; Sergeant Major Lindberg; Captains Silfversparre, Stenbeck, Sparreström, Arosenius, Charles Johnson, Eric Johnson, Lempke, Edvall, Wickstrum, Carl Gustavson, Enstrom, Cornelieson. Lund, Nelson, Eckström, Vanstrum,. Lindberg, Alfred Lanstrum, C. E. Landström, Linquist: First Lieutenants Hellström. Andberg, Eckdall, Nyberg, Ackerström, Johnson. Olson, Lindell, Oliver Erickson, Nels. Nelson, Hjalmar and Johan Alexis Edgren. Liljengren, Gustafson. Lundberg, and others.

To complete the list would involve research far too extensive for our present purpose.

Company C, Forty-Third Illinois Infantry

Under Lincoln's first call for troops a company was organized at Galesburg, consisting exclusively of Swedish-Americans. Leonard Holmberg was elected captain and tendered the services of the company to the governor of the state. Of three other companies organized in Knox county, one was accepted, but the other two, as also the Swedish company, were disbanded on the ground that no more troops were then thought needed. It soon became evident, however, that the troops at the government's disposal were totally inadequate to put down the rebellion, and congress authorized the issuance of a call for 300,000 volunteers for three years' service. The disbanded Swedish company now reorganized under new command, Captain Holmberg and many of the men having previously enlisted for service in other organizations. By the first of September, 1861, the company was at Camp Butler, near Springfield. It now consisted of one hundred Swedes and three Germans. The men elected their own officers, as follows, Dr. Hugo M. Starkloff, captain, Olof S. Edvall, first lieutenant, and Nels P. McCool, second lieutenant. Dr. Starkloff was a German, and his election to the captaincy was understood to be in reward for his material assistance in recruiting the company and only a step to the commission of surgeon in the regiment to which the company would be assigned. It was given the position of flag company in the Forty-third regiment and became known as Company C, of the Forty-third Illinois Infantry Volunteers, commanded by Julius Raith. Starkloff being made regimental surgeon, First Lieutenant Olof S. Edvall was commissioned captain of the company.

After remaining in camp for a short time, spent in company and regiment drills, the regiment was ordered to St. Louis on Oct. 13th, and quartered at Benton Barracks. There the men were given old Austrian muskets for exercising in the manual of arms, and just before leaving for Otterville, 150 miles west of St. Louis, they were armed with old Harper's Ferry and English Tower muskets, altered from flint lock to percussion guns. Arriving at Otterville Nov. 4th, they remained in that vicinity doing guard duty and perfecting themselves in military tactics until Jan. 20, 1862, when they were ordered back to St. Louis and there equipped with 54 caliber Belgian rifles, an excellent firearm, but very heavy.

There were only eight companies in the regiment, until now two more companies, I and K, were added, but many of the companies were so small that the regiment still fell 200 short of its full quota of one thousand men.

On Feb. 6th it was ordered to join General Grant's expedition against Fort Henry and Fort Donelson. The men embarked on the steamer Memphis, which carried them to Fort Henry, on the Tennessee River, where they were left to guard transports and supplies and thus prevented from taking part in the battle of Fort Donelson, only fifteen miles away. This proved a great disappointment to many of the Swedish boys who had an apprehension that the war would be over in a short time and they would have to return home without having taken part in any real battle.

On Feb. 24th the regiment was ordered to Fort Donelson and from there on March 4th back to the Tennessee River, and sent by transport steamers to Savannah, Tenn., where they disembarked and were ordered out in the country about twenty miles to disperse hostile detachments. The regiment was soon after encamped near Pittsburg Landing, a short distance from Shiloh church, as a part of the Third Brigade of General McClernand's Division of the Army of the Tennessee.

The boys of Company C had now been in the service about seven months, had become fair marksmen and were able to execute movements in approved military style. Sooner than expected, their skill was to be put to the test. The brigade had been in camp at Pittsburg Landing some three weeks, awaiting reinforcements in order to march on Corinth, Miss., and attack the enemy who were reported to be concentrating a large force there and strongly fortifying their position. Corinth was but twenty miles from the Union camp and skirmishes frequently took place between the cavalry scouts of the two opposing armies. On Friday evening, April 4th, troops were called out on the line in front of the camp and kept there till midnight, in consequence of a collision between the Union outposts and a rebel scouting party, but the alarm subsided. While the union forces were intent on moving upon the enemy's position at the opportune moment, no one in camp seemed to suspect that the enemy might have the same design.

On Saturday afternoon, April 5th, the 43rd Regiment was ordered to hold itself in readiness for inspection and review on Sunday morning at seven. As the men were awaiting orders that morning to form ranks, volleys of musketry fire were suddenly heard in front. While they were puzzling over the meaning of the firing on the picket line, the drummer beat the long roll of alarm. The pickets came rushing into camp barely in advance of the pursuing rebels. Seizing their guns and accoutrements, the boys of the 43rd formed ranks in company quarters, marched to the parade ground in front of the camp and formed in line of battle. Although it took but a few minutes for the regiment to form, yet the firing had increased so as to be continuous all along the line. Just as Company C swung into position, a shell from one of the rebel batteries came screaming over their heads and cut off a limb of a tree which struck Louis Nelson, disabling him for the fight. Col. Raith sent Lieut. Col. Engelman to General McClernand to inform him of the approaching battle. Engelman was instructed to tell Col. Reardon of the 29th Illinois to assume command of the brigade, as General Ross, the regular commander, was absent on furlough. Reardon being sick, the command devolved upon Raith, who left his own regiment in command of Engelman.

The Forty-third was one of the few regiments ready for action on that fatal morning. The general condition in the Union camp at the moment of attack is described by Greeley as follows: Some of the men were dressing, others washing or cooking, a few were eating breakfast, many, especially officers, had not yet risen. Neither officers nor men were aware of the approaching enemy until magnificent lines of battle poured out of the woods in front of the camps and at double-quick rushed in upon our bewildered, half-dressed and not yet half-formed men, firing deadly volleys at close range, then springing upon the coatless, musketless mob with the bayonets. Some fell as they ran, others as they emerged from the tents or strove to buckle on their accoutrements; some tried to surrender, but the rebels could not stop then to take prisoners.

Lieut. Col. Engelman had ordered out a line of skirmishers, but they hardly had time to deploy before the enemy appeared, marching in regimental divisions in such masses as to cover the ground over which the unionists had a clear view, and so close upon them that the skirmish line was pressed back on the regiment. The left flank of the 43rd was left exposed by the retirement of the 49th Illinois, whose members were driven out of their camp before they had time to form a line or fire a shot. Engelman then ordered the second battalion, five companies, including Company C, of his regiment to take the position left vacant by the demoralized 49th. The battalion, about 300 strong, moved into that position and held it probably ten minutes against a tenfold force of the enemy, then fell back to the first battalion, leaving many dead and wounded behind. Of Company C, Charles Samuelson was instantly killed here, and Swan Olson and Nels Bodelson were among the severely wounded. Prentiss' division, to the left of McClernand's, had been routed at the first onset before it could form in line of battle, and by ten o'clock it had been virtually demolished. Sherman's division, on McClernand's right, notwithstanding the desperate and untiring exertions of its leader, was practically out of the fight after the first hour.

McClernand stood firm, though the defection on both his flanks left the rebels free to hurl themselves against him in tremendous force. Two raw regiments, the 15th and 16th Iowa, which he brought to

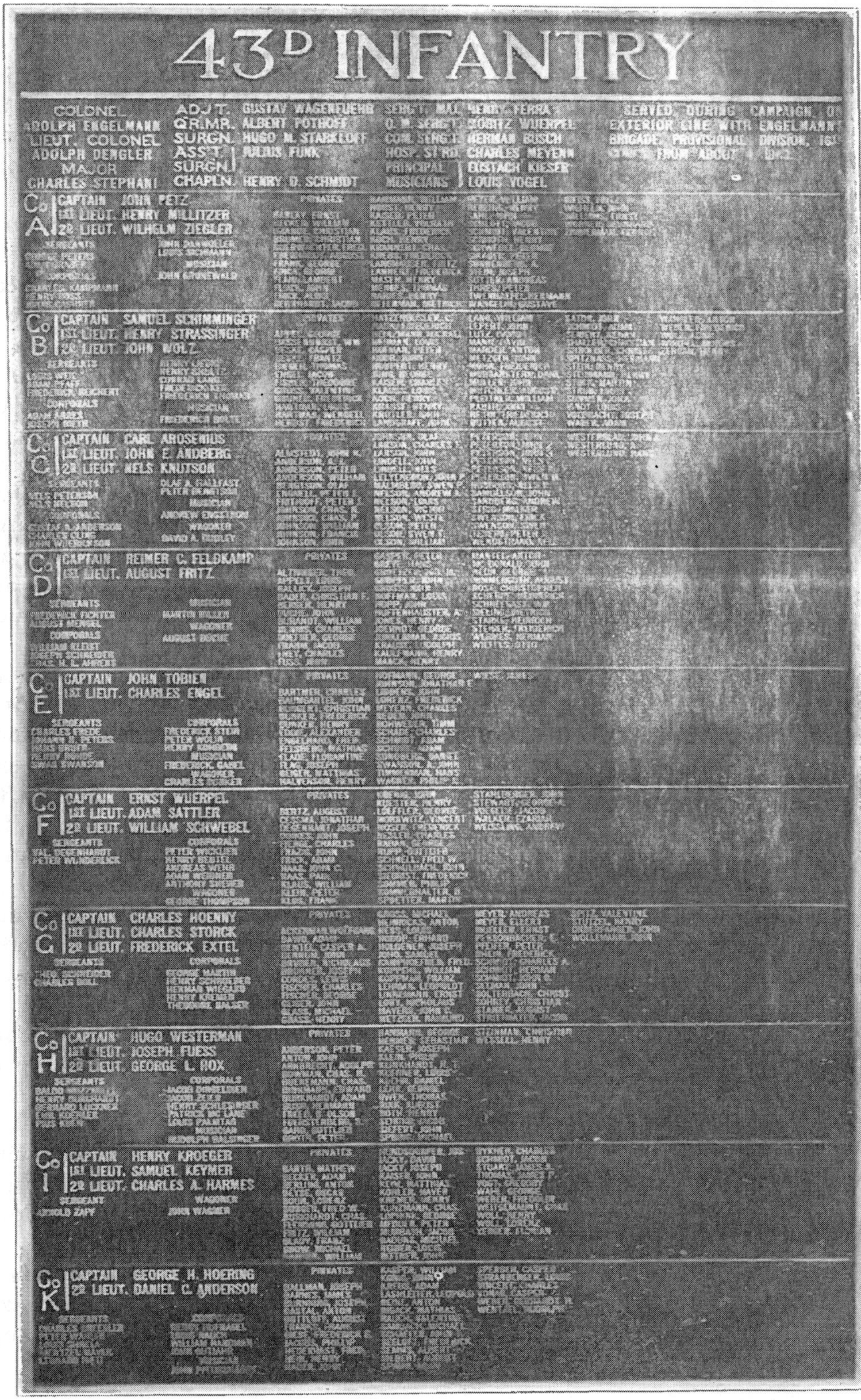

43ᴰ INFANTRY

COLONEL
ADOLPH ENGELMANN
LIEUT. COLONEL
ADOLPH DENGLER
MAJOR
CHARLES STEPHANI

ADJ'T. GUSTAV WAGENFUEHR
QR.MR. ALBERT POTHOFF
SURGN. HUGO M. STARKLOFF
ASS'T SURGN. JULIUS FUNK
CHAPLN. HENRY O. SCHMIDT

SERG'T MAJ. HENRY FERRA
Q. M. SERG'T. MORITZ WUERPEL
COM. SERG'T. HERMAN BUSCH
HOSP. ST'RD. CHARLES MEYENN
PRINCIPAL MUSICIANS EUSTACH KIESER / LOUIS VOGEL

SERVED DURING CAMPAIGN ON EXTERIOR LINE WITH ENGELMANN'S BRIGADE, PROVISIONAL DIVISION, 16 CORPS, FROM ABOUT JUNE 2.

Co. A CAPTAIN JOHN PETZ
1ST LIEUT. HENRY MILLITZER
2D LIEUT. WILHELM ZIEGLER

Co. B CAPTAIN SAMUEL SCHIMMINGER
1ST LIEUT. HENRY STRASSINGER
2D LIEUT. JOHN WOLZ

Co. C CAPTAIN CARL AROSENIUS
1ST LIEUT. JOHN E. ANDBERG
2D LIEUT. NELS KNUTSON

Co. D CAPTAIN REIMER C. FELDKAMP
1ST LIEUT. AUGUST FRITZ

Co. E CAPTAIN JOHN TOBIEN
1ST LIEUT. CHARLES ENGEL

Co. F CAPTAIN ERNST WUERPEL
1ST LIEUT. ADAM SATTLER
2D LIEUT. WILLIAM SCHWEBEL

Co. G CAPTAIN CHARLES HOENNY
1ST LIEUT. CHARLES STORCK
2D LIEUT. FREDERICK EXTEL

Co. H CAPTAIN HUGO WESTERMAN
1ST LIEUT. JOSEPH FUESS
2D LIEUT. GEORGE L. ROX

Co. I CAPTAIN HENRY KROEGER
1ST LIEUT. SAMUEL KEYMER
2D LIEUT. CHARLES A. HARMES

Co. K CAPTAIN GEORGE H. HOERING
2D LIEUT. DANIEL C. ANDERSON

the front under a heavy fire, gave way at once in disorder. The reunited battalions of the 43rd Illinois held their position for a time, alone supporting Capt. Waterhouse's Battery as long as protected against an enfilading fire, but after the troops on the right were forced back, they were compelled to give ground after stubborn resistance. With the enemy on their flanks and in their rear, they were squandering their lives to no purpose. In falling back they lost two guns of the battery and had to drag the others with them by hand. On their first position they left 36 dead, while many had been carried severely wounded to the rear. Retiring about a thousand feet, they formed anew and held their position a short time, punishing the enemy severely while themselves suffering heavy losses. Here Lars O. Berglöf of Co. C was killed and a number of the Swedish boys were severely wounded. With only one thin line our men were able to hold in check the several lines of the enemy because their Belgian rifles carried farther by about 200 feet than the rebel firearms. By this time there were but two other regiments left nearby, the other Union troops having retreated in disorder. These three regiments, sadly depleted, could not sustain the weight of more than half of the rebel army. After repulsing several determined attacks, sometimes advancing a little, but generally yielding ground, and losing three colonels of the line and three officers of his staff, with at least half the effective force of his batteries, McClernand by eleven o'clock A. M. was compelled to fall back. Col. Raith, the brigade commander, had been mortally wounded. With the foe on every side and occupying ground between this and other portions of the Union army, the retreat was slow and difficult. All camp equipage was abandoned and the dead and wounded were left where they fell.

By a circuitous route of about one mile the 43rd succeeded in connecting with other Union troops, and, taking a fresh stand, resisted the onslaught until far into the afternoon, cheered by the expectation of reinforcements. The position now held was near the road to Crump's Landing, where General Lew. Wallace was stationed with a large force. About 4:30 o'clock Generals Grant, Sherman and McClernand with many staff officers came up and inspected the position of the 43rd. They soon sent troops from the direction of the river, including two regiments and a battery. But Wallace's force marched a roundabout way, delaying his junction with the sorely pressed combatants until after nightfull, and thus a number of infantry regiments, batteries and battalions of cavalry remained useless throughout that day's bloody struggle.

Despite three desperate charges by the enemy that afternoon and evening, the 43rd stood firm and the Union forces still held their line, extending from this point to the landing, when darkness put an end to the day's carnage. The enemy withdrew a short distance for the night, in possession of the Union camps and most of their provisions and equipage together with many guns and thousands of prisoners. Albert Sydney Johnston, the Confederate commander-in-chief, had fallen and the rebel losses had been heavy, but Beauregard, the general commanding, that night reported that they had "gained a complete victory, driving the enemy from every position." He was not far wrong, for a large part of the Union army was in a demoralized state, a motley mob of skulkers, stragglers and fugitives crowded down to the river bank around the landing.

But that night the fortunes of war turned. Both Gen. Wallace and Gen. Buell arrived, the latter with 20,000 men. Next morning at daybreak the reinforced Union army was the first to advance, and the battle reopened anew. The field was hotly contested until about 4 o'clock in the afternoon, when the Confederates wavered and Beauregard withdrew in precipitous retreat to Corinth.

In every position held by the 43rd during the first day it had left its dead and wounded, who were the only men of the regiment to be reported missing. At the end of the second day's battle the regiment again stacked arms in front of its former camp. Out of a total of 500 actually engaged in the two day's fighting, it had lost 206, of whom 49 had been left dead on the field. Captain Edvall of Co. C received a mortal wound in the second day's conflict and died May 7th. The privates of Co. C who were killed in battle were: Lars O. Berglöf, Claes Danielson and Charles Samuelson, all of Andover. Many of the company were wounded, but we have no record of their names at hand. The total loss of the Swedish company in killed and wounded was 17. In addition to the three privates who died on the battlefield, others died soon afterward from wounds received there.

The 43rd participated in the advance on Corinth, which was evacuated by the Confederates May 29th; then it was sent to Bethel, Jackson and Bolivar, Tenn. At Bolivar they had their camp from July, 1862, to May 31, 1863, when they were ordered to Vicksburg, Miss. While at Bolivar, they made frequent expeditions to disperse detachments of Confederate troops and answered emergency calls where needed. Two hundred of the regiment, who were mounted, in the spring scoured the country dispersing or capturing Confederate raiders. Carl Arosenius, quartermaster sergeant of the 59th Ill., at Bolivar succeeded to the command of Co. C, being transferred and commissioned captain.

From June 2nd the company served around Vicksburg until July

4th, when the rebels surrendered that city, with 30,000 men and large quantities of ordnance stores.

Next the 43rd was ordered to Helena, Ark., to join Steele's expedition against the Confederates under General Sterling Price. A force of 12,000 men marched on Little Rock, arriving Sept. 11th. Simultaneous demonstrations on both sides of the river caused the enemy to abandon their intrenchments and take hurried leave of the city. The 43rd was the first regiment to enter* and was detailed to act as police guard during that fall. From now, until mustered out in November,

Captain Carl Arosenius

1865, the regiment was encamped at Little Rock, from whence numerous expeditions, up to 150 mile marches, were made to different sections, and frequent brushes with rebel guerrillas were had.

In December, 1863, eight months remaining of the three-year term of enlistment, the government offered the volunteers 30 days' furlough and free transportation to their homes and return on condition that they would re-enlist for a new term. This was to begin at once, and even though the war should close in the meantime, each man

* Col. Mattson makes the same claim for his regiment, the 3rd Minnesota. Lieut. Nelson is authority for our assertion on this rather unimportant point.

was to receive a bounty of $400 when mustered out. The money consideration may have influenced some, but most of those who re-enlisted doubtless did so from unselfish, patriotic motives. The majority of the men of Co. C, whose physical condition permitted them to continue in the service, re-enlisted and were given their furlough in February, 1864. While at home, they secured thirty recruits, all Swedish-Americans, to fill up their depleted ranks. They returned to the South just in time to join Steele's expedition to the Red River to reinforce Gen. Banks, but the latter was defeated by the rebels under Kirby Smith before assistance could reach him. The Confederates then massed their forces against Steele, whose force, far outnumbered, retreated to Little Rock after several encounters with the foe. After this set-to, which occurred in April, 1864, the boys of the 43rd fought in no regular battle.

After re-enlistment the regiment was reorganized, and Co. C was assigned to first position as Co. A and was so known thereafter. It was mustered out of the service at Little Rock on Nov. 30, 1865, and taken to Springfield, where the men received their final pay Dec. 14th. The Swedish company then returned home after a continuous service of 4 years and 3½ months.

The total number of men that served in this company was 168, of whom 103 enlisted Sept. 1, 1861, 30 as recruits early in 1864 and 35 were transferred to the company on reorganization. After three years' service 34 were mustered out; 29 died from disease or from wounds received in battle; 30 were discharged on account of disability.

In recapitulation, the following list will show the engagements and sieges in which the Swedish Company C, 43rd Illinois Infantry Volunteers, participated:

Battle of Shiloh, both days, April 6 and 7, 1862.
Siege and occupation of Corinth, Miss., May, 1862.
Battle of Salem Cemetery, Tenn., Dec. 18, 1862.
Skirmishes around Sommerville, Tenn., April and May, 1863.
Siege and capture of Vicksburg, Miss., June and July, 1863.
Occupation of Little Rock, Ark., Sept. 11, 1863.
Battle of Prairie D'Ahu, Ark., April 10, 1864.
Battle of Jenkin's Ferry, Ark., April 30, 1864.

The roster of Co. C is here given mainly according to the official "Report of the Adjutant-General of the State of Illinois," with minor corrections of names and dates.

Roster of Company C, 43d Infantry

Name and Rank	Residence	Date of rank or enlistment	Remarks
Captains			
Hugo M Starkloff..	Galesburg	Sept. 1, '61	Promoted Surgeon............
Olof S. Edvall.....	"	Oct. 1, '61	Died, May 7, '62; wounds.....
Carl Arosenius.....	"	Oct. 9, '62	Mustered out Nov. 30, '65.....
First Lieutenants			
Olof S. Edvall.....	Galesburg	Sept. 1, '61	Promoted......................
John P. Andberg...	"	Feb. 13, '62	Mustered out Feb. 13, '65.....
Nels P. McCool....	"	Oct. 1, '61	Died Jan. 13. '62.............
Second Lieutenants			
Nels P. McCool....	Galesburg....	Sept. 1, '61	Promoted 1st Lieutenant......
•Nels Knutson......	"	Feb. 13, '62	Mustered out Feb. 28, '65.....
John P. Andberg...	"	....	Promoted 1st Lieutenant......
First Sergeant			
Magnus M. Holt...	Galesburg......	Sept. 1. '61	Disch. June 14, '62; wounds..
Sergeants			
Nels Peterson......	Young America	Sept. 1, '61	Re-enlisted as Veteran....-..
Nels Knutson......	Galesburg......	"	Promoted 2d Lieutenant.......
Nels Nelson........	"	"	Re-enlisted as Veteran........
Nels Anderson.....	"	"	Disch. May 27, '62; disability.
Corporals			
Gustaf A. Anderson	Galesburg	Sept. 1, '61	Re-enlisted as Veteran........
Charles Cling......	"	"	"
John W. Erickson..	Andover.......	"	Mustered out Sept. 26, '64....
Olof A. Hallfast..	Galesburg	"	Re-enlisted as Veteran........
Peter Bengtson.....	"	"	" "
Adolph Larson.....	"	"	Disch. Sept 4. '62; disability..
Magnus M. Nelson.	Andover.......	"	Deserted Sept. 15, '64........
John Paulson.......	Galesburg	"	Mustered out Sept. 26, '64....
Musician			
Andrew Engstrom..	Wataga........	Sept. 1, '61	Re-enlisted as Veteran........
Wagoner			
David A. Dudley...	Galesburg	Sept. .1, '61	Mustered out Sept. 16, '64....
Privates			
Almstedt John N...	Moline	Sept. 1, '61	Mustered out Sept. 26, '64....
Anderson Andrew J.	Wataga........	"	Re-enlisted as Veteran........
Anderson Louis J..	Galesburg	"	Died, St. Louis June 14, '62..
Anderson William..	Wataga........	"	Died, Hebron, Miss., Aug. 15,'63
Anderson Peter.....	Andover.......	"	Tr. to Invalid Corps Nov. 15.'63
Anderson Alexander	"	"	Disch. June 30, '62; disability.
Axelson Nels P....	Berlin.........	"	" April 9. '63; "

Name and Rank	Residence	Date of rank or enlistment	Remarks
Privates			
Bengtson Olof......	Bishop Hill....	Sept. 1, '61	Re-enlisted as Veteran........
Berglof Lars O.....	Andover.......	"	Killed at Shiloh, April 6, '62..
Björk Gustaf.......	New Sweden Ia.	"	Died, St Louis, Nov. 13, '61....
Bodelson Nels......	Galesburg.....	"	Disch. Oct. 11, '62; wounds...
Chillberg Jacob.....	Berlin.........	"	Re-enlisted as Veteran........
Daniel Claes........	Andover.......	"	Missing after battle of Shiloh..
Denning Henry....	Galesburg.....	"	Disch. July 8, '62; disability..
Erickson John A...	"	"	" April 29, '62; "
Erickson Gustav W.	Andover.......	"	" July 26, '62; wounds...
Engnell Peter J....	"	"	Re-enlisted as Veteran........
Fjellstedt Swan J..	Moline........	"	Disch. Mar. 28, '63; disability.
Hallgren Nels N...	Andover.......	"	" Feb. 6, '62; disability..
Harpman William..	Victoria.......	"	" Aug. 14. '62; "
Hall Gustaf........	Andover.......	"	" May 15, '63; "
Johnson Andrew....	New Boston...	"	" June 17, '62; wounds...
Johnson Francis....	Berlin.........	"	Mustered out Sept. 26, '64....
Johnson Charles....	Galesburg.....	"	Dis. Sept. 9, '62; disability....
Johnson William...	Berlin.........	"	Re-enlisted as Veteran........
Johnson Charles N..	"	"	" "
Johnson Olof......	"	"	" "
Johnson John.......	Wataga........	"	Died, Helena, Ark., Aug. 21, '63
Johnson Charles P..	Ontario.......	"	Mustered out Sept. 26, '64....
Johnson Charles W.	Andover.......	"	Disch. July 4, '62; disability..
Larson John.......	Berlin.........	"	Mustered out Sept. 26, '64....
Larson Charles J...	Andover.......	"	Died, Bolivar. Tenn., Apr. 2, '63
Larson Charles E..	"	"	Re-enlisted as Veteran........
Larson Nels........	Berwick.......	"	Disch. Jun 18. '62; disability...
Lindell Nels.......	Andover.......	"	Re-enlisted as Veteran........
Lindell John.......	Berlin.........	"	" "
Liljengren John P..	Andover.......	"	Mustered out Sept. 26. '64....
Lundquist John....	Victoria.......	"	Died at St. Louis, Feb. 4. '62..
Malmberg Sven P..	Galesburg.....	"	Re-enlisted as Veteran........
Nelson Sven A.....	"	"	Died. Jackson, Tenn.,Sept 30.'62
Nelson Victor.....	Andover.......	"	Mustered out Sept. 26, '64....
Nelson Weste......	Galesburg.....	"	Died, Little Rock, Dec. 16, '63.
Nelson Louis.......	"	"	Re-enlisted as Veteran........
Nelson Andrew J...	Andover.......	"	" "
Nelson Gustaf W...	"	"	Died. Quincy, Ill.. June 30, '62..
Nelson Charles M..	"	"	Disch. March 3, '63; disability.
Norlinder Nels.....	Moline........	"	Died, Bolivar, Tenn., Nov. 5,'62
Nyberg Erick......	Kewanee.......	"	Died at St Louis, Jan. 24, 62..
Olson Sven.........	Knoxville......	"	Disch. June 21, '62; wounds....
Olson Peter.......	Galesburg.....	"	Mustered out Sept. 26, '64....
Olson Nels........	"	"	Died,Savannah,Tenn.,Apr.10 '62
Olson William.....	Wataga........	"	Re-enlisted as Veteran........
Olson Sven T......	Galesburg.....	"	" "
Peterson Nels C....	Knoxville......	"	" "
Peterson Jonas.....	Galesburg.....	"	" "
Peterson John......	Bishop Hill....	"	" "
Peterson John......	Galesburg.....	"	....
Peterson Olof......	"	"	Disch. Nov. 8, '62; disability...
Peterson Nels N...	"	"	Tr. to Invalid Corps Nov. 15, '63
Peterson Sven M...	"	"	Re-enlisted as Veteran........
Peterson Sven......	"	"	....
Rosburg Nels P....	Andover.......	"	Re-enlisted as Veteran........
Sandberg Andrew..	Galesburg.....	"	Mustered out Sept. 26, '64....
Samuelson Charles..	Andover.......	"	Killed at Shiloh April 6, '62....
SamuelsonAlexand'r	"	"	Disch. June 30, '62; disability..
Samuelson Andr. M.	Berlin.........	"	Died, Otterville, Mo., Jan 18,'62
Samuelson John....	"	"	M. O Sept. 26, '64, as Sergeant
Strid Walter.......	"	"	Mustered out Sept. 26, '64....

Name and Rank	Residence	Date of rank or enlistment	Remarks
Privates			
Sundberg Peter J..	Berlin.........	Sept. 1, '61	Disch. July 9, '62; disability..
Sundberg Gustaf...	"	"	Died at St. Louis Jan. 22, '62..
Svenson Sven G....	Andover.......	"	Disch. Aug. 28, '62; wounds...
Svenson Sven E....	Galesburg....	"	....
Svenson Erick....	Bishop Hill....	"	Re-enlisted as Veteran........
Svenson Sven......	Galesburg	"	" "
Svenson Bengt.....	"	"	Disch. Sept. 6, '62; disability.
Teberg Peter J.....	Andover.......	"	Re-enlisted as Veteran........
Wendstrand Nels P.	"	"	" "
Westerblad John A.	New Boston...	"	Mustered out Sept. 26, '64....
Westerlund Andrew	Andover......	"	" "
Westerlund Hans...	"	"	Re-enlisted as Veteran........
Wilberg Daniel	Chicago........	"	Disch. Jan. 1, '63; disability..
Veterans			
Mustered out Nov. 30, 1865, except as noted.			
Anderson Gustaf A.	Galesburg.....	Dec. 18, '63	Promoted Sergeant Jan. 5, '64
Anderson Andrew J.	Wataga........	Dec. 30, '63	" Corporal Jan. 5, '64
Bengtson Peter.....	Galesburg.....	Dec. 18, '63	Pro.Corp'l Dec.28,'63,M.O.Sergt
Bengtson Olof.....	Bishop Hill....	Dec. 30, '63	
Cling Charles......	Andover.......	"	Prom. Corporal, M. O. Sergeant
Chillberg Jacob	Berlin.........	"	" "
Engnell Peter J.....	Andover.......	"	Promoted Corporal...........
Engström Andrew..	Bishop Hill....	Nov. 18, '63	
Frithioff Peter J....	....	"	M. O. Corporal July 7, '65....
Hallfast Olof A....	Andover.......	Dec. 30, '63	
Johnson William...	Bishop Hill....	"	Died, Mound City, Oct. 25, '64.
Johnson Charles N.	Lima.........	"	
Johnson Olof......	"	"	
Larson Charles E..	Andover.......	"	
Lindell Nels.......	"	"	Died, Little Rock, Feb. 21, '65
Lindell John.......	Berlin.........	Jan. 5, '64	
Malmburg Sven P..	Galesburg.....	Nov. 18, '63	Disch. Sept 2, '65; disability..
Nelson Louis.......	"	Dec. 30, '63	
Nelson Andrew.....	Andover.......	"	
Nelson Nels.......	Galesburg....	"	Pr. 2d Sergt.Jan.5,'64; 1st Lieutenant Mar. 17, '65.......
Olson William......	Wataga........	"	M. O. as Corporal...........
Olson Sven T......	Galesburg.....	"	
Peterson Nels......	Young America	"	Transf. to Co. A, consolidated
Peterson Nels C...	Knoxville......	"	Died, Knoxville, Jan. 24, '65..
Peterson Sven M...	Andover.......	"	
Peterson Jonas.....	Galesburg.....	Dec. 18, '63	Promoted Corporal Dec. 28, '63
Peterson John......	Monmouth.....	Dec. 23, '63	M. O. as Corporal...........
Peterson John......	Galesburg.	Nov. 18, '63	
Rosberg Nels P....	Andover.......	Feb. 14, '64	Died, Little Rock, Sept. 22, '64
Svenson Sven......	Galesburg	Dec. 28, '63	" " 15, '64
Svenson Erick......	Bishop Hill....	Dec. 30, '63	
Svenson John E....	Galesburg	"	
Teberg Peter J.....	Andover.......	"	M. O. as Corporal...........
Westerlund Hans...	"	"	Prom. Sergeant Jan. 5, '64; 2d Lieut. Nov. 9,'65; M.O.as Sgt.
Wendstrand Nels P.	"	Feb. 14, '64	
Recruits			
Anderson James....	Galesburg	Feb. 11, '64	
Anderson John A...	Andover.......	Feb. 28, '64	
Anderson Peter D..	"	Feb. 29, '64	
Brown Thomas M..	Chicago	Feb. 19, '64	
Bergquist Sam A...	Andover.......	Feb. 29, '64	
Esping Axel........	Galesburg	"	

Name and Rank	Residence	Date of rank or enlistment	Remarks
Recruits			
Esping Carl........	....	....	
Esping Julius L....	Chicago........	March 16, '64	Disch. April 6, '65; disability..
Frithioff Peter......	....	Aug. 21, '62	Re-enlisted as Veteran........
Hammar Henry....	Chicago........	March 16, '64	
Hjertberg Fred. A..	Andover.......	"	Mustered out May 27, '65.....
Holt Magnus M....	Galesburg	Feb. 29, '64	Prom. July 10, '65, in 113 U.S.C.T.
Hanson Andrew M.	Andover.......	March 17. '64	
Hultberg Samuel P.	Galesburg	Feb. 29, '64	
Hockomb Magnus..	"	March 11, '64	Mustered out May 27, '65.....
Johnson William...	"	Jan. 15, '64	Transf. to Co. A as consol....
Jacobson John......	"	March 11, '64	
Johnson Charles....	"	March 1, '64	
Johnson John.......	"	March 21, '64	
Johnson Charles A..	Andover.......	March 16, '64	
Johnson John A....	Chicago........	"	Transf. to Co. A as consol....
Larson John........	Lynn..........	March 25, '64	
Mangerson Sam'l A.	Galesburg	March 27, '64	
Nelson John N.....	Chicago........	March 16. '64	
Norton Charles O..	Andover.......	Feb. 29. '64	
Nelson Benjamin...	Paxton........	March 24. '64	
Peterson Sven......	Galesburg	Nov. 25. '63	
Rosengren CharlesG.	Pulaski co. Ark.	Feb. 3, '64	
Samuelson Charles A.	Galesburg	March 11, '64	
Willman Gustaf.....	"	Feb. 29, '64	Died, Little Rock, Oct. 16, '64
Wager Henry B.....	Chicago........	Nov. 4. '63	" Dec. 11, '64.

Col. Oscar Malmborg and the Fifty-Fifth Illinois Volunteer Infantry Regiment

Early in the summer of 1861, David Stuart, a lawyer of Chicago, obtained authority from the war department to raise a body of troops to participate in the conflict just then assuming formidable proportions. At first, probably one regiment only was contemplated, but a surplus of recruits being tendered, a brigade was ultimately formed, which Stuart, himself a war democrat and a great admirer of Douglas, who had ardently declared in favor of the Union, christened the Douglas Brigade. It was made up of two regiments, the 42nd and 55th. When the first, organized from material already at hand, was mustered in and left for the field, Stuart went with it in the capacity of lieutenant-colonel. In his absence, the 55th regiment was gradually taking form under the hands of Oscar Malmborg, who declined the colonelcy of this and also another regiment, when tendered the commission by Governor Yates.

Malmborg, a native of Sweden, born in 1820 or 1821, was a nephew of Lieutenant General Otto August Malmborg of the Swedish army, who was raised to noble rank in 1842. Prepared by prior academic training, Oscar Malmborg entered the Karlberg Military Academy at Stockholm, from which he was graduated after completing the six years' course of study. He subsequently served for eight years in the Swedish army. When the war with Mexico broke out, he came to the United States to tender his services to our government. Embarrassed from an imperfect knowledge of English, he volunteered in the artillery corps as a private, although it is understood that at first the experienced soldier sought some grade above the ranks. He served for twenty-one months in garrison at Fort Brown on the Rio Grande, a position which, much to his chagrin, withheld him from more active service in the field. His military knowledge earned him promotion and he served till the close of the war. In 1852 Malmborg located in Chicago, and was in the employ of the emigrant department of the Illinois Central Railway Company when the Civil War broke out.

The 55th regiment was recruited mainly from the farmers and workingmen of the state, but during the summer and fall these raw recruits, under Malmborg as commander and drillmaster, were transformed into a military body whose fine bearing was commented upon and which later became noted for its good discipline and splendid fighting qualities and known as one of the model regiments of the volunteer army. Malmborg possessed thorough tactical knowledge, then a rare acquirement among volunteer officers, and was untiring in his efforts at drill and discipline. He was exacting to the utmost limit, and wholesome as his discipline was, it was too rigid to suit his subordinates, especially those among them who had enlisted to attain their ambition to command, not to obey, or under the erroneous impression that the campaign would be a continuous picnic. Malmborg's temper is said to have been irritable and, at times, violent, and this, combined with his relentless discipline, made him unpopular. Stuart himself had unbounded faith in the military skill of Malmborg, while distrusting his own ability in that direction, and, therefore, took little part in actually drilling the regiment. The result was that when he afterwards, as colonel, took the command, his lack of technical training generated a species of contempt always fatal to the respect due a superior officer. Thus it happened that the colonel and the lieutenant colonel of the 55th both came to be held in contempt by the rank and file, the one for knowing too little, the other for knowing more than the green citizen soldiers thought necessary.

The greatest source of dissatisfaction, however, lay in the manner in which the regiment was organized. For the most part the recruits had come to the rendezvous at Camp Douglas as embryo companies, headed by men who were ambitious to become captains, and provided with a full complement of prospective officers, but lacking the required quota of privates. In the transfers and consolidations necessary to the formation of ten full companies, many would-be officers were reduced to the ranks, while their respective handfuls of recruits helped to fill companies over which Stuart, arbitrarily, as they considered, placed others in command. Among those who had been most active in raising recruits were two Methodist preachers, Haney and Presson. Each was made captain of a company, and these men also exercised great influence over the rest of the regiment, the bulk of which apparently was made up of recruits of the same faith. Like most patriots, they also were "willing to serve as brigadiers," or, leastwise, regimental officers, and when Malmborg was made lieutenant colonel of the regiment, these reverend gentlemen and their friends felt grievously disappointed. If we are to believe "The Story of the Fifty-fifth Regiment," a book largely devoted to the task of defaming the name and character of Malmborg, and airing the grievances of those who vainly aspired to his position, the 55th regiment was on the verge of mutiny from the time of muster-in until near the end of the three-year term of service. And yet Col. Malmborg—ridiculed for his foreign brogue, denounced as a tyrant, hated for his "martinet discipline," branded as un-American and declared unfit to command free-born citizens, led this same regiment through a score of battles, in which none fought better and few won greener laurels. Whatever his shortcomings may have been, as a man or an officer, Malmborg proved himself a highly capable military leader, whose achievements on the field of battle, complimented by his superiors again and again, are the best answer to the charges of his scheming and envious traducers.

On the 31st day of October, 1861, the regiment was mustered into the United States service and on Dec. 9th left Chicago. Some time prior to the departure, the former colleagues of Lt. Col. Malmborg in the employ of the Illinois Central railroad presented him with an elegant sword, the whole ceremony tending to show that he was held in high esteem by his former associates. He was, as a matter of fact, a gentleman of more than ordinary culture and enjoyed the respect of his fellow countrymen in Chicago, from among whom he had just been appointed local consular representative of Sweden and Norway.

Upon reaching Benton Barracks, near St. Louis, the regiment continued its course of company and battalion drill, then became a part of Gen. William T. Sherman's division, and was sent south to join the Army of the Tennessee. While in camp near Pittsburg Landing, prior to the battle of Shiloh, the regiment was brigaded with the 54th and 71st Ohio and Col. Stuart was placed in command of the new brigade. Although a part of the fifth (Sherman's) division, the brigade was encamped two miles east of the other three brigades and formed the extreme and isolated left of the Union army in the first day's battle of Shiloh.

In the battle the three regiments were placed in line by Stuart. They were at first supported by a battery and by the 41st Ill. Inf. regiment. These and also the 71st Ohio retreated, leaving the 55th Illinois and 54th Ohio to fight, with a total of 800 men at the outset. With no federal forces in view, the two regiments fought for two hours against a Confederate force of five infantry regiments, a battery of four guns and a body of cavalry. After the cartridge boxes of the killed and wounded had been emptied, the ammunition was exhausted. They retreated in good order, although shelled, and stopped near the landing where they were promised ammunition. Col. Stuart was wounded, and turned the command over to Col. Thomas Kilby Smith of the 54th Ohio. Smith left the command to Lt. Col. Malmborg in order to find a part of his regiment which had been detached during the retreat. Gen. Grant, passing, ordered Malmborg to form a line near the batteries. Through Malmborg's efforts a battle line of some three thousand men was formed, composed largely of remnants of regiments retreating towards the landing. How splendidly Malmborg acquitted himself in the desperate struggle during the rest of the day may be inferred from these words in Stuart's report of the work of his brigade: ''I was under great obligations to Lieutenant Colonel Malmborg, whose military education and experience were of every importance to me. Comprehending at a glance the purpose and object of every movement of the enemy, he was able to advise me promptly and intelligently as to the disposition of my men. He was cool, observant, discreet and brave and of infinite service to me.'' After the battle, Malmborg reported to Col. Stuart a long list of names of officers and privates meriting special mention for bravery. Among them was First Lieutenant Lucien B. Crooker, whose elaborate villification of Col. Malmborg seven years after the death of the latter was doubtless his most noteworthy subsequent achievement.

In this, the initial engagement of the 55th regiment, its loss was the heaviest of any federal regiment engaged in that terrible conflict, except the 9th Illinois. The loss of the 55th was 1 officer and 51 enlisted men killed and 9 officers and 190 men wounded, being a total of 251, and 26 men captured. On the second day the regiment, commanded by Malmborg, fought in Sherman's division, under his very eye, sustaining but slight loss. During the advance on Corinth Malmborg had charge of the strategic movements of the brigade and later of the entire division, in the matter of picking the positions and planning and executing the fortifications. For this work he was complimented by his superiors, including Generals Grant and Thomas.

It may be added here that, although the extensive intrenchments thrown up during the advance on Corinth proved needless, owing to the demoralized condition of the Confederate army, yet it would have been the height of recklessness to continue hazarding the safety of

Tablet in Illinois State Memorial Temple, Vicksburg National Military Park

the Union army in exposed camps, while the enemy's strength was still unknown. After Shiloh, Grant's army learned the value of fortifications in the field, and Malmborg was the instructor. Seven different and complete lines of intrenchments, reaching for miles across the front of the army, were erected. They were solid, massive earthworks with log backing, and all scientific attachments, and were far superior to the rebel works around Corinth. They are yet to be seen with their outlines almost perfect. "The 55th did its full share of digging, and the fortifications built by the regiment were the pride of Lieutenant Colonel Malmborg's heart," says the aforesaid Crooker, who sneeringly adds: "He was never so happy as when displaying his alleged engineering skill." Other military writers, however, have taken a different view, deploring the absence of intrenchments on the Shiloh battlefield, and they probably would agree that a few prior lessons in digging might have wholly changed the aspect of that battle.

Malmborg and his command shared largely in the credit for the victory at Arkansas Post on Jan. 12, 1863. The 55th Illinois regiment disembarked from the transports in the Arkansas river and was led by Malmborg to a position ¾ mile east of the fort. At dark the regiment advanced and proceeded for a quarter of a mile through a thicket, to an open space a short distance from the fort. The enemy showered grape and shell, but did little damage. Here the men slept on their arms. One hour before daylight Malmborg directed the construction of earthworks for a battery of 20-pounder Parrott guns— formerly Silfversparre's battery. At noon, after a brisk bombardment, Malmborg with his regiment took part in the first assault upon the enemy's works. After an obstinate fight of three hours, a second assault was ordered, whereupon the enemy surrendered. In his report of the battle Col. Thomas Kilby Smith, the superior officer in command, says: "I desire to make special mention of Col. Malmborg, commanding the Fifty-fifth Illinois, whose zeal and unremitting diligence in superintending working parties and planting batteries, performing at the same time his whole duty to his regiment, demand compliment."

In the "Tallahatchie campaign" Malmborg and his command in less than 24 hours constructed a bridge 170 feet in length, on which Sherman's army and train crossed the Tallahatchie River. At Vicksburg Malmborg's command participated in the assaults of May 19th and 22nd, his regiment bearing its full share during the siege, losing 14 killed and 32 wounded. Col. Malmborg himself on the 19th was struck by a musket ball near the right eye and was stunned for a moment, but upon rallying he refused to withdraw from the fight, continuing to cheer his men on. In the second assault Malmborg participated against the advice of Gen. Sherman and was again wounded, being struck by a fragment of shell near the left eye. Notwithstanding his wounds, he was active throughout the siege, spending twenty whole nights from before sunset till after sunrise in prosecuting the work allotted to him by virtue of his training and experience.

During the siege and investment of the city Malmborg had charge of Brig.-Gen. Lightburn's work of advanced rifle pits and attacking

Stockade Redan before Vicksburg. The First Marker at the Right of the Road indicates the Position of the 55th Illinois during the Assault of May 19, 1863

the enemy's stockade. He conducted sap-rolling operations and was constantly superintending this perilous work in person. With his men he approached the enemy's stockade within 25 feet and was shelled severely during the nights of June 30th and July 1st and 2nd. After the saps could be advanced no farther, being within reach of the enemy's hand-grenades, with which his men were copiously served, Malmborg went to mining. He proceeded far with the mines, and on the night between July 3rd and 4th had 200 lbs. of powder and fuses ready to blow up the enemy's works. Half an hour after he had received these supplies, with instructions, the city surrendered. His achievements before Vicksburg at the head of the 55th regiment were no less noteworthy. During the assault on May 19th, the 55th at 2 P. M. advanced in line with other regiments under heavy fire to within 30 or 40 yards of the enemy's works and held their position until 3 A. M. next day, when they were withdrawn. On the 22nd, Malmborg, again taking part in the assault, remained near the enemy's rifle pits until ordered back on the morning of the 23rd.

Col. Thomas Kilby Smith, commander of the brigade, in his report of the operations before the city, said: "I shall make no apology for undue length of my report nor stint with measured praise the meed of the officers or the men of the Second Brigade. I only regret my own inability in language to do them full justice. With Col. Malmborg. of the Fifty-fifth Illinois, I have been side by side in seven battles; have stood with him literally among heaps of slain. He is always cool, prudent and of dauntless courage, and in the recent engagement, although wounded twice, and, by strange fatality, first in the right and next in the left eye, displayed those qualities with the ardor and cheer so necessary in a charge."

In the movements about Chattanooga in November, 1863, and in the final battle, Malmborg took a conspicious part. On the night of the 23rd, with the brigade now again commanded by Malmborg in the absence of the superior officer, he manned a fleet of pontoon boats in North Chickamauga Creek and during intense darkness descended and crossed the Tennessee and captured the enemy's pickets—a feat conceded to be one of the most daring operations of the war.

After the battle of Mission Ridge, in which Malmborg and his regiment fought, the 55th marched with Sherman the round trip to the relief of Knoxville, and after their return encamped during winter successively at Bridgeport, Bellefonte and Larkinsville. While at the latter place, after exacting the right to elect officers, the regiment veteranized. at which time the existing field officers all failed of election and at the end of their term quit the service.

The result is accounted for by the disaffection existing in the regiment from its organization. The relations between Stuart and Malmborg on the one hand and a number of the lower officers on the other grew more strained as time passed. The faults of the commanders were magnified and real or imaginary grievances accumulated. Stuart's failure to have the commissions issued was a legitimate cause for complaint. they being delayed for over a year.

In the fall of 1862, when Stuart's promotion seemed likely, steps were taken boldly and openly to get rid of Malmborg also. In a letter to Governor Yates, confessedly inspired by Chaplain Haney, twenty-one subordinate officers demanded a voice in the prospective selection of a colonel, urging unpopularity, military incapacity, harsh discipline and abusive treatment of his subordinates against Malmborg's succession to the coloneley. The action of the sub-officers was reported to Col. Stuart, who at once wrote to the governor to counteract the effect of the protest. From his letter we quote the following:

"Col. Malmborg is a strict disciplinarian, an exacting officer, who demands from every officer the active and complete discharge of all his duties. There are very few of them who do not feel pretty well contented with themselves when they somewhere near half perform their duties; such men are not only not patted on the back by him, but they are sternly and promptly reproved by him, and are driven up and compelled to do their duty. They would like to get rid of him and have a slip-shod, easy-going time of it. It is this vigilance, zeal and discipline, which has made this regiment in every regard today the best one in this army. I claim boldly for it (and it will be conceded by the commanding generals), that it is the most efficient, the best drilled, best disciplined, best behaved, cleanest, healthiest and most soldierly regiment in this army. This perfection has not been attained, nor these qualities acquired, without great labor and care, constant and earnest vigilance. I have, of course, the reputation of having accomplished this, amongst those who know only generally, that I am at the head of the regiment; they who know us more intimately are well informed of the consequence Col. Malmborg has been to me. It would be not alone ungenerous, but ungrateful in me to appropriate any share of the credit and honor, which so justly belongs to him, to myself.

"There was scarcely an officer in this regiment who, when he entered it, knew his facings; they have learned here all they know (and with some of them the stock of knowledge on hand is not burdensome even now), but by dint of hard work and doing their work for many of the officers, we can get along—and do. They ought to be grateful to Col. Malmborg for what he has done for them, but vanity, selfishness and that 'prurient ambition for fame not earned,' which afflicts most men, makes them insensible to the better, nobler and more generous sentiments of their nature.

"I desire frankly and truthfully to bear witness to you, as our chief, that this regiment, which has done and will do honor to your state, owes its efficiency, its proficiency, and everything which gives it superiority or a name, to Col. Malmborg—I owe most that I know to him—the officers owe all to him."

The governor replied by issuing a colonel's commission for Malmborg, to date from Dec. 19, 1862, which was received Jan. 27, 1863.

Stuart was promoted brigadier-general but the appointment by the President failed of confirmation, whereupon he left the service.

The opposition, having failed to oust Malmborg, bided their time.

Colonel Oscar Malmborg

after five officers had resigned in disgust at Malmborg's promotion. The mustering out of six first lieutenants for disability followed, at the colonel's recommendation, made likely in a spirit of retaliation. In the summer of 1863 an attempt was made to have Col. Malmborg tried before the general court-martial. The charges, alleging intoxication and the use of profanity at sundry times, were preferred and forwarded to the brigade commander, who detained and finally suppressed them. This document, which quotes certain offensive phrases ascribed to the colonel, but is silent as to the provocation, is remarkable in this, that it makes Malmborg speak very plain and correct English, while all other stories about "the d—d old Swede " make him speak an impossible German brogue, highly suggestive of fabrication.

But the real crisis did not come until the question of re-enlistment for a new term was urged on the regiment early in 1864. By this time the faction dominated by Chaplain Haney had grown to comprise almost the entire regiment. Contrary to usage, the malcontents insisted on the privilege of electing officers anew, and successfully frustrated every attempt to re-enlist the men until that special permission was accorded. Malmborg himself in a regimental order finally, under pressure, made the extraordinary and unmilitary concession, and on April 6th, the second anniversary of Shiloh, the regiment ousted the man who had helped them pluck laurels on that and many subsequent battlefields. Chaplain Milton L. Haney was elected colonel with 164 votes, as against 22 for Malmborg, and all the other regimental officers were sacrificed, no matter how bravely and well they had served. Haney had been captain of a company until the regiment reached the field in March, 1862, when he resigned to take the less perilous position of chaplain. He was entirely ignorant of military tactics and seemed to have had little faith in his own ability. for he preferred not to accept the command. To complete the reform, the principal musician was elected sergeant-major and a man hardly able to write his own name was made quarter-master. The whole procedure seems to have been looked upon by the superior officers as a ridiculous farce. General Logan, commander of the army corps, is quoted as having said to Col. Malmborg: "We have been accustomed to look upon the 55th as the best regiment in the army, and how shall I express my astonishment to find they are after all but a set of d— fools! Electing a chaplain, a civilian, a know-nothing for their colonel! Are they prepared to go into battle under such a man? Do you suppose that I, now on the eve of the most important campaign of the war, am going to send that regiment into battle under that man? Do you suppose the Governor and the Adjutant-General of Illinois will commission him?" As a matter of fact, only those officers elected, who were in line of promotion to their respective positions, ever received the sought-for commissions. Col. Malmborg expressed his intention of resigning soon to give place to the colonel-elect, but seems to have been prevailed upon to retain his commission while awaiting -developments, and did so until the end of the three-year term. After the election Malmborg, however, did not remain in active command of his regiment. He served as chief engineer of the 17th army corps until July 18th. Thinking to ease him of his exertions and divorce him from his difficulties, Sherman on July 24th commissioned him to visit posts on the Mississippi River. While the assertion that Malmborg resigned from his regiment owing to broken health is erroneous, it is nevertheless true that his health was on the decline. His condition did not improve by the combined light duty and recreation afforded by

55TH INFANTRY.

COL. OSCAR MALMBORG.
2D BRIG., 2D DIV., 15TH CORPS.

CASUALTIES:
ASSAULT, MAY 19, 1863,
KILLED 4, WOUNDED 22, TOTAL 26.
LIEUT. LEVI HILL KILLED:
ASSAULT, MAY 22, KILLED 5, WOUNDED
13, TOTAL 18
AGGREGATE, KILLED 9, WOUNDED 35,
TOTAL 44.

ILLINOIS

Monument at Vicksburg National Military Park

his new commission, wherefore he now resigned and was mustered out on Sept. 20, 1864, returning to his home in Chicago.

On Jan. 1, 1865, Malmborg was commissioned colonel in the First Veteran Army Corps then being organized under Gen. Hancock, and was ordered to superintend the recruiting in Illinois, with headquarters in Chicago. Soon after appointed head of the second regiment, with orders to be at Winchester, Va., at the beginning of April, Malmborg there became the commander of the only brigade of this corps that was ever organized. His impaired eye-sight weakened, and in order to avoid complete blindness Malmborg, acting upon medical advice, now asked for his dismissal, which was granted May 31, 1865. Thereupon he was given a position in the departments at Washington. In course of time his vision was still further impaired, and, almost wholly blind, Malmborg returned to Sweden, subsisting on his pension until the spring of 1880, when he died in the city of Visby, on Gotland, on April 29th, in the sixtieth year of his age.

After the retirement of Malmborg, the regiment continued to acquit itself creditably, at Jonesboro, Kenesaw Mountain and throughout the Atlanta campaign, but most of its fighting had been done under the intrepid Swedish colonel. This regiment was engaged in thirty-one battles and was 128 days under fire. It lost 108 men actually killed in battle, and its total wounded were 339, making an aggregate of 447 struck by the missiles of war. During the entire period of service it received less than fifty recruits, and the fact that it had only 49 men captured speaks well for the discipline and cohesion imparted to it by its gallant commander.

By their countrymen the Swedish commanders Major Stolbrand and Captain Silfversparre have been lionized, and deservedly so, for their military exploits, while for some inexplicable reason Col. Malmborg has received but meager credit at their hands. A diligent search of the war records, however, reveals the fact that in point of skill, brilliancy and personal bravery, the leadership of the latter was in no wise inferior to that of either of the other two, and all the facts point to the conclusion that there were but few, if any, better fighters of any nationality in the Union army than was Col. Oscar Malmborg.

The state of Illinois has erected in the Vicksburg National Military Park the Illinois State Memorial Temple. On the interior walls there are bronze tablets and basrelief portraits in memory of Lincoln, Grant and Logan. On the tablet giving the organization of the staff occurs the name of Charles Stolbrand, chief of artillery under General Logan. There is a bronze tablet for each regiment of Illinois troops, giving the names of all officers and privates who fought at the siege of Vicksburg. Among them may be remarked as of greatest interest to Swedish-American history those of the 43rd and 55th Infantry, and the 1st and 2nd Artillery. The 55th Illinois has a marble monument on Union ave., besides which it has five marble markers to designate the positions occupied on the firing line. Marble monuments are also erected to the 43rd Infantry and to Co. H, 1st Artillery and Co. G, 2nd Artillery.

Company D, Fifty-Seventh Illinois Infantry

In the summer of the year 1860 a certain martial spirit was aroused in and about the Bishop Hill settlement, resulting soon in the organization of a military company, with Eric Forsse as captain. With his

Swedish military training, combined with natural talent for leadership, he drilled the boys under his command to a fair degree of skill in the use of arms. At the time there was probably no serious thought of ever engaging in actual warfare, but the very next year momentous events called for the service of every patriot willing and able to bear arms. Not long after the first call for volunteers, the Bishop Hill military company tendered their services to the state and nation. On the 16th day of September, 1861, they enlisted, and on the 30th they boarded the train at Galva, bound for Camp Bureau, near Princeton, where Col. Winslow was in command.

At this time a number of regiments of sharpshooters were being organized at St. Louis, for the recruiting of which emissaries were sent to the various military camps. Several visited Camp Bureau and secretly persuaded the members of the regiment to join the sharpshooters, and made arrangements for their transportation to St. Louis on the quiet. A steamer named Musselman was moored at a convenient point in the Illinois River and before daylight dawned on the 23rd of October, the regiment broke camp, embarked and steamed away down the river. When Col. Winslow that morning found the camp vacated, he at once endeavored to intercept the deserters. These had taken the precaution to cut the telegraph wires, but messengers were dispatched to the nearest telegraph station in operation, from which the state authorities were notified of what had occurred. From Springfield a battery was ordered to Alton, there to await the arrival of the Musselman and capture those on board. When the steamer attempted to pass that point a blank shot was fired directly over the vessel as a signal to stop. The warning left unheeded, the prow of the Musselman was shattered by a well-aimed cannon ball. Then the engine was stopped, the boat lay to and all its passengers were lodged in the old state penitentiary at Alton. From there the absconders were brought to Camp Butler, at Springfield, for court martial. Through the intervention of influential friends all were acquitted and then sent to Camp Douglas, Chicago. where the regiment, which hitherto had but six companies and was known as the 56th, was made a part of the 57th. The change in the numeral was almost imperative, the stigma left on the 56th by the Camp Bureau episode making it well-nigh impossible to secure recruits for it. On Dec. 26, 1861, the 57th regiment was mustered in, with Col. Silas D. Baldwin in command.

On Feb. 8, 1862, the regiment left Chicago for Cairo, en route to the war scene. Reaching Fort Donelson on the 14th, it participated in the siege of the fort and its capture two days later. The regiment next took part in the battle of Shiloh.

The 57th was held in reserve for a time, then ordered to take up a position to the left, in support of a battery which was sharply engaged with the enemy. Here the regiment suffered little from the enemy's fire, but was soon to be tried in the crucible of hot conflict. Well along in the afternoon it took a position on the left of Gen. Hurlbut's division, and on the extreme left of the Union line, barring Stuart's isolated brigade. Here, about 4 o'clock, an advance was made, encountering the enemy in strong force directly in front. Firing began on both sides and for about 20 minutes there was a constant roar of musketry. Notwithstanding this was the first severe engagement of the 57th, they fought with all the heroism and valor that could have distinguished old and tried soldiers, but the contest was unequal. The old altered flint-lock muskets became foul after a few rounds, rendering it impossible to get a load down, though many of the men, in their effort to drive the charge home, drove the rammers against the trunks of trees; some, baffled in this attempt to reload, picked up the muskets of their fallen comrades and renewed the firing. Thus crippled by unserviceable arms, flanked on both sides and left without support under an enfilading fire, the gallant command was compelled to retire or suffer capture. . In falling back the regiment was subjected to a storm of grape and canister from the enemy's cannon until it passed the artillery line massed not far from the landing by Col. J. D. Webster, which checked the Confederate advance, ending the day's conflict. In this murderous engagement the 57th lost 187 of its officers and men in killed, wounded and missing, the losses of Co. D being Charles M. Green and Adolf Johnson killed and fourteen wounded, including Andrew G. Warner, who was promoted soon after. On the second day this regiment moved into position at daybreak and was in the fight until the enemy withdrew defeated late in the day.

From Pittsburg Landing the regiment joined in the advance on Corinth. The city having been occupied on May 30th, the 57th was garrisoned there.

On Oct. 3rd and 4th the Union army in and around Corinth fought back an attack of a large force of Confederates. In these engagements Co. D lost three men, Otto W. Peel and Andrew Anderson, who were killed on the battlefield, and Olof Wiekstrum, who was mortally wounded, dying on the 7th.

From Jan. 31st to Sept. 13th, 1863, while the regiment was still at Corinth, Co. D was assigned to garrison duty at Battery Robinet, just out of town, where the regiment had its winter quarters. The 57th remained at Corinth, except for an occasional raid or scout into the surrounding country, until the fall of 1863. On Nov. 4th this entire command, composing a part of Gen. Sherman's army, moved to middle Tennessee, where the 57th was assigned to outpost duty. Twenty days later Co. D was ordered to take possession of Mitchell's Mill, near Lynnville, where the company remained till Jan. 18, 1864, occupied in cutting timber and operating the sawmill.

The term of enlistment having expired, the regiment veteranized on Jan. 17, 1864, with the exception of Co. C and a few men of the other

Soldiers' Monument, Bishop Hill

companies. Of Co. D the men very generally re-enlisted. The next day the regiment started for Chicago on veteran furlough of 30 days, arriving Jan. 27th. The members of Co. D arrived at Galva Jan. 29th, receiving an enthusiastic reception at the hands of the townspeople. From the station they marched to Norton's Hall, where the ladies spread for them a banquet to which the army rations could nowise be compared. Returning south March 9th, with 250 recruits, the regiment went to Athens, Ala., thence to join Sherman's army at Chattanooga.

Henceforth the regiment was kept constantly moving, marching with the Army of the Tennessee_in the Atlanta campaign, taking part in the maneuvering against the rear of Gen. Johnston's retreating army and in the battle of Resaca. On May 16th, with the Third Brigade in advance, the line of march was taken up on the Calhoun road. The whole brigade, under the command of Major Forsse of the 57th, encountered the enemy in force near Rome Cross Roads, where the rebels had taken a stand to protect the train of the retreating army. The brigade was drawn up in battle array and soon became engaged, the fighting being at intervals quite severe and lasting until nearly night. Following the enemy's retreat the next day the division moved to Kingston, thence to Rome, where the 57th, with other regiments, was assigned to garrison duty, while the balance of Gen. Dodge's command continued with the advance on Atlanta. On Oct. 13th the regiment under command of Major Forsse moved out from Rome, with a brigade under Lieut. Col. Hurlbut, on the Cave Springs road, where a portion of Gen. Hood's army was encountered. resulting in driving the enemy four miles back, with a loss to the 57th of seven killed and wounded. Major Forsse resigned on Oct. 16, 1864, while at Rome.

The regiment, with 504 men in line, on Nov. 10th moved out from Rome four miles towards Kingston, being the initial movement on its part for what proved to be the famous "March to the Sea," and on Dec. 21st reached Savannah, just evacuated by the enemy without a fight.

Going up the Savannah River on Jan. 24, 1865, the 57th had its last encounter with the Confederates at Bentonville two months later, on March 20th and 21st. It took part in the final grand review at Washington May 24th. From the capital the 57th regiment was brought to Louisville, Ky., and there mustered out, but retained its organization and returned to Chicago. On July 14th it received final pay and was disbanded at Camp Douglas, its starting-point, after three years and five months of active service or three years and ten months from the time of enlistment of the greater portion of the regiment.

The roster of Co. D. exclusive of non-Swedish recruits, is here given.

Roster of Company D, 57th Illinois Infantry

Name and Rank	Residence	Date of rank or enlistment	Remarks
Captains			
Eric Forsse	Bishop Hill....	Dec. 26, 1861	Promoted Major.............
Eric Johnson.......	Galva.........	April 15, 1862	Resigned Sept. 3, 1862.....
Peter M. Wickstrum	Bishop Hill....	Sept. 3, 1862	Mustered out July 7, 1865.....
First Lieutenants			
Eric Johnson.......	Galva.........	Dec. 26, 1861	Promoted........
Eric Bergland......	Bishop Hill....	April 15, 1862	Mustered out July 7, 1865.....
Second Lieutenants			
Eric Bergland......	Bishop Hill....	Dec. 26, 1861	Promoted..................
Peter M. Wickstrum	"	August 15, 1862	" ....
George E. Rodeen..	"	Sept. 3, 1862	Died at Corinth, Aug. 7, 1862
Andrew G. Warner.	Andover.......	August 7, 1863	Promoted in Colored Regim'nt Commission canceled......
Olof Anderson......	Bishop Hill....	April 29, 1864	Mustered out July 7, 1865.....
First Sergeant			
Peter M. Wickstrum	Bishop Hill....	Sept. 14, 1861	Promoted 2d Lieutenant ......
Sergeants			
Olof Crans.........	Bishop Hill....	Sept. 14, 1861	Disch'ged June 3, '62, disability
Peter Nilson.......	"	"	Term expired, 1864...........
Olof Olson.........	Victoria........	Nov. 10, 1861	" " ....
George E. Rodeen..	Bishop Hill....	Sept. 14, 1861	Promoted 2d Lieutenant ......
Corporals			
Andrew G. Warner.	Andover.......	Sept. 16, 1861	Prom. 2d Lieut'nt Aug. 7, 1863
Peter Johnson......	Bishop Hill....	Sept. 14, 1861	Re-enlisted as Veteran........
Olof Wickstrum....	"	Sept. 16, 1861	Died at Corinth Oct. 7, '62 ...
Jonas M. Johnson..	"	Oct. 6, 1861	Re-enlisted as Veteran........
Jonas Allstrom.....	"	Sept. 25, 1861	Mustered out 1864............
Wagoner			
Eric Lindgren......	Bishop Hill....	Nov. 25, 1861	Disch'ged July 1, '62, disability. Louisville, Ky.............
Musicians			
Olof Anderson......	Bishop Hill....	Sept. 14, 1861	Re-enlisted as Veteran........
Swan J. Nordin....	"	"	Died, Mound City, Jan. 15, '64
Privates			
Anderson Andrew..	"	Sept. 25, 1861	Killed at Corinth, Oct. 4, '62
Anderson Peter E..	Galva.........	Oct. 8, 1861	Re-enlisted as Veteran........
Anderson Charles P.	Moline	Oct. 6, 1861	Disch'ged July 8, '62; disability
Anderson William..	Bishop Hill....	Oct. 11, 1861	....
Anderson Peter.....	"	Oct. 6, 1861	
Anderson Lars......	"	Sept. 25, 1861	Term expired 1864
Anderson Lars W...	"	Sept. 16, 1861	Disch. July 1, '62; wounds....
Anderson August...	Berlin.........	Dec. 7, 1861	Re enlisted as Veteran......
Broberg August	Gillson	Oct. 11, 1861	Term expired 1864 ....
Beck John.	Watertown.....	Dec. 5, 1861	" " ....
Crone Andrew......	Bishop Hill....	Sept. 25, 1861	....
Caline Eric.........	Galva.........	"	Re-enlisted as veteran ......
Danielson Daniel...	Bishop Hill....	Sept. 14, 1861	" " ....
Erickson Lars......	"	Sept. 25, 1861	" " ....
Forsell Jonas......	"	Sept. 16, 1861	" " ....
Granat John.......	Galesburg.. ..	Oct. 8, 1861	" " ....
Green Charles M...	Bishop Hill....	Sept. 25, 1861	Killed at Shiloh, April 6, '62..
Hanson Jonas	Wataga........	Oct. 8, 1861	Term expired 1864............
Hartz Andrew......	Bishop Hill....	Sept. 14, 1861	Re-enlisted as Veteran........
Hillstrom John E...	"	Sept. 25, 1861	Term expired 1864...........

Name and Rank	Residence	Date of rank or enlistment	Remarks
Privates			
Johnson Adolph....	Princeton......	Oct. 10, 1861	Killed at Shiloh, April 6, '62..
Johnson John O....	Andover.......	Sept. 20, 1861	Re-enlisted as Veteran... ....
Johnson Hans......	Bishop Hill....	Sept. 16, 1861	Term expired 1864...........
Johnson Andrew....	Moline	Sept. 25, 1861	" " ....
Johnson John......	Bishop Hill....	Oct. 3, 1861	
Johnson Nils......	Princeton......	Sept. 21, 1861	Re-enlisted as Veteran........
Johnson John......	Andover.......	Oct. 11, 1861	" " ....
Johnson N. J......	Henry.........	Oct. 8, 1861	Term expired 1864...........
Johnson John......	Moline	Sept. 25, 1861	Re-enlisted as Veteran........
Lind John.........	Berlin.........	"	Died at Hamburg, Tenn., May 13, 1862................
Lindgren Jonas.....	Bishop Hill ...	Oct. 6, 1861	Term expired 1864...........
Lock Andrew.......	"	Sept. 25, 1861	M. O. to date, Dec. 25, '64....
Larson Lars........	"	Dec. 7, 1861	Disch. July 5, '62; disability..
Matthews Olof......	"	Sept. 16, 1861	Re enlisted as Veteran........
Moberg Jonas......	Andover.......	Sept. 25, 1861	Died, Corinth. Aug. 24, '62...
Norstedt Olof......	Bishop Hill....	"	Re-enlisted as Veteran........
Neston Charles.....	"	"	" " ....
Norline Olof.......	"	Sept. 14, 1861	Term expired 1864...........
Norlund Lars......	Victoria........	Dec. 20, 1861	Disch. July 5, '62; disability..
Olson William O...	Moline	Sept. 25, 1881	Re-enlisted as Veteran........
Olson Peter........	Bishop Hill....	"	Term expired 1864...........
Olson Eric.........	"	Dec. 4, 1861	Discharged Feb 8, '62........
Peterson John P....	"	Oct. 7, 1861	" Sept. 9, '62; disability..
Peterson Lars F....	Swede Bend, Ia.	Oct. 10, 1861	" July 3, '62; wounds....
Peterson Peter.....	Bishop Hill....	Sept. 25, 1861	" July 10, '62; disability..
Peterson Nels......	"	Sept. 16, 1861	....
Peterson Andrew....	Princeton......	Oct. 22, 1861	
Peterson Magnus....	Bishop Hill ...	Nov. 25, 1861	Disch. July 12, '62; disability..
Peterson P. I......	Victoria........	Dec. 20, 1861	" May 29, '62; disability
Peel Otto W.......	Bishop Hill....	Sept. 16, 1861	Killed at Corinth, Oct. 3, '62..
Rudeman Olof......	Victoria	Dec. 19, 1861	Term expired 1864...........
Swanson Nils......	Bishop Hill....	Sept. 25, 1861	Re-enlisted as Veteran........
Tillman Nils........	Weller........	Oct. 10, 1861	" " ....
Tolin Charles......	Geneseo........	Sept. 22, 1861	" " ....
Trolin Eric J.......	Bishop Hill....	Dec. 7, 1861	....
Valentine Chas. J. Y.	Geneseo........	Sept. 29, 1861	Deserted..................
Westlund Jonas....	Bishop Hill....	Sept. 25, 1861	Died at Corinth July 9, '62....
Wickstrum Hans....	"	Sept. 16, 1861	Re-enlisted as Veteran........
Young Frank......	Princeton......	Dec. 15, 1861	" " ....
Veterans			
Anderson Olof.....	Bishop Hill....	Dec. 27, 1863	Promoted to 2d Lieutenant....
Anderson Peter E..	Galva.........	"	Mustered out July 7, '65......
Anderson August...	Berlin.........	"	Trans. to Co. F, Oct. 2, '64....
Anderson Andrew..	Galesburg.....	"	Mustered out July 7. '65......
Blom Gustaf.......	Chicago.......	"	" " ......
Caline Eric........	Galva.........	"	" " ......
Danielson Daniel...	Bishop Hill....	"	M. O. July 7, '65, as Corporal.
Erickson Lars......	"	"	" " ......
Erickson Eric......	Moline	"	Mustered out July 7. '65......
Erickson Charles J..	"	"	" " ......
Forsell Jonas.......	Bishop Hill....	"	Committed suicide. June 27, '65
Frederickson Claus.	Chicago.......	"	Mustered out July 7, '65......
Granat John........	Galesburg.....	"	" " ......
Hartz Andrew......	Bishop Hill....	"	" " ......
Johnson John......	Andover......	"	" " ......
Johnson Nils.......	Princeton......	"	M. O. July 7, '65............
Johnson John O....	Andover.......	"	M. O. July 7, '65, as Corporal...
Johnson Claus......	Chicago.......	"	" as Sergeant..
Johnson Peter......	Bishop Hill....	"	M. O. July 7, '65, as Sergeant..
Johnson Jonas M...	"	"	" July 7, '65, as 1st Sergt..

Name and Rank	Residence	Date of rank or enlistment	Remarks
Privates			
Johnson John.......	Moline	Dec. 27, 1863	Mustered out July 7, 1865 ....
Larson Andrew.....	Chicago.........	"	" "
Matthews Olof......	Bishop Hill....	"	M. O July 7, '65, as Sergeant..
Neston Charles......	"	"	M. O July 7, '65, as Corporal..
Norstedt Olof	"	"	Mustered out July 7, 1865.....
Olson William O...	Moline	"	M. O. July 7, '65. as Sergeant..
Peterson John......	Bishop Hill....	"	Mustered out July 7, 1865.....
Swanson Nils......	"	"	Died at Newark, N.J.,May16,'65
Swanson Peter......	Chicago......	"	Mustered out July 7, 1865.....
Tillman Nils.......	Weller........	"	Died, Rome, Ga., June 15, '65..
Tolin Charles.......	Geneseo........	"	Mustered out July 7. 1865.....
Warner Audrew G..	Andover......	"	Com'd 2d Leut.; not mustered; prom. Capt. 63d U. S. Col'd Inf. from Sergt. Apr. 5. '64.
Wickstrum Hans...	Bishop Hill...	"	M. O. July 7, '65, as Corporal..
Young Frank......	Princeton	"	" "
Recruits			
Anderson Nils P....	Bishop Hill....	Feb. 20,' 1864	Mustered out July 7, 1865.....
Anderson John G..	Berlin........	Feb. 13, 1864	" "
Anderson Peter.....	Princeton	Aug. 25, 1862	" "
Anderson Andrew..	....	....	Re-enlisted as Veteran........
Anglund Eric......	Galva.... ...	Feb. 12, 1864	Mustered out July 7, '65......
Almquist Eric......	Chicago........	Oct. 5, 1864	" "
Burnison Charles G	Berlin.........	Feb. 13, 1864	" "
Blom Gustaf........	Cook co......	Jan. 5, 1862	Re-enlisted as Veteran........
Beck John P.......	Watertown.....	Jan. 26, 1862	Disch. Oct. 19. '62; wounds....
Blom John	Bishop Hill....	Nov. 3. 1861	Disch. Aug. 23 '62; disability.
Erickson Jonas.....	"	Feb, 18, 1864	Mustered out July 7, 1865.....
Erickson John......	Truro..........	Feb. 15, 1864	" "
Erickson Andrew...	Chicago........	Feb. 29, 1864	" "
Erickson Erick.....	Moline	Jan. 6, 1862	Re-enlisted as Veteran........
Erickson Charles J.	"	July 11, 1862	" "
Eastlund Charles E.	Bishop Hill....	Feb. 18, 1864	Disch. Jan. 28, '65; disability..
Frederickson Claus.	Cook co......	Jan. 4, 1862	Re-enlisted as Veteran........
Forsse Olof........	Chicago........	Feb. 21, 1864	Mustered out July 7, 1865.....
Hanson Eric........	Galva..........	Dec. 1, 1862	" "
Haslett Peter.......	"	Sept. 6, 1862	" "
Hartsell John E....	Moline	Jan. 6, 1862	Disch. Aug. 23, '62; disability
Hedberg Eric......	Galva..........	....	Died at Corinth July 10. '62..
Imberg Peter......	Victoria........	Feb. 8, 1864	Mustered out July 7, 1865.....
Johnson Charles J..	Berlin.	Feb. 13, 1864	" "
Johnson Olof.......	Galesburg......	Feb. 12, 1864	" "
Johnson Andrew P..	Princeton.......	Sept. 9, 1862	" "
Johnson Swan P....	"	Aug. 25, 1862	" "
Johnson Claus......	Cook co........	Jan. 4, 1862	Re-enlisted as Veteran........
Johnson Gustaf.....	Moline	Jan. 26, 1862	Disch. June 18, '62; disability..
Jones Andrew......	Weller.........	Dec. 20, 1861	Disch. Aug. 23, '62; wounds...
Knuth William.....	Bureau	Dec. 28 1861	Disch. Oct. 20, '62; disability..
Lagerlof Frans O...	Andover.	Feb. 26, 1864	Mustered out July 7. 1865.....
Landgren Adolph...	Chicago........	March 16, 1864	Died, Rome, Ga., June 30, 1864
Larson Andrew.....	Cook co.......	Jan. 4, 1862	Re-enlisted as Veteran........
Martin Swan H....	Chicago........	Feb. 20, 1864	Mustered out July 7, 1865. ...
Nord Andrew.......	Galva..........	Nov. 15, 1861	....
Nord John M.......	Berlin.........	Feb. 13, 1864	Mustered out July 7, 1865.....
Nordstedt Frederick	Bishop Hill....	March 20, 1864	" "
Nordine Jonas......	....	Sept. 18, 1863	" "
Nordquist Louis....	Wataga........	Dec. 25, 1861	Term expired 1864...........
Nyberg Thomas....	Bishop Hill....		Disch June 16. '62; disability..
Olson Eric.........	Chicago........	Feb. 21, 1864	Mustered out July 7, 1865.....
Peterson John......	Bishop Hill....	Nov. 7, 1861	Re-enlisted as Veteran........

Name and Rank	Residence	Date of rank or enlistment	Remarks
Recruits			
Peterson Jacob G...	Chicago........	Feb. 20, 1861	Mustered out July 7, '65......
Pierson John......	"	" " "	" "
Peterson William...	Princeton......	Sept. 5, 1862	" "
Swanson August....	Chicago.......	March 15, 1864	" "
Swanson Peter......	Cook co.......	Jan. 4, 1862	Re-enlisted as Veteran........
Wood Andrew......	Bishop Hill....	....	Disch. Aug 7, '62; wounds ...
Young Fred........	Princeton......	Jan. 15, 1862	Term expired, 1864...........

Major Eric Forsse

Major Eric Forsse was a native of the Swedish province of Dalarne, where he was born March 4, 1819, in the parish of Malung. He served for twelve years in the Swedish army prior to his emigration in 1850. Coming to this country with his family, he landed at New Orleans and took a steamboat up the Mississippi to St. Louis, where he was laid up as a cholera patient for some time. After getting well, he proceeded with his family to Galesburg, and removed in turn to Knoxville, to Moline and to Bishop Hill, settling there in the winter of 1851-2 and remaining until after the colony had been dissolved. As already told, the organization in 1860 of a military company, which later became Co. D of the 57th Ill. Vol. Inf., was the work of Eric Forsse, who served as captain from its inception and was given the same rank in the army. He enlisted in the summer of 1861 and was mustered into service Sept. 14th the same year. When Major Norman B. Page of the 57th Regiment fell in the Battle of Shiloh, Captain Forsse was promoted major to take his place, the commission being dated April 15, 1862. His ability was recognized by his superiors and he was sometimes called upon to command as large a force as a brigade, which was the case at Allatoona Pass. He shared the hardships and triumphs of the campaign with his regiment until after the fall of Atlanta, when he resigned together with a large number of other officers, confident that their services were little needed from that time on. Having been mustered out Oct. 16, 1864, Major Forsse returned home, bought a 160-acre farm northwest of Galva and disposed of his share of the colony property at Bishop Hill. In November, 1869, he sold out and removed to Saline county, Kansas, where he had purchased a section of railroad land. Major Forsse headed a party of some 50 Swedes who located at or near Falun at this time, forming the nucleus of a large and prosperous Swedish-American settlement:

When a postoffice was established at Falun in 1870 Forsse was made postmaster and retained the position for seventeen consecutive years, serving all this time as township trustee and justice of the peace.

In the fall of 1872 he was elected to the Kansas legislature and served as a member for one term.

Major Forsse, gallant fighter and trusted citizen, passed away on

Major Eric Forsse

April 18, 1889. Of his family of five children three survive, including the oldest son, Olof, born July 8, 1842. He also served in Co. D, joining as a recruit in February, 1864, and remaining in the service, as high private in the rear rank, until mustered out July 7, 1865. Olof Forsse, who is a dealer in grain, coal and farm implements at Falun, has served the county for three years as county commissioner and seven years as sheriff.

Captain Eric Johnson

Captain Eric Johnson's military record is brief, but creditable. At the time of enlistment he was a puny stripling and would not have joined the army but for the military enthusiasm of the time and possibly a spark of the fighting spirit inherited from his grandfather on his mother's side, who was a veteran of Sweden's war with Russia. Johnson enlisted as a private, but at the organization of the company at Camp Bureau he was elected first lieutenant. After the battle of Shiloh, when Capt. Eric Forsse was promoted major of the regiment, Co. D held a new election April 15th, and Eric Johnson was chosen captain to fill the vacancy. During the siege of Corinth, he was stricken down with typhoid fever and brought so near death's door that arrangements were made to ship his body home. Somehow he rallied from the fever, but was attacked by another disease, and upon the urgent advice of the regimental surgeon resigned the captaincy and left the army Sept. 3, 1862, about one year after enlistment.

An incident which occurred in the summer of 1862 in Capt. Johnson's company is worthy of record as showing how the Swedish boys in the field, as well as the nationality in general, felt on the subject of slavery.

The Democratic party secured power in Illinois after so many Republicans had enlisted, and in order to make hay while the sun was shining they called a constitutional convention. Among the pro-slavery articles framed for the new constitution several were submitted to the voters in the form of separate propositions. To make a show of fairness, the Democrats allowed the Illinois soldiers in the field to vote upon the proposed constitution, and sent a commission of three Democrats, with the notorious "Sam" Buckmaster as chairman, to poll the vote of the soldiers. The balloting was not secret, but as each soldier appeared before the commissioners he was asked how he wished to vote on each separate proposition, and his answer was recorded on prepared tabular sheets. When it came to the negro propositions, if the vote of the soldier was not satisfactory to the commissioners, they would say, "You do not want to find your sister married to a negro, when you return from the war." Of course the soldier would answer "No," and this answer would be recorded as his vote on a proposition to which the voter at first assented. Company D was the fourth in order, and its members, having noticed how the soldiers were being confused and made to vote contrary to their convictions, went to Eric Johnson and said: "Captain, we want you to vote first, and when our turn eomes, we will have them record our votes the same as yours.'' Capt. Johnson voted not only against all the Democratic propositions on the negro question, but against the entire pro-slavery constitution as well. To a man his company voted the same way. When the last vote of Co. D had been polled, Buckmaster remarked with an oath: ''That was the d—dest black abolition company in the service.''

Another incident highly creditable to Co. D is a part of the record of the company during the first summer's campaigning, which might properly have been recorded in the official history of the regiment.

Prize Drill Flag, Co. D, 57th Ill. Infantry, Carried in 4th of July parade
at Bishop Hill

In the early part of the year (1862), Col. Baldwin of the 57th sent to Chicago and bought a beautiful silk flag for $125, which he offered as a reward to the best drilled company in the regiment. Several months were allowed for drill, and about half of the companies entered for the competition. Some time in July the exhibition drill took place, with three officers of the regular army acting as judges. In the regiment was a wholly German company (Co. G), and when this and the Swedish company had drilled, the companies still remaining withdrew from the competition, deeming further efforts hopeless. After comparing notes, the judges reported that as between the Germans and the

Swedes they were unable to decide. They therefore requested them to repeat their drill, which embraced marching and battalion movements in addition to the manual of arms. After the second drill the award was unanimously given to Co D, the Swedish company. This flag is still preserved at Bishop Hill—the trophy of a friendly contest in time of war.

Captain Peter M. Wickstrum

Capt. Peter M. Wickstrum was born March 3, 1827, in Mo parish, Helsingland, Sweden. He was a son of Mathias and Anna (Nelson) Wickstrum. When he was six years old his mother died, leaving two sons, of whom Peter was the younger. His early aptitude for learning made him the favorite child, and almost constant companion of his father. From him he acquired a love of legendary lore and a thirst for knowledge. His father was a man of more than average intellect, but fate had placed him where he must labor for his daily bread where the hours were long and the pay meager. Determined that his younger son should have some of the advantages denied himself, he sent him to school at Söderhamn. But as soon as he reached an age when he could be of use, he was taken out of school and put to work. At that time there were only two men in the whole parish who were readers of a newspaper, the young Peter and his employer, the two together subscribing for one paper. At the age of twenty-one he married Miss Ingrid Bergquist. Shortly after that he came in contact with an influence destined to shape his remaining life.

Helsingland was in a state of ferment over the teachings of Eric Jansson. Young Wickstrum became a convert, and with his wife and young child sailed for America in the spring of 1850. He became a member of the Bishop Hill Colony and worked there until its dissolution in 1860. He learned the English language with the aid of a small dictionary loaned him, and at night plugged the keyhole in the door to shut off the light that would have betrayed him, for at that time the study of English was frowned upon in the colony. Ten years of a deadening routine dampened his religious ardor and caused him to adopt more liberal views than those taught at Bishop Hill.

On Sept. 14, 1861, Mr. Wickstrum enlisted in the 57th Ill. Vol. Inf., Co. D, as a private, and was appointed orderly sergeant. After the battle of Shiloh he was promoted second lieutenant, and on Sept. 3rd of the same year he was again promoted, this time to the position of captain to succeed Eric Johnson, resigned, which rank he held until the close of the war, receiving an honorable discharge July 7, 1865. He participated in the battles of Fort Donelson, Shiloh, siege of Corinth, Sherman's campaign before Atlanta, and in his famous march from Atlanta to the sea. He fought in the battle of Bentonville while on the march to the sea, and also participated in many minor skirmishes and engagements.

After the war he returned home, purchased a farm of 210 acres near the village of Galva, and settled down to a peaceful rural life. For the first time he was now free to live his life according to his own dictates. His love for knowledge was revived. However hard the

Captain Peter M. Wickstrum

labors of the day, night found him with his beloved books and papers. He was more of a reader and thinker than a farmer; in fact, he had no relish for any work that took him away from his books. He left his children no greater heritage than this love of freedom, the desire to know and to grow. He believed that love is more than dogma, that humanity is the greatest church.

Capt. Wickstrum died at his home in Galva, Ill., Oct. 30, 1890, leaving a wife and four children, one daughter and three sons.

Politically he was a Democrat, socially he was a member of the G. A. R., belonging to Galva Post, No. 33.

Captain Andrew G. Warner

Captain A. G. Warner was born in northern Helsingland, Sweden, July 13, 1837. His parents emigrated in 1850 and located at Andover, Henry county, where the family, including the son and two daughters, engaged in farming. Young Warner was a member of the military company organized in and around Bishop Hill in 1860, which joined the army of volunteers in September, 1861, and was designated as Co. D in the 57th regiment of infantry, Warner being appointed first

Captain Andrew G. Warner

corporal at its organization as a part of the army. In the battle of Shiloh he received an ugly bullet wound in his right arm, but refused a furlough and staid with the company, performing his duties while carrying the arm in a sling. He was soon promoted first sergeant and subsequently second lieutenant. In 1864 the government organized regiments of colored troops officered by experienced white soldiers. These commands were not eagerly sought for, because in case of capture the rebels would show no mercy to either the colored soldiers or their officers. Warner, however, volunteered to accept one of these perilous posts, and on the 7th day of March, 1864, he was commissioned captain of Co. A, 63rd U. S. Colored Infantry. He served as such until the 9th day of January, 1866, when he was mustered out of the service at Duval's Bluff, Arkansas, after an honorable service of 4 years, 3 months and 15 days.

At the close of the war Captain Warner again settled down as a farmer at his old home in Andover. In the fall of 1868 he was called away from his agricultural pursuits by election to the office of sheriff, as an independent candidate running against the regular Republican candidate, winning by a majority of 116 votes, while the county gave General Grant for President a majority of over 2,700 votes. Warner was nominated by an independent convention of Swedish voters after their request for a place on the Republican county ticket had been denied, whereupon the Democrats refrained from making a nomination and assisted in electing Captain Warner. At the end of his term of office he took a trip west to find a new home and located in Page county, Iowa, where he removed with his family in the spring of 1871. On Dec. 4, 1865, Capt. Warner married Mathilda Johnson, the only daughter of Erik Jansson, founder of Bishop Hill. On Dec. 5, 1875, just ten years after, he died at his Page county home, leaving her a widow with two children—Charles A. Warner, who still lives at the old homestead, and Mamie Warner, now Mrs. Thomas.

Major Eric Bergland

Major Eric Bergland, Corps of Engineers U. S. Army, retired, enlisted at the age of seventeen in Company D, Fifty-seventh Illinois Volunteer Infantry, Sept. 14, 1861.

In December, 1861, he was mustered into U. S. service as second lieutenant and in April, 1862, was promoted to first lieutenant, in which capacity he served until the regiment was mustered out of service after the close of hostilities.

During his connection with the 57th Illinois Volunteer Infantry he took part in the capture of Fort Donelson, the battles of Shiloh, Corinth and Resaca, the latter part of this time being in command of his company. While in the field at Rome, Georgia, in the autumn of 1864, he received an appointment as cadet at the U. S. Military Academy at West Point, New York. On reporting to the superintendent of the military academy, Nov. 16, 1864, he was informed that his class, which had begun their studies September 1st, was already well advanced and that it would require considerable previous knowledge of mathematics to be able to make up before the January examination for the time lost.

As before enlisting in the army he had only enjoyed the advantages of a village school education, and knew nothing of higher mathematics, he thought it highly improbable that he would be able to prepare for the January examination after being nearly two months behind his classmates. On the advice of the superintendent he therefore applied to the Secretary of War to have his appointment extended to the following June, when he could enter on more nearly equal terms with other members of his class. This request was granted and he was in the meantime ordered to Johnson's Island, Ohio, for duty as assistant to Captain Tardy, Corps of Engineers, until June 1st, 1865.

He entered the military academy as a cadet July 1, 1865, and was graduated June 15, 1869, at the head of his class. The staff corps being then closed by Act of Congress, he was commissioned as second

Major Eric Bergland

lieutenant Fifth Artillery and stationed at Fort Warren, Mass.; at Fort Trumbull, Conn.; in the field on the Canadian boundary during the Fenian raid, 1870; at Artillery School, Fort Monroe, 1872. While there, he was transferred to the Corps of Engineers and promoted to first lieutenant. He was promoted captain January 10, 1884, and major Oct. 12, 1895.

Since his transfer to the Corps of Engineers, U. S. Army, he has served with the Engineer Battalion as a company officer; has been instructor of military engineering and mathematics and assistant professor of ethics and law at the U. S. Military Academy; assistant engineer on western surveys, under Capt. George M. Wheeler, for three years in California, Arizona, Nevada and Colorado; engineer in charge of river and harbor improvements in Tennessee, Mississippi, Arkansas,

Louisiana and Texas; in command of Company C, Battalion of Engineers, and instructor of civil engineering at U. S. Engineer School at Willets Point, New York; was ordered to Johnstown, Penn., a week after the great flood, in charge of a detachment and bridge train and ordered to replace by pontoon bridges those swept away by the flood.

In November, 1891, he was ordered to Baltimore as engineer of the 5th and 6th Light House District. During four years' service as above he built light houses at Cape Charles, Hog Island, Wolf Trap and other points. He retired from active service March 31, 1896, on his own application, after over 30 years' service. and resides, since retirement, at Baltimore, Md.

Major Eric Bergland is a native of the province of Helsingland, Sweden, born at Alfta April 21, 1844. In 1846 he was brought to the United States, his father, Anders Berglund. being one of the leaders of a party of Erik Janssonists, who emigrated that year. He was reared in the Bishop Hill Colony. At the age of twelve, Eric was put to work in the colony printing office at Galva and some years later was given the management of that modest establishment. He was thus employed up to 1861, when he enlisted for service in the Civil War. As shown, the young volunteer served with credit and he was the first cadet of Swedish birth to be admitted to West Point.

On June 5, 1878, Major Bergland was joined in marriage to Lucy Scott McFarland of Kentucky, a cousin of the wife of President Rutherford B. Hayes.

Charles John Stolbrand, Chief of Artillery, Brigadier General

Charles John Stolbrand was born at or near the city of Kristianstad, Sweden, May 11, 1821. His original name was Carl Johan Möller. At the age of eighteen he entered military service as a constable cadet in the Royal Vendes Artillery. At the time, according to common custom. he exchanged his patronymic for a more martial name and was enrolled as Carl Johan Ståhlbrand. In this country the name was written Stohlbrand or Stolbrand. sometimes preceded by Carlos John, but in these pages preference is given to the form found in the official war records. Prior to joining the army he was assistant to a surveyor.

Stolbrand was promoted 2nd constable in 1839. 1st constable in 1840 and sergeant in 1843. About two years later he was married to one Miss Pettersson. daughter of a non-commissioned officer. During the Danish-German War Stolbrand served in a battery attached to a Swedish army corps under Major-General Otto August Malmborg. which was encamped at Flensburg from August. 1849, until June the next year. This fact is probably responsible for the assertion made that Stolbrand served Denmark as a volunteer soldier. On July 12,

Brig.-General Charles John Stolbrand

1850, shortly after his return to Sweden, Stolbrand resigned, owing, it is alleged, to some differences with a superior officer, after having served for seven years as sergeant.

He came to this country in 1851, locating in Chicago, where after some time he secured a position in the office of the county recorder. During his residence in Chicago he was prominent in Swedish circles. When the Svea Society was organized, in 1857, he was chosen its president and was re-elected time and again. At the outbreak of the Civil War his martial spirit was rekindled, and at the first call for troops he raised a company, which, however, was not accepted, the quota of the state having been already filled. At the second call for volunteers, later in the same year, a second company was recruited by Stolbrand at Sycamore, where he was then engaged in making abstracts of DeKalb county land titles. This was mustered into service on Oct. 5. 1861, as Battery G, Second Ill. Light Artillery, with Stolbrand as captain, his commission being dated the day before.

On Dec. 31st Stolbrand was promoted major and subsequently he was made chief of artillery under General John A. Logan. In 1863, on Logan's succession to the command of the 15th army corps, Stolbrand was transferred to the command of its artillery brigade, virtually assuming the duties of brigadier-general. By Gen. Logan, Stolbrand was greatly admired as a fighter and was held inestimable to him as a military tactician. Sherman, who, as Gen. Wallace said, was "crazy on the subject of artillery," also accorded him unstinted praise, as told by Col. Mattson, who narrates the following:

The great General Sherman about 1866 visited St. Paul and a banquet was given to him at which I was present. During the conversation I asked about General Stolbrand. "Do you know him," he inquired. "Yes, sir, he is my countryman, and we served in the same regiment in Sweden," I replied. "Then," said he, "you may be proud of your old comrade, for a braver man and a better artillery officer than General Stolbrand could not be found in the entire army." At the same time the general told the story of Stolbrand's promotion to brigadier-general, which Mattson repeats as follows: Stolbrand had served in his corps for some time with the rank of major, and performed such services as properly belong to a colonel or brigadier-general without being promoted according to his merits, because there had been no vacancy in the regiment to which he belonged. Displeased with this, Stolbrand sent in his resignation, which was accepted, but Sherman had made up his mind not to let him leave the army, and asked him to go by way of Washington on his return home, pretending that he wished to send important dispatches to President Lincoln. In due time Stolbrand arrived in the capital and handed a sealed package to the President in person. Having looked the papers through. Lincoln ex-

General John A. Logan and Staff

tended his hand, exclaiming, "How do you do, General?" Stolbrand, correcting him, said, "I am no general; I am only a major." "You are mistaken," said Lincoln, "you are a general"—and he was from that moment. In a few hours he received his commission and later returned to the army with a rank three degrees higher than that held by him before.

After the war General Stolbrand took up his residence in South Carolina, locating at Beaufort, where he owned a plantation. In that once Confederate state the former Union commander attained prominence as a citizen, his allegiance to the Republican party always remaining unswerved. In 1868 he was elected secretary of the constitutional convention of the state. The same year he was delegate at large to the national Republican convention at Chicago and served as presidential elector. He was for some years superintendent of the state penitentiary and under Harrison's administration was superintendent of the United States government building in Charleston.

King Carl XV. of Sweden, in 1866, recognized Stolbrand's soldierly achievements by decorating him with the Royal Order of the Sword. While the latter part of his life was chiefly devoted to politics, Stolbrand was also engaged in mechanical inventions and made various improvements in steam engines and steam boilers.

He passed away in Charleston, Feb. 3, 1894, after having spent the winter months in New York. His remains were interred with military honors at Columbia, S. C., beside those of his wife. At the time of Stolbrand's death, three of his children were living in New York, and one married daughter, a Mrs. Strobel, in Atlanta, Ga.

One who was intimate with Gen. Stolbrand in his later years gave to the "News and Courier" of Charleston at the time of his death certain recollections, which tend to reveal some of the traits of the man. Stolbrand often spoke of his life in Sweden, particularly of his career as professor of horsemanship and sword exercises in the Swedish army, and claimed that he had drilled King Oscar II. while the latter was a cadet.* He said that the prince was very difficult to manage, but that he, Stolbrand, was upheld in his discipline of the young prince by the king, his father. Before entering the federal army, Stolbrand had been engaged in irrigation enterprises in the Northwest. He also related how he had invented a shoe of sufficient size to enable him to move about on water, carrying his military equipments, and had learned to use such a pair of shoes with dexterity and ease. While he resided in Columbia Stolbrand had fitted up in his watermelon patch a trap for thieves, so if they attempted to steal his melons the guns would go

* For this story the known facts in Stolbrand's life furnish not the slightest support. It merely betrays in him a fondness for making an impression in narrating past experiences, real or fancied.

off and kill them. In connection with stories of his army career in this country the general would show with great pride the burning-glass with which he claimed to have fired the gun that sent the first ball that struck the state-house in Columbia. He was an enthusiastic member of the Grand Army of the Republic and a firm believer in its patriotic objects.

To complete the account of Stolbrand's military career the following data, culled from the army records, are added as showing more precisely the functions performed by him during the war. As major, Stolbrand in September, 1862, is shown to have been in command of five batteries of Brig.-Gen. John A. Logan's artillery brigade in the district of Jackson, Tenn., and in November he had a brigade of nine batteries of Maj.-Gen. Stephen A. Hurlbut's division under him. He commanded five batteries in the siege of Vicksburg and the largest force under his command at any one time was ten batteries. Ample testimony of Stolbrand's usefulness in the operations before Vicksburg is given by Gen. Logan, who repeatedly compliments him in his report of May 26th, thus: "The admirable manner in which this battery was handled reflects the highest credit upon Maj. Stolbrand, my chief of artillery."—"The respective batteries. . . . under the personal supervision of Major Stolbrand rendered incalculable aid in effectually shelling the enemy."—"To Major Stolbrand, my chief of artillery, I am indebted for valuable aid."

In the Savannah, Ga., campaign, Nov. 15 to Dec. 31, 1864, Stolbrand took an efficient part. In the siege of Savannah, Stolbrand on Dec. 19th placed half of his batteries before the Confederate forts and uncovered and silenced the enemy's heavy batteries, whereupon the Confederates under cover of darkness abandoned the fort and the city, leaving guns and ammunition behind them. In his report a few days thereafter Maj. Gen. P. J. Osterhaus, of the 15th army corps, said: "To Major Stolbrand I have to acknowledge important services during the campaign as chief of artillery of the corps. Through his energy and skill that branch of the arms which was under his immediate care was in most excellent condition."

The one unfortunate incident in Stolbrand's army career occurred on May 19, 1864, when he fell into the hands of the enemy, while the Army of the Tennessee was encamped at Kingston, on the Etowah River. "While examining the surrounding country by my direction," says Maj. Gen. Logan in a report dated Sept. 4th, "Maj. C. J. Stolbrand, a gallant and untiring officer, was captured by a squad of the enemy's cavalry." No mention was then made of his return, but in October of that year he again figures in the reports as chief of artillery.

At his own request, Stolbrand was relieved from further duty as chief of artillery of the 15th army corps, at Beaufort, S. C., on Jan. 28,

1865, his three years' term of service having expired. In February his promotion to brigadier-general, as told by Sherman, took place. On March 30th, as brigadier-general, he was by the Secretary of War ordered to report in person to Maj. Gen. Sherman for assignment to duty. A month later he was placed in command of the second brigade, fourth division, 17th army corps, formed from the 14th, 15th and 32nd Ill. Vol. Inf. The brigade marched north from Raleigh, N. C., April 29th, passed in review through Washington May 24th, whence it was sent via Louisville and St. Louis to Fort Leavenworth. After brief service on the plains of the far West the three regiments were mustered out at Fort Leavenworth in September, terminating Stolbrand's command. One of his last assignments was to the temporary command of the Fort Leavenworth district in the absence of the general commanding. Brig.-Gen. Stolbrand continued to hold his commission until January, 1866, when he was mustered out of service.

The Swedish members of Stolbrand's Battery were: Oscar L. Ekvall of Chicago, enlisted Aug. 6, 1861, mustered in Oct. 5th, re-enlisted as veteran March 1, 1864, mustered out Sept. 4, 1865; Francis Lindebeck of Chicago, enlisted Aug. 6, 1861, mustered in Oct. 5th, drowned by sinking of the steamer Horizon on the Mississippi river, May 1, 1863; Claes Mathiason of Galesburg, enlisted Aug. 6, 1861, re-enlisted as veteran March 1, 1864, died at Montgomery, Ala., July 14, 1865; Charles J. Mellberg of Mendota, enlisted Aug. 6, 1861, re-enlisted as veteran March 1, 1864, discharged Aug. 7, 1865, as corporal, supernumerary; Sven August Videll of Chicago, enlisted Aug. 6, 1861, mustered out Oct. 4, 1864; Andrew Burgstrom of Chicago, enlisted Jan. 28, 1864, mustered out Sept. 4, 1865; Nicholas Carlson, enlisted and mustered in Jan. 1, 1862, drowned by sinking of the steamer Horizon on the Mississippi river May 1, 1863; Oscar Kelburg, enlisted and mustered in Sept. 13, 1864, mustered out June 3, 1865; Joseph Esbyorn of Chicago, enlisted Aug. 6, 1861, mustered in Oct. 5th, re-enlisted as veteran. Other members of the battery, apparently of Swedish blood, were, Olson L. Durkee of Chicago, Alfred Hall of Rockford and John Vehlen of Chicago.

Capt. Frederick Sparrestrom and Battery G, 2d Light Artillery

Frederick Sparrestrom enlisted at Chicago in the second company of artillery organized by Charles J. Stolbrand. When on Sept. 16, 1861, this company was mustered into service as Battery G, of the Second Light Artillery regiment, he was commissioned first lieutenant. The battery was recruited mostly from Sycamore, Chicago, DeKalb, Belvidere, Joliet and Rockford. Early in December the battery was ordered to Cairo, Ill., where it was assigned to Gen. Pain's division and furnished with two Napoleon and four Rodman guns. In the meantime the men were detailed to man the Howitzers used in the attacks on Forts Henry and Donelson.

Sparrestrom served as second in command until Dec. 31st, when, upon Stolbrand's promotion to major of the second artillery regiment,

Captain Frederick Sparrestrom

Sparrestrom succeeded to the captaincy. The battery served under Stolbrand, the chief of artillery in Logan's army, and was generally a part of the artillery brigades commanded by Stolbrand from time to time. On May 1, 1863, the battery was sunk in a collision, while being ferried across the Mississippi river to Bruinsburg, Miss. Two men and most of the horses were drowned. The battery was re-equipped at Memphis and returned to Gen. Logan by June 30th. In the interval Sparrestrom was detailed to take charge of Battery D, First Ill. Artillery, whose captain had been killed on May 29th, and whose lieutenant was sick. In this capacity he served during the month of June, participating in the siege of Vicksburg. About July 1st Sparrestrom resumed command of his own battery, which took part in several expeditions around Vicksburg. In December it moved to Union City and was engaged in the campaign against Gen. Forrest. Early the next spring it went to Columbus, Ky., where it was reorganized and veteranized. Returning, it took part in the expedition to Tupelo, Miss., and in July and August in the expeditions to Holly Springs and Oxford. In

BATTERY D, 1ST LIGHT ARTILLERY.

CAPT. HENRY A. ROGERS:
LIEUT. GEORGE J. WOOD;
CAPT. FREDERICK SPARRESTROM.
3D DIV., 17TH CORPS.

CASUALTIES:
CAPT. HENRY A. ROGERS WAS KILLED ON DUTY AT THE SITE OF THE ILLINOIS STATE MONUMENT, ABOUT MAY 29, 1863, WHERE THE "WHITE HOUSE BATTERY" SERVED, FIRING DURING THE SIEGE FROM THIS POSITION 5200 ROUNDS OF AMMUNITION.

ILLINOIS

Monument at Vicksburg National Military Park

September it joined Gen. A. J. Smith's army corps in pursuit of Gen. Price in Missouri. In November, 1864, it moved to Nashville and participated in the fighting of December 15th and 16th. From here it joined in the pursuit of the defeated Confederate army. The battery subsequently took part in the Mobile campaign and in the siege and capture of Fort Blakely. Sparrestrom resigned from the service Aug. 22, 1864, and the battery was mustered out Sept. 4, 1865. Sparrestrom, of whom we have no information beyond his military career, proved himself a gallant and skillful officer and rendered efficient service wherever placed during his three years in the army. Two of the Illinois monuments in the Vicksburg military park bear his name.

ARTILLERY

BATTERY "G" 2D ARTILLERY

SERVED DURING CAMPAIGN WITH 3D DIVISION, 17TH CORPS. MAY 1, 1863, IN A COLLISION OF TRANSPORTS LOST GUNS, EQUIPMENT AND HORSES. WENT TO MEMPHIS FOR REFITTING. RETURNED TO DIVISION ON INVESTMENT LINE JUNE 30. LOSS REPORTED: DROWNED 2.

CAPTAIN FRED. SPARRESTROM
1ST LIEUT. JOHN W. LOWELL

BATTERY "K" 2D ARTILLERY

SERVED DURING CAMPAIGN FROM ABOUT MAY 20, 1863, AND ON INVESTMENT LINE FROM ABOUT MAY 25, WITH 4TH DIVISION, 16TH CORPS

CAPTAIN BENJAMIN F. RODGERS
1ST LIEUT. FRANCIS M. ROSS
1ST LIEUT. ABEL S. GALE
2D LIEUT. WESLEY PLATT
2D LIEUT. JOHN PYATT

BATTERY "L" 2D ARTILLERY

SERVED DURING CAMPAIGN AND ON INVESTMENT LINE WITH 3D DIVISION, 17TH CORPS.

CAPTAIN WILLIAM H. BOLTON
1ST LIEUT. JABEZ H. MOORE
1ST LIEUT. SIMON P. TRACY
2D LIEUT. ORLANDO S. WOOD

CHICAGO MERCANTILE BATTERY

SERVED DURING CAMPAIGN AND ON INVESTMENT LINE WITH 10TH DIVISION, 13TH CORPS. LOSS REPORTED: WOUNDED 3.

CAPTAIN PATRICK H. WHITE
1ST LIEUT. GEORGE THROOP
1ST LIEUT. PINCKNEY S. CONE
2D LIEUT. JOSEPH W. BARR
2D LIEUT. HENRY ROE

COGSWELL'S BATTERY

SERVED DURING SIEGE ON EXTERIOR LINE, FROM ABOUT JUNE 12, 1863, WITH 1ST DIVISION, 16TH CORPS.

CAPTAIN WILLIAM COGSWELL
1ST LIEUT. HENRY G. EDDY
1ST LIEUT. WILLIAM R. ELTING

Tablet in Illinois State Memorial Temple, Vicksburg National Military Park

Lieutenant Joseph E. Osborn

Joseph E. Osborn has had a varied career in the army service as well as in civil life. He was born July 12, 1843, at Hille, Helsingland, Sweden, where his father, Rev. L. P. Esbjörn, then served as pastor and schoolmaster. The family came to America in 1849, locating in Andover, Ill. The son Joseph attended Capital University for a short period at the age of eleven, then worked on "Hemlandet" as typo and roller boy, when that paper was started in Galesburg. In 1858-60 he studied at the Illinois State University at Springfield, where his father taught.

Lieutenant Joseph E. Osborn

While there he became acquainted in a boyish way with Abraham Lincoln and more intimately so with his son Robert, who attended the same school. The Esbjörn family having removed to Chicago in 1860, Joseph worked at the printer's trade until the war broke out, when he enlisted immediately in a company recruited by Charles J. Stolbrand. The quota being already filled, the company was not accepted, but at the second call for volunteers Stolbrand again raised a company, which young Esbjörn joined Aug. 12, 1861. He served with this organization, known as Battery G., Second Ill. Light Artillery, until July, 1863, when, after the siege of Vicksburg, he was placed on detached service at Gen. Logan's headquarters, where he served for several months.

During this time Stolbrand offered Osborn the captaincy in the 11th Miss. Inf., a colored regiment, which he declined and rejoined the battery. Early in 1864 he applied to be examined for a commission in a colored regiment and, after passing the examination at Memphis, Tenn., was commissioned second lieutenant and assigned to Co. G., 4th U. S. Heavy Artillery, colored, in garrison at Columbus, Ky. He was at once appointed on the staff of Maj.-Gen. Ord, commander of the department of the Mississippi, and placed in charge of the U. S. ordnance depot at Columbus, a responsible place for a man of twenty-one. Relieved of the command after eight months, he was appointed post commissary at the same point, to succeed Maj. Overton. When relieved

Monument at Vicksburg National Military Park

of his duties as such, he was made provost marshal of the Freedmen's Bureau. He again rejoined the regiment late in the fall of 1865, when ordered to Arkansas, where it was mustered out Feb. 5, 1866, Osborn being at the time in command of a company, although not holding a captain's commission.

Osborn, after a visit north, took charge of a store in Corinth, Miss., owned by Gen. Eaton. In 1867 he visited his relatives in Sweden, returning the following year, when he became cashier and general book-keeper for the American Emigrant Co., and in 1869 traveling repre-

sentative for the company. He was sent to Sweden in 1871 by the
C. B. & Q. Railway Co., to advertise their lands in Iowa and Nebraska,
and remained two years. On his return he opened a steamship ticket
and foreign exchange office and importing and exporting agency, and
was laying the foundation for a very promising business when, during
his absence in the West, the stealings of a confidential clerk caused his
failure.

Osborn in 1874 associated himself with two clergymen, J. G.
Princell and A. Hult, for the purpose of founding "Barnvännen," a
juvenile paper published in Chicago for a number of years. In 1875-6
he was organist of the Swedish Lutheran Church of Boston. While
there he was married, Sept. 19, 1876, to Miss Anna I. Bergström. From
1877 to 1883 he served as school teacher and organist of his father's old
charge in Andover, Ill.

Osborn was associated with Capt. Eric Johnson in the publishing
of "The Swedish Citizen," a paper finally named "The Daily and
Weekly Moline Citizen." In 1883 he severed his connection with the
publication and removed to St. Paul to become manager of "Skaffaren" ("Minnesota Stats-Tidning"). In that city he now holds a position in the office of the State Auditor.

Captain Andrew Stenbeck

Captain Andrew Stenbeck, who commanded Battery H, 2nd Illinois
Light Artillery from date of muster Dec. 31, 1861, until his resignation
May 25, 1863, was a native of Hafvaröd, Skåne, Sweden, where he was
born Feb. 12, 1828. Emigrating in 1854, he settled in Galesburg. In
December, 1861, having enlisted as a volunteer, he organized the battery
at Camp Butler, Springfield, and on the last of the month received his
captain's commission, partly through the influence of C. J. Stolbrand,
then captain of Co. G, 2nd Ill. Artillery, and a former comrade in arms
in the Swedish army. Captain Stenbeck fought at Fort Donelson,
Shiloh, Clarksville, Nashville, and led his company through a number of other operations in the Tennessee campaign. After having
resigned his command, Stenbeck located in St. Louis, where he served
as superintendent of Benton Barracks until 1866, when in the piping
time of peace he removed to Chicago and became a piano tuner. Capt.
Stenbeck had a desire to enter the regular army, and after peace was
restored applied to Johnson for a captaincy, which was denied, the
President offering him the rank of first lieutenant, which Stenbeck
declined. All through his vocation as a tuner, Capt. Stenbeck worked
in connection with the firm of Julius Bauer and Company. He was an
amateur violinist of no mean talent. To relieve the strain on his nerves
and hearing incident to his vocation, he secured an appointment as

deputy under Sheriff Mattson, but failing health compelled him to resign the position after a few months, resuming his former employ-

Captain Andrew Stenbeck

ment. He passed away at his home in Chicago Dec. 14, 1891, leaving a widow, Mrs. Caroline Stenbeck, and three children, of whom a son, Edward Stenbeck, of Denver, Colo., survives.

Capt. Axel Silfversparre and Battery H, 1st Regt. Light Artillery

In 1861, at the outbreak of the war, Axel Silfversparre, a former lieutenant of the Svea Artillery Regiment in the Swedish Army, left in order to go to the United States to fight for the Union cause. He received his commission from Gen. John C. Fremont, who at once put the knowledge and experience of the young Swedish artillery officer to good use. Silfversparre was first sent to Fort

Fremont, at Cape Girardeau, Mo., to put a number of heavy artillery pieces in place. This duty done, Silfversparre, burning with an ambition to distinguish himself in the war, went to Illinois on leave, intent on organizing a Swedish battery. On Dec. 25, 1861, he secured from the state authorities a commission to that effect and during the next two months, accompanied by John A. Anderson of Chicago, he made a recruiting tour of the Swedish settlements in the state, starting with Chicago and visiting Rockford, St. Charles, Batavia, Geneva, Sycamore, DeKalb, Princeton, Galva, Bishop Hill, Andover, Moline, Knoxville, Victoria, Galesburg, and other places. Swedish-Americans to the number of fifty joined him, besides a larger number of men of ten other nationalities. These volunteers met in Chicago to complete the organization, when the organizer, Silfversparre himself, was elected captain, while all the subordinate offices were given to men of other than Swedish descent.

Silfversparre was a scion of the Swedish nobility. His parents were Viscount Gustaf Johan Silfversparre, an ex-lieut.-colonel of the Royal Horse Guards, and his wife, Countess Sophie Mörner of Morlanda. He was born in the city of Strängnäs May 8, 1834, and educated at the Upsala University. After his graduation from college in 1852 he became a non-commissioned officer of the Svea Artillery, and was promoted second lieutenant the following year. He served in the regiment at Stockholm, Vaxholm and Hernösand until 1858, when he entered the artillery academy of Marieberg, continuing his studies until 1860. He is said to have been one of a number of army officers who after having been engaged in a fracas with civilians in Stockholm, were court-martialed and degraded. Shortly thereafter he came to the United States and was employed in Missouri as army engineer before enlisting in the volunteer army.

Captain Silfversparre's Command

The battery was mustered in at Camp Douglas, Chicago, on Feb. 20th, 1862, as Battery H, First Illinois Light Artillery, commanded by Col. Joseph D. Webster. Early in March it was ordered to Benton Barracks, Mo., where the men were given three weeks' drill and the battery was provided with four 20-pound Parrott guns. By boat they were then sent south to join the army of the Tennessee. The battery reached Pittsburg Landing on April 5th, the day before the battle. It was given a place in the center of a line of artillery protecting the landing, and aided materially in beating back the last assaults of the rebels on the first day's battle. Silfversparre here put his Swedish military training to excellent use and displayed great skill and bravery.

Silfversparre had, according to his own memoranda of the battle, most carefully prepared for the reception of the enemy, differing in that respect, as we have seen, from most of the other Union officers in that fatal affray. At that time the Swedish artillery was in point of equipment rather in advance of that of the Union army. Patterning after the Svea Artillery, Silfversparre had furnished his men with spades, picks and axes, and having planted his cannon, he had them well protected by walls of earth and logs built up in front.* To those who thought he took needless pains he explained, "My battery is put to stay, not to run." Another arrangement of his was to mount his gunners on the horses hitched to the guns so as to be instantly on hand, instead of following with the ammunition wagons. By putting handles on the sponge-heads he made it possible to reload without danger while the guns were still hot from the last discharge, thereby enabling his men to fire about five shots in the time otherwise required for one. While in St. Louis he had procured at his own expense fuses of varied length, and when in this battle the enemy closed in on his position he used the shortest lengths, with the result that when General Chalmers' column charged the battery, it was met by a blizzard of shrapnel which made further advance impossible, and the enemy was forced back with great loss. Silfversparre was personally thanked by Grant and Sherman that day for his part in checking the advance of the enemy, but like most of the heroes of the day, received no mention in Grant's report of the battle.

These arrangements are said to have rendered him many compliments in the press, which in turn aroused the envy of the other artillery officers. Twice he was court-martialed on the trumped-up charge of cruelty to the horses and wasteful handling of the ordnance stores and material, but was acquitted both times, and complimented upon his skillful tactics.

Shortly after the battle of Shiloh the Silfversparre battery was transferred to General Sherman's division and subsequently belonged to the second division of the 15th army corps until the close of the war. At the first inspection Gen. Sherman rejected the "newfangled things" introduced by Silfversparre with instructions to equip the battery in the regular way. This was done, but after the second shot subsequently fired by the battery a man lost his hand in a premature explosion of a load, all because of the absence of the handle to the sponge-head.

In September, 1862, Capt. Silfversparre was assigned to Fort

* A survivor of Battery H states as his recollection that sacks of grain and feed from the commissary stores, stacked up in front of the guns, afforded the only protection against the enemy's fire. Major Reed's account of the battle corroborates the survivor's impression in these words: "We find at Shiloh that with three exceptions no breastworks were prepared by either side on Sunday night. Of these exceptions a Union battery near the Landing was protected by a few sacks of corn piled up in front of the guns."

Pickering, near Memphis, Tenn. He was detailed by Gen. Sherman on Sept. 16th to take charge of the fixed and permanent batteries in the fort and instructed to mount and equip heavy guns, besides supervising the appurtenances of the lighter guns. The officers of the

Captain Axel Silfversparre

batteries were to be instructed by him in the manual of the guns. Sherman further directed him to instruct or supervise the drill of two of the companies and to personally drill the other two companies daily. In case of action, Silfversparre was to command the four companies. About the beginning of the next year he was also assigned as drill-

Tablet in Illinois State Memorial Temple, Vicksburg National Military Park

ARTILLERY

BATTERY "H"- 1ST ARTILLERY

SERVED DURING CAMPAIGN AND ON INVESTMENT LINE WITH 2D DIVISION, 15TH CORPS.
LOSS REPORTED, KILLED 1.

BATTERY "I"- 1ST ARTILLERY

SERVED DURING SIEGE ON EXTERIOR LINE, FROM ABOUT JUNE 12, 1863,
WITH 1ST DIVISION, 16TH CORPS.

BATTERY "A" - 2D ARTILLERY

SERVED DURING CAMPAIGN AND ON INVESTMENT LINE WITH 14TH DIVISION, 13TH CORPS.
LOSS REPORTED, KILLED 1.

BATTERY "E"- 2D ARTILLERY

SERVED DURING CAMPAIGN FROM ABOUT MAY 20, 1863, AND ON INVESTMENT LINE
WITH 4TH DIVISION, 16TH CORPS.

BATTERY "F"- 2D ARTILLERY

SERVED DURING CAMPAIGN AND ON INVESTMENT LINE
WITH 6TH DIVISION, 17TH CORPS.

master of General Hurlbut's division, encamped four miles distant. Apparently doubtful of his ability to attend to his complex duties, he resigned his commission Feb. 22nd, to take a position in another department of the army. But before his transfer he had the misfortune of being captured by the Confederates.

Like many other officers, Silfversparre engaged in a little private speculation. While out in the country alone one day buying up cotton, which at that time brought high prices, he encountered a band of bush-whackers and was taken prisoner after killing one of his antagonists. He was threatened with hanging, when a squad of cavalry interfered and carried him off to Jackson, Miss. There he was granted an interview with Gen. Joseph E. Johnston, who sent him to the Libby prison at Richmond, with other prisoners of war. After having endured inhuman treatment there for ten months he made good his escape by bribing a guard, whose uniform he donned and, after having secured a pass at the military headquarters, went south to Wilmington, S. C. There he engaged as engineer on the blockade runner Cornubia, which was chased by Union vessels the better part of the way to the Bermudas. Such was the closing episode in Capt. Silfversparre's military career.

Death of Sergeant Wyman

Capt. Levi W. Hart, who succeeded to the command of the Silfversparre battery, was followed by Francis De Gress, from Cape Girardeau, Mo., the oldest second lieutenant, who was promoted to the chief command of the battery Dec. 25th of the same year. Under him the battery took active part in all the engagements of the second division of the 15th Army Corps and was one of its working batteries at Vicksburg, Mission Ridge and Atlanta. The battery especially distinguished itself for brilliant work at the taking of the latter city July 21-22, 1864, but lost in that engagement Sergeant Peter S. Wyman, one of its most efficient men. The batteries of the brigade were posted in a semi-circle, De Gress' battery holding one of the flanks. The unionists were confronted by a force of rebels five times their own number, which made an irresistible charge. The brigade commander therefore ordered a retreat, and all but Capt. De Gress and Sergeant Wyman fell back. The two stuck to the guns to give the rebels a few parting shots. This done, De Gress turned and ran, but Wyman, not yet satisfied, reloaded for a final warm farewell. Then he spiked the gun and sought safety in flight, but fell the next instant, pierced by three musket balls. The battery, captured by the enemy, was soon retaken, and its guns again pointed at the Confederates, who now made reverse tracks faster than they had stormed forward just before.

Under the command of De Gress, Battery H, henceforth known as De Gress' Battery, added to its laurels and became a very famous one in Gen. Sherman's command. From Atlanta, it participated in the march to the sea, and finally marched in review before the President at Washington and was mustered out at Springfield June 14, 1865. The surviving members of the battery are said to have been a unit in praise of Silfversparre as a commander as brave as any and a tactician of

Sergeant Peter S. Wyman

more than average skill, but they were of the opinion that his ironclad Swedish discipline was impracticable in a citizen army of volunteers.

Peter S. Wyman (Yman), who died a hero's death before Atlanta, was born at Ysanna, Blekinge, Sweden, in 1836, and emigrated in 1854, locating in Galesburg, where he was working as a blacksmith, when the war broke out. When on his recruiting tour Silfversparre reached Galesburg, Wyman was one of the first to apply. Enlisting as a private, he soon became sergeant. Had he lived one day longer, he would have been promoted, his appointment to a lieutenancy having reached his chief the very same day that Wyman lost his life. Capable, brave, patriotic, Wyman had the making of a good artillery officer, and his comrades in arms looked for him to rise to high rank in the service. His remains rest in an unmarked spot on the battlefield where he fell.

In the battle of Atlanta Peter Larson, Gustaf Ahlstrand and S. A. Lundgren fell into the enemy's hands. What became of the two last named is not recorded, but Larson had to spend several months amid the horrors of Andersonville prison, before he was transferred to more tolerable quarters.

BATTERY H,
1ST LIGHT ARTILLERY.

CAPT. LEVI W. HART.
2D DIV., 15TH CORPS.

CASUALTIES:
SKIRMISHES, MAY 18, 20 AND 21, 1863.
KILLED 1.

ILLINOIS

Monument at Vicksburg National Military Park

Peter B. Larson of Silfversparre's Battery, who was mustered out as corporal, located in Chicago after the war and as general agent of the National Line, became extensively known among his fellow countrymen. He was born at Axeltorp, Skåne, Sweden, March 31, 1843, and came along with his parents to this country in 1854. The family located in Galesburg, where Peter Larson enlisted. He was captured at Atlanta and was a prisoner at Andersonville, Charleston and Florence until the close of the war. Upon his return home he took a four years' course of study at the Illinois Soldiers' College at Fulton, prior to engaging in the steamship ticket business. He died about April, 1881.

From Atlanta the battery was ordered to Savannah, participating in the capture of Fort McAllister, and thence to Columbia, which was destroyed by fire supposed to have been started by a random shot fired by this battery. At Bentonville Battery H had its last fight.

While the battery lay at Savannah the term of enlistment expired and all but eight men of the battery re-enlisted. The eight took the steamer General Lyon for New York, but never reached home, the vessel being burned at sea March 31, 1865. All on board perished, including Charles Beckman and John Johanson of Chicago, Peter Olson Hult of St. Charles and Peter Munson of Knoxville.

About the time of re-enlistment, battery H was given a brief furlough. Its Swedish members then went home to Illinois in a body and were accorded a public reception in Chicago, and presented with a handsome parade flag, emblazoned with the names of the three great victories—Shiloh, Vicksburg, Atlanta.

Silfversparre's Civil Career

From the Bermudas Silfversparre betook himself to New York and there met Col. W. W. Adams, who promised to make him his assistant in the construction of the Union Pacific railway projected by Gen. Fremont and of which Adams was to have been chief engineer. When the project failed, owing to the murder of Fremont's chief financial backer, Adams and Silfversparre collaborated on plans for a suspension bridge across East River, which plans were afterwards used by the war department and the New York legislature in planning the Brooklyn bridge.

Toward the close of 1864 Silfversparre was engaged as engineer of the Quincy copper mine in Michigan. In 1865 he became assistant city engineer of Chicago, a place retained for several years. In the great fire he lost his home and everything he owned, including a number of instruments. The year following he helped to draw the new city plans. He was nominated on the police board that year, but failed of election, and also suffered defeat as a candidate for county surveyor in 1876. Having left the city engineer's office, he was engaged in preparing a commercial atlas of Illinois in 1877 and during part of the next two years worked under Gen. McDowell, who superintended the construction of the federal building in Chicago.

Going to Colorado in 1880, Capt. Silfversparre drew plans for the city of Denver that year, and the next made the survey for the Denver and Rio Grande railway over the Rockies to the Utah border. A map of the state of Colorado, with a supplement covering the mining districts, was worked out by him in 1882 and printed in Chicago under his supervision the following year. A map of the city of Washington was next undertaken, but the work being interrupted, he secured a position in 1886 as draftsman in the Department of Agriculture. The next year the map of the capital city was completed and published.

Owing to failing strength, Capt. Silfversparre in 1888 sought admittance to the soldiers' home at Hampton, Va., where the veteran spent eight years, being subsequently transferred to the home at Dayton, O., where he was chosen commandant in 1897. Having been pensioned, he made a trip to Sweden in 1898. After his return he was engaged in Chicago on a large wall map of Sweden, drawn according to the latest maps issued by the Swedish general staff.

Again laying down the draftsman's pen, he entered the soldiers' home at Danville, Ill., where he passed away March 2, 1906, and was buried with military honors. Capt. Axel Silfversparre was married in 1866 to Mary Jane Gunning of Chicago. Their union was dissolved in 1884. Of their three children, Servais Zacharias Silfversparre, a lawyer, is the publisher of a mining journal, "Ores and Metals," at Denver.

Roster of Battery H, First Illinois Artillery

With the exception of the officers, only Swedish names are given

Name and Rank	Residence	Date of rank or enlistment	Remarks
Captains			
Axel Silfversparre	Springfield	Dec. 25, '61	Resigned Feb. 22, '63
Levi W. Hart	Chicago	Feb. 22, '63	Discharged Dec. 25, '63
Francis DeGress	C. Girardeau Mo.	Dec. 25, '63	Pro. by President Brevet Major, Mar. 13, '65, M. O. June 14, '65
First Lieutenants			
Lewis B. Mitchell	Chicago	Feb. 1, '62	Resigned April 14, '65
George G. Knox	"	March 6, '62	Discharged Nov. 1, '62
Robert S. Gray	Erie, Penn	Dec. 25, '63	Promoted Senior 1st Lieuten't
Robert S. Gray	"	June 12, '65	Mustered out June 14, '65
Second Lieutenants			
Francis DeGress	C. Girardeau, Mo	Jan. 1, '62	Promoted Captain
Edward Adams	Springfield	Feb. 1, '62	Killed July 10, '63
Lewis Larson	Knoxville	June 13, '65	Mustered out June 14, '65
Henry Meyers	C. Girardeau Mo	"	M. O. June 14, '65, as Sergeant
First Sergeant			
John R. Scupham	Chicago	Feb. 5, '62	Re-enlisted as Veteran
Sergeants			
William E. Merritt	Chicago	Jan. 28, '62	Private. Drowned at sea by burning of steamer Gen'l Lyon, March 31, '65
John A. Anderson	"	Jan. 6, '62	Re-enlisted as Veteran
Lewis Larson	Knoxville	Jan. 27, '62	" "
Henry O. Olson	Chicago	Feb. 12, '62	" "
Peter Olson	Rockford	Jan. 13, '62	" "
Daniel E. Steward	Chicago	Feb. 20, '62	Discharged Dec. 14, '62, as private; disability

Name and Rank	Residence	Date of rank or enlistment	Remarks
Privates			
Abrahamson John..	Rockford......	Feb. 25, '62	Dis. Oct. 7, '62; disability....
Anderson Andrew..	Andover......	"	Dis. Sept. 14, '62; disability...
Anderson Peter.....	Galesburg.....	Jan. 15, '62	Died, Pittsburg Ldg. May 9, '62
Anderson John A...	Moline.........	Jan. 29, '62	Re-enlisted as Veteran........
Alstrand Gustav....	Andover......	Jan. 28, '62	" "
Anderson Thomas..	Chemung.....	Jan. 28, '62	Died, Memphis, Aug. 21, '62..
Anderson Anders E.	Chicago	Feb. 21, '62	Disch. Oct. 24, '62; disability.
Buckland John J....	Rockford......	Jan. 15, '62	Re-enlisted as Veteran........
Beckman Charles...	Chicago	Feb. 24, '62	Drowned at sea by burning of the steamer General Lyon, March 31, '65.............
Charleson N. Peter.	Rock Island...	Feb. 25, '62	Re-enlisted as Veteran........
Charleson Aaron ...	Andover......	Jan. 28, '62	" "
Erickson Sven.....	Knoxville.....	Feb. 26, '65	Died at Memphis, Sept. 19, '62.
Godee Seth........	Galena	March 2, '62	Deserted.....................
Hultgreen N John	Andover......	Jan. 28, '62	Disch. Oct. 20, '62; disability.
Hult Peter Olson...	St. Charles....	Feb. 5, '62	Drowned at sea by burning of the steamer General Lyon, March 31, '65.............
Hagerstrom John C.	Chicago	Feb. 4, '62	Re-enlisted as Veteran........
Högberg Olof......	"	Feb. 28, '62	Disch. June 19, '63; disability.
Johannson John....	"	Feb. 24, '62	Drowned at sea by burning of the steamer General Lyon, March 31, '65.............
Johnson Johannes..	....	Feb. 24, '62	....
Johann August.....	Chicago	Feb. 22, '62	
Johnson John A....	Rockford......	Jan. 13, '62	Deserted....................
Johnson Carl Peter.	Moline	Jan. 31, '62	Died near Corinth, May 17, '62
Johnson C. Julius..	Chicago	Jan. 20, '62	Re-enlisted as Veteran........
Johnson August....	....	Jan. 22, '62	" "
Johnson Axel......	Chicago	Jan. 23, '62	" "
Johnson Andrew J..	"	Jan. 26, '62	" "
Larson Peter......	Galesburg.....	Jan. 27, '62	" "
Larson Ch W......	Andover.......	"	" "
Lindman Axel.....	Moline	Jan. 30, '62	" "
Landström John....	Knoxville..:...	Feb. 26, '62	Deserted.....................
Löfgren Charles...	Andover.......	Feb. 25, '62	Re-enlisted as Veteran........
Lundgren S. A.....	"	"	" "
Lindquist C........	"	"	Died, Vicksburg, Nov. 20, '63.
Munson Peter......	Knoxville.....	Feb. 19, '62	Drowned at sea by burning of the steamer General Lyon, March 31, '65.............
Nelson August.....	Rock Island...	Feb. 25, '62	Deserted.....................
Nelson John.......	Galesburg.....	Feb. 25, '62	Re-enlisted as Veteran........
Nero Samuel John..	Geneva........	March 4, '62	" "
Olson Abraham....	Andover.......	Jan. 27, '62	" "
Oberg Peter Alfred.	Rockford......	Jan. 15, '62	" "
Olson Gustaf.......	Chicago	March 2, '62	" "
Peters John........	Rockford......	Feb. 25, '62	" "
Peterson Sven......	Chicago	Jan. 26, '62	" "
Swanson S. M.....	Andover.......	Jan. 28, '62	Died, Andover. Ill., Sept. 17,'63
Swanson Nels P....		"	Re-enlisted as Veteran........
Stark Peter........	Chicago	March 2, '62	" "
Winlöf N..........	"	Jan. 28, '62	Died, Memphis, Nov. 19, '62..
Wyman Peter S....	Galesburg.....	Feb. 26, '62	Re-enltsted as Veteran........
Westerland E A....	Andover.......	Jan. 28, '62	Died at Camp Sherman, Miss., Sept. 4, '63.............
Wahlborg Louis....	Rockford......	Jan. 15, '62	Re-enlisted as Veteran........
Veterans Mustered out June 14, 1865, except as noted.			
Anderson John A...	Chicago	Feb. 27, '64	Disch. Jan. 4, '65; disability..

Name and Rank	Residence	Date of rank or enlistment	Remarks
Veterans			
Anderson John A...	Chicago........	Feb. 27, '64	M. O. June 14, '65, as Corporal
Alstrand Gustaf....	"	"	
Buckland John J...	"	March 6, '64	M. O. June 14, '65, as Corporal
Benson Henk......	"	"	"
Charleson Aaron...	"	Feb. 27, '64	" "
Charleson N. Peter.	Rock Island...	"	Died in the field, Ga.,Oct. 4, '64
Hagerström John C.	Chicago	Feb. 27, '64	Died, Chattanooga, Nov. 15, '64
Johnson C. Julius..	"	"	
Johnson August....	"	"	
Johnson Andrew J.	"	"	
Johnson Axel......	"	"	Abs't, wounded, at M. O. of Bat.
Larson Peter.......	"	"	M. O. June 14, '65, as Corpor'l
Larson Louis.......	Knoxville.....	"	" " as Sergeant
			" " as Co. Q.
			M. Serg't. Com. 2d Lieut.,
Larson Charles N..	"	"	but not mustered........
Lindman Axel.....	"	"	
Löfgren Charles....	Andover.......	"	
Lemgren John A...	Chicago	"	
Nero Samuel J.....	"	March 6, '64	
Nelson John.......	"	Feb. 27, '64	
Olson Abraham....	"	"	
Olson H. Olof......	"	"	Disch. March 24, '65; disability
Oberg Peter Alfred.	Rockford.....	"	
Olson Peter........	Chicago	"	
Olson Gustaf......	"	March 6, '64	M. O. June 14, '65, as Sergeant.
Peters John........	"	Feb. 27, '64	
Peterson Sven......	"	"	
Stark Peter........	"	March 6, '64	
Swanson Nels P....	"	Feb. 27, '64	Corp'l. Died in Ala. June 7,'64
Wahlborg Louis....	"	"	M. O. June 14, '62, as Sergeant.
Wyman Peter S....	"	"	Serg't. Killed in battle July 22,'64
Recruits			
Anderson John.....	Chicago	March 30, '65	
Anderson Henry....	Rockford......	March 4, '62	Deserted April 6, '62.........
Anderson N J......	Chicago	March 2, '62	
Danielson August..	"	April 21, '64	
Godee Seth	"	Aug. 11, '64	M. O. June 14, '65, as Corporal
Johnson Samuel....	"	March 30, '64	
Johnson Sven J....	Galesburg	Feb. 1, '62	Deserted............
Lindwall August...	Rockford......	March 5, '62	"
Lindwall Lewis.....	Andover.......	March 2, '62	" ....
Nelson Peter.......	Geneva........	March 4, '62	" . April 6, '62.........
Olson John........	Chicago	March 30, '62	
Olson Nils........	"	March 6, '62	
Okerson William...	"	March 30, '64	
Peterson John G...	"	"	
Pearson Olof.......	Rockford......	March 5, '62	Deserted............
Svenson Sven......	Chicogo	March 30, '64	Disch. Oct. 20, '62; disability..
Sword Andrew.....	"	April 22, '64	Absent, sick, at M. O. of Batt'y
Trägårdh Lewis....	"	March 30, '64	Mustered out July 3. '65......

Captain Carl Arosenius

Carl Arosenius, whose antecedents we have been unable to trace, was a resident of Galesburg. In 1859 he became editor of "Frihets-vännen," a Swedish newspaper of Baptist tendencies, and appears to have been in charge of the paper until it ceased publication after a year. Arosenius was a college bred man from Sweden and has been credited with considerable ability as a writer. He had laid down the pen some time before taking up the sword in defense of the Union cause. On July 17, 1861, he enlisted and was mustered in as corporal of Co. A. in a regiment recruited in Missouri, and afterwards credited to Illinois as the 59th. Arosenius was promoted quartermaster sergeant Dec. 1st that year, serving as such until the following autumn, when, on Oct. 9th, at Bolivar, Tenn., he was transferred to the 43rd regiment and made captain of Co. C., to succeed Capt. Edvall, who had died of wounds received in the battle of Shiloh. At the end of his three-year term, he re-enlisted, as did almost all the members of Co. C., and remained in command of the company, which was known as Co. A., after consolidation of the 43rd regiment, until mustered out on Nov. 30, 1865. His war record is a part of the history of the company he so gallantly led. After the war Capt. Arosenius is known to have joined in establishing the Swedish weekly "Svenska Amerikanaren" of Chicago, in 1866, and he is said to have aspired to the editorial position with that paper which was tendered to Col. Mattson of Minnesota. The subsequent career of Arosenius we are unable to trace for want of data. He is said to have died in Chicago not many years after the close of the war.

Lieutenant John H. Ekstrand

One of those Swedish-American veterans, whose names deserve to grace the roll of honor for gallant service, was Lieutenant John H. Ekstrand. He was born Dec. 24, 1828, in Göteborg, Sweden, and there obtained a college education, then taught public school until he enlisted in the Göta Artillery, where he was promoted sergeant. He went to sea in 1851, was for a time in England, then shipped for Egypt and had a siege of severe illness at Alexandria. Returning to Liverpool, he shipped for the United States and came to New York early in 1854. At Buffalo he met Capt. C. M. Lindgren and sailed on one of his schooners that summer. After two years of errant existence he came to Chicago in 1856. Here he fell bravely to studying the English language, was soon married to a widowed lady, Katarina Johnson, whereupon the pair settled on a small farm at Beaver, Ill. There Ekstrand served as school teacher for two years. One Christmas morning he heard a stirring sermon by a Methodist preacher, which effected his conversion. In his spiritual exaltation he began preaching the same day and was soon duly licensed as a preacher of the Swedish Methodist Church. On Sept. 20th, 1861, Ekstrand enlisted for volunteer service as a private in the 51st Ill. Vol. Inf. regiment. At the muster-in Dec. 24, 1861, he was made sergeant of Co. C., and was detailed to service as orderly. He was with the regiment in the thick of the fight at Stone River, and after the battle of Mission Ridge, Nov. 24, 1863, Ekstrand's gallantry and military capacity were brought to the attention of his superiors. Upon Sherman's recommendation, Grant promoted him to second lieutenant in the 13th regiment of the regular army. In the battle of Franklin, Tenn., Nov. 30, 1864, he received an ugly wound in the leg, necessitating the amputation of the limb and compelling his retirement from the service. He resigned after having bravely served the Union for three years and three months. The mutilated veteran

Lieutenant John H. Ekstrand

re-entered the service of the church militant as a Methodist preacher, and during the next fifteen years served the Swedish churches in Leland, Victoria, Andover, Geneseo and Beaver. In 1879 he was retired, being declared superannuated when but fifty-one years old.

In the year 1890, or prior, he removed to Seattle, Wash., where he attained some consequence as a politician. Being a maimed veteran, he had little difficulty in securing fairly lucrative positions. He was alternately clerk of court, under Judge Ashburn, private secretary to Mayor

Phelps and held a position in the county clerk's office. Ekstrand passed away April 11, 1902, leaving a widow tolerably well provided for.

Even late in life Ekstrand, although an invalid, was an exceptionally agile man, and still bore the stamp of the rough and ready fighter, with no traces of the meek and sanctimonious divine. His gifts as a public speaker, which were not small, he devoted in his latter years to the cause of politics. He entered with great zest into the American Protective Association movement while that was at its height. He was an extreme and uncompromising Republican, and is said to have expressed a desire to forego the eternal bliss of heaven, should a single Democrat be admitted to that sacred realm.

Officers and Men of Various Regiments

Adjutant John E. Youngberg, who was of a pioneer Swedish family of Galesburg and Galva, enlisted in Co. H., 57th Ill., Oct. 2, 1861, and was mustered into the service on Dec. 26th. He was promoted sergeant-major Dec. 27, 1863, and mustered as such Jan. 17, 1864. On Dec. 30th of the same year he was promoted adjutant and served in that capacity until mustered out July 7, 1865.

Capt. Herman Lund enlisted as a private in Co. H, 16th Ill., from St. Joseph, Mo., on May 24, 1861; was promoted second lieutenant June 28th, 1862, and given a captain's commission Aug. 2nd the same year. His subsequent promotion to major of the regiment did not go into effect because he was not mustered in. On July 8, 1865, he was mustered out as captain of Co. H.

Lieutenant John Lindroth of Co. G., 43rd Ill., was killed in the first day's battle of Shiloh, April 6th, 1862. He enlisted Sept. 1, 1861, and was made 2nd lieutenant at the organization and muster-in of the regiment the following 16th day of December.

Capt. Axel F. Eckstrom, who commanded Co. G. of the 65th Ill. for two years, enlisted as a resident of Cook county. He held the rank of 1st lieutenant from Nov. 1, 1862, until May 31st the following year, when he succeeded to the captaincy to fill a vacancy caused by resignation. He was mustered out April 25, 1865.

Capt. Jonas F. Lempke began earning his shoulder-straps as a private in Battery B., First Ill. Artillery, which was organized in April, 1861, and mustered in July 16th. With this battery, which began its career at Belmont, going into the fight with six guns and coming out with eight after demolishing the balance of the enemy's battery, and did excellent work throughout the campaign, Lempke served until Nov. 30, 1863, when he was discharged as corporal for promotion. He afterwards attained the rank of captain.

Col. Steelhammar, mentioned in Mattson's memoirs, appears to
have entered the service in Illinois, though he is not shown to have
attained that rank in the rosters of this state. One Charles Stillham-
mer of McLean county enlisted July 25, 1861, as a private in Co. K. of
the Eight Ill. Inf., and re-enlisted as a veteran. He was promoted 2nd
lieutenant Nov. 25, 1864, or, according to another statement, 1st lieutenant from corporal. The adjutant-general's report of Illinois gives
no further record of promotion.

Lieut. Nels Nelson of Galesburg served in the ranks of Co. C. of
the 43rd Ill. Inf. until at the expiration of three years the regiment was

Lieutenant Nels Nelson   Corporal Peter Larson

consolidated, when he was promoted to the rank of 1st lieutenant of
the company, now Co. A., dating from March 3, 1865. He was mustered
out of the service Nov. 30, 1865. He was for many years a merchant
and subsequently managed the head office of a mutual life association,
as told elsewhere in a biographical sketch.

Private John J. Engberg, of a family well-known to the first
generation of Swedish settlers in the West, enlisted before attaining
military age. On his way to the recruiting office he chanced to cross
Kinzie street bridge, which had just been closed by the tender, Charles
Lindholm, an acquaintance from Minnesota. "Where are you bound
for, John?" said he. "To the recruiting office, to enlist." Lindholm
threw down the turning bar saying: "Wait till I get my coat, and I
am with you." Before that night, Nov. 12, 1863, the two were mustered
in Co. D, Eighty-ninth Illinois Infantry, popularly called "the Railroad
Regiment" because it was originally made up of railroad men.

After drilling two months at the instruction camp at Springfield, Engberg was sent to his regiment, then stationed at Chattanooga, preparatory to taking part in General Sherman's famous "March to the Sea." Engberg fought in the battles of Rocky Face, Resaca, Pickett's Mills, Kenesaw Mountain, and Peach Tree Creek. The latter engagement took place July 20, 1864, near Atlanta.

Having become sick, he was sent to the hospital in Chattanooga and later to Nashville. He was transferred to the Fifty-ninth Illinois Infantry and shortly after, about Dec. 1st, was transferred to Co. A,

Private John Engberg

Veteran Reserve Corps at Chicago, where he guarded Confederate prisoners at Camp Douglas until the close of the war.

Among the score or so of Swedes in the 55th regiment was Oliver Erickson, first lieutenant of Co. E, who died a hero's death before Atlanta in August, 1864. He was a gallant officer who had won promotion from the ranks, having entered the service as a corporal in Co. A. He was struck by three or more bullets, while at the head of his company, and died where he fell.

Lieutenant Jonas Eckdall enlisted from Macomb, Ill., on Dec. 1, 1861, and was mustered in with Battery H, Second Light Artillery, on the 31st of the same month. The next day he was promoted sergeant and on Aug. 21, 1862, became senior second lieutenant. He attained the rank of senior first lieutenant in the battery on May 25, 1863, and was mustered out July 29, 1865.

Swedes in the Spanish-American War

When in more recent years the Spanish-American War stirred the patriotic sentiment of our country, the Swedish-Americans gave prompt response to the call to arms. In the ten regiments of land troops furnished by this state there were more than four hundred men of Swedish extraction. Those in the naval reserves of Chicago and Moline brought the number safely beyond five hundred, making them about one-twentieth of the forces mustered into service. The great battles of the war being fought at sea, deciding the outcome of the conflict in a very short time, the volunteers did little or no fighting. These troops consisted largely of the National Guards, whose men, trained and disciplined as they were, needed but an opportunity to make the same distinguished record as the defenders of the Union thirty-five years before.

The greatest percentage of Swedes was found in the first and second regiments, from Chicago, in the third. where they were numerous in the Rockford companies, H and K, and others, and in the sixth. where the Swedes of Galesburg figured prominently in Companies C and D, and those of Moline in Co. F. A canvass of the names gives the following result:

Regt.	No. Swedes	Regt.	No. Swedes
1 Infantry	53	7 Infantry	9
2 "	78	8 "	12
3 "	104	9 "	3
4 "	6	1 Cavalry	37
5 "	22	1 Artillery, Battery A	9
6 "	95		
		Total	428

While war was imminent and before the actual outbreak, Carl A. W. Liljenstolpe of Chicago planned to organize an entire regiment of Swedish-Americans. Aided by Axel af Jocknick, another Swedish Chicagoan, he set about recruiting and on May 1, 1898, within ten days after war was declared, he was reported to have four hundred men enrolled. The recruiting continued for a number of weeks, and in July the regiment, which was named "The Blue and Gray Legion," had its officers appointed, including Liljenstolpe as lieutenant colonel and Jocknick and M. Theodore Mattson as majors of battalions. The son of a major in the Swedish army, Liljenstolpe entered the Karlberg

Brevet Lieutenant-Colonel Carl A. W. Liljenstolpe

military academy at the age of thirteen; became instructor in gymnastics and fencing; was graduated at twenty-two, as lieutenant; was offered a place as instructor in gymnastics in the Russian army, which he declined; served as lieutenant in the Kalmar regiment until 1882, when he resigned to devote himself to the care of his estate, Östrabo, in Småland, and in 1894 came to this country engaging in the practice of medical gymnastics and massage, a vocation he still pursues.

By short, sharp and decisive action, the American navy put a sudden end to the war, and the Swedish-American regiment of Illinois was one of many volunteer organizations who never were called into service. It appears, therefore, that no less than 1,500 Swedes had enlisted in this state, up to the time of the naval engagement at Santiago, which deprived two-thirds of them of the privilege of taking the field. But in the fact that among those who actually entered military service in Illinois in the year 1898 .one out of every twenty men was a Swede, while that nationality constituted little more than one-twentieth of the state population, the former record of the Swedish-Americans for loyalty and patriotism seems, nevertheless, well sustained.

CHAPTER XII

Music and Musicians

Music in the Early Days

WEDISH song on American soil dates from the arrival of the first Swedish immigrants who upon landing raised their voices in praise and thanksgiving to God for safe guidance across perilous seas. Strangers in a foreign land, they found their first comfort and cheer in the sacred hymns dear to them from childhood. Also for some length of time after settlement, their musical utterances were chiefly of a devotional character. But there were occasions even in hard pioneer times when the joy of life or recollections of the home land prompted the singing of merry folksongs or patriotic airs. The first harvest festival at Bishop Hill in 1847 and the visit of Fredrika Bremer to Pine Lake in 1850 are instances in point. We have noted that L. P. Esbjörn, the pioneer preacher, who had a musical education, early began drilling his congregations so as to improve their singing, which, even at its best, was not of a high order. Another musical pioneer was Jonas Engberg, who in 1855 formed and conducted a small Swedish choir in Galesburg, probably the first of its kind in this state, and during the winter of 1856-7 led the singing and conducted choral practice in the church at Vasa, Minn. About that time the first musical instruments were introduced in the Swedish churches. A primitive affair with one string, known as a psalmodikon or monochord, played with a bow, was used in 1853 in the Immanuel Church of Chicago. This was superseded in 1856 by a melodeon. An instrument of the latter kind was procured for the Moline Lutheran church in 1858. The Vasa, Minn., church bought a psalmodikon in 1859, the same being replaced the following year by a melodeon. Among the people at large, there were musical amateurs who loved the characteristic folksongs, ballads and romances of Sweden and sang them in their immediate circles, and probably some self-taught fiddler might be found to time the old-country dance at neighborhood gatherings. Most of the new-comers, however, were sternly religious folk, who disapproved of pleasures of a worldly sort, and in consequence secular music among Swedish-Americans is, on the whole, of a much later date. At the present day, when no Swedish home is considered well equipped without some musical instrument, and music is the art cultivated by Swedish-Americans with predilection, in all branches and to every degree of perfection, it is interesting to recall that it was from the very first a cultural factor among these people.

The Immanuel Church Choir

With the exception of the choir named Svenska Sångföreningen, which existed in August and September, 1855, in Galesburg, during the short sojourn of Jonas Engberg in that place, the Immanuel Church Choir of Chicago has the distinction of having been the first Swedish church choir in Illinois. It was formed at the instance of Jonas Engberg, who was organist 1863-67. The choir was the first Swedish-American chorus to sing a cantata. The work chosen, George F. Root's "Queen Esther," was sung at the opening of Augustana College at Paxton in the fall of 1863. The performers were Jonas Engberg, Emma Peterson, Anna Carlsson, Tilda Swedman, Hannah Carlson, John J. Engberg, L. E. Lindberg, and P. Lindberg. "Queen Esther" was later repeated at Chicago. Trips were made to the church conventions at Geneseo and Moline. Jonas Engberg was so interested in his choir that he provided it with music at his own expense. Among later choir leaders were Lars E. Lindberg, 1867, Joseph Osborn, 1869, K. Sandquist, 1870-74, J. F. Ring, 1874-79. In 1883 the choir was reorganized by Mrs. Emmy Evald, who drilled the augmented choir of about one hundred voices for a jubilee concert. This choir, together with the choirs of Salem Church and Gethsemane Church sang some Messiah choruses and several of Wennerberg's "Psalms of David" at the Luther Jubilee concert, Nov. 10, 1883, at Central Music Hall. Joseph Osborn was the director and the accompaniments were played by the Augustana Orchestra with Clarence Eddy at the organ. The choruses sung were "And the glory of the Lord," "Behold the Lamb of God," "Psalm XXIV," "Psalm LXXXIV," "Psalm XCVI," "Psalm CXXXVII" and "Psalm CL." Mr. Osborn and the orchestra had just assisted in similar celebrations Nov. 7th and 8th at Augustana College. C. Levinsen and Mrs. Ella Carlson were the soloists. The latter was one of the few excellent Swedish sopranos of that time. In 1889-90 she was soprano soloist of the Immanuel Church Choir. She is now soprano soloist of the Ravenswood M. E. Church Choir.

Victor J. Tengwald served as director from 1886-88 and was

The Immanuel Church Choir, 1896

followed by John L. Swenson, 1888-90. It was in 1889 that the choir sang Gaul's "The Holy City." The choir was brought to a high state of efficiency under Swenson's term and that of his successor, Samuel E. Carlsson, 1891-98. The latter had been trained under Dr. Stolpe, was highly musical, and prepared many artistic programs from time to time. On Nov. 14, 1894, the choral numbers were Farmer's "Gloria in Excelsis," Rossini's "Inflammatus" and Gounod's "Unfold, ye Portals." The choir sang on Jan. 22, 1896, Woodward's "The Radiant Morn Hath Passed Away," and Gounod's "By Babylon's Wave," with splendid effect. Mr. Carlsson organized during his incumbency an orchestra of twelve members which played both sacred and secular music. It existed about a year.

During the first eight months of 1897 Martin J. Engberg acted as director. The choir sang Gaul's "Ruth" on April 21, 1897. In the fall of 1898 William Dahlén became director, serving until 1907. During this period several cantatas have been sung, viz., Stainer's "Daughter of Jairus," Nov. 19, 1902, an abridged version of Gaul's "The Holy City," Nov. 3, 1903, Gaul's "The Ten Virgins," April 23, 1904, besides two revivals of Gaul's "Ruth."

Alfred Holmes, the organist, succeeded Dahlén in January, 1907. Some months later he directed a third revival of Gaul's "Ruth," with accompaniments by an orchestra. On June 3, 1908, he directed Haydn's "Creation," abridged, with orchestral accompaniment. Mrs. Christine Engstrom has been soprano soloist of the choir since 1890.

The annals of this organization have been given at some length because it is a typical Swedish-American church choir. Besides performing its chief function, viz., assisting in the congregational singing, it has generally prepared from one to three anthems for each Sunday, besides rehearsing special choruses and cantatas for numerous concerts during its long career.

Edward A. Wimmerstedt

The first professional musician among the Swedish Illinoisans was, without doubt, Edward Anders Wimmerstedt, who was born at Skärstad, near Jönköping, Sweden, Jan. 18, 1838. His father, Anders Wilhelm Wimmerstedt, was an organist and musical director, having attained both positions by examination. He was a prolific composer.

The son emigrated in 1863 and settled in Chicago, where he was a piano teacher for three years. In 1866 he moved to Jacksonville, Ill., where he became the director of the musical department of Illinois Female College. He also imparted instruction in the Illinois School for the Blind in the same city. Mr. Wimmerstedt married a fellow teacher in the college, Marion Phillips, a soprano and pianist. They gave many recitals during their career at the college. E. A. Wimmerstedt composed many songs and piano pieces which were popular in the sixties and seventies. On one of his programmes, dated Nov. 15, 1878, are to be found the titles "Shadows," a song, "Mirth and Prank," a rondo and "Polacca Sentimentale," Op. 156. He is said to have become wealthy through his musical talents.

Wimmerstedt became consumptive and went to Napa, Cal., in 1879 or 1880, where he bought a fruit farm which he cultivated successfully.

Edward A. Wimmerstedt

In the fall of 1883 a frost was threatened, whereupon he climbed to the top of a tree to cover it with a sheet and thus protect it from damage. The limb broke and Wimmerstedt fell to the ground and was hurt internally. He was taken to Oakland, where he lingered some time. He died on Oct. 28, 1883, leaving a widow, who still survives.

Oliver Larson

Oliver Larson was born in 1851 at Åhus, Skåne, Sweden. He emigrated in 1863 with his parents who settled in Chicago. The father purchased a melodeon and Oliver attained with its aid quite a proficiency in playing. His voice developed into a rich second bass. In 1869 he became identified with an organization known as the Scandinavian National Quartette, composed besides himself of two Swedes, John L. Swenson, C. J. Blomquist, and three Norwegians, Evert, Jacobsen and Olsen. They made a tour of Wisconsin and Minnesota, always appearing in provincial costumes. After returning they became the nucleus of the Freja Society.

Mr. Larson was a typographer and had worked in the "Hemlandet" and "Svenska Amerikanaren" offices. Leaving in 1873 for

Oliver Larson

Minneapolis, he worked there at his trade and married in that city.

Mr. Larson became active in the musical life of the twin cities, singing solos and leading quartettes and male choruses. For several years he was organist of the Augustana Sw. Luth. Church and besides gave instruction in vocal and instrumental music. He was drowned June 18, 1882, in the Mississippi river and left a widow and a daughter. Mr. Larson was a brother of Emil Larson, the well-known musician.

Joseph E. Osborn

One of the pioneer Swedish-American musicians is Jos. E. Osborn, son of the patriarch, Lars P. Esbjörn. During a portion of the year 1869 he was organist and choir leader of the Immanuel Church in Chicago. In 1875-6 he was organist of the Swedish Lutheran church in Boston. The next year he moved to Andover, Ill., where he served as school teacher and organist until 1883. It was at Andover in the summer of 1880 that the idea of the Augustana Oratorio Society was first broached. Joseph Osborn became leader of the society and conducted the "Messiah concerts" at various places during the next few years. From the proceeds of half a dozen concerts conducted under his direction at Lindsborg the first building of Bethany College was erected. Mr. Osborn has two daughters who have had musical careers. Constance Osborn has been well-known as a pianiste in Minnesota. Esther Osborn has not only appeared as a vocalist in this country but has prosecuted further studies at the Royal Conservatory of Music in Stockholm and has made a successful debut in the Royal Opera in that city.

Anna Frederika Magnusson Jewett

It was in 1855 that Lewis J. Magnusson came to Chicago with his family. He was a merchant, an early member of the Svea Society, and was a cousin of Consul von Schneidau's wife. He had once lived in New York, where he met Sarah Corning, a young lady of Huguenot and New England ancestry, who was becoming known in literary circles through her sketches, essays and verses. They were mutually attracted and were married. Moving to Stockholm, his birthplace, Mr. Magnusson embarked in business and prospered. Mrs. Magnusson became thoroughly acquainted with the Swedish language and translated many Swedish poems into English. The young couple mingled in the literary and musical circles of the day. Among the family friends were Crusenstolpe, Fredrika Bremer, Jenny Lind, and Ole Bull. Three children were born to the parents: Howard C. Magnusson, who became the founder of Northwestern College of Dental Surgery, Anna Frederika and Rosalie.

Anna Frederika began the study of the piano at the age of seven. The talented girl made rapid progress, for when only thirteen years old she played with orchestral accompaniment at the Saturday afternoon concerts instituted by Arne, an early Chicago musician. The next year she became organist of the St. Ansgarius Church, and subsequently had a similar position in Ascension Church. Having found that she had an unusually good voice, Anna went to New York, where she studied under the direction of Barille, the brother and teacher of the famous Patti. In 1860 she went to Hamburg to study with Mme. Cornet. It is said that she was the first Chicago girl to go abroad to seek instruction in music. She soon met Jenny Lind, who advised her to become a pupil of Lamperti at Milan. Anna went there and studied operatic singing with the famous Italian vocal teacher. She also studied dramatic art with Fiorvanti and the playing of accompaniments with Alberti, remaining three years in Italy.

Returning in 1864 to Chicago, Miss Magnusson sang at the Chicago

Philharmonic Society's concert in Bryan Hall and was enthusiastically welcomed. She also sang to the Swedish people at the St. Ansgarius and Immanuel churches. Engaged as prima donna by Strakosch for a season of grand opera, she was having great success when she was stricken with typhoid fever. Several recurrences of the illness induced

Anna Frederika Magnusson Jewett

her permanently to abandon the operatic stage. Miss Magnusson opened a studio in Crosby Opera House and entered upon a successful career as vocal teacher. Among the many pupils trained by her was Marie Engel, a grand opera singer. She married Frederick Jewett and thereafter was known as Mrs. Magnusson Jewett. While in Europe she had been correspondent for the "Evening Journal." She was a facile writer and prepared many articles for the musical journals. No less than six languages were familiar to her.

Mrs. Magnusson Jewett was seized with a stroke of apoplexy and died on May 8, 1894.

Rosalie Magnusson Lancaster

The younger daughter, Rosalie, was born in Stockholm and came to Chicago at a tender age. When she was six years old her parents took her to hear Ole Bull, the violinist. After they had returned home, the child asked her father to open the piano. Seating herself, she astonished her parents by playing through one of the Norwegian violinist's selections, "The Carnival of Venice." While still a young girl, she became a pupil of Louis Staab, a Chicago pianist, and continued with him several years. After a period of study in New York she went

Rosalie Magnusson Lancaster

to Berlin in 1871, where she was a student under the ablest masters. In Vienna she enjoyed the advantage of studying under the personal direction of Anton Rubinstein, who took a kind interest in her.

After three years of intense application, Miss Magnusson returned to this country. She was married to Alvin M. Lancaster and moved to southern California, where she achieved a reputation as a concert pianiste. She was generally regarded as the most successful piano teacher on the Pacific Coast, having trained a number of concert pianists and piano teachers. The Lancaster Musical Club, a southern California society, was named in her honor.

Mrs. Lancaster has recently returned to Chicago, where she, besides giving occasional recitals, imparts instruction on her chosen instrument. She is a fine linguist and is a writer of ability on musical subjects. Mrs. Lancaster's daughter Rosalie is also a professional pianiste.

The Freja Society

A singing society named Freja was organized in the fall of 1869 by Swedes and Norwegians in Chicago. The initiative was taken by John L. Swenson, together with a little company of Chicago singers upon their return from a concert tour in the Northwest. The fundamental idea was to unite the Scandinavian singers of Chicago into a common, powerful organization. Its first director was Mr. Swenson,

John L. Swenson

who led the choral society for ten years. A biographical sketch of him appears elsewhere in this work. .

The chorus numbered sixty singers on an average. Many excellent concerts were given, attracting audiences numbering as high as one thousand persons. The bulk of the membership in Freja was Swedish. A sick and death benefit was an added feature of the society, but the principal beneficiaries turned out to be "Bikupan" and Skow-Peterson, Isberg & Co.'s bank, two Swedish financial institutions, upon whose failure Freja lost respectively $500 and $200 of its funds. Among the early presidents of the organization were C. Bryde, G. Nyquist, Henry L. Hertz and Charles Ferm.

Svenska Sångföreningen

A society known by the name of Svenska Sångföreningen was formed in January, 1875, by Alfred Lagergren. Persons of both sexes were eligible to membership and there were no particular requirements, the organization being more of a singing school than a body of trained singers. Almost at the outset the membership was about one hundred.

The results obtained were commendable. Among the soloists who appeared were Emma Larson (Mrs. H. E. C. Peterson), soprano, Christine Britten (Mrs. Engstrom), soprano, and Emma Blanxius (Mrs. Hodge), alto. This chorus was continued until 1879, when it was dissolved, the burden of holding the organization together having grown too heavy for the shoulders of the director.

Alfred Lagergren was born in Kristianstad, Sweden, May 29, 1840. After having had employment in Malmö and Göteborg, he emigrated in 1869 and became identified with the White Star Line steamship ticket office in New York. In 1871 he established a branch office in Chicago and continued in the same business during the rest of his career in that city. Mr. Lagergren was active in musical circles in both New York and Chicago and did all that he could to keep alive the interest in Svenska Sångföreningen. He returned to Sweden in 1883 and has since lived near Göteborg, where he conducts a chicken farm.

D'Ailly and Owen

About 1876 there was in Chicago a tall, good looking young man by the name of D'Ailly. His grandfather had fled from France during the French revolution and settled in Stockholm so that the family became Swedish. D'Ailly had a sonorous bass-baritone voice and sang at concerts in Swedish and American circles. Grau, the impresario, was so struck with the quality of his voice that he paid D'Ailly one hundred dollars a month to aid him in preparing himself for the grand opera. D'Ailly did not appreciate his opportunity, and after a few months Grau's interest in him ceased.

One of the early Swedish musicians of Chicago was Benjamin Owen, (Ovén), who was organist of Plymouth Church about 1878. He retained this position for several years and was considered one of the leading organists of the city. Owen was a good musician, theorist and composer. Some of his anthems, as the "Ave Maria," are still sung. He moved to Wisconsin and died there in the early eighties.

The Swedish Lady Quartette

The woman's quartette which first toured this country, calling themselves the Swedish Lady Quartette, was organized at Stockholm, in 1873, by August Jahnke. They then styled themselves "Den nya svenska damkvartetten." Under Jahnke's management they toured Sweden, Norway, Denmark, Germany and Holland, returning to Stockholm. Continuing their studies for a year, they were graduated from the Royal Conservatory of Music. The two first sopranos now left and a single soprano was chosen in their stead. The members now were

Amanda Carlson, soprano, Ingeborg Löfgren, mezzo-soprano, Inga Ekström, alto, and Bertha Erixon, contralto. In 1875 they started on a tour through Sweden, Finland and Russia, where at St. Petersburg they sang at Nobel's reception given in honor of A. E. Nordenskiöld. They continued on through Germany, Belgium and Holland. There meeting the impresario Max Strakosch, the quartette came to America under his management, arriving in Boston, Sept. 5, 1876. Their

INGA EKSTRÖM   AMANDA CARLSON   BERTHA ERIXON
INGEBORG LÖFGREN
The Swedish Lady Quartette

first American concert was given at that place with the Philharmonic Club. After a concert at New York they went to Philadelphia, where they sang on Nov. 1st at one of the Centennial Musical Festival Concerts conducted by Theodore Thomas. Myron W. Whitney, the famous basso, and the Thomas Orchestra were on the same programme. After returning to New York and there singing, they went to Boston and on Nov. 24th appeared on the same stage with Ole Bull, Aptommas, the Welsh harpist, and the Mendelssohn Quintette Club. Not long after, they sang at the Worcester musical festival and continued their tour through the eastern states.

In the fall of 1877 the quartette went westward, stopping at Chicago. There, on Nov. 5th, they gave, in conjunction with Aptommas, a concert in McCormick's Hall, at Clark and Kinzie streets, then the largest hall in the city. In the east the quartette sang both Swedish and English songs. To their countrymen they sang only the cherished songs from the fatherland, such as Prince Gustaf's "Kälkarne fram," compositions by Lindblad, Wahlin, Söderman's "Wedding March," "Kjerulf's "Brudefærden i Hardangers Fiord," besides numerous folk-songs, among them being, "En gång i bredd med mig," "Å jänta å ja'," "Tänker du att jag förlorader är," "Vill int' du, så ska' fäll ja'," etc. It was the first time that a Swedish-American audience here heard the familiar songs interpreted by highly cultivated voices. Numerous bouquets of flowers besides frantic plaudits were bestowed upon the quartette by the enthusiastic audience.

After a second concert, given in the same hall, Nov. 7th, a banquet was tendered the Swedish Lady Quartette at Brand's Hall. Vice-consul C. J. Sundell, J. A. Enander, C. F. Peterson, O. G. Lange and C. G. Linderborg made addresses, while Freja and Svenska Sångföreningen sang several numbers.

The quartette was greeted with many poetic effusions in the Swedish and American press of the day. Continuing, they went as far west as San Francisco, where their tour was interrupted, for Bertha Erixon, in 1878, was there married to the violinist Christian Krause. Returning to Chicago, Miss Carlson left them and was engaged as soprano in a Reading, Pa., church. After a couple of years she married August Svenson of Kearney, Neb. In Chicago the remaining two met Emma Larson, a young soprano of rare musical ability and education, who was soon persuaded to join them. The three ladies sent to Stockholm and engaged Anna Cedergren, a contralto of very rich, deep voice. The quartette went on concert tours through Upper and Lower Canada, and all over the United States, until 1882, when Anna Cedergren left them. Bertha Erixon Krause, then widowed, rejoined her former companions, and the quartette traveled until 1883, when the Swedish Lady Quartette was disrupted by the double marriage of two of the members, the event taking place at the Palmer House, Chicago, on June 5th. Inga Ekström was united with Emil Olund, then a politician and business man at Red Wing, Minn. Emma Larson was married to Henry E. C. Peterson, a portrait artist of Chicago.

Anna Cedergren and Bertha Erixon Krause are both dead. Ingeborg Löfgren Schreiner lives at Palestine, Texas. Amanda Carlson Svenson in 1895 went to Salt Lake City where she trained a woman's chorus so well that it gained first prize at the Eisteddfods of 1895, '97 and '99. Mr. and Mrs. Olund moved to Hudson, Wis., and later to

Duluth, where Mr. Olund was collector of customs. They now reside
at St. Paul, where Mr. Olund is in the insurance business. Mrs. Olund
has continued to use her musical talents as vocal instructor and as

INGEBORG LÖFGREN   EMMA LARSON
                ANNA CEDERGREN   INGA EKSTRÖM
The Swedish Lady Quartette 1878—83.

concert singer. One of her five children, a daughter, is a student at
the Royal Conservatory of Music at Stockholm.

During its career the Swedish Lady Quartette was managed by the
Slayton Lyceum Bureau of Chicago, the Redpath Lyceum Bureau of

Boston, and then by their own management. They were among the most popular attractions of the day, for no other woman's quartettes had sung in this country prior. The sympathy of the singing and the perfect blending of their voices made them irresistible to their audiences. They had a standing invitation to sing at the Worcester Musical Festival. Their popularity caused several female quartettes to appear under similar names at various periods for years after.

Emma Larson

Mrs. Emma L. Peterson is the daughter of Anders and Sarah B. Larson, who came to this city in 1846, on the same ship with Eric Jansson, the Bishop Hill prophet. The family settled in Chicago and

Miss Emma Larson

it was there that the daughter Emma was born. From her eleventh year it was noticed that she had an unusual voice. When Christina Nilsson was banqueted by the Svea Society on the occasion of her first visit to Chicago in December, 1870, it was Emma Larson who, escorted by Vieuxtemps, the famous French violinist, placed in the Swedish singer's hands a magnificent bouquet. At a subsequent interview the little girl's voice was heard by Miss Nilsson, who advised her to have it cultivated. Miss Nilsson came to Chicago at various times until 1884, and at each visit Miss Larson was a welcome caller.

Miss Larson studied singing for two years with Sig. Carrozi. She sang solos at the public concerts of Freja and Svenska Sångföreningen in the St. Ansgarius Church, and was well known in the Swedish circles of that time. Besides singing at concerts in various American churches, she was soprano soloist at the Eighth Presbyterian Church and the Fullerton Avenue Presbyterian Church. A benefit concert was given to Miss Larson by Freja and Svenska Sångföreningen, after which she went to New York, where a year was spent in study with Mme. Rudersdorff, the mother of Richard Mansfield. During this period Miss Larson was soprano soloist of Dr. Scudder's church in Brooklyn. Returning to Chicago, she had, in 1878, just accepted an appointment as soloist in St. James' Episcopal Church, when she was asked by Inga Ekström and Ingeborg Löfgren to join with them in reorganizing the Swedish Lady Quartette, which had successfully toured this country for two seasons. The three ladies sent to Stockholm for the contralto, Anna Cedergren. They traveled many times through this country and three times through Canada. Ofttimes they were welcomed to the country towns by brass bands. They appeared on the same programmes with many notabilities, among whom may be mentioned Tagliapetri, Anne Louise Cary, Teresa Carrenno, Edwin Booth and Clara Morris. Among their pleasant recollections is the dinner given them at Washington by the Swedish minister, Count Lewenhaupt. Miss Larson had the leading part, that of first soprano, during her five years membership with the quartette. Their artistic triumphs were brought to a close by the marriage of two of the members. Miss Larson was married June 5, 1883, to Henry E. C. Peterson, the portrait artist, of Chicago, of whom a sketch appears elsewhere in this volume.

Since her marriage Mrs. Peterson has occasionally sung in public at charity concerts.

The Original Ladies' Quartette

The second woman's quartette which sang in the United States was the first one of its kind organized in Sweden and was there known as "Svenska damkvartetten." Hilda Wideberg, Amy Åberg, Wilhelmina Söderlund and Mrs. Maria Petterson, fellow students at the Royal Conservatory of Music at Stockholm, after a successful debut at the university seat, Upsala, toured through Norrland and Finland, sang at St. Petersburg and other Russian cities, at Rome, Leipsic, Berlin, Paris, London and other continental points. They sang at Wagner's home,

"Wahnfried," where they moved the master to tears by their beautiful singing.

The quartette made tours of the United States during the seasons 1878-79 and 1879-80, during which time they made several visits to Chicago and vicinity. Their first concert was held in Hershey Hall on Madison street.

Music at Augustana College—The College Band

The first band at a Swedish-American college was founded in 1874 by President Hasselquist. It played at various college celebrations. At one time it was called Augustana Silver Cornet Band. Like all student organizations, its membership has changed greatly each succeeding year. Prof. C. L. Krantz led the Augustana Band in 1903-4 whilst Prof. L. W. Kling was the director in 1907-8. The membership is usually about twenty.

The Augustana Orchestra

This student orchestra was first proposed by Henning Jacobson in 1879 to some of his musically inclined comrades. The idea caught fire and early in January, 1880, the boys had an orchestra composed as follows:—Samuel E. Carlsson and C. L. E. Esbjörn, first violins; F. A. Linder and J. A. Krantz, second violins; Fritz N. Andrén, viola; J. A. Udden, cello; Henning Jacobson, contra bass; Gustaf Andreen, flute; William Reck, second flute; G. N. Themanson, cornet; C. J. Freberg, clarinet, and Fritz Jacobson, trombone. Henning Jacobson's enthusiasm soon cooled and C. A. Bäckman took his place.

The accompanying illustration portrays the orchestra at this stage of its career.

The boys engaged Petersen, a Danish musician in Davenport, as instructor and chose S. E. Carlsson as director. They had no aid from the college, but bought their own instruments and music, and paid for their instruction themselves. The orchestra played overtures, marches and other light music at college entertainments and made short trips to various towns in Illinois and Iowa, playing in Swedish churches.

When it was decided to sing the "Messiah" at Rock Island, the orchestra was annexed to the chorus. The score, parts and books were imported from London, arriving early in January, 1881, after which rehearsals of the orchestra and chorus began. The story is told under the caption Augustana Oratorio Society.

Samuel E. Carlsson continued as leader of the orchestra until he left college in 1883. Dr. Stolpe now took active charge and introduced some of his orchestral compositions and other music to the members, besides having them play the accompaniments to the oratorios. During

Fritz N. Andrén   William Reck   C. J. Freberg   Gustaf Andreen   Fritz Jacobson   G. N. Themanson   C. A. Bäckman
F. A. Linder   J. A. Krantz   S. E. Carlsson   C. I. R. Esbjörn   J. A. Udden

The Augustana Orchestra, 1880

1888 S. E. Carlsson acted as assistant leader. After Stolpe's withdrawal from the Augustana Conservatory the orchestra had a precarious existence. It was revived by Franz Zedeler, who conducted it until 1904. For the next two years it was directed by Christian Oelschlaegel. During the school year 1907-08 Gertrude Housel, the violin instructor at the conservatory, has conducted the Augustana Orchestra. With the help of a few outside musicians they played the overtures to Rossini's "Barber of Seville" and Balfe's "Bohemian Girl" besides furnishing accompaniments for Gounod's "Gallia" and Mendelssohn's "Hymn of Praise." The membership is about sixteen.

Olof Olsson

Among our musical pioneers we may well include Dr. Olof Olsson. It was he who gave the first impulse to the rendering of the "Messiah" and other great oratorios, first at Augustana College and later at Bethany College, where the annual Messiah concerts have become a noted musical event. His glowing account of a Messiah concert attended by him in Exeter Hall, London, at Easter, 1879, inspired the organization of the Augustana Oratorio Society in February, 1881. The idea underlying the establishment of the Augustana Conservatory of Music is also traceable to Dr. Olsson, who that same year publicly expressed the desirability of having an orchestra, a trained chorus and a professor of music at the Rock Island institution. We quote the following words by way of characterizing his musical views and ideals: "If ever there was a place for an orchestra and a good chorus it is at a divinity school. There the great works of Handel, Bach and other masters ought to be most thoroughly studied. In the sacred compositions of Handel and Bach there is more genuine theology than in many a heavy tome of biblical exegeses and theological treatises. Had our congregations the correct conception of the matter, they would forthwith engage a competent professor of sacred music at our institution."

The Augustana Oratorio Society

In the summer of 1880 the preliminary steps toward the organization of an oratorio society were taken by the forming of choruses in various cities and communities, including Rock Island, Moline, Galesburg and Andover, but the actual organization was not completed before Feb. 25-26, 1881, when the various choruses and the orchestra met together to rehearse for the first time. They chose the name Augustana Oratorio Society. After a second general rehearsal the society gave its first public concerts April 11th and 12th, at Moline and Rock Island, respectively, this being the first time that the "Messiah" or any equally pretentious musical work was rendered by Swedish-

The Handel Oratorio Society, 1908

Americans. Encouraged by the first successful appearances, the chorus, orchestra and soloists at once started out on a tour of the neighborhood, appearing at Galva, Galesburg, Orion, Geneseo, Altona and Andover, large audiences being attracted at each place.

The participating members of the Oratorio Society numbered one hundred. Dr. Olsson was president and virtual manager; Joseph Osborn (Esbjörn), musical director; J. F. Ring, organist, and the soloists were, C. A. Bäckman, Wilhelmina Kohler, Sophie Fair, Cecilia Strömberg, Esther and Joshua Hasselquist and Maria Bergblom.

In April the following year the Messiah concerts were repeated. The society first appeared at Princeton and Geneseo, then rendered Handel's great masterpiece in the large Swedish Lutheran Church of Moline two successive evenings. These two events proved a most gratifying climax to the tour, the edifice being crowded to the doors both times, while, on an estimate, five hundred people were turned away.

That same spring the orchestra and soloists went to Kansas and participated in the first renditions of the "Messiah" in Lindsborg and vicinity. The entire society was also invited to Omaha, to several places in Iowa and to Minneapolis. It was found impracticable, however, to fill these engagements, but as a direct result of Dr. Olsson's successful efforts at Rock Island similar choruses were subsequently formed in Lindsborg, St. Paul and New York-City.

On Nov. 7 and 8, 1883, a grand Luther jubilee was celebrated at Augustana, and for that occasion there was erected on the slope of the college hill an amphitheatrical structure, named Jubilee Hall, with a seating capacity of several thousand. This rudimentary, yet serviceable structure, now torn down, was made necessary principally through the success of Dr. Olsson and the Oratorio Society in attracting large audiences. The "Messiah" was sung the first evening. The second concert was devoted chiefly to Wennerberg's "Psalms of David," Dr. T. N. Hasselquist figuring as one of the soloists. Two days after, the orchestra assisted at a similar celebration in Chicago. The following year P. A. Edquist became director of the chorus. Some of the choruses from "Messiah" were repeated in the annual concert. On June 10, 1885, selections from Haydn's "Creation" and Mendelssohn's "Elijah" were sung. Nov. 6th, the same year, selections from Wennerberg's "Psalms of David" were sung. Professor Stolpe directed the chorus in 1886 and was followed the next year by James Moody. In the latter part of 1887 Professor Stolpe again assumed direction of the society. At this period Stolpe composed and dedicated to the chorus "David's LXVIIth Psalm" for three solo voices, chorus and orchestra.

During 1888 there arose friction causing a division of the chorus,

Stolpe remaining, however, at the head of the college chorus and orchestra. The same year "Messiah" and Stainer's "Daughter of Jairus" were rendered by the chorus. On June 4, 1891, Bennett's "Woman of Samaria" was performed.

The other wing chose in 1888 Victor J. Tengwald as its director and then adopted the present name, Handel Oratorio Society. Mr. Tengwald rehearsed assiduously with his chorus and in 1889 the "Creation" was for the first time rendered in full, the concert taking place at Moline. At a later concert in Rock Island some of Wennerberg's "Psalms of David" were sung. The "Messiah" and "Creation" were also given.

In 1891 Prof. O. Olsson succeeded to the presidency of Augustana College. He effected the next year a union of the two choruses under the leadership of Prof. G. E. Griffith, who remained in this capacity until 1896. The organization retained the new name, Handel Oratorio Society. At the Jubilee Concert in 1893 the following works were rendered with the assistance of Strasser's Orchestra, Augustana Brass Band and Bethany Brass Band; Stolpe's "Jubel-kantat" for baritone, alto, chorus, organ and orchestra; Gade's "Zion," a cantata for baritone, chorus, orchestra and organ; Cowen's "Song of Thanksgiving;" excerpts from "Messiah," and Wennerberg's "Psalm CL." Other works sung in 1892-6 are Mercadante's "Seven Last Words," Wennerberg's "Jesu Födelse," Gaul's "Holy City," Spohr's "Last Judgment," "Creation," "Elijah," Bach's "God's Time is Best," besides other works of a high order. During 1896 and 1897 Prof. A. D. Bodfors directed the society, presumably drilling several of the above works. In the fall of 1898 Prof. F. E. Peterson took charge of the chorus and directed the performance of the following oratorios: 1889, Apr. and Dec., "Messiah"; 1900, "Creation"; 1901, "Elijah"; 1902, "Creation"; Founder's Day, 1903, "Messiah"; 1904, "Messiah"; 1905, "Creation". Prof. Christian Oelschlaegel was the next leader, repeating the "Messiah" in 1906. Emil Larson, the conservatory director, next assumed charge, and in the spring of 1907 Gaul's "Holy City" was performed. On May 7, 1908, Mendelssohn's "Hymn of Praise" and Gounod's "Gallia" were rendered by the chorus, which on this occasion consisted of 75 voices, accompanied by organ, piano and the Augustana Orchestra of 20 pieces. Mr. Larson in July, 1908, severed his connection with the Augustana Conservatory of Music and thereby with the chorus. The above list of works performed would be creditable to any musical society, but is especially so to a college chorus, whose membership changes from year to year, a large percentage each year being lost to it.

The Chapel Choir

The Chapel Choir at Augustana College has been led for quite a number of years by Edla Lund, the vocal instructor. Many good compositions have been artistically rendered by it in the course of time. Among them may be mentioned Söderman's smaller mass with Latin text called "Andeliga Sånger," Söderman's "Hjertesorg," Gade's "Spring Song" and MacDowell's "Barcarolle." Mrs. Lund has also been conductor of the Choral Union of Moline, which among other things has sung the Söderman Mass, the "Messiah" and Goring-Thomas' "The Swan and the Skylark."

The Wennerberg Chorus

The first male quartette at Augustana College was formed in 1867 when the school was still at Paxton. In that year the 350th anniversary of the sixteenth century Reformation was celebrated very generally in the Swedish Lutheran churches. Professor Hasselquist lectured in many of the Illinois churches and the male quartette, which accompanied him, sang at each place to appreciative audiences. From time to time similar student quartettes arose, so that when the first college building at Rock Island was dedicated in 1875, the students could furnish both band and vocal music to enrich the exercises.

It was not until 1901 that a student male chorus was permanently organized. Gunnar Wennerberg had died that year and memorial concerts were held in many of the Swedish communities. The Svea Male Chorus of Moline asked the aid of the students for such a concert and the Wennerberg Chorus was accordingly organized Oct. 21, 1901. A. S. Hamilton, the first director, was succeeded by Prof. C. J. Södergren the next year. In September, 1903, E. C. Bloomquist was chosen leader. The following April. the chorus gave concerts in Rockford, Aurora, Batavia and Elgin. In January, 1905, Emil Larson, the conservatory director, became the musical head of the chorus. During April, concerts were given in Rockford, DeKalb, Joliet, Aurora, Paxton and Chicago. After commencement, a tour was made, beginning with Galesburg and extending as far west as Stromsburg, Neb., concerts being held in twelve places. Since then the Wennerberg Chorus has sung in Michigan, Indiana, Illinois, Iowa and Nebraska.

The repertory comprises the standard Swedish student songs and also many selections with English text. It is noteworthy, that there is an entire absence of the burlesque and vaudeville features characteristic of the usual college glee club programme. Under Mr. Larson's leadership the Wennerberg Chorus has so gained in precision of attack, intonation, enunciation and general musical effect, that it is perhaps the peer of any similar student body in the West.

The Wennerberg Chorus, 1908

Gustaf Stolpe

Gustaf Erik Stolpe was born Sept. 26, 1833, in Torsåker parish, Gestrikland, Sweden, where his forefathers had been organists for a period of one hundred and forty years. At the early age of five years he began to receive instructions in piano and violin from his father, Johan Stolpe. Three years later he was sent to the athenaeum at Gefle, which he attended for seven years. When ten years old, he played the organ at the regular services one Sunday and also appeared in

Dr. Gustaf Stolpe

concert with some visiting musicians. His mother died when he was twelve years old. The young boy relieved his father of playing at the funeral service and performed a funeral march which he himself composed for the occasion. The father preserved at the homestead a pile of musical manuscripts composed by the son from his tenth to his sixteenth year.

At the age of fifteen Gustaf was entered in the Royal Conservatory of Music at Stockholm. After a year he passed the organist's examination with credit and, continuing, graduated at the age of twenty-two, with the degree of Director Musices et Cantus. At this period he acted as accompanist and piano soloist to Jenny Lind during her tour through Sweden.

At the age of twenty-three he was united in marriage with Engel Aurore, daughter of Per Johan Pålman and his wife Brita Engel Ihrfors of Vesterås. The same year, 1856, Stolpe succeeded the composer J. N. Ahlström as director of the orchestra at the Ladugårdsland and Humlegård Theatres in Stockholm. It is interesting to note that the present royal kapellmeister, Conrad Nordqvist, then played second violin in his orchestra. Stolpe either composed or arranged most of the musical repertory during his connection with the theatre. He composed thirty-eight operettas, each containing from fifteen to twenty-four pieces. Among them may be mentioned "Sven och liten Anna," a three act piece.

Removing in 1863 to Varberg, Halland, Stolpe was engaged as organist of the city church, besides teaching vocal and instrumental music at two institutions of learning in that city. These positions he retained for many years, meanwhile making frequent concert tours in Sweden as a skilled performer upon organ, piano and violin.

During 1879-80 Stolpe had a year's leave of absence which was spent in Stockholm. Much of this time was passed in companionship with his friends, Ludvig Norman and P. A. Oppfeldt. It was at this time that his twenty-four studies for the piano were published.

In 1881 Stolpe left for a concert tour of the United States. The enterprise did not prove a financial success, and he was facing actual want when called to the professorship of music at Augustana College in 1882. He accepted the position, and his connection with the institution resulted three years later in the establishment of the Augustana Conservatory of Music, of which he thus was the virtual founder.

Stolpe gave instruction to advanced pupils in piano, organ, violin, violoncello, voice and harmony. His lectures on musical history were no less fascinating for their style than for the musical illustrations with which they were embellished. Prof. Stolpe was a capable writer on topics pertaining to his art and contributed on occasion to various periodicals.

His ethical views Dr. Stolpe set forth in "En Examinerad Musikdirektör," a monograph written in 1894 to the memory of his deceased friend P. A. Oppfeldt, the contents of the book being an indirect, but none the less vigorous protest against the pretentions of cheap dilettantism.

From 1883 until the end of his Rock Island career, Prof. Stolpe was organist of the Swedish Lutheran Church in Moline. He had wonderful skill in improvisation and his chorale playing has been declared by musicians to be well-nigh matchless. He refused to play music of a "gospel hymn" character at the Sunday evening services, deeming it unchurchly. Consequently a substitute had to perform the objectionable melodies.

During 1888 the Stolpe Trio existed. Stolpe played the piano, Samuel E. Carlsson the violin and A. D. Bodfors the cello. They played many classic compositions. The degree of Doctor of Music was conferred upon Stolpe in 1891 by the New York Conservatory of Music in recognition of his talent in composition.

Dr. Gustaf Stolpe

During the school year 1893-94 differences of opinion arose between Dr. Stolpe and the president of the college, which culminated in the resignation of the former. Dr. Stolpe remained in Rock Island, giving instruction to advanced students. In 1895 he opened in Rock Island a music school of very modest proportions, which existed for several years. In 1900 Dr. Stolpe was called to head the department of music at Upsala College, Kenilworth, New Jersey, and taught there for two terms. The following year his health failed and on October 3, 1901, he breathed his last.

Dr. Stolpe had a son in his first marriage, viz., Rev. Johan Gustaf Mauritz Stolpe, D. D., Knight of the Order of Vasa, pastor of the Gustavus Adolphus Swedish Lutheran Church in New York City. In his second marriage, with an American lady, he had two sons, George Vitus, a naval veteran of the Spanish-American war, now dead, and David Evald. The widow, Mrs. Malvina Stolpe, resides in Kenilworth, N. J.

Professor Stolpe was a pious man, who spent his Sunday afternoons in the study of the Scriptures. It is said that he read his Bible through about two hundred times. This undoubtedly had a great influence upon his literary style.

An idea of Dr. Stolpe's productiveness and versatility is afforded by the following schedule of his published works:

Thirty-eight operettas, all of them rendered in Stockholm; about twenty-five orchestral works, among them "Marche Militaire," "Festival Overture," "Mazurka," "Fantasia on Swedish Melodies," "Arrangement of Gavotte from J. S. Bach's Second Violin Sonata," "The Lark in the Sky," "Tone Sketches," a suite, and several more overtures; twenty-five pieces for brass band; a string quartette; a trio for violin, cello and piano; a trio for violin, piano and organ, entitled, "Over the Forest, Over the Sea;" three duets for violin and piano, among them "Vue;" several piano duets; for organ: "Fantasia Heroica," "Symphony," "Concertino," "Preludium and Fuga," fifty "Preludes," "En moders bön;" for piano: "20 Originalpolskor från Gestrikland," composed by Per Stolpe, 1756, Johan Stolpe, 1792, and by Gustaf Stolpe in his youth, and harmonized by him; "24 Pianostudier," about twenty-five piano solos, including "Vinterkvällarne," "Matrossång," "Gondoliersång," "Guldfjärilarne," "Ballad vid hafvet," "Sonja," "Den gamla, goda tiden," "Prärieskizzer," "En tonsaga," "Hedvig Vals," "Konsertvals," "Humoresk," "Irländsk Dans," "Malvina," "A Dream of Haydn," "Soldatkör;" for mixed chorus: "Körer för Blandade Röster," comprising twenty-four sacred choruses; "Davids LXVII Psalm" for solo voices, chorus and orchestra; "Ordet," for alternating choirs; a cantata for chorus and organ; "Jubelkantat," for baritone and alto, chorus, organ, and orchestra; a cantata for baritone solo, chorus, and orchestra; for male chorus: "Tjugufyra sånger för Manskör," with sacred text; "Dolda ting," "Sverige och Norge"; "100 Sångstycken," for children's voices; about fifteen songs with piano accompaniment, among them being, "Mina dagar," "En lyra är hjärtat," with violin obligato, "Uppå Gud hoppas jag," "På blomsterdoft," "Ängen står slagen," "Paa Fjeldet,"

"When the grass shall cover me," "Hur skönt det är att komma i Herrens tempelgård," besides a sacred duet for soprano and alto, and "Dagar komma, dagar flykta," for soprano, female quartette and piano.

Stolpe's Opus 94 was published in 1895, and the opus number since reached was undoubtedly over 100, as various songs and piano com-

Emil Larson

positions were published in this country during his last years. If the individual compositions in these were counted they would amount to far more than one thousand numbers.

Emil Larson

One of the most prominent figures in Swedish musical life in this country is that of Emil Larson. Schooled under teachers like Creswold, Mathews, Eddy and Sherwood, he has developed into an able musician, whose influence has been far-reaching.

Emil Larson's career as organist, professor of music at North Park College, director of the Augustana Conservatory of Music and as private instructor in Chicago has served to impart the principles of good musicianship to hundreds of earnest pupils, many of whom, in turn, have themselves become music teachers in various parts of the country.

Many odd moments during his busy life have been devoted to composition. Perceiving the dearth of good music for Swedish church choirs, he has written or arranged numerous anthems. About twenty-five of these were published in the collection called "Kyrkokören." A fresh series collected under the title "Sångkören" has just been issued. The new series has also been published in English, German and Norwegian editions. Larson's choral arrangements are characterized by the melodiousness of not only the leading air but also of the inner parts. Many short airs have also been prepared for children's choruses and collected in annuals called "Bethlehemsstjärnan" and "Påskliljan."

The folksongs of the fatherland have appealed to Emil Larson to so great a degree that he has taken some of the melodies as themes and built larger musical structures therefrom. "Konsertfantasi öfver svenska folkvisor," "Second Fantasia on Swedish Folk Songs" and "Variations on an Old Swedish Lullaby" show considerable powers of invention and originality, and are very brilliant and effective concert pieces. They are not to be classed with the general run of variations and fantasies on operatic or other airs.

In July, 1908, Emil Larson severed his connection with the Augustana Conservatory of Music, moving to Chicago, where he has resumed his career as a musician. A biographical sketch is given elsewhere in this work.

The Swedish Festival Chorus, Chicago

The May Festival Chorus was organized in 1894 as a part of a movement to provide funds to prosecute the murderers of the unfortunate Swan Nelson. A concert was given in May in the Auditorium and proved a musical as well as a financial success. The chorus numbered several hundred men and women, enlisted mostly from the church choirs and the male choruses. John R. Örtengren acted as director and Emil Larson was accompanist. Early in 1895 rehearsals began for another concert which was held in the Auditorium the following May. "The Heavens are telling" was sung with orchestral accompaniment, besides several melodies a capella. In February, 1896, the name Swedish Festival Chorus was adopted. The membership varied from three to four hundred. A concert was given May 23rd in the Auditorium, one of the numbers being Abt's ''Neckrosen,'' arranged for the chorus by Emil Larson. Haydn's chorus from the ''Creation,'' ''Achieved is the Glorious Work'' was also sung.

The next concert took place May 8, 1897, in the same hall. Wennerberg's largest chorus, ''Psalm CXIII,'' was one of the numbers. Concerts were held in various churches and halls during the season of 1897-98. The attendance at the rehearsals flagged during the last two seasons and the chorus wound up its existence in the fall of 1898.

The Gunnar Wennerberg Memorial Choruses, Chicago

The Gunnar Wennerberg Memorial Chorus, for the most part composed of the same material as the Swedish Festival Chorus, was organized to assist in a concert to be held in memory of the then recently departed poet and composer, Gunnar Wennerberg. John R. Örtengren was the director of the chorus of five hundred voices. The concert, held Oct. 2, 1901, in the Auditorium, began with an organ fantasia on Wennerberg melodies arranged by Emil Larson. The mixed chorus sang ''Psalm XXIV'' and ''Psalm CL,'' whilst the male chorus sang ''Hör oss, Svea,'' ''Stå stark'' and ''O Gud, som styrer folkens öden.'' The other Wennerberg numbers were two duets from ''Gluntarne'' and three solos. Four-fifths of the proceeds were distributed to local charities, the balance being sent to Sweden in 1907 to go toward the erection of a statue of Wennerberg at Upsala University.

In August, 1907, John R. Örtengren gathered a chorus of five hundred voices from the various church choirs and male choruses in order to add to the fund for the proposed Wennerberg statue. The concert was held at the Casino. The mixed chorus sang ''Psalm CL,'' ''Psalm XXIV,'' ''Sommarsöndag'' and ''Trasten i höstkvällen.'' The male chorus sang ''Hör oss, Svea'' and ''Stå stark, du ljusets riddarvakt.'' A duet and a solo by Wennerberg were also on the programme.

Baptist Choirs

The choir of the First Swedish Baptist Church of Chicago was founded in 1871 but had a somewhat irregular existence until reorganized in 1891, when it assumed the name Symphony Singing Society. A. P. Nelson, who had been leader since 1889, translated the text to Baker's cantata ''The Storm King'' and conducted its production on Dec. 4, 1891. It was repeated in 1892 and 1893. Among the later leaders were Axel Francke 1899, John E. Spann 1895-8, 1900-3, and 1908.

A male chorus, Sångarbröderna, was organized among the Swedish Baptists of Chicago by A. P. Nelson in 1900. It has sung at several large celebrations, as the Golden Jubilee concert in 1902, and the concert for the benefit of the Swedish famine sufferers in 1903.

The Swedish Baptist Jubilee Chorus of Chicago is a union choir, organized in 1902 with John E. Spann as director, for the purpose of singing at the Golden Jubilee of the Swedish Baptists on Sept. 27, 1902. The chorus has since been permanently organized. It has taken part in the benefit concert for the famine sufferers of Sweden, April 4, 1903, and in several local charity concerts. The chorus numbers about 250 mixed voices and rehearses about ten weeks previous to the annual fall concert. Among the works sung are Wennerberg's "Psalm CL," Costa's "Zion, Awake," Bellini's "Lofsång," Berens' "Vid älfvarne i Babylon," Gounod's "Unfold, ye Portals," Cowen's "Bridal Chorus," Gounod's "By Babylon's Wave" and Gounod's "Zion's ways do languish."

Mission Choirs

The energetic Axel L. Hvassman was chorister of the Lake View Mission Choir 1890-92, the Swedish Tabernacle Choir 1892-96, 1899-1902 and of the North Side Mission Choir 1896-99, 1902—. In the Tabernacle Church the choir sang P. U. Stenhammar's "Höstpsalm" on Nov. 20, 1892, H. Berens' "Fader vår" on May 25, 1895, L. Norman's "Det gudomliga ljuset" on Dec. 14, 1895, and Gounod's "Vid Babylons älfvar" on Nov. 15, 1902. Several of the above works have been sung by the North Side Mission Choir under Mr. Hvassman's leadership. In 1895 many members of the above choruses sang at the Covenant concerts in St. Paul and Minneapolis.

Mr. Hvassman organized, in 1892, the Swedish Mission Festival Chorus of Chicago. Under his direction the chorus, varying from 350 to 500 voices, has sung at the Auditorium during various seasons such works as Gounod's "Gallia," P. U. Stenhammar's "David och Saul" and "Höstpsalm," A. F. Lindblad's "Drömmarne," Gounod's "Nazareth" and parts of "Messiah" and "Elijah."

The Asaph Singing Society was organized in 1894 by Mr. Hvassman from among the male singers in Mission choirs. The usual quartettes are sung, often furnished with religious text. On Nov. 28, 1896, Petterson-Berger's cycle, "Fjällfärd," was sung to words written by D. Nyvall. The chorus, numbering about thirty-five members, sang at Minneapolis and various points in Iowa in 1900.

Mr. Hvassman is indefatigable in his efforts to provide for his audiences a high grade of choral music, both as to content and vocal quality. He is one of the best Swedish chorus directors in the state.

One of the excellent Swedish choirmasters in Illinois is Andrew G. Hvass, who led the Lake View Mission Choir in the singing of P. U.

Stenhammar's fine "Höstpsalm" on Nov. 29, 1900. For several years he had a union chorus in Lake View, Chicago. Since 1906 he has been leader of the Swedish Tabernacle Choir. This excellent chorus sang Stenhammar's "Höstpsalm" and part I. of Gaul's "Ruth" Nov. 29, 1906, while on June 29, 1907, it sang A. F. Lindblad's "Drömmarne." Mr. Hvass has organized the South Side Choral Union which sang Van Boom's "Lofsång" and Stolpe's "Davids LXVII Psalm" on April 9, 1908, in the Swedish Tabernacle.

Lutheran Choirs

John Peters, organist and choir leader of Salem Sw. Luth. Church in Chicago was educated in Oberlin and New England musical conservatories. Besides the usual work, he has prepared many programmes with excerpts from standard oratorios and cantatas.

The Trinity Sw. Luth. Church in Lake View, Chicago, sang "Bethlehem" under Robert Anderson in 1904. The next year, when Otto Carlson became leader, the choir sang Stainer's "Crucifixion." This was repeated in 1906 and 1908. In 1907 Gaul's "The Holy City" and Mercadante's "The Seven Last Words" were sung. The choir numbers sixty-five voices.

On Feb. 20, 1908, the Swedish Lutheran churches of Chicago had a "national festival" in Orchestra Hall, where the Swedish-American National Chorus, composed of church choir members, under the leadership of Alfred Holmes, sang Stolpe's "Ordet," a composition for male chorus, female chorus, mixed chorus and final eight part chorus, Wennerberg's "När Herren Zions fångar" and "Aftonklockan," besides several numbers with English text. Emil Larson has been appointed director for 1909.

Many church choirs in various parts of the state have done similar good work. Owing to their preparing from one to four anthems for each Sunday they do not, as a rule, have the leisure to obtain that finesse in singing which the male choruses sometimes attain. Taking this into consideration, the results obtained are praiseworthy. It is worthy of remark that with but two or three exceptions the male choruses have devoted themselves to the singing of small quartettes. The church choirs have not hesitated to learn and perform large choral works, such as cantatas and oratorios, quite often scoring brilliant results. In this respect they may well be emulated by the male choruses.

It is doubtless a fact that one of the greatest influences toward a popular elevation of musical taste in the Swedish communities in this country has been exerted by the church choirs.

The Svithiod Singing Club

The present organization known as the Svithiod Singing Club is the outgrowth of a male chorus formed in 1882 among the early members of the Independent Order of Svithiod. It was directed successively by Björnholzt, E. Becker, August Elfåker and others. On Feb. 11, 1893, the chorus was organized under its present name

The Home of the Svithiod Singing Club

and charter as a singing and social club. Theodore Sjöquist, then chosen as leader of the chorus, shortly gave place to John L. Swenson, who remained as director until 1906, when John R. Örtengren became his successor. The new organization took an active part in the preparations for the song festival on Swedish Day at the World's Fair.

Jan. 11, 1896, was a memorable day in the history of the Svithiod Singing Club. On that date a tournament of song was held at the

The Svithiod Singing Club, 1896

Auditorium, participated in by male choruses of seven nationalities. The Svithiod, with its twenty-four voices, had to compete with choruses three times its size, but they sang Jahnke's "Sjömannen" with such spirit, such consummate finish, that when the contest was over, the prize was theirs. This consisted of a costly banner, bearing the inscription: "The Champion Singers of Chicago." The judges of the contest were three noted musicians of Chicago. The director, John L. Swenson, was awarded a gold medal.

Besides numerous concerts and public entertainments, this club has made two successful attempts in the operatic line. The first was a rendition of Sullivan's "Pinafore," in Swedish, at McVicker's Theater, in 1897, followed some years later by "The Little Saint," a Swedish operetta, presented at the Studebaker Theater. "Pinafore" was repeated several times, the last being Dec. 29, 1899, and Jan. 7, 1900, with the aid of the Swedish Glee Club. The two choruses played Gustaf Wicklund's "En afton på Tre Byttor" Dec. 30, 1899.

To the select chorus that toured Sweden in 1897 Svithiod contributed sixteen members, being one of the two clubs to appear independently at the concerts given in the old country.

The Svithiod Singing Club owns its clubhouse, located at 1768 Wrightwood avenue, to which was added in 1901 a concert hall with a seating capacity of several hundred.

The Swedish Glee Club

A male chorus called Svenska Sångsällskapet, founded in 1887, was led by John L. Swenson for two years. In 1889 it was consolidated with a social organization known as the Swedish Club, and renamed the Swedish Glee Club. Having secured John R. Örtengren as director, it soon proved itself a splendid aggregation of singers. At the Scandinavian singing festival held in 1891 at Minneapolis, they took second honors, but for a long period thereafter were accorded foremost rank among the clubs of the Swedish-American singers' union. The Glee Club furnished many of the best voices that went to make up the picked chorus for the Sweden tour in 1897.

Among the more notable numbers in its repertory may be mentioned Söderman's "Ett bondbröllop," Hedenblad's "På knä," Witt's "I natten," Körling's "Sten Sture," Grieg's "Landkjending," Norén's "Styrbjörn Starke," Hallström's "Hymn till fosterlandet," and portions of Bruch's "Scenes from Frithiof's Saga." The operetta "Doktor Dulcamara" has been given several times by the club.

A few years back the club was demoralized, partly by the loss of men who had become leaders of other clubs, but chiefly on account of flagging interest in the rehearsals on the part of the remaining members. It was in excellent form at the festival held in Chicago in 1905,

but shortly thereafter discontinued regular practice. It was revived
in the fall of 1906, under the leadership of William Dahlén.

The Swedish Glee Club occupies leased quarters at 470 La Salle
avenue. Its club house has been the scene of many a notable event
in the Swedish-American musical and social circles of the city
during the past quarter century. In the early part of the year .

The Swedish Glee Club, Chicago, 1902

1907 the club celebrated its silver anniversary, the nucleus of the
organization having been formed in 1882.

The American Union of Swedish Singers

A generation back little groups of Swedish-American singers began
to organize themselves into male choruses after the manner of those
of the mother country. At private or public gatherings, in lodge halls
and at social assemblages, a singer or two would be present who would
be asked to give a solo or try a duet together—some old favorite tune
familiar to all. A step farther, and the result would be a quartette.
This last would frequently form the nucleus for a male chorus, formed
to sing, for their own pleasure and the entertainment of their friends,
the favorite songs of the home-land. At a later stage, when the

choruses would grow to a score or more of voices, fairly trained under the direction of the most competent one from among their own number, they would attempt the more difficult task of rendering the characteristic creations of Wennerberg, Söderman and others, written originally for the world-renowned student choruses at the Swedish universities.

The Club House of the Swedish Glee Club

A like movement had been going on among the other Scandinavians of the United States. Norwegian and Danish male choruses had been formed in various localities, east and west. In the eastern states a union of Scandinavian fraternal and mutual aid societies was effected in the middle eighties. Why not a similar organization of singing societies? The idea was taken up by the Scandinavian Society of Philadelphia at the instance of Capt. C. M. Machold, on whose initiative an association known as the United Scandinavian Singers of America was organized on the lines of the German-American Sängerbund. The organization took place in the city of New York May 16, 1886, at a meeting of delegates from five choruses, in Philadelphia, New York, Brooklyn and Boston.

Their first singing festival was held at Philadelphia the following year. This was attended by a strong Norwegian male chorus from Chicago, which was forthwith admitted to membership in the union. The association now grew so rapidly that at the next festival, held in

Carl Fredrik Lundqvist

Chicago in 1889, about six hundred singers were in attendance. When the singers met in Minneapolis after another interval of two years, about two hundred more had been added. Up to this time harmony had been the predominant note in the united choruses, but the attempt, auspicious at first, to keep the organization intact from the traditional strife between Swedes and Norwegians, was destined to fail. Quarrels arose between these two factions, while the Danes held aloof and made unsuccessful overtures for peace. Close upon the Minneapolis festival followed the dissolution of the organization.

The Swedish choruses having gained many triumphs at the song festivals, were desirous of continuing mutual relations among themselves, and soon conceived the idea of forming a federation of their own. The Lyran Singing Club of New York took the initiative in calling the choruses together, and at a meeting held in the club house of the Swedish Glee Club of Chicago on Thanksgiving Day, Nov. 24, 1892, there was organized the American Union of Swedish Singers. Charles K. Johansen, a member of the Lyran, is the acknowledged father of the organization, having been the first to propose the idea and one of the most zealous promoters of the singers' union from that day to this. Other men taking a prominent part in the work from the start were, Magnus Olson, John R. Örtengren, Olof Nelson, William Dahlén, John L. Swenson, Fred Franson, Arvid Åkerlind, Edward Molin, Alfred G. Larson and Gustaf Hallbom.

The first singing festival of the new organization took place the following summer and the first of the three concerts formed the crowning feature of "Swedish Day," July 20th, at the World's Columbian Exposition in Chicago. The union had engaged three famous Swedish vocalists for the occasion, viz., Caroline Östberg and Carl Fredrik Lundqvist of the Royal Opera at Stockholm, and Conrad Behrens, a grand opera basso. The concerts were held in Festival Hall, which seated 6,500 people and was filled at each concert, thousands vainly striving to gain admittance. The Thomas Orchestra of 140 pieces, led by Theodore Thomas and his assistant, Oscar Ringwall, a native of Sweden, furnished the accompaniments. John R. Örtengren was director of the chorus of about 500 voices from the American Union of Swedish Singers. On account of the importance and interest of the occasion the programmes for the three concerts are given in full.

The First Concert, Thursday, 4 p. m., July 20, 1893

Overture, "Orleanska Jungfrun"......................................August Söderman
Thomas Orchestra

"Hör oss, Svea"...Gunnar Wennerberg
American Union of Swedish Singers

Hymn from "Gustaf Wasa"...J. G. Naumann
Carl Fr. Lundqvist

"The Countess' Aria," from "The Marriage of Figaro"..............W. A. Mozart
Mme. Carolina Östberg

"Swedish Dances"..Max Bruch
Thomas Orchestra

"Tannhäuser"...Aug. Söderman
Carl Fr. Lundqvist

a) "Neckens Polska"..Folksong
b) "I Bröllopsgården"...Aug. Söderman
Swedish Glee Club, Chicago

"Fjorton år tror jag visst att jag var"............................Swedish Folksong
Mme. Carolina Östberg

"Du gamla, du friska, du fjällhöga nord"..........................Swedish Folksong
Carl Fr. Lundqvist, with Chorus

"Hell dig, du höga nord"...B. Crusell
American Union of Swedish Singers

Second Concert, Friday, 3 p. m., July 21, 1893

'Stridsbön''...O. Lindblad
American Union of Swedish Singers
Symphony...:.August Elfåker
Thomas Orchestra
Aria from ''The Magic Flute''..W. A. Mozart
Conrad Behrens
Aria from ''Der Freischütz''............................. ... ... .C. M. von Weber
Mme. Carolina Östberg
''Sjömannens Farväl''...Meurling
Lyran, New York
''Svensk Rhapsodie''..A. Hallén
Thomas Orchestra
a) ''Don Juans Serenad''... ...Tschaikowski
b) ''I djupa källarhvalfvet''.. * * *
Conrad Behrens
a) ''Still wie die Nacht''.. * * *
b) ''La Fioraja''.'... * * *
c) ''Klara stjärnor med de ögon snälla''...........................I. Dannström
Mme. Carolina Östberg
''Fäderneslandet''...J. E. Nordblom
American Union of Swedish Singers
''America''...S. F. Smith
American Union of Swedish Singers, and the Audience

Third Concert, Saturday, 3 p. m., July 22, 1893

''Svensk Rhapsodie''..Lalo
Thomas Orchestra
''Vårt Land''..J. A. Josephson
American Union of Swedish Singers
''Qvarnruinen''...Aug. Söderman
Carl Fr. Lundqvist
Aria from ''The Jewess''..Halevy
Conrad Behrens
''Naturen och hjärtat''..O. Lindblad
Svithiod Singing Club
a) ''Sjung, sjung''...J. A. Josephson
b) ''Vandring i skogen''..G. E. Geijer
c) ''Sover du, min Sjæl?''...E. Sjögren
Carl Fr. Lundqvist
''Swedish Folksong''..A. Hamerik
Thomas Orchestra
''Bröllopsmarsch''..Aug. Söderman
Swedish Glee Club, Chicago
a) ''Trollhättan''...O. Lindblad
b) ''Nu är det natt''..F. Abt
c) ''Per Svinaherde''...Swedish Folksong
Conrad Behrens
a) ''Vermlandsvisan''...Swedish Folksong
b) ''Du gamla, du friska, du fjällhöga nord''..................Swedish Folksong
Carl Fr. Lundqvist, with Chorus
''Stå stark, du ljusets riddarvakt''.......................... .....G. Wennerberg
American Union of Swedish Singers

The above programmes show a preponderance of compositions by Swedish composers, particularly some of the best of the works of the brilliant Aug. Söderman. The symphony by August Elfåker, a Chicago organist, was an overambitious attempt at orchestral writing. The three soloists were superior in vocal gifts to any subsequent visitors from Sweden. They all had taken part in a concert on July 18th, given at Central Music Hall by the union. Mr. Lundqvist gave a parting concert with the Swedish Glee Club on Sept. 2, 1893, at the same place.

It having been decided to hold quadrennial conventions and festivals, the union next met in 1897, at New York City. Immediately thereafter, according to a pre-arranged plan, a select chorus of fifty men, with John R. Örtengren as musical director, sailed for Sweden to visit the Northern Industrial Exposition at Stockholm and give a series of concerts in the principal Swedish cities. Their reception in the old country was as cordial as could be wished, and the tour, besides being a highly enjoyable pleasure trip for the participants, served the additional purpose of dispelling the too prevalent skepticism in Sweden as to the status of general culture among the Swedish people in the United States. The work of the chorus, while not up to the high standard attained by the famous student singers of Sweden, nevertheless did not fall so far below that standard as not to be characterized as an artistic triumph.

Jamestown, New York, was the scene of the next convention, in 1901. In addition to the regular concerts given there, the chorus of four hundred voices sang at the Chautauqua Assembly, to an audience that filled the great amphitheater to overflowing. This occasion was one of the highest significance for the singers' union, demonstrating, as it did, that their renditions were listened to with the greatest zest by a discriminating audience not made up of their own fellow countrymen and to whom both the words and music of the songs were foreign. Add to this that the event carried the fame of the singers into wide circles never reached before, and it is apparent that this was a most notable triumph in the history of the American Union of Swedish Singers.

The 1905 convention was held in Chicago, and the grand concerts, given in the Auditorium, proved highly artistic events. At a subsequent Bellman festival, held in one of Chicago's summer gardens, the chorus sang before a still larger and more cosmopolitan audience than that assembled at the Auditorium.

For these song festivals the singers' union has brought over from Sweden a number of its most renowned artists of the operatic stage, such as Caroline Östberg, Carl Fredrik Lundqvist, Conrad Behrens, John Forsell and Anna Hellström, besides bringing out many Swedish-

American soloists, not a few of whom have risen from the rank and file of the male choruses.

The singers' union is divided into two sections, an eastern and a western division, each holding a quadrennial convention and song festival, so that the singers meet every two years, either jointly or in two separate bodies. The joint festivals are held in the East and West alternately, and heretofore the concerts have been directed in turn by Arvid Åkerlind of New York and John R. Örtengren of Chicago.

In 1908 the singers' union decided to send, in 1910, a select chorus of fifty voices from their body on a concert tour of Sweden, under the direction of John R. Örtengren.

John R. Örtengren, 1893

At the present time the singers' union numbers about sixty clubs, those in Illinois forming one-fifth of the entire constituency. No less than nine of these are found in Chicago, while Rockford and Moline boast two each. Outside of this state the union has the bulk of its membership in New York, New England and Minnesota. The Rockford choruses are the Lyran Singing Society, John L. Swenson, director, and Sveas Söner, John R. Örtengren, director. The Moline Societies are the Svea Male Chorus, Petrus Brodin, director, and the Olive Male Chorus, Adolph Erickson, director.

The Chicago male choruses made numerous public appearances under the leadership of John R. Örtengren before they were incorporated in 1906 as the Swedish Singers' Union of Chicago. The Chicago

choruses, with their respective leaders, are: Svithiod Singing Club, John
R. Örtengren; Swedish Glee Club, Lyran and Norden, William Dahlén;
Harmoni, Iduna and Orpheus, Joel Mossberg; Zephyr, E. D. Ytterberg;
Nordstjernan, Ernst Lindblom.

John R. Örtengren

From the time John R. Örtengren came to this country, in 1889,
he has been soloist at several prominent churches, and one of the
principal teachers of a large musical conservatory. Leader in turn of
the best two Swedish male choruses in the state, several mixed choruses,
director-in-chief of the American Union of Swedish Singers, of the
western division of the union, and of the Swedish Singers' Union of
Chicago, he is the best known musician among his countrymen in the
land of their adoption. He enjoys the universal respect and confidence
of the Swedish people of Chicago as evinced on more than one occasion.
In recognition of his eminent services to the cause of Swedish music
in. America, Mr. Örtengren was decorated in September, 1908, with
the medal of Vasa by King Gustaf V. of Sweden.

The Lund Students' Chorus

Sweden is a country devoted for almost a century to a capella male
chorus singing. All of its prominent composers have written music
in this style and it may well be questioned whether any land has
produced so many beautiful melodies and stirring march songs set for
male voices as has Sweden. Although cultivated everywhere, the
traditional seats of this style of chorus singing have been at the universities of Upsala and Lund. The Lund Students' Chorus was founded in
1838 by Otto Lindblad, who composed many now famous songs for it
and made it, at that time, the best chorus in the North.

From time to time during the last decade there were rumors that
either the Upsala chorus or the Lund chorus would tour America.
The former body had made tours in Russia, Germany and France,
taking grand prizes in the Paris Expositions of 1867, 1878 and 1900.
It was the fortune of the latter chorus, however, to take the long trip
across the Atlantic before its famous rival. The Lund Students' Chorus
of sixty-eight men came to Chicago after a tour of New England and
some of the central western states. Their concert was held in the Auditorium on July 7, 1904, under the leadership of Alfred Berg. With the
chorus appeared John Forsell, a baritone from the Royal Opera at
Stockholm.

The Lund Students' Chorus Programme
Organ, "Variations on Du gamla, du fria, du fjällhöga Nord".......Emil Larson
Emil Larson
"Hör oss, Svea".. ....G. Wennerberg
"Glad såsom fågeln"...Prince Gustaf

"Stridsbön"...Otto Lindblad
"Den store, hvide Flok"......................................Edv. Grieg
The Lund Students' Chorus
"Naturen och hjärtat".................................... ....Otto Lindblad
Swedish Singers' Union of Chicago
"Dalmarsch"..I. Widéen
"Blommande, sköna dalar".............................. ....Herm. Palm
The Lund Students' Chorus
Organ, "Variations on an American Air"...............................Flagler
Emil Larson
"Undan, ur vägen"..C. M. Bellman
"Sten Sture"..Aug. Körling
The Lund Students' Chorus
"Björneborgarnes Marsch"................................... * * *
Swedish Singers' Union of Chicago
"Olav Trygvason"..F. A. Reissiger
"Till svenska fosterjorden".....................................Arr. af Alfr. Berg
"Ett Bondbröllop"...Aug. Söderman
 a) "Bröllopsmarsch;" b) "I kyrkan;" c) "Önskevisa;" d) "I bröllopsgården"
The Lund Students' Chorus

Besides the eleven numbers indicated, the chorus sang several extra numbers. The first tenors had a beauteous lyrical quality of voice whilst the second basses gave forth a smooth and resonant tone. The distinct articulation, the good pronunciation, the precision of attack and steadiness of pitch were remarkable. The nuances and climaxes attained can be compared to the effect produced by a fine string orchestra. This was most marked in "Undan, ur vägen." Grieg's "Den store, hvide Flok" was new to the audience and was greatly admired. The noble but difficult ballad "Sten Sture" was brilliantly rendered. The tempi chosen had a tendency of being rather fast in certain numbers. The general impression made, however, is that such splendid a capella singing had probably never before been attained by any chorus in this country.

Concerts were given July 8th at Rock Island, July 9th at Rockford and again on July 10th at Chicago.

The Swedish Y. M. C. A. Chorus

This male chorus was first organized in Sweden to sing at the International Y. M. C. A. conference at London in 1894. It is composed, for the most part, of professional men from various parts of Sweden, who have sung in university choruses, but it includes also several laborers in its ranks. For several years past the Swedish Y. M. C. A. Chorus has been considered one of the best choruses in Sweden. Leaving Stockholm May 28, 1906, it made a short tour of the southern cities of Sweden. Its American tour began June 17th in New York. The chorus sang in Rockford June 25th, and the next day in DeKalb. On June 27th a large audience was assembled in the Chicago Auditorium to attend the festival of song. Hugo Lindquist was the director and John Husberg the baritone soloist. The chorus consisted of fifty singers.

The Swedish Y. M. C. A. Chorus Programme

Organ, Overture to "Raymond"...A. Thomas
     A. Alfred Holmes
"Stå stark, du ljusets riddarvakt".......................................G. Wennerberg
"Hör oss, Svea"...G. Wennerberg
"Öfver skogen, öfver sjön"...A. F. Lindblad
"Og jeg vil ha mig en hjertenskjer"...Aug. Söderman
"Nog mins jag, hur det var"...Aug. Söderman
"Afsked" ....Hermes
    The Swedish Y. M. C. A. Chorus
Fides' Aria from "The Prophet"..G. Meyerbeer
    Elisabeth Bruce Wickström
Violin and Piano Duet, a) "Romance"....................................Hugo Alfvén
    b) "Norwegian Dance".................Johan Halvorsen
    Mr. and Mrs. Frederik Frederiksen
"Glad såsom fågeln"...Prince Gustaf
"Ack, Värmeland, du sköna"...Swedish Folksong
"Dalmarsch"..I. Widéen
"Styrbjörn Starke"..G. Norén
    The Swedish Y. M. C. A. Chorus
Organ, Overture to "Semiramide" ....G. Rossini
    A. Alfred Holmes
Svenska Folkvisor.. * * *
    Elisabeth Bruce Wickström
"Guds lof i naturen"..L. Beethoven
"Solnedgång i hafvet"...E. G. Geijer
"Israels herde"...Bortniansky
"Den store, hvide Flok"...Edv. Grieg
    The Swedish Y. M. C. A. Chorus

The same entrancing effect as that produced by the Lund Students' Chorus was again experienced by the audience. The beautiful timbre of the first and second tenors, the splendor of the first basses and the velvety smoothness of the second basses may be fitly compared to the effect produced by a stringed orchestra or by a brilliantly voiced organ. Several da capo numbers were sung, among them being a novelty, "Stenbocks gossar," by Aug. Körling, which was sung in a spirited fashion and afforded the tenors an opportunity to display their limpid high tones.

After a tour of the central western states a second concert was given in Chicago on July 7th.

The well nigh perfect rendition attained by the two choruses from Sweden will long be a criterion to the Swedish male and mixed choruses in this country.

The Svea Male Chorus, Moline

One of the oldest male choruses in the state is the Svea Male Chorus of Moline, which was organized Aug. 23, 1887. The nucleus was formed from the sixteen male voices in the Swedish Lutheran Church Choir. It remained a church organization for a number of years, until it engaged its own quarters. Its musical directors have been William

The Svea Male Chorus, Moline, 1907

Ljung, 1887-91, P. Hartsough, 1891-2, William Svensson, then teacher at Augustana Conservatory, 1892-3, Joseph Lindstrom, 1893-4, C. M. Carlstedt, 1894, D. S. Davies, 1894-6, Adolf Hult, 1896-7, C. M. Carlstedt, 1898-1902, Edla Lund, 1902-5, Emil Larson, 1905-8. In August, 1908, Petrus Brodin was chosen leader. During the last few years the chorus has gained so much in precision, in surety of pitch, in shading and phrasing, as to make it one of the best male choruses in the singers' union.

Gustaf Holmquist

Doubtless Gustaf Holmquist is the Swedish-American vocalist who is best known to the American music loving public. Gifted with an imposing presence and a rich and sympathetic voice, he is rapidly becoming a favorite oratorio singer, for he is engaged by the leading choral societies of the country, from the central West to the East. Having sung the bass solo in the production of Gabriel Pierne's "The

Gustaf Holmquist

Children's Crusade," by the Apollo Club of Chicago, he has been engaged to take the same part on Feb. 19, 1909, with the Minneapolis Philharmonic Society.

Ever since 1900, when he moved to Chicago, Mr. Holmquist's voice has been a familiar one to Swedish concert audiences in Illinois. An extended biographical sketch of Mr. Holmquist is given in another part of this work.

The Orion Quartette

The Orion Quartette has existed since 1887, when it made its first public appearance in Chicago. William Dahlén is first tenor, Mauritz Hultin, second tenor, Peter Westerberg, first bass, and Emil Granath, second bass. They have been principals at scores of concerts during the last twenty years and probably form the oldest existing Swedish male quartette in the state. Many similar organizations are to be found in all Swedish communities.

The Swedish Ladies' Octette

The Swedish Ladies' Octette was organized in 1888 and came to New York in the fall of that year from Sweden. The members were:

M. HULTIN   W. DAHLEN   E. GRANATH   P. WESTERBERG
The Orion Quartette

first sopranos, Agnes Stabergh, Wilma Sundborg; second sopranos, Maria Hedén, Amanda Carlson-Svenson; first altos, Elizabeth Bruce, Maria Solberg; second altos, Amelia Hedén, Hilma Zetterstrand. After touring the eastern states throughout the winter, they went west and gave concerts in Chicago, March 19 and 20, 1889, after which they sang in various Swedish communities in Illinois the rest of the season. They toured the country from coast to coast twice and also sang their way through Canada and British Columbia. The octette's last concert was in Englewood, Chicago, on May 12, 1891. Jenny Norelius, a native of Helsingland, was a substitute for a sick member for almost one season. Miss Norelius is very generally known as Mme. Norelli, a prima donna of the Italian Grand Opera Company of New York.

The Swedish Ladies' Quartette

For several years past there has existed in Chicago the Swedish Ladies' Quartette, composed as follows: Ida Linn-Cooley, first soprano, Maria Solberg-Sinn, second soprano, Stephanie Hedén, first alto, and

MARGARET DAHLSTROM   STEPHANIE HEDEN   MARIA SOLBERG-SINN
                            IDA LINN-COOLEY
The Swedish Ladies' Quartette

Margaret Dahlstrom, second alto. Their repertory comprises many of the Swedish student songs, besides songs in English, especially arranged for women's voices. Mrs. Cooley and Miss Dahlstrom have appeared with credit as soloists on numerous occasions. Mrs. Solberg-Sinn was a member of the Swedish Ladies' Octette.

The Carlsson Trio

The Carlsson Trio has existed since 1907. It is composed of Samuel E. Carlsson, Gustaf Engstrom and Axel D. Smith. S. E. Carlsson, the violinist, was leader of the Augustana College Orchestra at its organization in 1880. After moving to Lindsborg, Kans., he organized an orchestra of fourteen players, which developed into the Bethany College Orchestra. In Chicago he conducted an amateur orchestra for a year in the early nineties. He has played in several chamber music organiza-

The Carlsson Trio, Chicago

tions from time to time. From 1902 until 1905 he was first violinist of a string quartette composed of Messrs. Carlsson, Hoyt, Carr and Carpenter.

Gustaf Engstrom devoted his studies to the violin from his eighth year. Conceiving a liking for the violoncello he derived instruction in that instrument from several teachers, finishing under Carl Brueckner. Mr. Engstrom has played in several trios and orchestras.

Axel D. Smith has studied the organ and piano under the able musicians Emil Larson, Thorwald Otterström, W. C. E. Seeboeck and Dr. Julius Fuchs. He has devoted his whole life to musical art and has made a special study of chamber music and is familiar with the works of the great masters in this genre. At present he is organist of the Rogers Park English Lutheran Church, where Mr. Carlsson is choir director.

The Carlsson Trio has appeared in concert at various times during the season of 1907-08. Its repertory consists of the piano trios of Beethoven, Mendelssohn, Haydn, Hummel, Gade and Chopin.

Sigfrid Laurin

Sigfrid Laurin is the best equipped pianist who has come from Sweden to this country. His technique is adequate to all demands, and his repertory is enormous. His playing is sympathetic, though, at times, extremely erratic.

Sigfrid Laurin

The works of Laurin, most of which are still in manuscript, comprise eighteen songs, romances and ballads for the voice and six compositions for the piano, several of the latter being quite large works. The vocal solos are: songs—"Bön," "Mitt hjertas vittnesbörd," "Julens stjerna;" romances—"Vid grafven," "Solen sjunker," "Hemlös," "I Gethsemane," "Sorgen," "Den döende krigaren," "I höstlig tid," "Bön;" ballads—"Vid hafvet," "Farväl," "It Is Done," "Från mitt hjertas lyra," "At Eventide," "Till döds;" romantic ballad— "Brustna strängar." The piano compositions are: "Mitt lif," a rhapsody; "Excelsior," a symphonic fantasia, requiring some two hours for its execution; "I drömmar," berceuse; "Öfver djupen," fantasia;

"På örnevingar," concert etude; "Tempelminnen," an arrangement of sacred melodies for piano, in four parts.

A biographical sketch of Laurin is given in another part of this work. Mr. Laurin severed his connection with Augustana College in June, 1908, and has returned to Sweden.

Minor Mention

Eleonore L. M. Wigström was born in Upland, Sweden in 1835. An actress in 1856-7 of the Royal Opera at Stockholm, she was married to V. Planckh. It is related that he sold her to a Russian, Petroff, who had fallen in love with her. After their marriage, Mme. Petroff is said to have studied with the best European masters and to have appeared in concert and opera with many renowned artists, attaining great success. Petroff died in 1869 after spending his fortune. The widow assumed the name Mme. Eleonore Petrelli and gave concerts in Russia, Poland and Germany for many years. Returning in 1886 to Stockholm, she did not thrive, and therefore left the next year for this country. After various adventures she settled in 1888 in Chicago as a singing teacher. Mme. Petrelli gave numerous recitals, although her voice had lost whatever beauty it once possessed. She died Feb. 21, 1904.

Several singers of Swedish birth have sung in grand opera at Chicago, as Christina Nilsson, Sigrid Arnoldson, Conrad Behrens, Olive Fremstad, Mme. Forstrom, Johannes Elmblad.

About 1885 there arrived in Chicago two young ladies from Sweden, Ellen Svendblad and Mimmi Lindström. The former was a soprano from the Royal Opera in Stockholm. Miss Svendblad had a good dramatic voice and appeared successfully in many Swedish concerts during the following three years, after which she moved to New York where she was engaged by various opera companies.

Miss Lindström was successful as a teacher and accompanist. She married John R. Örtengren after a few years and has since then occasionally appeared as accompanist.

C. H. E. Öberg lived in Rockford for several years, where he was organist, music teacher and musical conductor. He was a graduate of the Royal Conservatory of Music at Stockholm, being one of the few to receive the degree of Director Musices et Cantus. Öberg composed several male choruses and edited two collections for male voices, entitled "När och fjärran" and "Skandia." He died in Minneapolis about 1894.

During the past few years A. D. Bodfors, formerly connected with the Augustana Conservatory of Music, has conducted music schools in two or three Illinois cities, including Moline and Rockford. Mr. Bodfors, who is an accomplished performer on the piano and the organ, received his musical training chiefly at the hands of Dr. Stolpe.

De Celle was an amateur Swedish tenor of French extraction who sang in the Swedish church concerts in the early eighties.

One of the Swedish pianists sojourning in Chicago in the early eighties was one Dahlberg, who gave concerts in Swedish circles and aroused considerable enthusiasm through his technique.

Augusta Öhrström sang in Central Music Hall on Sept. 22, 1891. She had but lately come to this country from Europe, where she had sung with considerable success.

About 1890-93 the Lütteman Sextette, organized in Stockholm by Hugo Lütteman, traveled in this country. The male sextette gave concerts at many points in Illinois, and sang with finish.

Wilhelm Lindberg was piano teacher at North Park College 1895-96. He had a small tenor voice and played his own accompaniments on a harp. His piano playing was of a high order.

Ernst Swedelius was in Chicago from about 1895 to 1898. He had a tremendous bass-baritone voice and sometimes appeared at public concerts. More recently he has sung in grand opera at Stockholm.

In the nineties a young Swedish Chicago girl, Miss Helma Nilson, came before the public. Gifted with a fine voice and a charming appearance, she played the star parts and sang the interpolated songs in a number of Swedish dramatic productions in Chicago and other American cities, and subsequently appeared successfully in Sweden.

"Frithiof and Ingeborg," an opera whose plot is founded on Tegnér's "Frithiof's Saga," was produced in the Chicago Auditorium for three consecutive night in February, 1900. The composer, Charles L. Hanson, of Worcester, Mass., adapted the music largely from extant compositions, such as Donizetti's sextette from "Lucia," Söderman's "Ett bondbröllop" and other well-known works.

Martina Johnstone, the New York violinist, and Anna Hellström, the opera singer from Stockholm, appeared at the American Union of Swedish Singers' concerts in Chicago July 20 and 21, 1905.

Ebba Hjertstedt, a Chicago girl, received her first violin instruction in her home city. She has finished her education in Europe and has appeared as soloist with several continental orchestras.

A tour that awakened much interest was that made by the Royal Kronoberg Regiment Band of thirty-five players led by Erik Högberg. Two concerts were given in Chicago in April, 1908.

Among professional musicians of Swedish extraction in Chicago whose biographical sketches are given elsewhere in this work are John R. Örtengren, Gustaf Holmquist, Rudolph Engberg, Olof Valley, Hannah Butler, Ragna Linné, Ellyn Swanson, Lydia Hallberg, Elvira Wennerskold and Axel B. C. Carlstedt.

Other Swedish professional musicians in Chicago are Mrs. Christine

Engstrom, Anna Chinlund, Arthur Granquist, Hilma Enander, Edgar Nelson, Johannes Olsson, Karin Lindskog, John Newstrom, John Fr. Ring, Axel Francke, Ernst Fristrom and Sara Nordstrom.

Sketches of the musicians Emil Larson, Sigfrid Laurin, Edla Lund and Frank E. Peterson will be found under the heading Rock Island, in another part of this work.

Many musicianly amateurs are to be found in the Swedish population of this state. Swedish pupils are to be counted by the hundreds, divided between the various music schools and the private teachers. This bespeaks a general spread of culture which was not possible in the first generation of Swedish life in Illinois.

CHAPTER XIII

Press and Literature

Illinois the Producing Center

SURVEY of the whole field of Swedish-American literature establishes some interesting facts with respect to Illinois. The first Swedish printing-press on this continent was started within the borders of this state. From it was issued the pioneer Swedish newspaper in the United States and the second Swedish periodical in the New World.* Chicago early became the publishing center as well as the center of literary activity among the Swedish people, a position it still retains. Until twenty years ago no Swedish newspapers published elsewhere in this country could compare favorably with those issued from Chicago or dispute the field with them. Even now, with a number of formidable rivals in the East and the Northwest, the Swedish newspapers of Chicago are not outclassed. All the leading organs of the Swedish denominations were founded in Illinois and are being published from Chicago, except one, the Lutheran mouthpiece, which issues from Rock Island. In the matter of book publishing, the production of Swedish books outside of this state is insignificant as compared with that of the Swedish publishing houses here.

The great bulk of the literary output has passed through journalistic channels. To a marked degree the Swedish people have relied on their newspapers to furnish them with reading matter of whatever sort. The result has been, in a number of instances, that around some newspaper has grown up a considerable publishing business. Certain of the secular papers have put out good-sized editions of standard

* Reference is had to the weekly "Report of St. Bartholomew," 154 numbers of which were published in 1804—12, in English, by Anders Bergstedt, at Gustavia, on the sland of St. Bartholomew, then a Swedish possession.

works for premium purposes, while the publishers of religious journals have been called upon to supply the respective churches with books of a devotional and liturgical character. Many journalists have devoted themselves partially to independent authorship, as have also certain educators, clergymen and other professional men, but their number has been regulated by the rather limited demand for original works' by Swedish-American writers. The literary production of this character, however, embraces a few works of indisputable merit in the field of history, church and profane, religion, civics, biography and memoirs, travel, prose fiction and poetry.

In their literary activities the Swedish-Americans are not, however, confined to their mother tongue. Some of the first and many more of the second generation have devoted themselves to literary pursuits in the language of the land of their adoption. Back in the sixties we find in Illinois newspapers of a distinctively Swedish-American character published in the English language. In communities largely Swedish, here and in other states, one frequently finds young men of Swedish descent in editorial charge of the local English newspapers, while Swedish names also are found in the list of writers on the metropolitan papers and contributors to literary magazines and scientific journals. Among several Swedish names noted in American fiction, one is borne by a young novelist of Chicago.

Early Publications

Many of the earlier Swedish books and pamphlets were published in Illinois. The first one appears to be L. P. Esbjörn's four-page pamphlet entitled "Några enkla Frågor och Svar rörande Döpelsen," which was printed in the beginning of 1854. In the same year was issued the proceedings of the joint meeting of the Chicago Conference and the Mississippi Conference, in Chicago.

When Tuve N. Hasselquist issued his prospectus for the newspaper which, on publication, was called "Hemlandet," he suggested that the readers should each contribute fifty cents toward purchasing a complete Swedish printery which would become the property of the Mississippi Conference. The proposal won favor, and, by degrees, the appurtenances of a small printing shop were purchased and set up at Galesburg. The first material had been bought by Hasselquist in New York for $500. In addition to the papers "Hemlandet" and "Det Rätta Hemlandet," several small books and pamphlets were printed at Hasselquist's shop, which was called "Svenska Boktryckeriet." Among them are, "50 Andliga Sånger" by O. Ahnfelt, 1856; "Enchiridion. Dr. M. Luthers Lilla Cateches, För Allmänna Kyrkoherdar och Predikanter. Noggrann öfversättning Af L. P. E. Med ett upplysande företal,"

42 pages, 1856. In the preface, L. P. Esbjörn asserted that the common Swedish editions of the catechism had many alterations, additions and omissions, resulting from the whims of various translators. Now that he was free from the influence of the Swedish state church, he thought it high time that a faithful and correct translation be made. An English translation of the catechism appeared on the pages opposite to those containing the Swedish text. In the same year another English and Swedish edition of Luther's catechism was printed, but this time the

Rev. Tuve N. Hasselquist

usual Swedish text was employed. Other books issued from the Swedish printery are, "Förslag till Constitution för Evangelisk-Lutherska församlingar i Norra Amerika," 12 pages, 1857; "A-B-C-bok," or primer, by Dr. A. R. Cervin, 1856 or 1857; "Augsburgiska Bekännelsen," 15 pages, 1857; "Doktor Martin Luthers Sändebref till tvenne kyrkoherdar om vederdopet, 1528," 38 pages, 1857; several small tracts; "Plan för Dr. C. H. Grans Skandinaviska Kansas-koloni;" "Luther-Boken eller Den dyre Gudsmannen Doktor Martin Luthers Lefverne och Gerningar af Herman Fick," translated from the German by Mrs. Eva Hasselquist, 68 pages, 1858.

The Swedish Lutheran Publication Society

At the meeting of the Mississippi Conference held at Galesburg in October, 1856, attention was called to the fact that the Swedish printery founded by Hasselquist was its own property. A committee appointed to examine the condition of affairs recommended that a power press be purchased and used in place of the hand press. At the meeting of the conference in April, 1858, it was announced that Hasselquist desired to be relieved of the responsibility of publishing "Hemlandet," owing to the pressure of his pastoral duties. It was therefore decided to organize "The Swedish Lutheran Publication Society." The following September, the conference, then in session at Princeton, appointed Erland Carlsson, Jonas Swensson and John Johnson to confer with Hasselquist as to the purchase of his newspapers and the stock of books and pamphlets on hand. They were also to order a stock of books from Sweden and to attempt to unite "Minnesota-Posten" with "Hemlandet." The first-named newspaper had been published fortnightly at Red Wing, Minn., since Nov. 7, 1857, by Erik Norelius and Jonas Engberg. When the Mississippi Conference met in Chicago on Dec. 6-9, it was reported that Norelius and Engberg had agreed to sell their printing office and newspaper to the society and become its employees. Hasselquist had also made arrangements to turn over his publications to the society. It was decided to move the newspapers to Chicago before the end of the year. Norelius was chosen editor of the newspapers and Erland Carlsson was appointed business manager of the society.

By New Year's, 1859, the society had moved its possessions into a small schoolhouse in the rear of the Immanuel Church at 190-192 E. Superior street. After the basement of the church was renovated, the concern was installed there. Jonas Engberg, who had been a book colporteur when he first came here, attended to the store and assisted on the newspapers until 1864. From time to time, shipments of books arrived from Sweden to replenish the supply, for there was a brisk demand for reading matter. Engberg left in October, 1864, to engage in another line of business. Erland Carlsson apparently remained in the capacity of business manager until 1868, when he was replaced by Jonas Engberg, who was elected secretary and treasurer. The office was moved in 1869 to better quarters at 139 North Clark street. About this time the society published "Luthers lilla cateches, försedd med bibelspråk," "Hemlandssånger," text edition, "Svenska Psalmboken," text edition, and in 1869 and 1870. "Hemlandssånger," music edition.

In the Chicago fire of 1871 the society lost its entire stock, printery and book plates, and even its account books which were stored in a safe. Fortunately, Mr. Engberg happened to have a trial balance of the accounts at his home, which had been spared from the flames, and with the aid of that he could make up the accounts. The property, valued at $18,000, had been insured for $10,000, of which $5,000 was collected. This sum was divided between the bookstore and the newspapers. Mr. Engberg had been in Sweden that summer and purchased a lot of books filling eleven cases, which arrived at Chicago shortly after the fire. A basement was now rented on Milwaukee avenue, where the business continued for almost a year, after which it was moved to 94 E. Chicago avenue. The society's publications were now issued anew, and in 1872 Dr. M. Luther's smaller catechism was printed with Swedish and English text.

In the meantime, opposition to the society's activity arose within the Augustana Synod, which was in control, and on Sept. 29, 1874, the book department was sold for $17,000, to the new firm of Engberg, Holmberg and Lindell. It was arranged that this should continue to be regarded as the official synodical bookstore, the synod stipulating that standard works of the Lutheran confession should be kept in stock. The proceeds of the sale went to Augustana College and Theological Seminary.

The Engberg-Holmberg Publishing Company

The new firm, Engberg, Holmberg and Lindell, continued the business at 94 E. Chicago avenue, for two years. In 1874 the firm moved into a new building at 119 E. Chicago avenue, which it has ever since occupied. Charles O. Lindell sold out his interest to his partners in 1876. Soon after, he organized the Star Printing Co., which was bought out later by the book firm. Engberg and Holmberg have, at various times, bought out the stock and book plates of the following publishing firms: De Lang and Osterlind, Julin and Hedenschoug, Wistrand and Thulin, I. T. Relling and Co., Enander and Bohman, P. A. Norstedt and Sons' Chicago branch and Sången Publishing Co.

In 1884 the firm was incorporated as The Engberg-Holmberg Publishing Company. Jonas Engberg, the pioneer publisher, died Jan. 1, 1890. Charles P. Holmberg remained in active charge of the business until 1900, when he retired. He died May 20, 1903. Since 1900 the firm has been managed by Oscar and Martin J. Engberg, sons of Jonas Engberg.

Besides maintaining a large assortment of imported Swedish books they have produced several hundreds of their own. Of these, twenty-eight are language methods and school books; ten are histories and books of travel; thirty-nine are devotional and other religious works; one hundred and four are Sunday school storybooks; thirty-five are other works of fiction; fourteen are hymnals; eighteen are poems

K. WALLEN   C. P. HOLMBERG   C. O. LINDELL
F. N. ANDREN   JONAS ENGBERG

The Engberg and Holmberg Book Store, 1884

and collections of poetry; fifty-five are music books and pamphlets, in addition to which there are ninety-one pieces of sheet music; while sixty-one publications are of a miscellaneous character. The total, four hundred and fifty-five, does not include reprints of short stories from collections, nor reprints of songs from collections. Of the latter over two hundred separate numbers are issued. Many of the songs are provided with English text, but otherwise almost all of the publications are in Swedish only. Artistically designed book covers adorn many of the books, especially the poetical collections and the various bindings of "Den Svenska Psalmboken." One collection of choir anthems is issued in four languages. Owing to the large and varied stock carried, they are the central depot of supplies for the Swedish book and music trade in this country. The most notable of their original publications are: Olof Olsson's "Till Rom och Hem Igen," C. F. Peterson's "Ett Hundra År," Mrs. Woods-Baker's "Pictures of Swedish Life," and the present work. The firm has published the following papers: "Nåd och Sanning," 1877-86, "Vårt Land och Folk," a weekly newspaper, 1886-88, "Land och Folk," a semi-monthly illustrated story paper, 1898-1901, "Barnvännen," 1880-88, and the "Children's Friend," 1886-88.

Jonas Engberg

Jonas Engberg was born March 31, 1837, in Berge, Bergsjö parish, Helsingland, Sweden. He spent three years in the collegiate institute at Hudiksvall, obtaining several prizes for proficiency in his studies. Thereafter he was clerk to the crown tax collector. Emigrating Sept. 29, 1854, he landed in New York on Dec. 20th, and there met O. G. Hedström. An account-book and diary dating from Sept. 1, 1854, relates this and other incidents. Engberg went to Columbus, Ohio, where he remained a couple of weeks with his cousin, Erik Norelius, then a student in that city. Continuing his journey to Chicago he there became a book colporteur, for he had brought with him some Swedish books. From May until July he taught school at West Point, Ind. The Swedish Lutheran church of that place was too poor to retain him any longer. Resuming his former occupation he sold books until in August, when, after a visit to Bishop Hill, he went to Galesburg and began working in Hasselquist's printing shop. Engberg aided in the setting up of No. 9 of "Hemlandet" and continued in the printery until Oct. 3, 1855. Once more he became a book colporteur and traveled about selling English and Swedish books until September, 1856, when the balance of the Engberg family came from Sweden. From Chicago they went to Red Wing, Minn. From November until January, Engberg was teacher in the first parochial school at Vasa. He taught singing and the rudiments of English and Swedish grammar, besides the usual branches. His pay, $35.00 a month, was tendered in the form of potatoes. Engberg unfortunately stored his salary in the schoolroom where it froze, whereupon he gave up the vocation. The next summer Engberg worked as a compositor on a newspaper in Cannon Falls. On Nov. 7, 1857, Norelius and Engberg issued No. 1 of "Minnesota-Posten," the former as editor, the latter as printer. Engberg and his brother John, who then began learning the trade, subsisted mainly on

Jonas Engberg

crackers and molasses and slept in the printery. The subscriptions were paid in provisions, silver coin and wildcat currency. In December, 1859, the paper was consolidated with "Hemlandet" and both editor and printer went to the Chicago office. Engberg assisted in the editing and attended to the bookstore. After nine months Norelius left and Rev. Erland Carlsson took his place, soon, however, leaving all of the editorial work to Engberg. The latter remained editor until 1864. During the next four years he was associated with Peter L. Hawkinson as insurance agent and printer. In their office on Lake street they reprinted, in 1865, the first part of "Fänrik Ståls Sägner," 84 pages. This little booklet was dedicated to the Scandinavian soldiers who fought in the Union Army. In the same year they printed "Läsebok för Barn och Ungdom, utgifven af B. J. Glasell," 160 pages. In 1860 Engberg, together with Sven Gibson, had published "Konung Oskar den fridsälles minne," 91 pages.

In 1868 Engberg became secretary and treasurer of the Swedish Lutheran Publication Society. The next year he also became town clerk for North Chicago. In the summer of 1871 he went to Sweden to make purchases for the bookstore.

While there, he made a visit to Bergsjö, his birthplace, and copied from the church register the names and dates of birth and death of his forbears as far back as possible. He traced his ancestry to Peder Anderson from Savolax or Tavastland, Finland, who was born about 1540 or 1550, settled in 1598 at Rickmäki, also called Rigåsen, and in 1600 received permission from Charles IX. to build and live at Sörgården, on the crown estate of Kjölsjö. Jonas Engberg was the seventh in descent from Peder Anderson, being a grandson of Anderson's great-grandson's granddaughter. In this well-authenticated instance, there were eight generations in a span of three hundred and fifty years, an average of about forty-three years for each generation.

It has already been related how Jonas Engberg came to organize the firm of Engberg and Holmberg. He labored assiduously with his account books and proof sheets, habitually arising at 3 or 4 o'clock in the morning to begin his work. He compiled the old edition of "Hemlandssånger" and translated numerous hymns from the German and English for various songbooks. "Engelsk-svenska Brefställaren för Svenska Folket i Amerika," with mathematical tables and a course in bookkeeping, was written by him.

Mr. Engberg was one of the founders of the Augustana Synod in 1860. It has been related how he was one of the Swedish-American musical pioneers. In the sixties he was a member of Hans Balatka's Chicago Oratorio Society and sang with that chorus when Lincoln's body was on view in Chicago. His musical tastes resulted in the publication of numerous music collections by his firm.

Mr. Engberg's health was undermined by too constant application to work. After a week's illness he died on Jan. 1, 1890.

Mr. Engerg was married March 11, 1861, to Elizabeth Zimmerman, a native of Nussloch, Baden, Germany, born Dec. 10, 1841, who came to this country in 1853, and to Chicago in 1857. She still survives, together with eight of her children. They are: Oscar P. F. Engberg, Helga E. C. (Mrs. Mauritz Stolpe), Vendela B. E. (Mrs. Emil Larson), Martin J. G. A. Engberg, Lucia E. R. (Mrs. Aksel G. S. Josephson), Sigrid M. H. (Mrs. Joseph G. Sheldon), Emil N. J. Engberg and Ruth T. E. Engberg.

Charles Peter Holmberg

Charles Peter Holmberg was born March 8, 1840, in Fjärrestad, Skåne, Sweden. He learned the mason's trade and became a contractor. In this capacity he spent some time in Copenhagen, removing thence to Stockholm, where he lived several years. In 1865 he emigrated and settled in Chicago, pursuing the same trade. From 1869 until 1874, he was engaged in the insurance and real estate business. In the last-

Charles Peter Holmberg

named year he became a partner in the publishing firm of Engberg, Holmberg and Lindell. The latter retiring, the firm became Engberg and Holmberg. Mr. Holmberg eventually became president of the Engberg-Holmberg Publishing Company. He retired from active participation in business in 1900.

Mr. Holmberg was a member of the first board of trustees of Augustana Hospital and was active in church work. He died May 20, 1903, his wife Wilhelmina, née Vetterlund, surviving him.

Carl Oscar Lindell

Carl Oscar Lindell was born Feb. 19, 1847, in Hvena parish, Småland, Sweden. His parents were Carl Johan Roos and Ingeborg Roos.

At the age of ten years, the boy emigrated to this country with his uncle. Going to Andover, Ill., he found a fosterfather in S. P. Lindell, and adopted his surname in place of his own. On the recommendation of the Rev. Jonas Swensson, young Lindell entered the Augustana Theological Seminary at Chicago in 1862. After finishing his studies in the same seminary at Paxton, he was ordained at the synodical meeting in 1868. His first pastorate was at Geneva, Ill. Rev. C. O.

Rev. Carl Oscar Lindell

Lindell was married the same year to Otilia Linner. In 1874 he moved to Chicago and became a partner in the book firm of Engberg, Holmberg and Lindell. He remained with the firm two years, in the meantime having pastoral care of three churches.

Lindell organized the Star Printing Co. about 1877, and published several books. After selling his business to Engberg and Holmberg, he was the chief editor of their periodicals until they were sold in 1888. During 1890-91 he was assistant editor of "Augustana." Rev. Lindell was the founder of Bethlehem Swedish Lutheran Church in Englewood,

Chicago, and served as a mission pastor at various places. From 1903 on, he was assistant pastor to Dr. E. Norelius at Vasa, Minn. On Aug. 16, 1905, while at Red Wing, on the way to attend his daughter's funeral, he was stricken with heart disease and died instantly. The remains, together with those of the daughter, were buried from the old home in Chicago.

Gamla och Nya Hemlandet

One of the first men to realize the need of a newspaper for the Swedish-American immigrants was Rev. T. N. Hasselquist, pastor of the Swedish Lutheran Church of Galesburg. Undeterred by an abortive attempt a few years before to establish a Swedish newspaper in New York City—named "Skandinaven" and published for a short time in 1851-1852—Hasselquist in October, 1854, issued the prospectus of a new paper to be called "Den Svenska Posten." On January 3, 1855, the first number was issued from Galesburg, bearing the name of "Hemlandet, Det Gamla och det Nya," as a substitute for the name originally proposed. The paper was a sheet of four pages, 10 inches by 14 inches, printed at the office of a local weekly in Knoxville. It was at first issued fortnightly and the subscription price was two dollars per year. During the first half-year it acquired about four hundred subscribers, and by the end of the year it had over one thousand subscribers, principally among the members of the ten Lutheran churches founded up to that time, the contents being from the outset and for a number of years to come essentially religious in character and Lutheran in tone. From 1856 a companion paper called "Det Rätta Hemlandet," a sixteen page monthly, purely religious, was also published. The editorial assistant of Hasselquist was his brother-in-law, A. R. Cervin. After running at a loss for over two years this newspaper enterprise was transferred from Galesburg to Chicago, where a publishing concern styled "The Swedish Lutheran Publication Society" was organized, with the energetic Erland Carlsson at the head.

Late in the year 1858 the new company took charge and the first number of "Hemlandet" issued in Chicago was published Jan. 7, 1859, from 192 East Superior street, a small schoolhouse, and later the basement of the Swedish Lutheran church serving as office and printing shop. The "Minnesota Posten" was merged with the "Hemlandet," and the latter became a weekly, with a department for Minnesota news. Eric Norelius, assisted by Jonas Engberg, assumed the editorial duties of the combined papers. The size of the paper was increased twice during the same year.

After nine months of strenuous work Norelius' health gave way and he resigned. Erland Carlsson then acted as editor, assisted by Jonas Engberg. The former soon after turned the editorial work over to the latter, owing to pressure of other duties. Jonas Engberg was editor during the greater part of the Civil War. He inserted a large number of letters from Swedish-American volunteers in the paper. The originals were preserved by him as long as he lived. A feature of the monthly "Det Rätta Hemlandet" was the hymns provided with numerical notation, sometimes in four part harmony. A. R. Cervin succeeded him as editor on Oct. 26, 1864, and remained until the close of 1868, then left J. G. Princell, his assistant, in charge of both papers until July, 1869, when P. A. Sundelius became editor of "Hemlandet."

Rev. Anders R. Cervin

"Hemlandet" now inaugurated a new epoch in its development. Doubtless spurred by competition with the secular weekly "Svenska Amerikanaren," started in 1866, it changed from a mainly religious to a general newspaper, remaining, however, loyal to the Lutheran Church. The office was later removed to 139 North Clark street, where it was destroyed by the fire in 1871. Three or four days after the fire the paper appeared as a small sheet, printed on one side, being issued from a printing office in Aurora. On Nov. 21st of the same year "Hemlandet" was again issued from its own office, it being the first Swedish newspaper to be issued from Chicago after the fire.

In December, 1869, Sundelius, whose relations with the leading men in the printing company and the Lutheran Church had become strained, resigned and went over to the competitive paper, "Svenska Amerikanaren." Johan A. Enander was at once chosen his successor. He was in the service of the company until 1872, when the printing concern was turned over to the directors of Augustana College to help support that institution at Paxton. The directors, deriving little, if any, revenue from the business, soon sold the newspaper plant, the

purchasers being Enander, the editor, and G. A. Bohman, another employee. The purchase price was $10,000, payable at the rate of $500
every six months without interest. The directors of the Paxton institution entered into a formal agreement not to start any other political
newspaper and never to give their support to any such paper other
than "Hemlandet." The purchasers held that the directors acted
also for the entire Augustana Synod.

The firm of Enander and Bohman published "Hemlandet" as a
"Republican political newspaper for the Swedish nationality in the
United States." Notwithstanding many reverses, such as the panic of
1873, and successive losses through the failure of Ferdinand Winslow's
and Skow-Peterson, Isberg and Co.'s Scandinavian banks in the late
seventies, the enterprise was successfully carried on by Enander and
Bohman until 1889, when the firm was dissolved.

In 1874—77 the firm published an illustrated monthly, entitled
"När och Fjerran," and from 1871 to 1881 "Ungdomsvännen," a
monthly paper devoted to the interests of the young people. The firm
was not, as it had supposed, protected against competition from within
the Augustana Synod, rival newspapers appearing from time to time,
including "Skandia" of Moline, founded in 1876 by Prof. Melin of
Augustana College, and "Skaffaren" of Red Wing, Minn., later of St.
Paul. To meet competition in the Minnesota field, "Hemlandet" in
1883 established a branch office at St. Paul and for a long term of
years published a Northwest edition, edited by Herman Stockenström.
In 1874—77 the firm published fortnightly a special edition for Sweden
and later for a short time maintained a small weekly at Lindsborg,
Kans., named "Kansas-Posten." In May, 1886, the firm started a
bookstore in connection with its newspaper office.

The firm of Enander and Bohman went into the general publishing
business quite extensively. The principal original works put out by
them was Enander's "Förenta Staternas historia," vols. I-IV, 1,358
pages, begun in 1873 and completed in 1880. The next in importance
was an edition of D'Aubigne's "Det sextonde århundradets Reforma-
tionshistoria," vols. I-III, 1,962 pages. Other publications, original
works and reprints, by this firm are: "Frithiofs Saga," with illustrations by Malmström; "På Lifvets Vädjobana" (Matthews' "Getting
On in the World"); several editions of "Den svenska psalmboken,"
with and without music; "Zions sångbok," both text and music
editions; "Eterneller och Vårblommor," a collection of standard poems
of Sweden; "Linnea," a collection of Swedish-American verse.

Several of the above named works were used to increase the
circulation of the paper. In more recent years "Hemlandet" has published a number of the books given as premiums year by year, including

the following: "Bilder från Gamla Hemlandet;" "Hemlandets Krigsbilder;" "Sveriges Folk;" "Panorama öfver Amerika;" and Odhner's "Sveriges Historia."

When in 1889 the firm of Enander and Bohman was dissolved, the paper was taken over by a stock company, The Hemlandet Publishing Co., comprising Enander, Bohman, J. N. Söderholm, A. L. Gyllenhaal and several others. This company, formed in 1890, was dissolved the following year, when "Hemlandet" was sold to A. E. Johnson of New York. The new owner entered into partnership with Söderholm, who for the next five years acted in the double capacity of editor-in-chief and business manager. Dr. Enander accepted a professorship at Augustana College and later associated himself with a newspaper enterprise in Omaha, Neb. In January, 1896, Mr. Johnson bought out his partner and then organized the present Hemlandet Company, with himself as president, Enander vice president, A. Schön secretary and C. Th. Strandberg treasurer and business manager. Enander again assumed the position of editor-in-chief of the paper. The principal co-editors engaged from time to time have been the following: Magnus Elmblad 1871-1873; Gottfried Cronwall; A. L. Gyllenhaal, 1874-91; C. G. Linderborg; Alfred Heyne, 1881-82; Aron Edström, since 1883; Gustaf Sjöström, 1890-93, and Anders Schön, since 1891.

Johan Alfred Enander

As a publisher, editor and author, Johan Alfred Enander has rendered eminent service to the Swedish press and literature in this country, as shown in a full sketch of his life appearing elsewhere in this work. As a young man he came to this country swelling with pride in the country and people from which he sprung, and in his career of almost forty years in the United States he has made his mark as the foremost champion of Swedish letters and culture on American soil. While a splendid type of the ultra-patriotic Swede, he has shown too little receptiveness to American influences to be a true exemplar of the Swedish-American citizen. Coming here at a time when there was among his countrymen a scarcity of able wielders of the pen, Enander had an enviable opportunity to assert himself and he did so. For the work of educating the immigrants and their children up to a love and a taste for the language and literature of Sweden he unquestionably deserves greater credit than any other man. As his paper enlarged its field beyond the pale of the church, so he propagated his sentiments in widened circles. In this mission, his eloquent tongue has ably seconded the efforts of his pen. Countless are the times he has given to Swedish audiences his ringing orations on festal days or recounted in carefully prepared lectures the virtues of the ancient Northmen and the deeds of Swedish heroes in modern times.

The history of the United States compiled by Enander in the seventies was a laudable attempt on his part to acquaint the Swedes with the land of their choice. While the four-volume work was a creditable performance for a man who was simultaneously editing a weekly paper and, part of the time, a monthly magazine in addition, it has faults which are not condoned by the acknowledged lack of ability,

Johan Alfred Enander

sources and time. The author gives almost the whole of the first volume to the discoveries of the Northmen and the history of their civilization, or thrice the space accorded to the earliest races on this continent. This can be attributed only to a faulty sense of proportion and a false historical perspective, caused by nationalistic bias.

Among the works of Enander, elsewhere mentioned, the second in importance is a volume of selections from his writing in verse and prose, entitled ''Valda Skrifter.'' As a verse writer he is not voluminous, and he has been charged with a lack of originality, but we concede to his verses a quality and finish that is rare in Swedish-American poets.

Gustaf A. Bohman

Gustaf A. Bohman was born Dec. 24, 1838, in Skellefteå, Vesterbotten, Sweden. After finishing his school studies, he was a clerk and thereafter was a seaman for several years. In 1866 he came to this country and roved about for some time. After two years he obtained a position with the Swedish Lutheran Publication Society in Chicago,

Gustaf A. Bohman

later becoming the circulation manager of its paper. While Jonas Engberg was in Sweden in 1871, Bohman superintended the bookstore. After December, 1872, when the firm of Enander and Bohman took over "Hemlandet," Bohman acted as the business manager, remaining in that capacity until the dissolution of the firm in 1889. For a number of years thereafter Bohman was a clerk in the county recorder's office and subsequently was employed in the office of "Svenska Tribunen" until the death of Andrew Chaiser. Mr. Bohman was a member of the board of trustees of Augustana Hospital in 1884, and at various other times was honored with positions of trust in his church denomination and elsewhere. On July 5, 1906, Mr. Bohman died from heart disease, leaving a widow, three sons and a daughter.

Eric Norelius

In 1872—73 Eric Norelius published "Luthersk Kyrkotidning" and during the year 1878 "Evangelisk Luthersk Tidskrift," which he continued in 1879—82 under the name of "Skaffaren."

Ever since he came to this country Norelius has followed with keen interest the progress of the Swedish Lutheran Church and has collected material for Swedish-American history. Possessing an intimate knowledge of the church and a capable pen, Norelius was elected historian of the Augustana Synod, and the result of his work as such is a compendious volume, entitled, ''De svenska luterska församlingarnes och svenskarnes historia i Amerika.'' This volume, issued in

Rev. Eric Norelius

1890, gives a very complete account of Swedish settlement in the West up to 1860 and of the activities of the Swedish-Americans, especially the Lutherans, during this formative period. One or more additional volumes of this valuable work are awaited.

From the pen of Norelius have issued a number of published works, including ''Salems Sånger'' (1859), ''Handbok för söndagsskolan'' (1865), ''Evangelisk-Lutherska Augustanasynoden i Nord-Amerika och dess mission'' (1870).

Alfred Heyne

Alfred Heyne, a member of the ''Hemlandet'' staff of editors for two years, up to August, 1883, excelled as a music and art critic. He was connected with ''Öresunds-Posten'' of Helsingborg both before and after the period spent in Chicago. His pen was fluent in prose and verse alike. Heyne was born in Skåne, Sweden, in 1855 and died there in 1889.

Aron Edstrom

Aron Edstrom has held a position as associate editor of "Hemlandet" since May, 1883, with the exception of eight months spent in editing "Nordens Medborgare" at Manistee, Mich. Prior to his engagement in Chicago he was editor of "Skaffaren" of St. Paul from 1880. Edström is an interesting narrator of personal experiences, but has done little original literary work. A few sketches by him have appeared, however, in "Hemlandet," "Prärieblomman" and elsewhere.

Gustaf Sjöström

Gustaf Sjöström attained wide popularity in the early '90s through a series of humorous articles in "Hemlandet," headed "Bref från Jan Olson" and subsequently published in book form under the title, "Jan Olsons Äfventyr." By critics Sjöström is given front rank among Swedish-American writers. He wrote in a characteristic style, all his own, and, whether in humorous or sober vein, he spoke in simple and homely fashion, his products abounding in apt comment and wholesome homespun philosophy.

Sjöström came to America in 1890, equipped with a university education obtained at Upsala, Sweden. In an editorial capacity he was in turn connected with "Hemlandet," "Tribunen," "Vårt Land" of Jamestown, N. Y., and "Österns Härold" of Brooklyn. Abandoning journalism, he took up the study of theology and was ordained to the ministry of the Episcopal Church. For a time he was in charge of a Swedish Episcopal church in Chicago, then left for Sweden, where he entered the service of the State Church.

Sjöström was a fluent versifier and a successful humorous lecturer, touring the country in 1897 in the latter capacity.

Anders Schön

Anders Schön was educated for the teacher's vocation in Sweden and taught public school for four years, subsequently serving for a year and a half on the police force of Stockholm. He came to this country in 1889. In the fall of 1891, with some prior experience as a newspaper correspondent, he was engaged on the staff of "Hemlandet" in the editorial position he still holds. Few men have served the Swedish press in the United States more ably and with greater energy than has Mr. Schön. His pen is capable of any literary task, except versification, and alongside of practical journalism he has for years pursued literary and historical studies, the latter bearing on the Swedish colonial periods in America in the seventeenth and nineteenth centuries. He has edited eight editions of the literary annual "Prärieblomman," also "Bilder från Gamla Hemlandet," and was the translator of "Coin's Financial School" and "The Cross and the Crescent."

Anders Schön

In the present historical work Mr. Schön has collaborated on the first eight chapters.

Svenska Republikanen

In the year 1856 the leaders of the Bishop Hill colony added a newspaper to their other numerous enterprises. At Galva a printing office was fitted up, from which was issued a weekly paper called "Svenska Republikanen," the full title being "Den Svenska Republikanen i Norra Amerika," edited by S. Cronsioe. In this same shop Andrew Chaiser and Eric Berglund (Bergland), two well-known Swedish-Americans, began their careers, as "printer's devils." "Svenska Republikanen" was the first competitor of "Gamla och Nya Hemlandet" in the Swedish newspaper field. It was, as the name indicates, Republican in politics, and in church matters it was, at least at the outset, as non-partisan as could be expected of a paper dependent upon a religious colony for its chief support. The first issue was dated July 4th, 1856. The paper proved fairly prosperous for a time, but on being turned over to Cronsioe, as his private property, it lost its main backing and, after a short struggle for existence, ceased publication. Prior thereto, in 1857, it was removed to Chicago, where it was issued until

July, 1858. According to C. F. Peterson, it was the first Swedish newspaper published in this city. Toward the last, the paper seems to have deviated from its course as a non-partisan in church matters, for we have it from the same authority that it "succumbed in the fight with the Lutheran Church," while Cronsioe, the editor and publisher, explained, that publication ceased because the enterprise "did not yield and income proportionate to the toil and labor expended on it."

Swedish Baptist Papers.—Nya Wecko-Posten

"Frihetsvännen," published in Galesburg from January, 1859, to March, 1861, was a fortnightly paper, started by a company of Swed-

Rev. Eric Wingren

ish Baptists. The publishers were a number of adherents of that denomination, including L. Ahnberg, Jonas Peterson and Louis Peterson. It was edited in turn by Peterson, Wilborg and Arosenius. During the latter part of its existence it was issued weekly. The paper suspended publication for lack of paying subscribers. "Frihetsvännen" was not classed as a denominational organ, but in 1860 a paper called "Evangelisten" was started in the same city as the recognized mouthpiece of the Baptists. Its span of life was about one year. This was an almost exact reproduction of a paper of the same name, published in Stockholm, Sweden, by Rev. Anders Wiberg. L. Ahnberg was business manager, but the name of the editor is not known. "Evangelisten" was the first Swedish Baptist paper here, followed by "Zions Vakt," in 1873, and "Evangelisk Tidskrift," in 1877, both edited by Dr. J. A. Edgren. The former was shortlived; the latter was turned over in

1880 to Rev. E. Wingren. Before the appearance of Edgren's first paper, an abortive publication, named "Facklan," was published by K. A. Östergren.

After a year, Wingren enlarged "Evangelisk Tidskrift" and changed it from a monthly to a semi-monthly paper. The church had need of a weekly newspaper, and from Jan. 1, 1885, the paper has been published weekly under the new name, "Nya Wecko-Posten," adopted from "Wecko-Posten," the organ of the Baptist church in Sweden. In recent years several minor Baptist papers have been started in Chicago in the interest of missions and the Sunday school. Rev. Erik Wingren came over from Sweden in 1880 on a call from the Second Swedish Baptist Church of Chicago. He preached and assisted Dr. Edgren in teaching and editing his paper, until he began to devote all his attention to the publishing business.

The books published by Rev. Wingren in connection with "Nya Wecko-Posten" are: "Femtio år i romerska kyrkan;" "Skapelsens under;" "Bröderna Alvarez;" "Birmas apostel;" "Elvira eller Evangelii makt;" "Spurgeons lif och verksamhet;" "Spurgeons predikningar," vols. I-II; "Klosterlifvet afslöjadt;" "Det heliga kriget;" "Illustrerad kalender," issued yearly from 1904 to 1909, and "Sånger för Söndagsskolan och hemmet," text and music editions.

Sändebudet

In July, 1862, Rev. Victor Witting, of Rockford, commenced to publish a small church newspaper, named "Sändebudet," which became the official organ of the Swedish Methodists. It was started as a 6-col. 4-page paper, the first issue being dated July 18th. Rev. Witting, as chief editor, was assisted by Revs. N. O. Westergreen and A. J. Anderson. Notwithstanding the loyal support of the laity and clergy, the paper did not prove self-sustaining, and the ministers often had to go down into their own pockets to meet balances. After a year and a half Rev. Albert Ericson, Witting's successor as pastor at Rockford, assumed the editorship, filling the position until Nov., 1864, when the M. E. Book Concern of Cincinnati was induced to take over the publication. The paper was now removed to Chicago and published by Poe and Hitchcock, 66 Washington street, the western branch of the publishing house, the first issue after the removal appearing Dec. 8th. In August, 1863, it was changed from a fortnightly to a weekly paper. In 1865 Rev. Witting again became its editor, and two years later he was succeeded a second time by Rev. Ericson, who edited "Sändebudet" up to Oct., 1871, when the great fire put an end to publication. One year elapsed before the paper was resurrected. It appeared again on Oct. 14, 1872, in a new dress, with Rev. N. O. Westergreen as editor.

Dr. William Henschen assumed editorial charge in September, 1875, remaining in the editorial chair until 1882, when Rev. Witting for the third time took the position. Dissatisfaction with the manner in which the American concern managed the paper prompted the organization in September, 1888, of the Swedish M. E. Book Concern in Chicago, with a view to put the publication under Swedish control. Their request that the paper be turned over to them was at first refused, but when, three months after, the new concern started a competitive paper, named "Väktaren," the Americans yielded the control to the Swedes, and the new paper was merged with "Sändebudet," which has since remained the official organ of the Swedish Methodists, under the control of the General Conference. Since 1889 Dr.

Dr. William Henschen

Henschen has been in editorial charge, except for the interval from June, 1898, to October, 1902, when Rev. H. K. Elmström occupied the editorial chair.

In connection with the office of "Sändebudet" is maintained the Swedish M. E. Book Concern, which carries on a general publishing business for the church. Besides "Sändebudet," two periodicals are published, viz., "Epworth-Klockan," a semi-monthly paper for the Epworth League, and "Söndagsskolbaneret," a monthly Sunday school paper. From a long list of books published by this house we quote the titles of some of the more noteworthy, such as: "Svenska Metodismen i Amerika," a history by Rev. C. G. Wallenius et al.; "Vinterrosor," a Christmas annual published every year from 1903 on; "Biblisk Historia," by Dr. William Henschen; "Bilder från Bibel-Länder," by J. E. Hillberg; "Where the Mississippi Flows," by Mrs. Emma Shogren-Farman; "Metodistkyrkans Nya Psalmbok" and "Herdestämman," a songbook, each of which is published in both text and music editions. Their other publications are chiefly Sunday school booklets.

Svenska Amerikanaren, I.

Up to 1866 no fruitful attempt had been made to start a Swedish-American newspaper that was not the organ of some church denomination. "Skandinaven," started in New York City in 1851, aimed to be an independent secular journal, but lacking both vitality and a definite tendency, it died the following year. For a long time after this venture those who were without church connections, either by choice or because membership in secret societies disqualified them, waited in vain for the launching of an independent and entirely secular newspaper in the Swedish language. Finally, on April 16, 1866, a number of men in Chicago and elsewhere in Illinois issued a circular, inviting their countrymen to join in forming a stock company for the purpose of publishing a weekly newspaper that would champion more liberal ideas in opposition to the intolerance of the church element at that period. Those who issued the call and organized the stock company were: John A. Nelson, president; N. E. Nelson, vice president; P. J. Hussander, treasurer; P. L. Hawkinson, secretary; Charles J. Strömberg, P. L. Eastman, C. F. Billing, F. T. Engström, P. M. Almini, all of Chicago; John Peterson, Galesburg; A. A. Schenlund, Princeton, and Olof Johnson, Galva. Behind the enterprise and in strong sympathy with it stood two well-known Chicago Swedes, Consul Charles J. Sundell and Captain Oscar G. Lange. The business was incorporated under the name of The Swedish-American Publishing Company.

At this time most Swedish-Americans possessed of more than a common school education were affiliated with the churches and denominational schools as ministers and teachers, making it difficult to secure, first, a suitable editor, and second, the support of the more intelligent class of readers. Herman Roos af Hjelmsäter, a young Swedish nobleman, employed in the Chicago office of the Inman Line, was slated for the position of editor, he being a forceful, sometimes even a virulent and vitriolic writer, who had had prior experience as a contributor to some of the daily papers in Stockholm. Yet his irregular habits counted against him so that the company decided on another man for the position. This was Hans Mattson, then a young lawyer in Minnesota. He was editor of the new paper, styled "Svenska Amerikanaren," from its first day, Sept. 8, 1866, to Feb. 6, 1867. Mattson was little more than nominal editor, but he commanded respect, as did also his associates. Many liberal-minded Swedish-Americans gladly supported the new weekly, which at once became a formidable opponent of "Hemlandet," the mouthpiece of the Augustana

Synod. There was continual warfare between the two papers, the principal casus belli being the secret societies. Roos, who was the virtual editor from the start and also nominal head of the editorial staff from February, 1867, to December, 1869, conducted an aggressive campaign in defense of the fraternities until his return to Sweden. His place was then filled by Peter A. Sundelius, who from July, 1868, to December, 1869, had been editor of the rival newspaper, "Hemlandet." Sundelius, however, hewed closely to the line marked out by his predecessor. His was a caustic style, and despite his impaired health he was a forceful and able journalist whose greatest delight was to fight his opponents, mostly politicians holding views different from his own. He was editor during the year 1870 and again from September, 1871, to April, 1873, when the company sold out to Charles J. Stenquist, a jeweler, who changed the name of the paper to "Nya Svenska Amerikanaren." In the interregnum from January to August, 1871, the paper was edited by A. W. Schalin.

In the Chicago fire the office and composing room of "Svenska Amerikanaren" were destroyed. Ten weeks later the almost ruined company resumed publication, issuing a smaller sheet, which led a struggling existence and was sold to Mr. Stenquist. He was publisher and sole proprietor until September, 1877, when he disposed of the paper to Hans Mattson, who shortly afterward acquired stock in the Swedish Publishing Company, transferred the paper to that company, and on the ruins of "Nya Svenska Amerikanaren" and "Nya Verlden," of Chicago, and "Skandia," of Moline, a new weekly by the name of "Svenska Tribunen" was built up.

"Nya Svenska Amerikanaren" was edited first by Magnus Elmblad, a poet and fluent, imaginative writer, who had formerly been assistant on "Hemlandet" and co-editor of "Skandia" of Moline and "Nya Verlden" of Chicago. He was succeeded by Gottfried Cronwall and he in turn by A. L. Gyllenhaal, in April, 1874. The following September Herman Roos upon his return from Sweden was appointed co-editor with Gyllenhaal. The two, assisted by Elmblad, edited the paper up to the time of its sale to Hans Mattson.

Hans Mattson

Except for a brief residence in Moline shortly after immigrating, and his aforesaid connection with the first "Svenska Amerikanaren" and later with "Svenska Tribunen," Col. Hans Mattson was a Minnesota man and attained great prominence in that state. He was born in Önnestad, Skåne, Dec. 23, 1832, educated at Kristianstad and was in the Swedish military service for a year and a half. Having emigrated from Sweden in 1851, he came West the year following and worked as a common laborer in and about Galesburg, Moline and neighboring places. In August, 1853, he headed a party of newcomers who went to Minnesota to pick out suitable land for a Swedish settlement. They chose a tract in Goodhue county, and Mattson with two others built the first dwelling in the Vasa settlement, of which he became the founder. Mattson tried farming and business, then studied law and

Hans Mattson

was admitted to the bar, but abandoned legal practice for the office of auditor of Goodhue county. At the outbreak of the Civil War Mattson organized a Scandinavian company which took the field in November, 1861. In April, 1863, Mattson was promoted to the rank of colonel. He was editor of "Amerikanaren" 1866-67; the latter year he became secretary of the Immigration Bureau of Minnesota, was elected Secretary of State in 1869, removed with his family to Sweden before the term expired and remained there as representative of the Northern Pacific Railway until 1876. From January, 1877, to May, 1881, he published "Minnesota Stats Tidning," a Swedish weekly, and aided in the establishment of ''Svenska Tribunen'' in Chicago in 1877, being a director of the publishing company until 1879. In June, 1881, Mattson was appointed United States Consul General for India by President Garfield and served in that capacity at Calcutta for about two years, afterwards accepting a position as manager of a land company in New Mexico. He was again elected Secretary of State in Minnesota in 1887 and served four years. The same year he started a bank in Minneapolis and two years later established ''The North,'' a newspaper in the English language, devoted to the interests of the Scandinavians. Col. Hans Mattson died March 5, 1893. Two years prior he published his memoirs in two languages, the English edition bearing the title, ''The Story of an Emigrant,'' the Swedish, ''Minnen.''

Herman Roos

One of the pioneers in Swedish-American journalism was Herman Roos (af Hjelmsäter.) As the scion of a noble family in Sweden, he obtained a university education, and thus prepared he ought to have made a successful career in his native country, but for the fact that in some way, never revealed even to his intimates, he had closed to himself the door of opportunity. He turned up in Chicago shortly after the close of the Civil War, in which he fought. He was one of the unassimilative class of Swedish immigrants who never learn the language of the land or take any real interest in things American, but are content to flock by themselves in little ultra Swedish circles, hardly meriting the name of Swedish-Americans. When Col. Hans Mattson retired from the editorship of ''Svenska Amerikanaren,'' Roos became his successor. Opinions differ as to whether he was a man of more than average talent. He was not a studious man and lacked that interest in the living issues of the day, which, coupled with his undeniable ability to wield the pen, might have made him a journalist of the highest rank. The popularity he attained rested mainly on the attitude the paper assumed versus ''Hemlandet.'' Among the anti-church element this paper, being partly of a religious character, was held to be the organ of ignorance and bigotry. When it trained its guns on the new liberal organ, Roos got a splendid opportunity to pose as the defender of free thought — or, as he put it, the right to your own views, whether right or wrong. In the wordy war that raged between the representatives of the two factions, Roos gained a number of polemical triumphs and came to be looked upon by many as the foremost champion of liberalism among the Swedish people in the West. But the part he played was not natural to him. While he fought for liberalism and human rights in the abstract, he always remained the born aristocrat. In his lowly

editorial chair he had the same high regard for the traditions and pre-
rogatives of the nobility as if he had held a seat in some feudal house
of lords. His aristocratic sentiments were skillfully concealed under
the cloak of democracy, and it was less from choice than by force of
circumstances that he became the spokesman for popular views.

After a few years Roos tired of his editorial duties and returned

Herman Roos

to his old home in Göteborg. His fair editorial salary appears to have
been inadequate to the demand made by his habits and appetites. In
1873 he returned, now more than ever enslaved by the drink habit.
Securing a position with "Nya Verlden," he did editorial work at intervals between frequent rampages, in which all sense of duty and
moral responsibility was drowned in the flowing bowl.

He now worked on "Nya Verlden" and later on the new "Svenska Amerikanaren" for upwards of seven years. To a biographer who
met Roos for the last time just before New Year's, 1880, his last words

were, "Do you know, I am tired of life." A few days afterward it was reported that Roos had disappeared. On Jan. 2nd his dead body was found on a railway track within the city, mangled by the wheels of a passing train. Whether his death was accidental or self-inflicted, no one knows. At the funeral of the agnostic, Captain Lange, a brother agnostic, officiated, and no clergyman was present. While tabooing the Christian service, Lange nevertheless felt constrained to use the formula of the Swedish Lutheran Church, but in the following corrupted form: "Of earth thou art come; to earth thou returnest; if there be a God, He shall resurrect thee on the last day."

Herman Roos, although a champion of liberal views, was intolerant with respect to the opinions of others, and was himself without any pronounced beliefs. He was a formidable opponent, whether in a polemical skirmish over personal matters, or a sustained campaign in defense of some general cause. While overestimated by his admirers and underrated by his antagonists, Roos cannot justly be denied a place of prominence among Swedish-American journalists, earned by him as one of the frontier fighters in the struggle for an unbiased press and an untrammeled public opinion.

Peter A. Sundelius

Peter A. Sundelius, one of the veteran Swedish newspaper men in the United States, was born at Uddevalla, Sweden, in 1839 or 1840; studied in Uddevalla and Göteborg; spent several months traveling in Denmark, Germany and Great Britain; crossed the Atlantic in 1864, and at once enlisted in the Union army. The following spring, in the battle of Petersburg, he received a bullet wound from which he did not recover for a year and a half. In the late fall of 1866 he came to Chicago and passed the winter teaching. The next fall he went to Augustana College, at Paxton, where he taught classes for two years while studying theology himself.

In July, 1868, Sundelius entered upon his journalistic career. He was editor of "Hemlandet" from July, 1868, to December, 1869; of the first "Svenska Amerikanaren," its bitter rival, in 1870, and from September, 1871, to April, 1873, and of "Nya Verlden" from February to April, 1871. After four years in the U. S. internal revenue office and seven in the recorder's office, Sundelius, with C. F. Peterson, G. Hjertquist and N. P. Nelson as partners, purchased the second "Svenska Amerikanaren" and was one of its editors up to May, 1888, when he sold his interest to F. A. Lindstrand.

In 1884 Sundelius was elected to the state legislature and served for three terms. His most noted achievement as a legislator was the framing of the compulsory education bill. During his last years Sunde lius was employed in the office of the county clerk. He died in Chicago, Feb. 18, 1896.

The bullet which Sundelius received in battle was never removed, but caused him constant discomfort and pain. The acerbity that characterized the products of his pen, which otherwise were models of style and cogency, doubtless was due to the same cause. Sundelius was the

Peter A. Sundelius

first Swedish political writer to master the subject of American politics, local and national.

Magnus Elmblad

Magnus Elmblad was recognized while in the United States as the foremost poet among the Swedish-Americans, others having attained to the same high rank only in later years. Elmblad's authorship, however, was not characteristically Swedish-American. He was educated in Sweden and there began his career as a writer and poet. He was therefore essentially a product of that country. His writings bear but faint, if any, evidence that the author was impressed with American life and conditions. His poetry touches both extremes of idealism and realism.

Although remembered chiefly as a poet, Elmblad's thirteen years in the United States were devoted mainly to journalism. Coming to Chicago in the fall of 1871, while the fire-swept city was still a charred ruin, he soon obtained employment in the Swedish weekly press and was in its service until 1884. His genius was of the errant type. He

Magnus Elmblad

wrote mostly according to his own whims and fancies, and the poetical contributions were by far his best.

Elmblad was a versatile writer and his pen was phenomenally productive and fluent. In six hours he is said to have composed "Gunnar och Anna," a lengthy epic poem of decided merit. His verse is characterized by ease and fluency of rhyme and rythm, lucidity and beauty of thought and elegance of diction. He was master of the art of translation, a sharp satirist and a highly entertaining commentator of passing events.

Besides some five hundred lyric poems and bits of light verse, Elmblad wrote a number of stories and sketches, a play which was produced on a Chicago scene, five epic poems, "Allan Roini," "Azilla," "Kristina Nilsson," "Pehr Thomasson" and the aforementioned "Gunnar and Anna"—the first-named having been awarded a prize by the Swedish Academy. He translated "Brand," by Ibsen, and a number of American poems. A volume of patriotic songs by Elmblad was published in Sweden in 1871; Ibsen's "Brand" and a translation of Kristofer Janson's "Han och Hon" were published the same year. A second volume of verse was published in Sweden in 1887. In this country two books of verse by Elmblad have been published, one in 1875, reprinted in 1890,.simultaneously with a second collection.

Magnus Henrik Elmblad was born Sept. 12, 1848, at Herrestad, Småland, the son of a country parson named P. M. Elmblad, who afterward became lector, or professor, at the Stockholm Gymnasium. He had a college and university education when he came to this country in 1871. Here he was employed first on "Hemlandet," then, in 1873, became associate editor of "Nya Svenska Amerikanaren;" edited "Vårt Nya Hem," published at Kearney, Neb., during the early months of 1877; was subsequently editor of "Skandia" in Moline up to April, 1878, and soon after became associate editor of "Svenska Amerikanaren," a position retained by him until he left for Sweden in 1884. There he was a free lance contributor to various journals and periodicals until his death, April 9, 1888.

Svenska Tribunen

On January 4, 1869, Eric Johnson, son of the founder of the Bishop Hill colony, started a newspaper at Galva, entitled "The Illinois Swede." It was printed in both English and Swedish. The salutatory said in part: "The idea of a weekly journal printed in both languages, devoted to the interests of the 50,000 Swedes residing in Illinois, has been the subject of our thought for a number of years, and now we rejoice that it is to be a reality. The establishment of an organ for the Swedish population of Illinois, printed mainly in the English language, is the forerunner of the true Americanization of this class of our citizens, and to that end will our efforts be directed. We shall strive to make foreign and native born citizens better acquainted. Our adopted country, first and last, is our motto."

At this time Eric Johnson was publishing two other papers, the "Galva Republican" and the "Altona Mirror." Finding that he had undertaken a bigger job than he could well attend to alone, he in July 1869 took in Andrew Chaiser as a partner. Chaiser brought no capital into the business, but he was a practical printer. In August, 1870, the firm was still further strengthened by the addition of C. F. Peterson, whose only capital was his ability as a writer. In November of that year the name of the paper was changed to "Nya Verlden." The paper was now published exclusively in the Swedish language, the two-language hobby of Mr. Johnson having been overruled by his two partners. It was also at their suggestion that the paper was moved to Chicago in January, 1871. In Chicago "Nya Verlden" met with a favorable reception. P. A. Sundelius, a journalist of experience and recognized ability, became associated with Mr. Peterson in the editorial management. Sundelius, by his sharp and caustic pen, got the paper involved in two libel suits for $25,000 each, and the two editors were arrested until released on bonds. Having been involved in expensive law suits through no fault of his own, Johnson decided to sever his connection with "Nya Verlden" and transferred his interest to Andrew Chaiser.

In the matter of policy "Nya Verlden" steered its course between two extremes, viz., "Gamla och Nya Hemlandet," the Lutheran Church paper, on the one side, and "Svenska Amerikanaren," which was anything but friendly to the church, on the other. With the exception of "Sändebudet," the organ of the Methodists, these papers were its only competitors.

After the great fire of 1871, when all the Swedish newspaper offices were destroyed, "Nya Verlden" was removed to Galesburg where it was issued within the week. It was moved back to Chicago in March, 1872. The proprietors remained the same, Mr. Chaiser having charge of the business and Mr. Peterson of the editorial office. In the spring of 1873 Frank A. Anderson, a brother-in-law of Mr. Chaiser, was admitted to partnership, and Herman Roos (af Hjelmsäter), who was formerly associated with Col. Hans Mattson in "Svenska Amerikanaren," became associate editor.

In the early spring of 1876 "Nya Verlden" was turned over to a corporation known as the Swedish Publishing Company, with Frank. Anderson as president and Chaiser and Peterson as the other main stockholders. The following year Col. Mattson became a member of the company. He was the first editor of "Svenska Amerikanaren," and the company now purchased this paper from its owner, Mr. Stenquist, and consolidated it with "Nya Verlden" under the new name of "Svenska Tribunen." In 1878 two small papers, "Skandia" of Moline and "Nya Folkets Tidning," were absorbed. The fact that another newspaper has been published ever since under the name of "Svenska Amerikanaren" is explained in this way, that the company neglected to subjoin the old names to the new one by way of protection against infringement of their proprietary rights. The opportunity was quickly grasped by Nils Anderson and Herman Roos, who had started a new paper that same year, and they forthwith changed the name of their publication from "Svenska Posten" to "Svenska Amerikanaren."

In 1880 Col. Mattson sold his stock in "Svenska Tribunen" to Carl Gustaf Linderborg, who thus acquired practically a half interest in the paper, Chaiser retaining the other half. Without breaking with the former views and policies of the paper, Linderborg made dominant the principles of liberalism, religious tolerance and political independence with Republican tendencies. Its political color was rather variegated, for while Republican candidates were generally supported, most of the editorials were written by C. F. Peterson, who was a Greeley man in 1872, continuing independent after that; furthermore, P. P.

Clark and Kinzie streets, where "Tribunen," "Fosterlandet," "Hemlandet" and "Kuriren" once centered, the last two still retaining the location

Svenson, a good writer and an astute Democrat, defended in its columns the Democratic doctrine of state sovereignty.

Linderborg exercised editorial supervision as long as he was connected with the paper. He is said to have combined diplomacy and literary judgment with good business sense, with the result that the paper gained friends and prospered in a higher degree than ever before or after. Among his editorial associates from time to time were Magnus Lunnow, afterwards for many years editor of "Svenska Folkets Tidning," of Minneapolis; Ernst Skarstedt, now well known as an author, poet and essayist; Carl Anton Mellander, who afterward became editor-in-chief; Herman Lennmalm, who later turned to dental surgery; Valdemar Torsell, a capable local news writer, and Ernst Lindblom.

Owing to ill health, Linderborg sold out to his business partner in September, 1890, and retired to private life, having accumulated in ten years of journalism a modest fortune.

In January, 1891, Anders Leonard Gyllenhaal, for seventeen years a member of the editorial staff of "Hemlandet," took the place made vacant by Ernst Lindblom's departure for Sweden. The staff now consisted of Mellander, chief editor, Mannow, Lennmalm and Gyllenhaal, associate editors, besides special correspondents and contributors, such as Jenny Braun, the novelist, and Anderson-Edenberg, in Sweden, and, in this country, Konni Zilliacus, Johan Person and Harald Beckström. Shortly after the World's Fair, Mellander died and was succeeded by Gyllenhaal.

At the end of the century Chaiser passed away and C. F. Peterson was appointed administrator of the estate. This included the management of the newspaper until the plant was sold in August, 1900, to John E. Norling, P. O. Norling and Samuel E. Carlsson. The chief editorship, temporarily assumed by Mr. Peterson, was now entrusted to Ernst W. Olson, former stockholder and editor of "Fosterlandet," with Messrs. Gyllenhaal and P. C. Pearson as his associates. Later, Anders Tofft was added to the staff. Mr. Pearson had been connected with "Fosterlandet" from its inception, most of the time as editor-in-chief, and Mr. Tofft had previously worked on Swedish newspapers in Minnesota. In the autumn of 1901 Mr. Norling became sole proprietor of "Svenska Tribunen," and continued as its publisher until May, 1905, when the paper was sold to C. F. Erikson, late advertising manager of "Svenska Nyheter." One year later "Svenska Tribunen" was consolidated with "Svenska Nyheter," a weekly published by Gus Broberg. The combination was named "Svenska Tribunen-Nyheter." After a few months Mr. Broberg withdrew from the partnership, having sold his half interest to Mr. Erikson.

Mr. Norling had kept the paper Republican, even at the sacrifice of his personal views, which for a number of years had been in sympathy with the democracy, and was entirely in accord with the editors in this matter. His successor, who held radical views, attempted to make a gradual change in its politics, but had no success, so long as either Mr. Olson or Mr. Gyllenhaal remained as editorial writers. Their positions on the staff were reversed shortly after the change in ownership, Mr. Gyllenhaal being again made editor-in-chief. His physical powers had been undermined by an illness of several years' duration, and on October 17, 1905, he succumbed to heart disease. One month later Mr. Olson left his position. With temporary assistants Mr. Tofft edited the paper until the following spring, when Carl G. Norman, editor of "Svea," at Worcester, Mass., was engaged.

Among the premium books employed to swell the circulation of "Svenska Tribunen" are found the following works, of which the publishers put out their own editions: "Bibliotek för allmänbildning;" "Från vår Konstverld;" "Nittonde Århundradet," by O. H. Dumrath, three volumes in two; "Kunskapernas Skattkammare" by Trumbull White, Swedish edition revised and augmented, and a book of views of Sweden.

Eric Johnson

Of Swedish-American newspaper men, few, if any, have had so varied a career as Captain Eric Johnson. With him publishing has been a sort of intermittent fever, he having been sole or joint proprietor of no less than half a score of newspapers at different periods. In the intervals he has been engaged in various private pursuits or in public life.

The son of the founder of the religious community of Bishop Hill, Eric Johnson was born in Vestmanland, Sweden, July 15, 1838, eight years before the beginning of the exodus of his father's adherents, the Erik Janssonists, to the United States. The family left Sweden in January, 1846, going via Christiania, Copenhagen, Kiel, Hamburg, Hull and Liverpool, to New York, where they arrived in the early spring and remained several months before proceeding to Victoria, Ill. The first houses in Bishop Hill completed, the family located there in September. The boy's early schooling was limited to the instruction received from S. B. Randall, who taught in the colony in 1854.

When the Bishop Hill colony corporation was dissolved in 1861, Eric Johnson began to cultivate the eleven acres of land allotted to him, together with some rented land. On Sept. 16th of the same year he enlisted in the volunteer army, and was chosen lieutenant at the organization of Company D, 57th Ill. Regiment. After the battle of Shiloh he was promoted captain of the company, which was composed entirely of Swedes. During the siege of Corinth in the summer of 1862 Captain Johnson was taken sick with typhoid fever and at the advice of the army surgeon he resigned and returned North. In 1864 he was induced by the Republican leaders at Galva to become editor and publisher of the Galva "Union." The venture was new to him and a year of that work was enough, but in 1868 he was again attracted to the newspaper field, assuming the editorship of the Altona "Mirror." After the election he became owner of the Galva "Union," which name was changed to "Republican." His connection with the "Illinois Swede" and "Nya Verlden" has been shown.

In January, 1871, Johnson was made journal clerk in the House of Representatives at Springfield, serving during the regular session and also the called session just following the Chicago fire and the adjourned session early in 1872. The year after, he engaged in mercantile and land business at White City, Kans., but failed after three years, owing to drought and grasshoppers, and returned to Illinois, starting in business anew at Nekoma, as a hardware and lumber dealer.

In 1879 he was engaged in gathering material for "Svenskarne i Illinois"—a book published by him and C. F. Peterson. The same year, in partnership with Joseph E. Osborn, Johnson began publishing "The Citizen," a weekly paper at Galva and later at Moline, but sold his interest to his partner in 1882, following a disagreement as to the political policy of the paper. Next Captain Johnson held a position in the war department at Washington, resigning which he became editor of "The Republican" at Stromsburg, Neb., for one year, and subsequently was in the newspaper business at Holdrege, Neb., until 1891. While there he was elected to the General Assembly in 1888, being the only Independent in that legislature. In 1891 he was made chief clerk of the House of Representatives and was reelected unanimously two years later.

After having been operating in Texas lands for a time, Captain Johnson in 1896 became the editor of the "Saunders County New Era," established 1890 at Wahoo, Neb., as a Populist paper. With the subsidence of that movement the paper lost prestige, turned Republican and was continued by Capt. Johnson until the spring of 1906, when he suspended publication of the paper and sold the plant. His next, and last, venture in journalism was "The Viking," a Swedish-American monthly in the English language, published at Fremont, Neb., from July, 1906, to August, 1907, when lack of support prompted its discontinuance. Capt. Johnson in October, 1907, removed to Clearwater, Cal., his present place of residence.

Mr. Johnson was married Jan. 31, 1863, to Mary Octavia Troil, who died in 1890. Of their eight children three are living, viz., Axel T., of St. Louis, Julia C., of Omaha, and Ernest G., publisher of the "Lindsay (Neb.) Opinion." A son, Sixtus Erik, died in the Spanish-American War. On July 15, 1902, Mr. Johnson married his second wife, Georgia A. Tillinghast, who has aided him in his recent editorial work.

Andrew Chaiser

Andrew Chaiser had a pecuniary interest in "The Illinois Swede —Nya Verlden—Svenska Tribunen" from 1869 and was its sole owner from 1890 until his death in 1899. Chaiser was born in Bälinge parish, Upland, Sweden, Aug. 5, 1841. His father, who had served in the Upland Dragoons, emigrated in 1850 and joined the Erik Jansson colony at Bishop Hill. He worked for three years, 1855-58, in the colony's newspaper office at Galva, and in 1869 associated himself with Captain Eric Johnson in publishing the "Illinois Swede" at that place. After the paper was removed to Chicago and converted into the all-Swedish weekly "Nya Verlden," Chaiser was one of the several men who took the paper through the financial crisis in the seventies. In the eighties he and Linderborg as joint proprietors of the paper, now "Svenska Tribunen," pushed it ahead until it outdistanced all its competitors. After Chaiser had become sole owner in 1890 he soon had to pilot the enterprise through the financial straits of 1893 and follow-

Andrew Chaiser

ing years. In this he succeeded, but in the last few years before his death the enterprise seems to have suffered through lack of vigilance in the management. Mr. Chaiser was a public-spirited man and had the interests of his countrymen at heart. The credit for the erection of the Linné monument in Lincoln Park, Chicago, is due in a large measure to his energetic work in securing the needed funds. His death occurred March 31, 1899.

Carl Fredrik Peterson

Carl Fredrik Peterson was born at Fittja, Södermanland, Sweden, April 16, 1843. His parents were poor and could afford him but little schooling. The boy was sent to relatives in Falun at an early age, and there worked as a dyer's apprentice. As a young man of eighteen he emigrated to the United States. Intending to fight for the liberation of the slaves, the newcomer enlisted, but was rejected on account of nearsightedness after having had but a taste of camp life. He then joined the crew on a Mississippi steamer plying between St. Louis and New Orleans. After that he worked successively as section hand on the railroad, wood-cutter, farm laborer and factory hand. His desire for knowledge caused him to improve every opportunity to repair the defects in his education.

In January, 1870, he became editor of "Minnesota Tidning" at St. Paul, Minn. With that he entered upon the journalistic and literary career which he subsequently followed through life. He left this paper in May of the same year and in August assumed the editorship of "The Illinois Swede," published at Galva, Ill. Peterson remained with the paper through various changes until 1880, as editor-in-chief,

Carl Fredrik Peterson

and continued another four years as associate editor. Then he went over to "Svenska Amerikanaren" and was until 1888 editor and part owner of that paper. After that he edited "Svea," a newspaper which ceased publication in 1889. For a short period in 1890-91 a Swedish daily newspaper was published in Chicago, with Mr. Peterson at the head of the editorial department. When this venture failed he devoted himself for a number of years to independent literary work, producing several volumes on historical, political and kindred topics. As administrator of the estate of his old friend and partner, Andrew Chaiser, Peterson was in 1899 called back to the field of journalism and for a time directed both the business and the editorial policy of the paper. In the early part of the year 1901 he edited "National-Tidningen." Its existence was cut short in April, when Mr. Peterson was stricken with an illness that ended his life June 11th following.

Up to 1885 Peterson was a Republican, with independent tendencies. That year he embraced the tenets of the Democratic party, and later, when populism was at its flood-tide, accepted its political doc-tries, and he in turn championed these various views with a vigor that seemed born of long established conviction. Never a strong partisan, he could do' this without much readjustment of his own position. It is admitted that his political articles were characterized by a depth and thoroughness seldom if ever found in the work of other Swedish-American journalists.

Being of a speculative bend, Peterson gave a great deal of thought to the higher problems of this and the future life, and his views were freely expressed in the press and on the platform. A biographer has said of him that he was "by far a greater poet than thinker, and a greater orator than poet"—an estimate probably based on the fact that his mind was not free from bias and the trammels of various -isms, including spiritualism, with all its accessories of slate-writing, materialization, etc. Astrology was a real science to his mind and he faithfully believed in it. As a public speaker and a poet, on the other hand, he moved in a freer atmosphere, bounded only by the limitations of his fertile brain and a vivid imagination. Peterson handled English with almost as great fluency as his mother tongue, and translated a large number of the best Swedish poems into English.

The published works of C. F. Peterson are: "Svenskarne i Illinois," edited in collaboration with Eric Johnson; "Förenta Staternas Historia," which has been translated into Norwegian and Finnish and used as a text-book in schools; "Republiken och dess Institutioner;" "Amerikanska Vältalare;" "Kärlek och Pligt," a novel; "Lärobok i Geografi;" "Ett Hundra År," a recapitulation of the nineteenth century; "Politisk Handbok;" "Sverige i Amerika," besides contributions to Swedish periodicals and magazines. Among his unpublished works may be mentioned a "History of Sweden" in the English language; about one hundred Swedish poems translated into English; a number of original essays and translations on philosophical, political and economic questions; a work on the various doctrines and views on the future life; a collection of Swedish-American short stories; lectures on religio-philosophical subjects; a work on the occult phase of science, and the first chapters of a novel dealing with Swedish-American labor conditions.

Self-taught as he was, Peterson attained a remarkably high intellectual development and his name will be written large in the annals of his fellow countrymen. Yet, with a better start, and under more favorable conditions, his unusual talents ought to have made him still more noted and influential.

Carl Gustaf Linderborg

Carl Gustaf Linderborg, who directed the policy of "Tribunen" from 1880 to 1890, when he sold his interest and retired, was a newspaper man of extraordinary ability. True, he wrote very little, if anything, for the paper, but he knew so well wherewith to fill its columns, that under his regime "Tribunen" attained phenomenal financial success, purely on the strength of its high standard. He chose to rely on the merit of the paper alone, scorning to increase its revenues by means of the questionable and dishonest advertisements only too common to the press. If his paper was open to criticism it was for over-cautiousness. Far from fearless and outspoken, it was extremely guarded in tone, lest any reader should take offense. This policy, however,

Carl Gustaf Linderborg

proved benevolent in the main, and Linderborg is given credit for greater ability than any other Swedish-American publisher in increasing the circulation and profits of his paper without sacrificing its reputation.

Linderborg was born March 26, 1844, in Skellefteå, Sweden. Having gone through college, he taught in Sweden publicly and privately for three years and spent one year at the University of Helsingfors, Finland. He came over to this country in 1867, and taught at Augustana College, in Paxton, Ill., and at an academy in Hillsboro. After two years he engaged in business and in 1871 became advertising solicitor and assistant editor of "Hemlandet." He was a member of the Illinois legislature in 1874, and in 1880 purchased a half interest in "Svenska Tribunen." After 1890 Linderborg lived in retirement in Chicago, until his death on July 10, 1901. While with "Hemlandet," he translated William Matthew's "Getting On in the World," the Swedish version of which has been published in several editions, entitled "På lifvets vädjobana." This and other works he rendered into Swedish showed him to be an excellent translator.

Jacob Valdemar Torsell

Jacob Valdemar Torsell was added to the editorial force of "Svenska Tribunen" shortly after his removal to Chicago from the East in 1882 and served until his death, which occurred Jan. 2, 1900. He ranks with the foremost journalists employed on this or any other Swedish newspaper in this country. He was a wit and satirist, capable of dealing the most stinging blows with his rhetorical lash. As a critic he was keen, unrelenting and sometimes unjust. A skillful translator, he

Jacob Valdemar Torsell

turned into Swedish a number of English novels, published serially in his paper.

Torsell was born in Stockholm Nov. 20, 1849. In addition to a general education, he took a thorough course in music, but engaged in business on reaching mature years. In 1870 he emigrated to New England. He lived principally in Boston and Worcester, earning his living as music teacher, bookkeeper and otherwise. For a couple of months in 1875 he edited an ephemeral Swedish newspaper named "Fäderneslandet."

Johan Peter Swenson

Johan Peter Swenson was one of the editors of "Svenska Tribunen" for two years, 1885-87. For several years prior he had been a regular contributor to "Svenska-Amerikanaren" while living in Boston. In 1876—77 he lived for a time in Chicago. He then wrote over the name of Carl Johan Stenquist, the publisher, several polemical articles, reputed to have been masterpieces of journalistic insolence. Swenson made a fair translation of Longfellow's "Evangeline" and was the author of a published treatise on the jury system. He wrote verse of a mediocre sort. Swenson was born in 1818 and was king's bailiff (länsman) in Redväg county before emigrating to Boston in 1865.

Carl Anton Mellander

Carl Anton Mellander began his journalistic career in Chicago as editor of "Fäderneslandet," published here in 1878-79. He joined

Carl Anton Mellander

the editorial force of "Tribunen" in 1880, remaining with the paper until his death Jan 9, 1899. Mellander was principally a news editor and did much. to sustain "Tribunen's" enviable reputation as the newsiest of the Swedish-American papers. Mellander was born in Göteborg on Dec. 5, 1849, and educated at a college in Malmö and at the Lund University. He came to America in 1873.

Anders Leonard Gyllenhaal

Anders Leonard Gyllenhaal was connected with the Swedish-American press of Chicago for about thirty-one years. In April, 1874, he was engaged on the staff of "Nya Svenska Amerikanaren." The following October, when that paper changed from Republican to Democratic, Gyllenhaal, who was a staunch Republican, resigned and at once was added to the editorial force of "Hemlandet." On Jan. 1. 1891, he joined the staff of "Svenska Tribunen" and remained with that paper until his death, which occurred Oct. 17, 1905. Gyllenhaal pursued no independent authorship, limiting himself entirely to the routine of the newspaper office, editing the news, writing editorials and compiling and assorting the miscellaneous contents of the paper. He was a model in his way. prompt, methodical and faithful in his work

Anders Leonard Gyllenhaal

to the highest degree. Since his entry into journalism, his life was rather uneventful.

He was born July 1, 1842, in Vestmanland, Sweden. After preliminary studies at the elementary school in Östersund he entered Upsala University, taking the bachelor's degree in 1860. He went to sea for two years, then returned to the university for post-graduate work, but was prevented by lack of funds from completing the course. In 1866 he came to this country and for several years engaged in a variety of occupations. He was in the employ of the Western News Company in Chicago for five years just prior to going into journalism. Gyllenhaal came of noble Swedish stock. He was married in 1880 and with his family lived in a New Church settlement at Glen View, he himself being a firm believer in the teachings of Swedenborg.

Konni Zilliacus

Konni Zilliacus, associate editor of "Tribunen" in 1889—90 and of "Kuriren" in 1892, while in Chicago and afterward, wrote a good al of fiction and several historical and descriptive works. In 1891 ; published a book of general information for immigrants, entitled ,Amerika,'' the following year a collection of emigrant stories, ''Ut- andrarehistorier,'' which was published in Helsingfors, while an illus- .rated book, descriptive of Chicago, was put out in this city. His most important work, however, was a book of a thousand pages on the United States, historical, descriptive and pictorial, entitled ''Ameri- kas Förenta Stater.'' This was published in New York City. Zillia- cus, who was a native of Finland, had traveled extensively and gave interesting accounts of his journeys in many lands. He returned to Finland, where in recent years several books by him have been pub- lished, including ''Nya utvandrarehistorier'' and ''Det revolutionära Ryssland.''

Svenska Amerikanaren, II.

When ''Svenska Amerikanaren'' was purchased by Hans Mattson and absorbed by ''Svenska Tribunen,'' the old name was adopted in October, 1877, by Nels Anderson and Herman Roos for a new weekly started by them under the name of ''Svenska Posten.'' Anderson was at the time Scandinavian clerk in the Inman Line office. It may be mentioned in passing that a single issue of a Swedish newspaper named in English ''The Swedish-American,'' is said to have been published Aug. 21, 1875, but who the editors and publishers were has not been ascertained. Herman Roos was at first sole editor of Nels Anderson's paper. He and Elmblad were joint editors from June, 1878, to Jan. 2, 1880, when Roos met his death under the wheels of a railway train. Elmblad continued as editor until June, 1884, when he left for his native country. His associates were: Ernst Skarstedt, 1880-84, Gustaf Wicklund, 1882-4, Jakob Bonggren, from 1882, and O. A. Linder, 1883-4. On Sept. 1, 1884, Anderson sold out to P. A. Sundelius, N. P. Nelson of Salina, Kansas, and Gabriel Hjertquist, foreman of the composing room of ''Svenska Tribunen.'' The firm was styled the Swedish- American Printing Company. In October, 1884, C. F. Peterson, one of the editors of ''Svenska Tribunen,'' joined the company. From that time till 1888 the editors were Sundelius, Peterson and Bonggren. In April, 1886, Hjertquist sold his stock to A. E. G. Wingård, then advertising agent of the paper, and on May 3, 1888, Mr. Sundelius, impelled by ill health, sold out to Frans A. Lindstrand, a watchmaker and jeweler, and well known in fraternal society circles, who soon after took over the stock owned by C. F. Peterson and N. P. Nelson and thus became three-fourths owner of the paper.

Frans Albin Lindstrand

In assuming control Mr. Lindstrand determined to make "Svenska Amerikanaren" a popular paper, non-partisan, liberal, tolerant. It then had about 3,000 paying subscribers and a debt of $16,500. It was apparent that it required strong pushing to put the enterprise on its legs, financially, but this the new proprietor did, and soon made good his determination to make the paper a financial success.

He retained Mr. Bonggren as editor, and soon after added to the staff Ninian Waerner, formerly associate editor of "Kurre," a comic paper, which was the forerunner of "Svenska Kuriren." Waerner, who was a poet and humorist, rather than a journalist, remained until

Frans A. Lindstrand

Oct. 1, 1889, when he assumed the editorship of "Svenska Korrespondenten" in Denver, Colo. Mr. Linder was re-engaged on the paper in 1892. Another man engaged was Edwin Björkman, a capable writer, who subsequently became editor of "Minnesota-Posten," at Saint Paul, and then in turn reporter and writer on daily newspapers in that city and in New York.

Mr. Lindstrand himself, although unschooled, took up the pen and began to contribute profusely to the columns of his paper. Possessing a goodly fund of personal experience, an inexhaustible vein of popular humor and a firm determination to "make good," his writings struck a responsive chord. His series of articles under the caption, "Bref från Onkel Ola," was continued for almost twenty years, making him extremely popular with the readers of the paper. In wide circles, in fact, Mr. Lindstrand is hardly known by any other than his pen name, "Onkel Ola." After twenty years Lindstrand withdrew from journalism, his paper being purchased in February, 1908, by F. A. Larson, a young business man.

The first "Svenska Amerikanaren" was founded as a non-sectarian paper intended as the mouthpiece of those Swedish-Americans who did not belong to the churches or, if they did, were liberal-minded and favored free discussion of all questions, including religious ones. Not only because its policy was condemned by the clergy, but owing still more to the fact that its earliest editors, Roos and Elmblad, had been too abusive in their antagonism, while personally they were not as strict and sober as might be expected of men intent on improving the teachings and morals of the church, a certain odium theologicum had clung to the name from the first. Those who purchased the second paper of that name in 1884 did what they could to eradicate this antipathy by moderating the tone of the paper and adopting a policy of fairness and tolerance toward all. This policy was strictly adhered to by Mr. Lindstrand and his staff of editors, so that now the old prejudice from the side of the church people toward "Svenska Amerikanaren" is practically a thing of the past.

"Svenska Amerikanaren" has been most prolific in the production of books for premium purposes. While Mr. Lindstrand was at the head of the paper, he published reprints and original works, as follows: "Verldshistoria," by Ernst Wallis, vols. I-III; Rosander's "Den Kunskapsrike Skolmästaren;" "Fältskärns Berättelser," by Z. Topelius, vols. I-II; "I öster- och vesterland," by F. A. Lindstrand; "Pennteckningar och reseskildringar af Onkel Ola;" "Kunskap för alla," vols. I-IV; O. Sjögren's "Karl XII och hans män;" "Kriget med Spanien. Frithiofs Saga. Fänrik Ståls Sägner," and "Ur det fördoldas verld."

In 1896 Mr. Lindstrand started a comic weekly paper named "Broder Lustig." In November of that year, it was replaced by an illustrated literary weekly, "Iduna," which ran until February, 1899.

Ernst Skarstedt

Ernst Skarstedt, in June, 1880, became the associate of Magnus Elmblad as editor of "Svenska Amerikanaren." In 1884 he was employed by Engberg and Holmberg as editor and proof-reader; shortly thereafter he took a position with "Svenska Tribunen" and early in 1885 left for the Pacific coast, where he has since resided in various localities. From 1891 to 1896 he was editor and part owner of "Vestkusten" of San Francisco. He then went to farming, but did not abandon literary work on that account. Numberless newspaper articles by him have appeared all along, and he has published a number of larger or smaller books on a variety of subjects, namely: "Oregon and

Washington,'' historical and descriptive of the two states; ''Svensk-Amerikanska poeter;'' a collection of poems by Magnus Elmblad; ''Enskilda skrifter of A. A. Swärd;'' ''Rosor och törnen,'' a collection of short stories, translated and revised; ''Från vilda vestern,'' and ''Den gamle smeden,'' stories; ''Våra pennfäktare,'' a biographical work on Swedish-American writers, and most recently an illustrated volume entitled ''Washington och dess svenska befolkning.'' Skarstedt is a poet of recognized merit, and a collection of verse by him appeared in book form in 1907. He is held to be an eminent critic, but disclaims that title. Be this as it may, he has played an important part in the

Ernst Skarstedt

matter of calling attention to and encouraging writers, thereby rendering great service to the young Swedish-American literature.

Ernst Teofil Skarstedt was born in Solberga, Bohuslän, Sweden, April 14, 1857; obtained a college education in Lund where his father became professor of theology in 1865; was a sailor in 1875, visiting England and the arctic regions, and studied for a short time at the Technical High School of Stockholm before emigrating in December, 1878. During his first year in the United States he worked at farming, carpentry, etc., and then, in partnership with one E. Lundquist, published ''Kansas Stats-Tidning'' at Lindsborg for three months, in 1879-80. From his childhood Skarstedt had a penchant for writing, having composed little sermons at seven and essays and sketches on nature at nine.

Skarstedt is a man of peculiar views and habits. He scorns conventionality, etiquette and luxury as the curses of civilization. An apostle of the simple life, he lived for years the life of a hermit in a small clearing in the primeval forests of the far Northwest. In his voluntary exile he kept in close touch with events, particularly those among his own countrymen. An enthusiastic literary collector, he has amassed an enormous amount of material, the bulk of which unfortunately was lost in the great San Francisco fire.

Jakob Bonggren

Jakob Bonggren has made himself well known as a journalist in the quarter century he has been connected with "Svenska Amerikana-

Jakob Bonggren

ren," but as a poet he is still more familiar to Swedish-American readers. By many he is accorded first place among Swedish poets in this country, and there is no one to dispute the fact that he ranks abreast with our best imaginative writers. His fertile mind and facile pen have produced a great amount of verse on a limitless range of themes, his poems being uniformly readable, ofttimes the brilliant crystallization of some fine thought or sentiment, and not infrequently precious gems from the diamond fields of fancy. Whether from necessity or not, Bonggren has stuck to the prosaic routine of journalism these many years, despite his marked predilection for belles lettres and research and for speculation in the field of the occult. Bonggren has written numerous literary reviews and critical estimates, in which, it has been charged, his opinion is unduly influenced by his likes and dislikes. He is a profound student, who in his reading has invaded almost every field of human culture. The services rendered by him to the Swedish-American literature as a critic and compiler are of permanent value, even aside from the opinions expressed to which others have taken exception. The following series of literary critiques and notices in "Svenska Amerikanaren" are from Bonggren's pen: "Litteraturhistoriska anteckningar," I—XXXVI; the same, series I—LII; "Svensk-amerikansk litteratur, I—XXXVIII; "Svenska litterära karaktärsdrag," and "Vår litterära värld," two series, 1898 and 1899. If it be true that he has bitterly denounced certain writers whose style and subject matter have been odious to him, it is also true that he is almost the patron saint of the lesser knights of the quill, whose efforts he has freely and charitably encouraged. Besides his others works, elsewhere mentioned, Bonggren has translated "Caesar's Column," by Ignatius Donnelly, and contributed a number of articles to a biographical volume entitled "Framstående män och qvinnor i vår tid." His published collections of verse, "Förstlingar" and "Sånger och Sagor," contain but a part of the profusion of verse that has flowed from his pen.

Oliver A. Linder

Oliver A. Linder is one of the most distinctive of Swedish-American writers. Until recent years these were, almost without exception, educated in Sweden, and their products varied little in character, style and subject matter from the literary products of the old country. Linder early began to depart from the well-trodden paths and has been growing more thoroughly American in sentiment with the passing years. This fact is reflected in his verse, which is American in tone and atmosphere, in fact, in all its essentials, except the vehicle of expression. He is one of a handful of poets of force and originality among a motley mass of vapid versifiers or mere rhymesters. Linder is a keen critic and an able reviewer, intimately familiar with the field of Swedish-American literature and its cultivators. In an essay on pseudonyms he has given apt and terse characterizations of many of their bearers.

In the eighties several series of humorous letters and sketches by Linder subjected their author to the charge of imitation or plagiarism of certain noted American humorists, the accusation being preferred by persons ignorant of, or unwilling to admit, the fact that Linder was himself a humorist. He himself owned to an affinity in style with Bill Nye, but that was the whole extent of it. In taking up historic research pertaining to the Swedish Delaware colony, Linder again displayed his keenness by discovering and correcting several grave errors in the

Oliver A. Linder

biography of John Morton, prevalent in works of reference. Mr. Linder has been entrusted with the responsible task of writing the biographies of those Swedish-Americans deemed worthy of a place in the new revised edition of "Nordisk Familjebok," the Swedish encyclopedia, a new edition of which is now in course of publication.

Other Staff Members and Contributors

Edwin Björkman had had sketches published in "Dagens Nyheter" and had been a member of the staff of "Aftonbladet" in his native city of Stockholm before coming to America in 1891. He obtained a situation on "Svenska Amerikanaren" as local news editor and wrote for the paper a series of original sketches under the common head, "Teckningar i sanden." In ease and elegance of style Björkman had few equals. The failure of "Minnesota-Posten," of St. Paul, which he was called to edit in 1892, transferred Björkman to the American press. He began by writing Scandinavian news for the Minneapolis "Times," and later became its music critic, besides writing feature articles and other "stories" for that paper. Before engaging in journalism Edwin Björkman spent three years on the Swedish theatrical stage.

For a time Bengt Åkerlund was a member of "Amerikanaren's" staff. He died as editor in chief of "Skandinavia," published at Worcester, Mass. More recently Emil Amelin was attached to the paper for a number of years. The latest acquisition was Frithiof Malmquist, for five years editor in chief of "Svenska Nyheter," a writer of strong, trenchant prose and similar verse, and an all-round practical newspaper man.

Frithiof Malmquist, conjointly with Edward Fjellander, founded "Forskaren," an organ of socialism and free thought, and a rabid antagonist of church and clergy, in 1893, at Rockford, and remained with that publication for several years after its removal to Minneapolis in 1894. In 1900 he was connected with "Svenska Tribunen," which he left to take the position of editor of "Svenska Nyheter" in 1901. For the next few years he gave this paper wide reputation as an outspoken and radical labor organ. When "Nyheter" was consolidated with "Svenska Tribunen" in 1906, Malmquist resigned and soon after joined the staff of "Svenska Amerikanaren." Malmquist is a writer of bristling and unkempt verse as shown in a volume appropriately entitled "Törnen och Tistlar." The author's literary ability is self-acquired, he having left the public school in Sweden at the age of fourteen to become a joiner's apprentice and never after had an opportunity for systematic study.

Missions-Vännen

In July, 1874, the Mission Synod founded in Chicago a church paper, called "Missions-Vännen," which was at first published once a month. The first editors were A. W. Hedenschoug and L. J. Peterson. In 1880 Rev. Andrew Hallner assumed the editorship of the paper, which was then made a weekly. A stock company, consisting of members of the North Side Mission Church of Chicago, and known as the Mission Friends Publishing Co., purchased the paper in 1882, doubled its size and added political and general news departments. Prior to this change, Hallner had been succeeded by Rev. A. E. Wenstrand, and now Gustaf Theden was made news and political editor. Some time after, Hallner again edited "Missions-Vännen," assisted by Gustaf Sjöström. In 1888 Rev. O. Högfeldt took charge of the church department, and prior thereto A. F. Boring had been engaged. Hallner continued as political editor, and for several years made the paper a champion of prohibition, until succeeded by Rev. John Hagström. Högfeldt and Boring remain with the paper in an editorial capacity, while the business management is entrusted to C. G. Petterson. Although private property, "Missions-Vännen" is the recognized organ of the Mission Covenant. Much of its prestige is due to the contributions of P. P. Waldenström, the leader of the Mission Covenant of Sweden, who has written for its columns for many years past.

The Mission Friends Publishing Company conducts a bookstore, and has published the following books: "Sionsharpan," text and music editions; "Dagligt Manna," by F. Risberg; "Lifvet, döden och evigheten," by A. Mellander; "Bibelbilder," by F. Risberg, and "Vinterros," an annual for children.

Rev. Otto Högfeldt

In 1891 Otto Högfeldt began publishing an annual, entitled "Hemåt," which is still being issued. A. F. Boring is the editor of two juvenile annuals, "Barnens Kalender" and "Vinterros."

At North Park College the Mission Covenant conducts a book and publishing business, from which is issued "Missionären," a semimonthly mission paper. Several books have been published by the same concern, chief of which is a 500-page book on Palestine, by Prof. Axel Mellander. "Aurora," a Christmas annual, edited by him, also has been issued from this office.

Johan Alfred Almkvist

Johan Alfred Almkvist, who was associate editor of "Missions-Vännen" for three months and of "Kuriren" for eight months, developed an extensive literary activity as a translator while in Chicago. He rendered into Swedish several religious works by J. R. McDuff,

published under the following titles:"Eskolsdrufvor,""Eldsprofeten,"
"Klårare än solen"; also "Trenne Familjer" and the following books
by Dwight L. Moody: "Förborgad Kraft," "Segervinnande bön,"
"Vägen till Gud" and "Till verksamhet, till verksamhet!" His poetic
ability stood him in good stead in rendering into Swedish the many
religious songs quoted in these works. Almkvist has given several
proofs of his talent as a writer of very readable prose fiction. In
Sweden he published in serial form a number of stories, including "Vid
kusten," "En syndares väg" and "Svindlaren i Stollnäs," the latter
attracting considerable attention at the time.

Almkvist was born at Tanum, Sweden, in 1847. He studied in
Uddevalla and, after his coming to the United States in 1872, took
theological courses at Decorah College, Decorah, Iowa, and Concordia
College in St. Louis. He returned to Sweden in 1874, continued divinity
studies at the Ahlberg school and served as a pastor for one year. In
1878 he became editor of "Gestrikland," a paper published in Gefle,
and later published "Folkets Vän" and "Norrlands Annonsblad,"
two radical organs. After having been imprisoned for infringing the
libel law he abandoned journalism in Sweden and returned to this
country.

The Augustana Book Concern

The beginning of this publishing house may be traced back to
December, 1877, when a society called "Ungdomens Vänner" was
founded by President Hasselquist, Professors O. Olsson, C. O. Granere,
C. P. Rydholm and the five members of the first senior class of Augustana College. Their aim was to foster the young people's societies
which began to form at that time in many of the churches. Besides
printing several tracts and pamphlets, the society began publishing the
monthly "Ungdoms-Vännen" in January, 1879. Two years later,
"Korsbanéret," a Christmas annual, was turned over to the society
by its publishers, O. Olsson and C. A. Swensson, who had started it in
1880. The name of the society was changed in February, 1883, to the
Augustana Tract Society. The membership fees not sufficing to meet
expenses, the business was incorporated under the name of Augustana
Book Concern the same year and capitalized at $15,000, divided in
300 shares. One of the provisions was that two-thirds of any net profits
should go to Augustana College and Theological Seminary. The following year the new firm purchased Thulin and Anderson's printing shop
in Moline, and also secured possession of the old society's publications
and other property. The firm started a bookstore at 7th avenue and
38th street, Rock Island. Prof. C. P. Rydholm, the first manager, was
succeeded in September of the same year by Jonas Westling. He re-

mained until 1886, when Rev. P. J. Källström took charge. The following July the monthly "Ungdomsvännen," was changed to a weekly and named "Hemvännen." In the fall of 1887 C. G. Thulin sold his bookstore to the Augustana Book Concern and assumed the management of affairs. The following year one of the publications of the Concordia Pub. Co., Chicago, was bought by the Augustana Book Concern and united with its own periodical, "Hemvännen."

In 1889 the board of directors offered to turn its property over

The Augustana Book Concern Building

to the Augustana Synod, provided the latter would establish a board of publication and reimburse those stockholders who might be unwilling to donate their capital stock to the synod. A few days later the synod appointed a board of publication and instructed it, if possible, to buy out the Augustana Book Concern in the interest of the synod. The synod recognized that its duty was to compensate Engberg and Holmberg, who had bought out the synod's book business and had assumed its liabilities, with the understanding that it was to continue as the official supply house, and therefore resolved that a satisfactory agreement should be made with Engberg and Holmberg. It may be observed, in passing, that no attempt has been made on the part of the synod to carry out its resolution.

The board of publication incorporated in August, 1889, under the name of the Lutheran Augustana Book Concern, and took possession of the property of its predecessor, promising to pay to the stockholders in five years eighty per cent. of the value of the paid up stock, with interest. This was accomplished within the stated time.

Dr. S. P. A. Lindahl became president of the publishing house, and remained in this capacity until his death in 1908. A. G. Anderson has been manager from the first. In 1895 the Globe Bindery was purchased and united with the plant. Two years later a commodious

Carl G. Thulin

brick building was erected, sufficient to house all the departments. Branches have been established, in St. Paul, 1891, New York, 1904, and Chicago, 1907. In 1906 the corporate name was changed back to Augustana Book Concern.

The periodicals published by the institution are: "Augustana," the weekly church organ, "Tidskrift för teologi och kyrkliga frågor," "Ungdomsvännen," "Barnens tidning." "Textblad för söndagssko-lan," "Solstrålen," "Solglimten," "The Olive Leaf," and "The Young Lutheran's Companion." Of their book publications, approximately two hundred and fifty-three in number, about fifteen are school books, seven are historical and biographical works, fifty-two are devotional and other religious works, ninety are Sunday school storybooks, four are hymnals, eight are collections of poetry, ten are music books, while sixty-eight are of a miscellaneous character. Their most notable original publications are Norelius' "De svenska luterska församlingarnas och svenskarnes historia i Amerika'' and the annuals ''Korsbaneret'' and ''Prärieblomman.''

Augustana

''Augustana,'' the official paper of the Augustana Synod, was founded in 1856 as a small monthly devotional paper bearing the name of ''Det Rätta Hemlandet.'' In 1873 it was made a weekly and the name changed to ''Augustana och Missionären.'' In 1876 the weekly was divided into two fortnightly papers, named, respectively, ''Augustana'' and ''Missionären.'' This experiment was abandoned the following year and the paper was issued weekly as before. The paper was enlarged in 1885, and named simply ''Augustana.'' Another enlarge-

Rev. Sven P. A. Lindahl

ment took place in 1890, since which time the paper has been issued in 4-column, 16-page form. Dr. Hasselquist, the founder and first editor, was succeeded in 1858 by Eric Norelius, who was followed shortly by Erland Carlsson, nominal editor until 1864, with the material assistance of Jonas Engberg. From the last-named year A. R. Cervin was in charge until the end of 1868, when his assistant, J. G. Princell, did all the editorial work for six months, or until July, 1869, when Hasselquist again took up the work. During subsequent years the editorial work was divided among Hasselquist, Norelius, O. Olsson, Cervin, C. P. Rydholm, C. M. Esbjörn and L. G. Abrahamson. From 1890 until his death in 1908, Dr. S. P. A. Lindahl was editor-in-chief, assisted by Abrahamson, C. O. Lindell, A. Rodell, O. V. Holmgrain, C. J. Bengston and others. To succeed Lindahl, the synod in 1908 chose Dr. Abrahamson, who at present directs the editorial policy of the synodical organ.

Life sketches of almost every one of these men appear in various parts of this work.

Besides "Augustana," the most consequential periodicals issued from the synodical publishing house are "Ungdomsvännen," an illustrated monthly, much of the contents of which is of general interest and has more than transient value, and "Augustana Theological Quarterly: Tidskrift för teologi och kyrkliga frågor," a dignified two-language publication.

Chicago-Bladet

As a result of a division of opinion among the Mission Friends in the middle seventies on church government, John Martenson in

John Martenson

February, 1877, started a fortnightly religious paper in Chicago, which was named "Chicago-Bladet." In 1879 it combined with it "Zions Banér," and was thenceforth issued weekly. Rev. K. Erixon, the publisher of the latter paper, became a partner in the business, and later Victor Rylander joined the firm. About 1882, Martenson bought out both his partners, and since then has been sole proprietor of the newspaper. Himself managing editor, he has from time to time had the assistance of Hjalmar Anderson, Rev. J. G. Princell, Gustaf Sjöström, K. Newquist, Andrew Anderson and C. G. Nilsson. After having worked in the printing office for nine years, Andrew Anderson was engaged on the editorial staff, a position he still retains. By a sort of tacit consent, "Chicago-Bladet" holds an official position in the denomination of Free Mission Friends.

A book and publishing concern is maintained in connection with the newspaper. A monthly Sunday school paper, named "Columba," is published, and among the books issued from this office may be mentioned: "Blad ur Naturens Historia;" "Märkvärdigheter ur Naturen, Historien och Lifvet;" "Himla-Uret;" "The Reconciliation," and "The Blood of Jesus." The book "Himla-Uret" (Heaven's Clock) is remarkable as an effort by its author, Rev. F. Franson, to establish the time of the Last Judgment.

Fosterlandet

For more than fifteen years a paper called "Fosterlandet" was published in Chicago by private enterprise, in the interest of the Swedish Lutherans. It was founded by Dr. Carl Swensson at Lindsborg, Kansas, under the name of "Framåt," and removed to Chicago prior to 1890. Petrus C. Pearson was the editor and Dr. Swensson the chief contributor. In October, 1890, Ernst W. Olson was added to the staff, the paper was doubled in size to eight pages of seven columns each, and the name changed to "Fosterlandet." In 1896 "Nya Pressen" was consolidated with "Fosterlandet," and Mr. Olson again joined Mr. Pearson in the editorial work, after an absence of four years. The stock company owning the newspaper transferred the property to the new publishers of "Svenska Tribunen" in 1900, who published both papers with the aid of the same editorial staff for several years, afterwards putting Rev. J. W. Nyvall in editorial charge of "Fosterlandet." After a second change of ownership, which removed the paper entirely from churchly influence, it died by slow stages, its nominal successor being a story paper, named "Fylgia." Until his death, in 1904, Dr. Carl Swensson was a constant contributor to the paper, which acquired strength and influence largely through his popular weekly letters. Dr. Carl A. Evald's able pen was also enlisted in the service of "Fosterlandet" for a number of years. Two different editions of "Fosterländskt Album," edited by E. W. Olson, were published in 1897 and 1898, as premiums.

Carl Aaron Swensson

In Swedish-American literature Carl Swensson holds a prominent place. While a student at Augustana College, Swensson began to contribute to "Hemlandet" and one or two periodicals, and he wrote for the current press continually almost up to the day of his death. He started "Framåt" at Lindsborg, in 1884, edited the paper for a time and made weekly contributions to it for twenty years. His articles under the caption "Vid Skrifbordet" in "Framåt," later "Fosterlandet," were probably more generally read than anything written for

Swedish-American newspapers, religious or secular, before or after. For long periods he also contributed weekly letters and articles to "Hemlandet," "Svenska Tribunen" and from three to six other papers, besides furnishing articles for the American press from time to time. In Lindsborg he was the principal stockholder in a book-store and the proprietor of two weeklies, "Lindsborgs-Posten" and the "Record," and did more or less editorial work on both.

It is readily understood that in such a mass of copy furnished, some would be inferior and trivial. To judge his literary ability by what he wrote on board trains in his extensive travels, or in moments

Rev. Carl A. Swensson

when a hundred cares stood waiting at his elbow, or in the weary hours after a strenuous day's work, would not be fair. But take him at his best, in his books "I Sverige" and "Åter i Sverige," both giving his impressions of Sweden, and he will be found an alert observer, a skillful word-painter, a brilliant narrator, and altogether a charming writer. The last-named book by him was published also in an English edition, and the first was published both in Chicago and in Stockholm. Other works by Swensson are: "Vid hemmets härd," an illustrated volume of miscellany; "I Morgonstund," brief discourses on Bible texts; "Förgät-mig-ej," with contributions by others, and "Ju-bel-Album," an illustrated historical account of the Augustana Synod, compiled in collaboration with Dr. L. G. Abrahamson and published by the National Publishing Company of Chicago. Together with others, he edited "Korsbaneret," a church annual, for five years, and "Ungdomsvännen" from 1880 to 1887.

Carl Aaron Swensson was born at Sugar Grove, Pa., June 25, 1857, and reared at Andover, Ill., where his father, Jonas Swensson, was pastor of the Swedish Lutheran church. He was educated at Augustana College, graduating from its college department in 1877 and from the theological seminary two years later. Having been ordained minister of the Augustana Synod, he was called to the church in Lindsborg. In 1881 he founded Bethany Academy, the modest forerunner of Bethany College, an institution which grew large and influential under his charge and stands as a monument to his remarkable energy. At the time of Swensson's death the institution had twelve departments of instruction, half a hundred professors and instructors, 950 students and property valued at $200,000.

In addition to his work as a preacher, educator and writer, Swensson accomplished much work in other fields. When the temperance agitation stirred Kansas, he was in the thickest of the fight and did as much as any man to secure the adoption of the prohibition law in that state. He served in the state legislature in 1889-90. In politics a progressive Republican, Swensson was a successful campaign speaker and did yeoman service in behalf of presidential and gubernatorial candidates.

In the pulpit, on the lecture platform, or on the political "stump," Swensson had few equals in his ability to sway an audience. Whether in English or Swedish, he spoke with the same spontaneous eloquence. His great public activity is reflected in the large number of offices and appointments filled by him in the church and the state. Augustana and Thiel Colleges conferred on him the degree of D. D., Upsala University that of Ph. D., and by King Oscar II. he was created a Knight of the Order of the Polar Star. Swensson passed away at Los Angeles, Cal., Feb. 16, 1904.

Svenska Kuriren

A weekly comic paper named "Kurre" was started in Chicago in May, 1884, by F. W. Ankarfelt. In December, 1887, it was changed to a news sheet. About this time Bredtschneider, the illustrator of "Kurre," and one Turk acquired an interest in the plant. By intrigue, it is claimed, the two soon after mortgaged the property to John Marder, of Marder, Luse and Co., in settlement for printers' supplies furnished by him on account, and he took over and ran the paper in a fashion for a number of months.

Having learnt that the paper was for sale, Alex J. Johnson, then an employee of a crockery firm, made inquiries looking toward a purchase. The price asked was far above his own means, but on Aug. 8, 1888, a contract was entered into by which Johnson assumed the management of the paper, the owner agreeing to advance the money needed for the balance of the year. The paper ran at a loss, and by Jan. 1, 1889, it stood Mr. Johnson at about $7,000. By giving notes for almost the whole of that amount, Johnson secured possession and soon put the business on a paying basis. During his twenty years as publisher of ''Svenska Kuriren,'' Mr. Johnson has had personal charge of the editorial work as well as the business management of his paper.

Alex J. Johnson

In point of ready wit, clearness of style and all-round knowledge, Mr. Johnson has no superior and few equals in the field of Swedish-American journalism. His conception of editing a newspaper is to

Alex J. Johnson

talk to the public as a friend to another, discussing any topic of the day, but leaving every one to follow his own opinion. He has little respect for popular opinion, and, as a sort of temperamental oppositionist, seemingly likes to go against it, thereby often stirring up a hornet's nest. He can give and take with the same evenness of temper, and has the rare faculty of retaining as readers even those whose views differ radically from his own. His criticisms would be more feared, if less certain, but as it is, an approval from him is never expected. His bristling editorials are very generally read and enjoyed, and have aided greatly in the making of Mr. Johnson's paper.

For a number of years a book of fiction and humor, named ''Kurre-Kalender,'' was published by Mr. Johnson and given free to the subscribers of ''Svenska Kuriren.''

Gustaf Wicklund

Gustaf Wicklund, born in Gefle, Sweden, Dec. 8, 1852, enriched our poetical and humorous literature measurably during the twenty odd years he was engaged in newspaper work. He came over in 1878 and tried diverse occupations for four years, including that of tailor, then secured employment on "Svenska Amerikanaren." He was associated with Ninian Waerner in editing the comic weekly "Kurre" from May, 1884, to December, 1887, when that publication was metamorphosed into "Svenska Kuriren." After working on papers in Minneapolis for five years, he returned to Chicago and edited "Humor-

Gustaf Wicklund

isten" for a number of years. Having been connected with "Tribunen" for some time, he lost his position when the paper was sold in 1900. He then went back to Minneapolis, where he was connected with "Svenska Amerikanska Posten" until his death, Oct. 10, 1905.

Wicklund was a facile writer of witty verse and humorous prose sketches. He wrote clever topical songs and improvised verses for numberless occasions with the same ease that characterizes the flow of language from a fluent public speaker. Wicklund was a playwright of no mean order. Five comedies were written by him in Chicago and produced in this and other cities. One of these, entitled "En afton på Tre Byttor," was played at the People's Theatre of Stockholm. where it enjoyed a month's run. It was published by Albert Bonnier. of Stockholm. Wicklund's Swedish rendition of "Pinafore" has been given publicly both in Chicago and in Sweden. After his death, Wicklund's verses were published in a collection entitled "Gnistor från rimsmedjan."

Otto Pallin

Otto Pallin for a few months in 1884 was editor and publisher of "Rockfords Allehanda" and subsequently was assistant editor of "Kurre," "Svenska Kuriren" and "Svenska Tribunen." Pallin possessed rare versatility. He was a good singer, a talented actor in the comedy class and a good writer of short stories and witty verse. He was a college man and had begun studying medicine when in 1880 he suddenly abandoned his studies to emigrate. In this country he tried his hand at many things—he was druggist, doctor, concert singer, grocery salesman, bartender, actor and cook, before engaging in

Otto Pallin

journalism. Pallin passed away on the 21st of May, 1904, soon after having been reengaged on the staff of "Svenska Kuriren."

Wilhelm Åkerberg

Wilhelm Åkerberg, a Stockholmian by birth, on his third visit to Chicago about 1888 was engaged as associate editor of "Kuriren" and in 1890 went over to "Humoristen" as its editor. The next year he left for Sweden and started a paper in Stockholm, which was shortlived; came back to Chicago in 1892, was reengaged on "Humoristen" for a few months, then, with Higgins, the artist, started a comic paper called "Skämt," in August, 1893, and when its short course was run, another called "Den svensk-amerikanska Söndags-

Nisse,'' whose career was likewise brief, being cut short after five
months by the death of Åkerberg in June, 1894.

Åkerberg was a talented but unprincipled and erratic young man.
Drink was the bane of his life, and in a spirit of bravado he owned
to having "soaked" a large part of his inheritance at certain Stockholm inns. He wrote a mass of well-turned rhymes, mostly of the
anacreontic variety. He was fond of stage life, often took part in
the production of Swedish theatricals here, and himself wrote a play,
"En folktalare," produced in Chicago in 1888.

Otto Crælius

Otto Craelius, associate editor of "Svenska Kuriren" for some
twelve years, took rank as a very capable journalist and a clever

Otto Crælius

writer of verse and short stories of Swedish-American life, mostly in
a humorous vein. Craelius was born in Fliseryd parish, Småland,
Sept. 10, 1863. He studied at the collegiate school in Oskarshamn,
being always at the head of his class and making splendid progress.
He aimed to graduate ahead of the class, but, failing in that, abandoned
his studies and accepted a proffered position on "Oskarshamns-
Tidningen" in January, 1885. In 1887 he leased "Hvad nytt?"—a
liberal newspaper about to fail—and published it for three years in
the conservative province of Småland, not without success. After
having been made defendant in a libel suit, he gave up the business,
although acquitted of the charge, and emigrated. He died in Chicago
March 4, 1903.

Johan Person

Johan Person's pen is one of the most capable enlisted in the service of the Swedish press in this country. He began as a casual contributor to "Svenska Tribunen," writing humorous comments, verses, and translating serial stories. Afterwards he was added to the regular staff. He has taken turns at editing "Svea," of Worcester, and "Svenska Folkets Tidning," of Minneapolis, and is at present second to Mr. Johnson as editor of "Svenska Kuriren." While in Worcester, Mr. Person had published a volume of short stories entitled "I Svensk-Amerika," dealing with Swedish-American life, and this has been followed by many well-written stories, sketches and essays on kindred topics. His style is forceful, inclined to be caustic, but tempered by more than the usual modicum of wit and humor. His depiction of the Swedish immigrant's life in this country is tinged with a sort of sentimental pessimism common to most Swedish writers on American conditions, conveying the impression that, despite prosperity and success, the Swedish-American lacks contentment and real happiness in the land of his choice.

Humoristen—Svenska Nyheter

The first issue of a comic weekly, known as "Humoristen," was published Jan. 13, 1890, from the office of Gus Broberg, steamship and immigration agent. Two other comic papers, "Friskytten," of Minneapolis, and "Frisk Luft," of New York, were absorbed by "Humoristen," which ran as a comic sheet for half a score of years, whereupon a general newspaper, named "Svenska Nyheter," took its place. The new and enlarged paper was published by Mr. Broberg under the editorial management of Frithiof Malmquist and others, until consolidated with "Svenska Tribunen" in July, 1906. The following year Mr. Broberg sold his interest in the combination and retired from the newspaper field.

As editor of "Humoristen" in 1890-92, Ernst Lindblom added much to our humorous literature. A published collection of his verse bears the title "På försök." A comedy in three acts by him, entitled "Pelle Pihlqvists Amerika-resa," was produced in Chicago. His humor is often grotesque and not always clean. As a versifier he is at his best in the serious strain. In an editorial capacity Lindblom was connected with "Svenska Folkets Tidning" of Minneapolis, "Tribunen," "Amerikanaren" and "Humoristen" for eleven years in all. He is now a newspaper writer in Stockholm, his native city.

Gus Higgins is known as a humorist, a writer of bacchanalian verse, a la Bellman, and an artist and illustrator, excelling in portraiture. Being a cynic and a sot, he produced little else than coarse, though witty, comic stuff in verse and prose, mostly published in "Humoristen" and sung or recited at low class entertainments. The products of his pen are so uniformly repulsive to good taste that a biographer of Higgins, wishing to quote him, had difficulty in finding an inoffensive specimen.

Aftonbladet

Scores of Swedish periodical publications, in this state, varying from annuals to dailies, which it were tedious to make note of in these pages, have each had their day. The greatest number were born and died in Chicago, while the cities of Rockford, Galesburg, Moline and Rock Island have had a goodly share. One of the most pretentious enterprises in Swedish newspaperdom was the launching of a daily, named "Aftonbladet," in 1892, by Pehr W. Nilsson. Having thrown out a feeler in the shape of a weekly, called "Skandia," started a month prior, Nilsson and his associates, C. F. Peterson and Axel Burman, turned out their first daily on Sept. 2nd. It was a 7-column, 4-page sheet. Peterson and Burman were the editors and Carl Anred and C. F. Erikson the advertising solicitors. "Aftonbladet" is said to have reached a circulation of 6,000. The weekly "Skandia," feeding on the same material used in the daily, attained great size, ranging from 16 to 32 pages. Like the men in charge, the papers were Democratic, and it is not denied that the new enterprise was nurtured partly with campaign funds. Nilsson ran the papers for eight months, after which time the business is said to have passed into the hands of Burman. Publication ceased some time in the spring or summer of 1893, to the best recollection of Mr. Nilsson.

Other Journalists and Authors—Theodore Hessel

Theodore Hessel is a unique character in the Swedish press of the United States. Being a man of uncommon versatility, he has been active as a teacher, preacher, playwright, poet, critic, political speaker, editor and publisher. He was born in Skönberga, Östergötland, Sweden, in the forties, graduated from the technical school of Norrköping, studied for three years at the dramatic school of the Royal Theater in Stockholm, taught privately in Gotland, then emigrated and became a Baptist preacher in the United States. In 1870 he edited "Skandinavisk Härold," a religio-political paper, at Omaha, Neb., and in 1879-80 "Evangeliskt Magasin" at Council Bluffs, Ia. After twelve years in the ministry he abandoned that profession, declaring it a "religious humbug," and from that time on he has been a violent persecutor of the clergy. In 1883 he started "Svenska Vecko-Bladet" in Omaha, removed with the paper to Kansas City after four years, and in 1892 to Chicago, having changed the name to "Facklan"—The Torch. Its light went out in 1894 and shortly thereafter Hessel started an English publication, named "The Swedish-American Review." It was a 9x19, 16-page paper, quoting freely from Swedish-American newspapers and containing articles and comments from Hessel's caustic pen. Its first issue, published in Nov., 1894, was soon followed by the last. The "Review" was published from Svea Music Hall, 456 31st street, Chicago.

The features of Hessel's paper were for many years a series of "Epistles" signed with his pen name, "Farbror Slokum," and "Letters from Washington," supposedly written by himself over the signature "Swedish Department Clerk."

Hessel is a wit and a satirist, but, lacking in heart qualities, falls short of being a genuine humorist. While in Sweden, Hessel contributed to "Svenska Familje-Journalen" and wrote several plays.

Isidor Kjellberg

Isidor Kjellberg in 1871 published in Chicago a newspaper named "Justitia." Its span of life was from March to October. Talent

Isidor Kjellberg

was not lacking, for Kjellberg, as the publisher and editor of "Östgöten," a newspaper founded by him in 1872, at Linköping, Sweden, proved himself an excellent newspaper man. He was born in Stockholm, where he obtained a technical education. He came over in 1869, worked as draughtsman in Philadelphia, traversed the Northwest as correspondent for "Göteborgs-Posten," and for a few months in 1870 edited "Svenska Monitoren" at St. Paul. In Sweden he published books of verse in 1878 and 1892, the latter year also a book descriptive of his American tour in 1890. A posthumous collection of verse was published shortly after his death, which occurred in 1895.

Kjellberg is described as a wide awake, fearless journalist. He was a republican at heart, an outspoken anti-royalist, a reformer and humanitarian, who voiced his views both on the platform and in the press.

Axel August Swärd

Axel August Swärd, while a student of theology at Rock Island, produced a volume of verse entitled "Vilda Blommor från Prärien," which, when published in 1887, was hailed as a significant contribution to Swedish-American literature. It was, in fact, one of the first collections of Swedish verse brought out in this country, the very earliest poetical volume of any consequence having been a book of poems by Magnus Elmblad, published in 1878. A second volume of poems by Swärd was published two years later, named "Från Vestanskog," with reference to the poet's residence in Oregon, where, after his ordination to the ministry, he obtained his first charge at Marshfield. Among his most noteworthy productions are the epics "Moses begrafning eller En natt på Nebo," and "Guldormen," and such lyric poems as "Vattnet," "Gatpojken," "Det förlorade paradiset" and "Poesien." Wirsén, poet and critic, and secretary of the Swedish Academy, found Swärd's shorter poems especially characterized by much poetic sincerity, and held that the author of the "Wild Flowers of the Prairies" was at his best in his religious songs. Another literary connoisseur of Sweden, Montgomery-Cederhjelm, gives him his full meed of praise by speaking of him as "a noble, poetic genius, a singer worthy of an exalted place on Sweden's Parnassus."

Following are the outlines of the poet's life: born at Snaflunda, Nerike, Sweden, March 27, 1854, the son of an old soldier in limited circumstances; enjoyed ordinary schooling in his boyhood; hired out at eighteen as a farmhand; entered Ahlberg's mission school at Örebro in 1881; came to the United States in 1883; studied at Augustana College and Theological Seminary until 1887, when he was ordained a Lutheran minister; as such he served at Marshfield, Ore., and Templeton, Cal., four years in all; in the latter place he succumbed to a pulmonary disease of long standing on July 20, 1891, in his thirty-eighth year.

Although imbued with the Christian spirit, Swärd's authorship is by no means limited to the religious sphere. But his secular verses, whether sentimental, humorous, or satirical, never fall below the moral standard, never offend the sense of beauty and propriety, and are always in good taste—which cannot truthfully be said of all poets in clerical robe. Swärd was also somewhat of a philosopher and philologist. Certain of his speculative views have been published by Ernst Skarstedt in a small pamphlet, under the title, ''Enskilda skrifter.'' From his youth and for a score of years Swärd was engaged in the task of perfecting a universal language. The manuscripts of his grammar,

Rev. Axel August Swärd

comprising 1,130 pages, and of an extensive glossary, he left to one E. Shiffelin, of New York, who had interested himself in the work, even to the extent of lending pecuniary aid in a small way. But for his untimely death, Swärd undoubtedly would have added much to the literary heritage left by him to posterity.

Ninian Wærner

Ninian Wærner, humorist and poet, was connected with Swedish newspapers in the United States from 1884, the year he came over, up to 1895, when he returned to Sweden. There he edited newspapers in Motala and Stockholm for ten years and died Oct. 10, 1905, as editor of ''Fäderneslandet.'' As second man to Gustaf Wicklund, he worked on "Kurre" for three years from 1884, then on "Svenska Kuriren" in 1888, until joining the staff of "Svenska Amerikanaren" the same year. In 1889 he accepted an editorial position with "Korrespondenten" of Denver. Two years later he and Wicklund started "Friskytten," a comic paper, in Minneapolis. When it was absorbed by "Humoristen" in 1894, Waerner worked for short periods on "Svenska Folkets Tidning" and "Svenska Amerikanska Posten," both of Minneapolis, until his return to Sweden, in November, 1895.

Waerner's original contributions to the newspapers on which he was employed were numberless. A small part of them is included in his

Ninian Wærner

published books: "I höst- och vinterkväll," verses and sketches; "Pennstreck," stories, and "C. A. Tolléens jul- och nyårskalender," a collection of humor in prose and verse. A poem by him received mention honorable by the Swedish Academy.

As a poet Waerner oscillated between the two extremes of burlesque humor and lachrymose pathos. As a humorist he is best known through the ludicrous and highly grotesque sketches purporting to be "letters from C. A. Tolléen." In these the author affects illiteracy and arouses one's risibilities by the old trick of bad spelling, employed by Artemus Ward and Josh Billings, only to a more preposterous degree than any of these writers. Except for his poems, Waerner seemed incapable of serious writing. He was reckless with truth at all times and never hesitated to distort facts to serve his purpose, as witness his sketches of American life and conditions, given with a pretense of truth, to the reading public of Sweden. Waerner's humorous writings abound in equivocations and phraseology suggestive of an impure mind, and his personal morals were not the best, but to deny his exceptional literary talent on grounds of morality would be like denying the genius of a Byron, a Bellman or a Poe. Swedish-American critics differ widely in their estimate of Waerner, Skarstedt touching one extreme in unreserved laudation, Bonggren the other by begrudging him even the scantest credit.

His serious verses, albeit smooth-flowing and pleasing in style, lack the originality of his humorous sketches, and those who knew him personally say his poems of feeling were affectation pure and simple, the grossness of his nature precluding all the finer sensibilities.

Ninian Waerner was born in Norrköping Dec. 12, 1856, and educated at a collegiate school in Nyköping and at Upsala University. He had a musical training and was an accomplished cellist.

Leonard Strömberg

Leonard Strömberg, who was for three years associate editor of "Sändebudet," the organ of the Swedish Methodist Church, besides editing "Söndagsskolbaneret," is the most prolific Swedish-American writer of prose fiction. At the age of fifteen he began sending modest contributions of prose and verse to the papers and soon found a demand for the products of his pen. Short stories and verses by him were published in half a score of newspapers in Sweden, and since his coming to this country in 1895 Strömberg has been a frequent contributor to the Swedish-American press.

The list of published works by Leonard Strömberg comprises a dozen novels and novelettes, several collections of short stories. two books of juvenile stories, one of juvenile verse, two collections of poems and two of verses and prose sketches. Several of the novels are rather voluminous, one running through 1,450 pages, while others reach 700 to 900 pages. Mr. Strömberg has found publishers for his books in Sköfde and Östersund, Sweden, and in Chicago and Minneapolis.

The titles of Strömberg's principal works are: novels and novelettes—"Olycksbarnet," "Ett dystert arf," "I tunga fjättrar," "Enkans son," I brytningstid," "Ljus och skuggor," "På törnestig," "Viktor Boring." "Tiggardrottningen." "Hederns vägar," "Genom strider," "Dygd och brott," "Församlingen i Grand View," "I Mästarens tjänst," "Erik Vedhuggare," "Efter striderna," "Satans spel," "Feg;" collections of verse—"Ett klöfverblad" and "Unga Röster;" collections of prose and verse—"Små blommor" and "Festtalaren." He has compiled several other books, including "Sångbok för söndagsskolor." The book entitled, "Erik Vedhuggare," has been published in three editions in Sweden and two in this country, and has been translated into English.

Strömberg has a light and flowing style. His stories are generally founded on actual experiences and events, make entertaining reading, are serious in tone and have an ennobling tendency. From his poetic vein have flowed many poems to warm the soul and awaken the reader to sober thought.

Strömberg was born in Arboga, Sweden, July 11, 1871. He studied theology at the Methodist Episcopal Seminary at Upsala and

Leonard Strömberg

entered the service of the church as minister. In this country he has served Swedish M. E. churches in Chicago and at points in Iowa and Nebraska.

David Nyvall

David Nyvall ranks well to the front among Swedish writers in the United States. Identified with the denomination of Mission Friends, he is prominent as a champion of higher education, and his main work has been and is to promote schools and disseminate knowledge among that church element. This cause he has sought to further partly by his writings and popular lectures. Nyvall is a deep thinker, an excellent stylist and a man of practical views. The following works by him have been published: "Vers och saga" (1890); "Minnesblad, sex ungdomstal" (1892); "Reformationen i Sverige. Reformationens bakgrund. Svenskhet i Amerika. Tre uppsatser" (1893); "Medsols.

Tre fosterländska tal för ungdom" (1898); "Söken Guds rike. Tjugufyra tal för ungdom" (1901); "Skogsdrillar. Lyriska dikter" (1901);
"My Business. Talks to Young People" (1906); "Roosevelt och konung Oscar såsom fredsvänner och deras relativa anspråk på Nobel-
priset" (1906).

David Nyvall is the son of the late Carl Johan Nyvall, a noted
lay preacher who lived at Vall, Karlskoga parish, Vermland, Sweden,

Dr. David Nyvall

where the son was born Jan. 19, 1863. He studied at Vesterås and
Gefle, graduating from college in the latter city in 1882, with the
highest mark for scholarship, and subsequently pursued medical studies
for four years at Upsala University and the Carolinian Institute of
Stockholm. His professional studies were interrupted in 1886, when,
discouraged by failing health, he emigrated. In this country he began by teaching at a mission school in Minneapolis, but detecting in
this position no promise for the future, entered the ministry. Shortly
thereafter he was elected by the Mission Covenant as associate teacher

of its department of the Congregationalist theological seminary in Chicago. After two years he joined in a movement to found a school exclusively for the Covenant, and, with Rev. E. A. Skogsbergh, established a school on these lines at Minneapolis. When this was turned over to the Covenant, in 1891, Nyvall was made president and continued in that position after the school was removed to Chicago and named North Park College, until 1905, whereupon he served several years at the head of Walden College, at McPherson, Kansas. Prof. Nyvall has edited church and educational papers from time to time, including "Missionären" and "The Walden Volunteer," and is the author of a number of articles scattered through annuals and other Swedish publications. For nine years he was secretary of the Mission Covenant, and has been active in other capacities as a churchman.

Anna Olsson

Miss Anna Olsson of Rock Island is the author of a goodly number of short stories and sketches that are as pleasant reading as anything

Miss Anna Olsson

that has flowed from a Swedish-American pen. A volume published in 1903, containing some of her best work, was well named "Från Solsidan," for there is a wealth of sunshine in everything she writes. Her serious sketches are toothsome mental dishes daintily served, while her Swedish-American dialect stories, the most genuine of their kind, disprove the old tradition that there are no feminine humorists. Unlike many who have put to literary use the mixed and grotesque lingo of the immigrant, Miss Olsson tells a story that has a value aside from the dialect. Contributions by her are of frequent occurrence in the Swedish periodicals ''Ungdomsvännen'' and ''Prärieblomman.'' Sketches by her in English are no less enjoyable than those in her mother tongue.

Ludvig Holmes

By some, Ludvig Holmes has been ranked superior to all other Swedish-American poets, while the average critic is satisfied to raise

Dr. Ludvig Holmes

him to the peerage, without making him king in this particular realm of the Muses. As a singer he is melodious, dignified, solemn, pure. His Pegasus is carefully groomed and seldom cuts capers in the way of wit, satire or epigram, but paces in measured tread as if hitched to a carriage of state. Many of his poems on festive occasions are fine examples of poetic oratory and almost all of his verse is characterized by nobility of thought and tenderness of sentiment. He has had two collections of verse published by the Augustana Book Concern, one in 1896, entitled ''Dikter af Ludvig,'' another in 1905, entitled ''Nya

Dikter af Ludvig.'' A poetic tribute to King Oscar II. on the occasion of the twenty-fifth anniversary of his reign was issued privately. Holmes has contributed generously to various publications, including ''Augustana,'' ''Ungdomsvännen,'' ''Korsbaneret'' and ''Valkyrian.'' In recognition of his work as an author and a churchman, Bethany College has awarded him the degrees of A. M. and L. H. D., Wittenberg College that of D. D., and ''Augustana College that of L. H. D. By the King of Sweden he has been repeatedly honored, having received the following marks of distinction: the silver jubilee medal, the gold medal ''Litteris et Artibus'' and the insignia of the Order of Vasa.

Dr. Holmes is a native of Ströfvelstorp, Skåne, Sweden, where he was born Sept. 7, 1858. He came to this country in 1879 and pursued studies at Augustana College and Theological Seminary for five years, until ordained to the ministry in 1886. After having had pastoral charges at Burlington, Ia., Jamestown, N. Y., and North Grosvenordale and Portland, Conn., he is now pastor of the Swedish Lutheran Church of Evanston, Ill.

Miscellaneous Writers

P. E. Melin, while professor at Augustana College, in January, 1877, started the weekly ''Skandia'' in Moline, which he himself edited for the first few months, then entrusted that task to Magnus Elmblad and Herman Stockenström. His partner in the enterprise was Gustaf Swenson, to whom Melin sold his interest the following July, making him sole proprietor. Melin was an excellent teacher, particularly successful in inspiring the students with a love for the Swedish language and patriotic enthusiasm for Sweden's history and literature. While a student at Upsala, Melin had a book of poems published and while assistant dean of Hernösand College made a translation of the Book of Proverbs from the original text. He left Sweden in 1875 on a call to Augustana College and returned in 1878, entering the ministry of the state church.

Carl Ebbesen, born in Stockholm in 1855, emigrated to the United States in 1880, and worked as typographer in a number of newspaper offices. In Chicago he formed the acquaintance of Herman Lindskog, then pastor of the Swedish M. E. Church in Rockford, and accompanied him to that city, where Lindskog started ''Rockfords Allehanda.'' When this venture failed, Ebbesen for a time was a reporter on the city dailies, ''Gazette'' and ''Star,'' then established ''Rockfords-Posten,'' which he conducted for more than ten years. Afterwards he sold his interest and went east, engaging in a similar enterprise in New England.

Bruno E. Höckert has been a constant contributor to ''Frihetsklockan'' and has developed great activity as a correspondent and general contributor to newspapers on both sides of the Atlantic. He came to this country in 1889 as a delegate from the grand lodge of Sweden to the world's grand lodge of Good Templars, and has since been a very prominent temperance worker here. He is the author of a score of short theatrical sketches written for production at society and lodge entertainments, but the principal work of his pen consists of newspaper articles on political, sociological and temperance topics. Höckert is a graduate of the Pharmaceutical Institute in Stockholm. He has lectured on a wide range of subjects, such as hypnotism, faith cure, cremation, suffrage, and on various phases of religion, hygiene, temperance and sociology. He spoke at the peace congress, the parliament of religions and the agricultural congress of the World's Columbian Exposition.

A most promising poet and writer was Oscar M. Benzon. He was born in Moline, Ill., Dec. 10, 1870, the son of a Swedish Lutheran clergyman; was graduated from Augustana College in 1891; continued his studies at Leland Stanford University, where he received the master's degree two years later. His extreme ambition led to overwork at college, causing a physical and mental collapse in the spring of 1891. He rallied sufficiently to pursue the university course, but had a relapse and in a moment of mental aberration put a tragic end to his young life on Oct. 13, 1893, by leaping from a rowboat into the waters of San Francisco Bay.

As an upper classman at Augustana he began literary pursuits, one of his first published efforts being a translation from ''Martyrerna'' by the Swedish poet Stagnelius, appearing in ''Balder,'' the students' literary annual. While in California he indited a number of poems of exquisite diction and profound depth of thought and feeling. One of these, entitled ''Illusions,'' is pronounced by Ernst Skarstedt, ''the finest English poem ever written by a Swede.'' Other highly meritorious poems by Benzon are entitled ''Kärlek'' and ''Till den förtviflade.'' While at Leland Stanford University, where he made a specialty of German, Benzon wrote verse in that language too, evincing skill in the art of versification in three different languages. As a student Benzon showed remarkable brilliancy, and had he lived to fulfill his promise, great gain would doubtless have accrued to Swedish-American literature.

Charles Edward Thornmark did splendid service to the press for some five years, 1889-1894. After working in the lumber camps and sawmills of Michigan and writing some excellent sketches of life in the frontier settlements, he became editor of ''Nordens Medborgare,'' published at Manistee, Mich., and three months later founded a newspaper of his own, named ''Arbetaren,'' at Cadillac, Mich. It was one of the very few minor Swedish-American papers edited with talent. The enterprise, however, did not prove a financial success. In 1894 Thornmark threw down his pen, discontinued the paper and became subscription agent for "Svenska Amerikanaren" of Chicago. Since then he has occasionally resumed the discarded implement to write an article, story or poem for that paper. Recently he has contributed articles to "The Public," a weekly political journal of Chicago.

Though self-taught, Thornmark handles the language with admirable mastery, whether he writes prose or verse. Among his poems, which are not many, one entitled "Är du med?" must be classed with the gems of the Swedish-American Muse. Thornmark is a humorist whose sweet good-nature is spiced with a dash of satire.

William Larson is a combination of author and artist. Poems and short stories by him which have appeared in different publications are characterized by objective truth, trenchant diction and a vivid sense of humor. A notable poem by him is entitled "Svarta Ridån." Under the caption "Från torngluggen" he has written current comment in the lighter vein for "Frihetsklockan," a temperance paper. Holiday numbers of "Svenska Amerikanaren," in whose business office he has been employed, have contained a number of drawings and sketches by him.

Carl Gustaf Norman while studying at Augustana College began to court the Muse. As early as 1883, while teaching at Bethany College, he contributed verses to Swedish periodicals, and for the next few years "Ungdomsvännen," "Augustana" and "Korsbaneret" published poems by him. These are uniformly well modeled and often sentimental in tone. Norman edited "Framåt" at Lindsborg, Kans., in 1886-8, and another paper of the same name at Providence, R. I., 1892-5. After editing "Svea," of Worcester, Mass., for a number of years, he took an editorial position on "Svenska Tribunen" in 1906 and remains with "Tribunen-Nyheter" as its chief writer.

Literary Work in English

In concluding this chapter, some of the evidences of English literary activity among the Swedish-Americans of the state may be pointed out. Reference has been made to newspapers in English with Swedish-Americans at the head. A noteworthy enterprise of this kind was the daily "Press" of Chicago, the chief, if not the sole, backer of which was Robert Lindblom. It was published for a brief period in the early nineties. In the eighties there was published in Chicago the monthly "Scandinavia," directed principally by Norwegians, and devoted to the publishing in English of the current events and chief features of Scandinavian literature, history, religion, science and art.

It had Swedish contributors and published not a few articles specifically Swedish-American.

The translation of selections from Swedish standard poets and prose writers has been pursued here for upwards of forty years, both by Swedes and others. Among translations published in Chicago in book form are: Tegnér's "Axel," translated by Major J. Swainson, published together with the original text of the poem, by the Lakeside Pub. Co. in 1870; Tegnér's "Frithiofs Saga" by Thomas and Martha Holcomb, in 1876; "The Surgeon's Stories," vols. I-VI, by Zacharias Topelius, translated by Marie A. Brown and Selma Borg, and published by Jansen & McClurg in 1882; "The Father," a tragedy by August Strindberg, translated by N. Ericksen and published in London and Chicago, 1899; "Swedish Fairy Tales," by Hofberg, translated by Willard H. Myers, second edition published here in 1890; "The Play of Fate," a novel by Herman Bjursten, by the same translator, 1892; "Swedish Fairy Tales," by Anna Wahlenberg, translated by Axel Wahlenberg, published in 1901; a prose translation of Tegnér's "Frithiofs Saga," done by John B. Miller and printed privately in 1905; a metrical translation of the same, about to be published in a profusely illustrated edition by Clement B. Shaw, the translator. Albert Alberg during his fifteen years in Chicago translated a number of Swedish, Norwegian and Danish works into English, besides writing several books in English published here. His original writings, while here, were: "Imaginary Travels," "Vacation Days," "Sophos, or, Kidnapping the Kings," "How I Twice Eloped" and "The Future Emperor of the United States," a satirical romance. His translations are: "The Pilgrimage of Truth," from the Danish of Erik Bögh, "High Aims and Other Tales," and "Marriage," by August Strindberg, "Antichrist," a drama by Victor Hugo Wickström, "George Stephenson," a drama, from the Norwegian of L. Dietrichson, and Holberg's comedy, "Jeppe paa Bjerget," from the Danish. Altogether Alberg has translated thirty or more books from Scandinavian languages into English, most of them published in London during the fourteen years he spent in England. His original writings, published in book form, are twelve in number.

Hundreds of Swedish poems in English garb have appeared in the Swedish papers, as well as numberless translations from the English. The translators of this class of literature are very many, and out of the whole number not a few have evinced ability to produce well-turned and musical lyrics in English. A volume of "Poems and Swedish Translations" by Frederick Peterson, M. D., of Buffalo, N. Y., was published in 1883 by S. A. Maxwell & Co., of Chicago. It contains a number of original poems of merit.

"The Ward of King Canute," "The Thrall of Leif the Lucky" and "Randvar, the Songsmith," well-known romances of old Norse life, are the work of a young Chicago woman, Ottilie Liljencrantz, whose Swedish father furnished her with the subject matter, while her American mother supplied the vehicle of expression, for her charming stories.

Turning from belles lettres to other fields of literary endeavor, we find several notable examples of works in English by Illinois Swedes. Dr. Oscar Oldberg of Northwestern University is the author of several textbooks on chemistry, pharmacy, metrology and related subjects and

Ottilie A. Liljencrantz

has served for almost thirty years on the committee of revision and publication of the "Pharmacopœa of the United States." Dr. Carl S. N. Hallberg of the Chicago College of Pharmacy, another authority on pharmaceutical science, was for eight years editor of the "Western Druggist," and has done a great deal of work in various sections of the American Medical Association, and contributed numerous papers to scientific journals. Dr. Josua Lindahl and Dr. John A. Udden are two other Swedish-American scientists whose names are familiar to readers of scientific journals. The latter has written quite extensively on geological subjects and also dipped into the archæology of America, as witness a publication by him entitled "An Old Indian Village." In the field of geology he has had a number of treatises published, four of which are the results of his investigations bearing on the wind as a geological agent, namely, "Dust and Sandstorms in the West," "Loess as a Land Deposit," "Erosion, Transportation and Sedimentation Performed by the Atmosphere" and "The Mechanical Composition of Wind Deposits." Among other scientific papers by Dr. Udden published separately is one entitled, "On the Cyclonic Distribution of Rainfall." A history of Sweden, in two volumes, published some years ago in English, is by N. N. Cronholm, a Chicago lawyer of Swedish birth, and the laborious task of compiling the genealogy of all the ruling houses of Europe has been performed in this same city by Carl Magnus Allström, who has had his compendious "Dictionary of Genealogy" published in two volumes. Herman Lennmalm, who abandoned journalism for dental surgery, in the early nineties compiled a work on dentistry which was published at Chicago under the title of "World's History and Review of Dentistry," in 1894. Dr. Olof Toffteen, of Western Theological Seminary, is the author of a book on "Myths of the Bible." The results of his researches in the past few years are found in three recent volumes from the University of Chicago Press, namely, "Ancient Chronology" and vol. V. of "Ancient Records of Egypt." The first volume of a third orientalist work by him, entitled "Researches in Assyrian and Babylonian Geography," appeared in 1908. To bibliographical literature Aksel G. S. Josephson has made several contributions, including "List of Bibliographies of Bibliographies," published by the Bibliographical Society of Chicago, and "Bibliography of Union Lists of Serials," published by the John Crerar Library. Josephson has edited four volumes of the yearbook of the Bibliographical Society of America and to the "Nation" he has contributed notes and reviews of bibliographical works and of notable books from Sweden.

Recent years have shown an increased demand for English reading matter that is no less characteristically Swedish-American for being in the language of the land. This is especially true of the church field, and the various publishing houses are meeting these requirements. The Augustana Book Concern has published for years an English Sunday School paper, "The Olive Leaf," to which was added a few years back a second English paper, "The Augustana Journal," now named "The Young Lutheran's Companion." A collection of Swedish songs and hymns in English, entitled "Hymnal," is from the same house, also a collection of "Masterpieces from Swedish Literature," six small volumes of "Stories for Children," being translations made by C. W. Foss, from "Läsning för barn," by Z. Topelius, an English edition of Nils Lövgren's "Kyrkohistoria till skolornas tjenst," translated by M. Wahlström and C. W. Foss, and "The Law of the Westgoths," done into English by Alfred Bergin. The Engberg-Holmberg Publishing

Company has been going gradually into English work by adding English text to its later editions of Swedish sheet music and song collections, and in publishing Woods-Baker's "Stories of Swedish Life," an edition of "Frithiofs saga" for colleges and universities, annotated by George T. Flom, and several juvenile books, while its largest undertaking in the English language is represented by the work in hand, "History of the Swedes of Illinois."

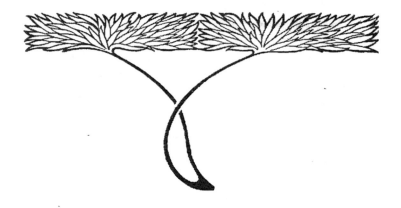

CHAPTER XIV

Art and Artists

The First American Artist a Swede

S early as the beginning of the eighteenth century Swedish artists have lived and flourished in the United States. According to researches in the history of American art, there lived at that early period one Gustaf Hesselius, a Swedish painter, whose works are admitted to be the first artistically executed paintings produced in America. The father of American art, therefore, was a Swedish-American.

A sketch of this pioneer artist may serve as a fitting preface to the following account of Swedish-American artists and their works in more recent times, the greater number of whom have centered about the city of Chicago.

Gustaf Hesselius was a native of the province of Dalarne, where he was born in 1682. His father, who was a clergyman, gave his five sons a thorough education. The other four all entered the ministry, while Gustaf pursued art studies under the direction of masters both in Sweden and other countries of Europe. In May, 1711, he came over to America together with his eldest brother, Andreas Hesselius, whom King Charles the Twelfth had appointed pastor of the Swedish Holy Trinity Church in present Wilmington, Delaware. Shortly after his arrival Gustaf Hesselius removed to Philadelphia, where he established himself as an artist and was married a few years later. About 1723 he removed to Maryland. Among the works executed there was an altar-piece representing the Lord's Supper, painted for the Queen Ann Episcopal Church, which was torn down in 1773. In 1735 we find Hesselius back in Philadelphia, where he now remained for a score of years. The demand for portraits and other works of art being limited, he was compelled to wield his brush as a common artisan, doing house and sign painting, decorating, gilding, and occasionally repairing and illuminating an old painting. He was in partnership with an

Englishman, John Minter, from London, the firm's advertisements appearing in the primitive newspapers of the time.

Hesselius was a man of many-sided talent. He possessed musical ability and was probably the first organ builder in the colonies. It is known that an instrument was built by him for the church of the Brethren in Bethlehem, Pa.

From paintings by Hesselius, still extant, it appears that he was the equal, if not the superior, of contemporary artists in Europe. Among the collections of the Pennsylvania Historical Society are found two of his paintings, one a portrait of himself, the other one of his wife, Lydia Hesselius. ''The works of Hesselius are characterized by clear colors and strong light effects,'' says Charles Henry Hart, to whom we are indebted for researches that have saved the name of Hesselius from oblivion. A few other portraits from his hand are still in existence. This pioneer artist died in Philadelphia May 25, 1755, and lies buried in the churchyard of the old Gloria Dei Church, of which he was a member. His son, John Hesselius, followed in the footsteps of his father and was, according to Hart, the first native American artist.

John Hesselius doubtless obtained his artistic education from his father, and did not go to Europe until late in life. He was engaged at Philadelphia and Annapolis as a portrait and miniature painter, and his name occurs frequently in the history of the colonial period. In 1763 he was married to one Mrs. Woodward, a lady of beauty and refinement.

The two Hesselii were the only Swedish artists in America in colonial times, of whom there is any record.

Another early American painter of Swedish birth was Adolf Ulrik Wertmuller, who flourished in the latter part of the eighteenth and the beginning of the nineteenth century. He was born in Stockholm in 1751, came to Philadelphia in 1794 and died in 1811.

Early Swedish Artists in Illinois

From this time down to the middle of the nineteenth century, we find no Swedish names in the annals of American art. When in the '50s and '60s Swedes in large numbers settled in the Mississippi Valley, they were mostly sons of toil, yet there was a sprinkling of professional men, among whom were a few artists. For these the field was far from promising. In the sodhouse and the log cabin there was no demand for art works, not even in the little frame churches with which these godfearing people soon studded the prairies. Daily bread, for body and spirit, that was their first need. It was not until the second period of development had set in, when the primitive huts gave way to more comfortable homes, and houses of worship assumed a more churchly aspect, that a craving for the beautiful awoke in the minds of the settlers. About this time the first frescoes and altar-pieces appeared in their churches and the decoration of the private homes began to betray the artistic instinct.

The artists of this period were Peter M. Almini, Henry E. C. Peterson, Axel William Torgerson and Fredrik B. Blombergson, all of Chicago, and Lars Axel Blombergson, of Moline.

Peter M. Almini

Almini was born in Linderås, Småland, Sweden, March 21, 1825, and learned the painter's trade in .Eksjö. He worked at his trade in Russia and Finland, in the meantime acquiring great skill with the

Peter M. Almini

brush. For six years he lived in Stockholm, during two of which he was assistant superintendent in the decorating of the royal palace. In 1852 he came over to the United States, settled in Chicago and there opened in business the following year. He soon made himself known as a skillful fresco painter, and was engaged to do the interior decorating and mural painting of numerous church edifices, assembly halls and public buildings in this and other American cities.

A work in twenty-four small parts, entitled ''Chicago Illustrated'', was published in the years 1868-71 by Almini and Jevne. This series was almost completed, when the Chicago fire put an end to the publication. Each part of the series contained four illustrations lithographed in colors, and descriptive text. The grandfather of Almini was an Italian artist, who was called to Stockholm by King Carl XIV. Johan to decorate the interior of the royal palace and who liked the country so well that he remained in Sweden.

In the early days of the Swedes in Chicago, Almini was a prominent figure among them. He was a member of the Academy of Design and one of the charter members of the Svea Society, organized in 1857, and in 1866 aided in founding the liberal Swedish weekly "Svenska Amerikanaren." The business established by him in 1853 is still continued in Chicago under the name of the Almini Company. Almini was chiefly a commercial artist, who painted pictures and sketches merely for study or pastime. He had made a profound study of both ancient and modern art, and stood at the head of his profession in Chicago. He was the vice-president of the Master Painters and Decorators' Association of Chicago and the treasurer of the National Association of Painters and Decorators when they were founded. Peter M. Almini died in October, 1890.

Henry E. C. Peterson

The Academy of Design was made up of members of several nationalities. Another Swedish member, besides Almini, was Henry E. C. Peterson, the portrait painter, who for a time taught the life class of the academy, resigning afterwards to go abroad for further study. The Academy of Design flourished remarkably and was in the sixties a noted social organization of Chicago. It held its meetings in Crosby's Opera House before the great fire, and later in the Academy of Design building on Michigan avenue. The artists' ball was the great society event of the season in those days, tickets selling as high as twenty dollars. After the fire, many of the artists left Chicago, some locating in New York, others going to Europe.

Henry E. C. Peterson was born May 20, 1841, on Skeppsholmen in Stockholm. His father was a ship builder. The son was educated at the Sloyd School at Brunkebergstorg and the Royal Academy of Arts. After having lost both parents in a cholera epidemic, he went for a tour around the world with his brother, who was a sea captain. He came to New York at the outbreak of the Civil War and at once enlisted in the Union navy. He served on the frigate Roanoke and was present at the great naval duel between the Monitor and the Merrimac. After serving the Union for three years and one month, Peterson located in Chicago and took up painting as a profession. He made two trips to Paris and there studied at the Julien school, with artists of fame. In the pursuit of his specialty of portraiture, Mr. Peterson has painted many people prominent in Chicago and elsewhere. Among those in Chicago were the McCormicks, the Farwells, and John and Moses Wentworth. Among other Americans, who have sat for him, are Brigham Young, president of the Mormons, and many bishops and leading men of the Catholic and Protestant churches. For libraries, universities, colleges and banks he has executed a large number of portraits of men of fame. In recent years Mr. Peterson has had the bulk of his work in New York, where, with his family, he spends the

Henry E. C. Peterson

greater part of his time. His wife Emma, née Larson, made a name for herself as a singer in the seventies and early eighties.

Fredrik B. Blombergson

About the years 1868-73 there lived in Chicago a landscape painter named Fredrik B. Blombergson. Finding here little demand for his work, he returned to Sweden. In the possession of his old friends are found a small number of canvases from which we are enabled to judge of his skill as an artist. He was painstaking to a high degree

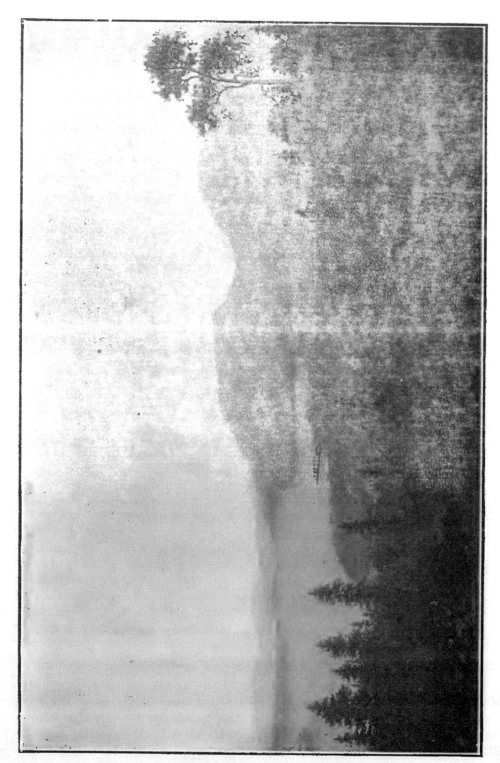

View of Bergsjö, Helsingland. By Fredrik B. Blombergson

and there is about his landscapes an almost photographic exactness. His tints are modest and natural, and he left nothing to be guessed at in his pictures. The canvas here reproduced is a view of Bergsjö, Helsingland, the artist's home parish. Another painting, also executed by Blombergson for Jonas Engberg, is "A Norwegian Fiord," a splendid reproduction of a most majestic scene. In the possession of John G. Malmgren of Chicago is a view of Upsala, also a replica of the scene from Bergsjö, while another copy of the latter is owned by John J. Engberg and a different scene from the same locality by Eos Hegström. Blombergson was born in the city of Söderhamn and located there after his return from this country.

Axel William Torgerson

Still another of the early Swedish artists of Chicago was Axel William Torgerson, who was born in Stockholm in the year 1833. He

Axel William Torgerson

was educated at Upsala University, and at the age of twenty-three came to the United States, locating in Chicago. At first he was engaged in the manufacture of cigars, but, possessing talent and ambition, he took up painting in 1870, and soon developed into a marine

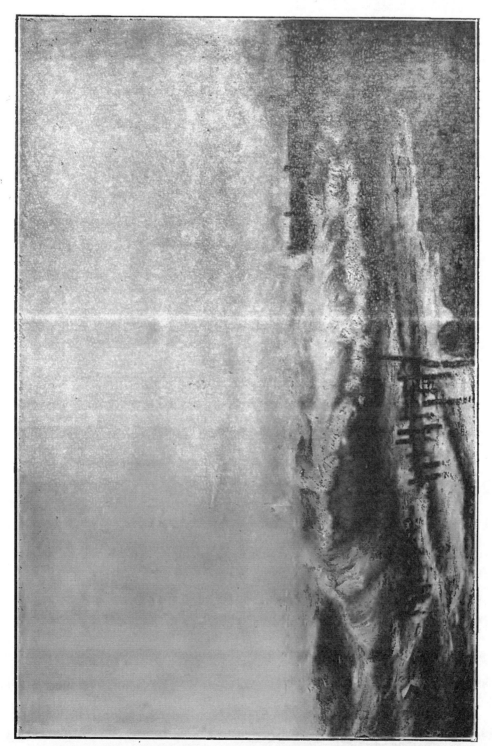

A Lake Michigan Scene. By Axel W. Torgerson

artist of recognized ability. He executed a great many commissions and his work was greatly admired. Torgerson died in January, 1890.

Lars Axel Blombergson

Blombergson was born Aug. 17, 1841, in the Swedish city of Söderhamn, where he learned the painter's trade from his father. He emigrated in 1868, coming to Moline, Ill., where he lived for eleven years. During that time he worked at interior decorating, and specimens of his skill could be seen in a number of the Swedish churches in that section. He died in Moline Nov. 18, 1879. According to our best information, the two Blombergsons were cousins.

Artists of a Later Period

In the '80s and '90s Swedish artists of repute came to this country in considerable number, many of whom made their homes here and successfully engaged each in his special line of work, some as illustrators, others as plastic artists and sculptors, still others as painters. Besides, quite a number of native Swedish-Americans have entered the field of art in late years, and almost every art exhibition catalogue will show a goodly number of Swedish names. As a rule, their contributions to art possess that merit and dignity which characterizes modern art productions in Sweden.

Swedish-American artists, however, in many cases are unknown to their own countrymen, both in this country and in Sweden. Most of them left the old country in early life, and here they have met with greater appreciation and found readier sale for their works among the general American public, few Swedish-Americans heretofore having attained that point of financial independence and love of art, at which people usually begin to patronize the studios and exhibitions. Progress in this direction has been made in the last few years, and the art schools established at various institutions of learning supported by the Swedish people bespeak a growing appreciation as well as a more general cultivation of art among them. Such art schools were opened in 1890 and 1895, respectively, at Bethany College, Lindsborg, Kansas, and Augustana College, Rock Island, Illinois.

Peter Roos

The chair of industrial art and design at the University of Illinois during the decade of 1880-90 was occupied by a Swedish artist, Peter Roos, who prior to his election to the professorship was instructor at the university in 1876-77 and in the winter and spring terms of 1880.

Peter Roos is a native of Skåne, Sweden, born at Lyngby, Feb. 22, 1850. He was educated in his native place and at Kristianstad, and came to America in 1872, establishing himself in Boston as fresco-

painter and designer. The following year he was instructor in the
evening drawing schools of the city, and in 1874 he established an art
school, the Boston Art Academy.

After leaving the University of Illinois Roos studied and prac-
ticed landscape art for the next six years, or until 1896, when he took
the position of director of art study in the public schools of Cambridge, Mass., the position he now holds. Roos became a member of
the Boston Art Club in 1874; N. E. A., 1903; the Cambridge Municipal
Art Society and the Illinois University Club, 1903.

C. F. von Saltza

C. F. von Saltza, deceased, was a noted portrait painter. His work
is characterized by that touch of genius which makes his pictures not

C. F. von Saltza

merely likenesses of persons, but works of art. Von Saltza took great
pride in numbering himself among "the rank and file of those that
champion the cause of Sweden and strive to bring honor and respect
to her name in all parts of the world." And in his position as in-

structor in three different art schools in the United States at various periods, he doubtless had a greater opportunity than most of his Swedish-American colleagues to make his influence felt.

C. F. von Saltza was born at Sörby, Östergötland, Sweden, in 1858, the son of Count K. A. F. von Saltza and his wife, née De la Gardie. After pursuing general studies at Upsala and Stockholm, he entered the Royal Academy of Fine Arts, studying for six years under the instruction of Boklund, von Rosen, Wallander, Kjellberg and Winge. Among his contemporaries at the academy were Zorn, Liljefors, Nordström and Eriksson, names later known to fame. The years 1880 and 1881 von Saltza spent at the art academy of Brussels, going from there to Paris, where during the next three years he developed his talent as a portrait painter. Returning to Sweden, he was engaged in his chosen line for a few years before coming to the United States in 1891. After a short stay in New York, he came west to Chicago and soon formed the acquaintance of Halsey C. Ives, commissioner of art at the World's Columbian Exposition, who induced von Saltza to assume charge of the department of painting at the Museum of Fine Arts in St. Louis. For six years he held that position, in the meantime painting portraits of a number of persons of prominence in that city.

In the Swedish department of the Chicago exposition in 1893 von Saltza had on view an excellent portrait of his wife. He took part also in the successive art exhibitions at Berlin in 1896 and at Stockholm the following year.

In 1898 von Saltza accepted a call to become the head of the department of painting at the Art Institute of Chicago. After one year, however, he left to accept a like position with the Columbia University and Teachers' College of New York. This he retained up to the time of his death, which occurred Dec. 10, 1905.

Olof Grafström

Olof Grafström was a contemporary of Anders Zorn, Bruno Liljefors and Richard Bergh at the Academy of Arts in Stockholm. At an early stage of his career he made himself known as a deft wielder of the brush, and his fine landscapes from northern Sweden exhibited at the Artists' Club found a ready sale. One of these found its way to the private art collection of king Oscar himself. Grafström is keenly sensible of the beauty of nature in the far North, which he reproduces with painstaking accuracy, down to the smallest fleck of cloud in its glorious sky and the minutest detail of the sunlit crags in the magnificent distance. The weird twilight of the northern summer night has had few better interpreters than he.

During the score of years spent in this country, Grafström has been an ardent student of all that is grand in our western forests, mountains, lakes and prairies.   He spent a number of years in the Pacific states, and many of his pictures grace the homes of wealthy westerners. In Portland, Oregon, where he first located, Grafström soon became noted for his splendid depiction of the sceneries in that section, and his pictures were much sought after both for private homes and public buildings.   Three years later he removed to Spokane, where he dupli-

Olof Grafström

cated his success.   He was well represented at the expositions in both cities the next few years, and a landscape of his, a scene from Lapland, won the grand silver medal in Portland.

In 1893 Grafström accepted a call to become the head of the art school in connection with Bethany College, at Lindsborg, Kans., and after four years took a similar position at Augustana College.   In these two positions he has exerted a marked influence in behalf of art among the Swedish-Americans.   This has not been limited to the classroom and the studio, for as a skillful painter of altar-pieces he has

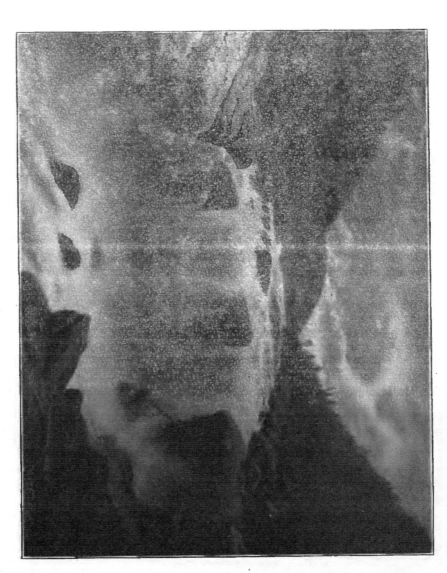

Ljunga River Rapids.　By Olof Grafström

been instrumental in disseminating art far and wide among the Swedish people in this country.

Grafström is a most versatile artist, capable of making a pastelle, water color, pencil or pen and ink sketch, as well as producing a fine

Mount Rainier, Washington. By Olof Grafström

portrait or landscape in oil. The last, however, is his forte. He delights particularly in reproducing the majesty of nature, as exemplified in mountains with caps of snow or bathing in opalescent sunlight, placid expanses of water, the gloom of the primeval forest, skies of delicate tints and atmosphere of remarkable translucence. Many of his canvases are very large, and justly so, in conformity to the magnitude of the artist's motifs.

Axel Elias Olsson

Axel Elias Olsson is one of the very few Swedish-American artists who have adopted the chisel in preference to the brush. A farmer boy, born in Blekinge, Sweden, in 1857, he went to Stockholm in 1870

Axel E. Olsson

and soon found employment in the studio of a sculptor. Not satisfied with what he was able to learn from his employer, he entered the sloyd school and from there went to the Academy of Arts. His education finished as to theoretical schooling, he went to work as a modeler and architectural sculptor, and in 1881 decided to go to France for further study. Changing his plan, he came to the United States and remained here. During the quarter century Olsson has spent in this country he has developed from artisan to artist.

We give here a partial list of his productions, all of which possess merit, some taking high rank as works of art:

Two reliefs, representing Spring and Autumn; the plastic groups that adorned the Hall of Animal Industry and Machinery Hall at the Columbian Exposition in Chicago; models for ornamental sculptures and wood carvings for the new building of the Chicago Athletic Club, including a large group in relief, representing a Football Scrimmage; two decorative groups for a circus building in Chicago; the model for

Art and Music. Relief by Axel E. Olsson

an art fountain in bronze for the Chicago Public Library; exterior and interior ornaments for the new Normal school in DeKalb, Ill., and a marble bust of one of the donors to the building fund for said school; over one hundred allegorical and portrait figures for the new court house at Fort Wayne, Ind., including 16 large gable friezes, each 40 feet in length; models for granite sculptures in the Edison Building in Chicago, also for the Carnegie Library at Muncie, Ind., besides a large number of low reliefs, sculptured figures for graveyard monuments, church ornaments, etc.

In 1903 Olsson completed a marble group in high relief, representing Psyche and the Zephyrs, also a statuette, entitled "The Whisper." Both were exhibited at the Chicago Art Institute, where they met with general appreciation. The Psyche group had a place in the Art Hall of the Louisiana Purchase Exposition at St. Louis in the same year, while "The Whisper" adorned the art room of the Swedish

Building. To the foregoing list should be added the sculpture decorations in the splendid Vanderbilt summer home at Newport, "The Breakers", and one of his latest groups, "Friends", a plaster bas relief, shown at the nineteenth exhibition of American paintings and sculptures, at the Chicago Art Institute in 1906.

An art critic has told the story of Mr. Olsson's Psyche and characterized the work of the sculptor in words worthy of quotation:

"His Psyche bas relief is proof of the capabilities of an artist in the plastic, if he possesses the 'divine spark'. This bit of sculptural decoration is so charmingly well balanced in composition and so truly tender in treatment, that one lingers in its presence, if but to admire the delicacy and refinement suggested. For all the nude figures by Mr. Olsson are characterized by this purity of expression. He believes in the beauty of form, but it is a divine beauty, chaste and pure. There is quite an interesting story of mishaps related by the sculptor in connection with the creation of this delightful mythical creature, that has for generations suggested to sculptor, painter and poet alike a theme whereby to express his art. When the idea of executing such a work first suggested itself to Mr. Olsson, he can scarcely recall, it was so long ago—a sort of cherished dream that the time might come when he could set aside so much of the commercial sculptural effects, by which he had been kept busy and by which he existed, and create something for the very love of it. In 1893 he made his first elaborate sketch of the work in wax, but alas, while it was resting on a chair, some one sat down on it and destroyed it. Then a year passed away, and he began the modeling in full size, taking it to a place for final treatment and casting. Mr. Olsson in the meanwhile had to go to a terra cotta factory to model a mantel. When he returned, he found, contrary to promises made, the clay model of his Psyche relief dry and almost ruined by falling apart. Almost discouraged, he again set to work and restored it and cast it in plaster, but the witticisms indulged in by the men about the misfortunes to which the work had been subjected made him abandon it in disgust, and Psyche was hung on the wall of the shop, there to await—not the coming of Cupid—but Fate. Two fires visited the building, and although the structure was almost destroyed, Psyche still clung to the wall, but with her beautiful arms and shapely feet amputated, and her attending Zephyrs wafted afar. During the spring of 1903 the sculptor was taken ill and, after recovering, had decided to go upon a vacation to last the whole summer through. He made a better recovery than expected and the thought occurred to him that he would spend his vacation time in the restoration and completion of his Psyche. In the sculptor's own words: 'Now or never—and I finished it. The poor girl masqueraded at the Art Insti-

Autumn.   Bas Relief by Axel E. Olsson

tute in a domino of bronze—a mud spot on the wall, practically unseen and unknown. But after due whitewashing she was sent to St. Louis and considered a good enough girl to be seen there'."

The writer affirmed that "Psyche and the Zephyrs" would be one of the sculptural attractions of the Exposition, continuing:

"How could it be otherwise? Note the wonderful beauty of form and the energy displayed by the Zephyrs, or Cupids, as others might term them, while the figure of Psyche herself and the suggestion of air amid the bit of drapery is superb. Mr. Olsson has the true art temperament, creating his own art atmosphere, rather than seeking for it elsewhere."

"The Whisper" is a delicately modeled creation, extremely refined, showing the little love god whispering his message in the ear of a young maiden whose figure, slightly draped and exquisitely posed, presents a fine conception of virgin beauty and modesty.

Carl Olof Erik Lindin

Carl Olof Erik Lindin is a landscape painter whose works have gained recognition not only in the United States, but in Sweden and France as well. A native of Fellingsbro, Sweden, he came to Chicago in the fall of 1888, at the age of nineteen. In the following spring he got a situation with a Swedish painter and decorator, but such work was far from a realization of his early ambition to become an artist. Shortly afterward he secured a place as coachman to a physician in Wisconsin. Both the doctor and his wife, learning of the young man's ambition, assisted him as best they could, the former by giving him instruction in the English language, the latter by defraying his expenses at the local art school. After a year he was advised to go back to Chicago to continue art studies. He entered the evening school at the Art Institute and besides took private lessons in painting. In the meantime he formed the acquaintance of a business man and art lover, who not only encouraged him, but aided him in a material way, making it possible for him to go to Paris in 1893 for further study. From there he visited his native land before returning to the United States. In Sweden he now formed the acquaintance of influential persons, who became interested in his future, ordered pictures and assured him of their support in the further prosecution of his studies. Postponing his return to America, Lindin now went back to Paris and spent the next four years studying with Jean Paul Laurens, Benjamin Constant and Aman-Jean in the winter and spring, passing the summer and fall in Sweden. By now, Lindin's name was known and his art recognized in artist circles there, and many of his landscape paintings were left behind, in the possession of art collectors, when he returned to the United States in 1897.

In Chicago, his home city, Lindin holds a prominent place in art circles and his pictures grace almost every exposition at the Art Institute. His works have been shown in Philadelphia, Detroit, at the St. Louis Exposition, in Munich, at the Stockholm Exposition of 1897, and his pictures were among those hung in the Paris Salon of 1900.

Carl Olof Erik Lindin

In his landscapes Lindin delights in soft, subdued color effects and, although an athlete in build, he paints with almost feminine delicacy.

Carl Johan Nilsson

Carl Johan Nilsson, who studied in the private studio of Oscar Berg, the Stockholm sculptor, and later at the Academy of Liberal Arts, under the direction of John Börjeson, came to the United States in November, 1899. His purpose was to exhibit in American cities a biblical gallery, comprising sixteen groups of statuary, illustrating

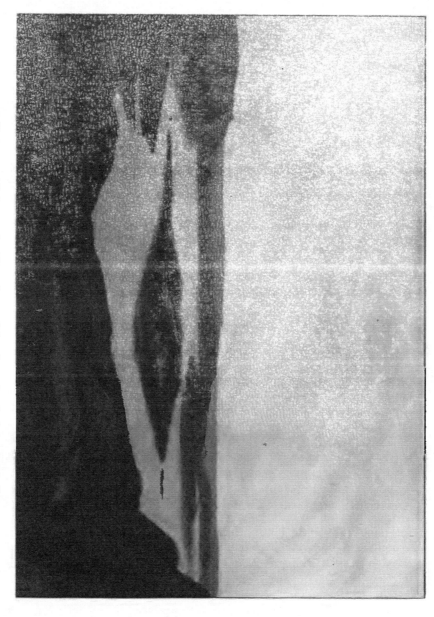

Midsummer Night on the West Coast of Sweden.   By Carl O. E. Lindin

incidents in the life of Christ, the gallery having been originally produced for the Stockholm Exposition of 1897.   The gallery was first
exhibited in Boston, then at the successive expositions in Buffalo and
St. Louis.   In January, 1905, Nilsson removed to Chicago, taking a
permanent position as modeler for a large terra cotta plant.   Since
then he has executed a large number of decorative groups and reliefs
for architectural purposes.   One of these is a statuary group representing ''Justice, Law and Bondage'', designed for a new county court-

Carl Johan Nilsson

house at Greensburg, Pa.   Another typical work of his is a life size
bust of King Oscar, first exhibited in Chicago in 1905, at the Swedish-
American art exhibition.   This included also a design for a proposed
John Ericsson monument, executed by Nilsson.

    While in Sweden, Nilsson produced a large number of portrait
busts and groups for the Swedish Panopticon of Stockholm, executed
plastic and sculptural work for the Northern Museum, the Royal Ar-
mory, the Royal Artillery Museum, the Gothenburg Museum and other
institutions.   For two years he was assistant to Prof. Börjeson, Sweden's foremost monumental sculptor, in modeling the statues of Carl

X. Gustaf and Magnus Stenbock, for the cities of Malmö and Helsing-borg, respectively. For the Russian ministry of war Nilsson designed a collection of plastic figures to be part of the Russian exhibit at Paris in 1900. The aforesaid biblical gallery, which was executed by Nilsson and his instructor, Prof. Berg, was taken abroad after the close of the Stockholm Exposition and exhibited for a season in Helsingfors. There,

Justice, Law and Bondage.   Decorative Group by Carl J. Nilsson

as in the Swedish capital, it attracted great interest, while in American cities it met with a rather indifferent reception.

Henning Rydén

Henning Rydén, born in Blekinge, Sweden, in 1869, the son of a schoolmaster, was thrown on his own resources early in life and learned the engraver's art. At this he worked in Stockholm and Co-

penhagen, devoting his leisure moments to art studies.   In 1891 he
crossed the ocean, and at the World's Fair in Chicago he had an exhibition of artistically engraved medals of the presidents of the United
States.   Finding little demand for this kind of work in this country,
Ryden gradually turned his attention to sculpture, and later turned
from sculpture to painting.   Following the pursuit of art studies in
Paris, Berlin and London, he located in Chicago and made a reputation

Henning Rydén

as one of the most skillful medal engravers in the West.   For a time
he devoted himself to relief portraiture in plaques and bronzes,
producing a number of excellent specimens of such work.
     In late years hardly an exhibition has taken place in Chicago at
which Ryden has not been represented with one or more paintings.
At the exhibition of American painters at the Art Institute in 1901
three of Ryden's pictures, "The Edge of the Woods", "Autumn
Tones", and "The Close of Day", were the objects of much favorable
comment.   The summer seasons the artist spends in Wisconsin, making
sketches for canvases, which are later finished in time for the winter's
exhibitions.

Arvid F. Nyholm

Arvid Nyholm is a pupil of Anders Zorn, whose school in Stockholm he entered after studying for more than two years at the Royal Academy of Fine Arts. In the fall of 1891 Nyholm came to the United States and located in New York City. For twelve years he maintained a studio there, devoting himself both to portrait and landscape painting. His canvases were frequently seen at the exhibitions of the New

Arvid F. Nyholm

York Water Color Society and the National Academy of Design.

In October, 1903, Mr. Nyholm removed to Chicago, where he has since resided. Here he has taken part in all the different exhibitions of water colors and oil paintings at the Art Institute. He is a popular member of the Palette and Chisel Club of Chicago.

In his personality Mr. Nyholm is a combination of northern rigor and strength and the sanguine fire of the south. The same traits are reflected in his art. Before leaving Sweden, Nyholm was a skillful

water color artist, and to-day he is a recognized master in this line of
work. His portraits and landscapes in oil display the genuine art instinct, coupled with technic of a high order.

Arvid F. Nyholm is a native of the Swedish capital, where he was
born in 1866, the son of the manager of the Central printing establish-

Old Appletrees.   Water Color by Arvid F. Nyholm

ment. Having finished college, he entered the Royal Technical High
School in 1886, his father intending to make an architect of him.
Draftsmanship did not appeal to the young man's taste, however, and
in a year he left to enter the employ of Brolin, a scene painter. In the
meantime Nyholm took private lessons in drawing from Gösta Grehl,
preparatory to entering the Academy of Fine Arts.

Hugo von Hofsten

In 1885, at the age of twenty, Hugo von Hofsten came to the United States, equipped with an art education acquired in the studios and art schools of Stockholm. In 1890 we find him on the staff of illustrators of the New York Graphic. After three years he came to Chicago and was successively employed on the Evening Post, the

Hugo von Hofsten and Child

Journal and the Tribune, until 1895, when he took a position as head of the illustrating department of the Times-Herald. When, after six years, there was a change in the ownership and name of the paper, Hofsten was supplanted by another man, but continued as a member of the illustrators' staff, remaining until 1906.

Mr. Hofsten excels in the line of portraiture, of which he has made a specialty. Aside from the routine work in the illustrating department of a great newspaper, he has devoted himself to legitimate art. The result has appeared in the form of wash drawings and oil paintings, shown at various local art exhibitions. Hofsten has tried his hand successfully at illustrating juvenile books. His pictures for the "Mother Goose Jungle Book", published some years back, betrayed a sense of humor as keen in the artist as in the author.

Hugo von Hofsten comes from a family ennobled in 1726. He was born in Vermland, in 1865, his father being a large manufacturer in Karlskoga. Many of the family have attained positions of high honor in the state, others have made a name for themselves in commerce and the industries. Still others have devoted themselves to literary pursuits. Among the latter is J. C. von Hofsten, an authoress who has enriched the literature of Sweden with many delightful sketches and stories of life in the province of Vermland.

Charles Edward Hallberg

Charles E. Hallberg has acquired considerable fame as a marine painter under the name of "the janitor-artist". In 1900 he had his first picture accepted by the Chicago Art Institute, and since that time his marines have graced every art exhibition in Chicago.

The encouragement given him by two great artists, Alexander H. Harrison and Anders Zorn, furnished Hallberg the impetus to take up painting as a profession—alongside of his work as janitor in a bank and apartment building in the suburb of Austin.

Dabbling with colors since a boy, Hallberg sought to fasten his memories of the sea on canvas. Seventeen years of service before the mast had taught him all the moods and foibles of the ocean. Ambitious to earn a little extra money, he began to copy a little marine sketch by the late Edward Moran, of Philadelphia. But when it was finished, the self-taught artist was sadly disappointed with his work and, throwing down the canvas, vowed never to touch paints again.

Yet the next day a newspaper item changed his purpose. It stated that Anders Zorn was visiting the family of Charles Deering in Evanston. Hallberg at once determined to submit his case to the great Swedish master. Putting the Moran copy under his arm, with another little attempt at painting, he set out for the Deering mansion. There the liveried servants informed him that Zorn was away for the day. While the two were talking, a guest rode up on a bicycle. "There's Alexander Harrison. He's a painter. Why don't you ask him, as Mr. Zorn is not here?" urged the servant. Hallberg looked first at his sketches, then at his mean apparel, and shook his head in hesitation. Finally he consented to send word in to Mr. Harrison, and in a few minutes the artist came down. Asked to look at the sketches, he said he had not time. Hallberg insisted, only to get no for an answer. When the little janitor turned away in disappointment, the artist finally relented, calling him back with the words, "Come on, then, I'll look at your sketches." He looked, not a second, but for several minutes, and said, "There's good in this stuff. Go on, paint."

Encouraged by the commendation of Alexander Harrison, Mr. Hallberg still craved the approval of his fellow countryman, the famous Zorn. Again he sought the Deering home. This time he found a house party in possession. Leaving his sketches at the carriage house, Hallberg timidly went up to the house and sent in for Mr. Zorn. The renowned artist came out to meet the unknown, and the two greeted each other in the mother tongue.

Charles Edward Hallberg

"Would the great Zorn see the sketches of the humble janitor?" The great Zorn would. But the sketches were at the carriage house. No matter—the two went there together, and Hallberg displayed his treasured pictures. Zorn looked at them a long time, then said, "There is good stuff in you. Keep on—paint." It was the advice of Mr. Harrison over again.

Hallberg told of his rare fortune. It reached the ears of a Chicago editor with artistic tendencies and human sympathy, and he brought Hallberg to the notice of the public. Some of his pictures were sold for small sums, and finally the attention of the Art Institute officials was directed to the artistic janitor.

Mr. French, the director, was induced to ask Hallberg to bring in some of his work. He at once recognized the merit and strength of the untutored artist. This was in February, 1901. It was then too late to include Hallberg's picture in the annual exhibition of the Chicago artists, yet so impressed was Mr. French with his canvas, ''The Open Sea'', that a special arrangement was made, whereby this picture was hung in the room of old masters. There it attracted great attention and was finally sold for $150.

Storm on the Sea of Galilee. By Charles E. Hallberg

With this impetus, Hallberg worked at his easel every spare moment, and the next spring sent nine pictures to the institute for competition. Three of these were admitted to the exhibition. They are entitled, ''Dawn at Sea Off the Coast of France'', painted from memory, with the aid of a sketch made on shipboard while Mr. Hallberg was a sailor; "A Summer Day on Lake Michigan", showing the placid beauty and vivid coloring of the great fresh water sea, basking in the summer sun; and "Sunrise on Lake Michigan", a canvas of delicate coloring and deft handling.

"Summer Day on Lake Michigan" was exhibited at the St. Louis

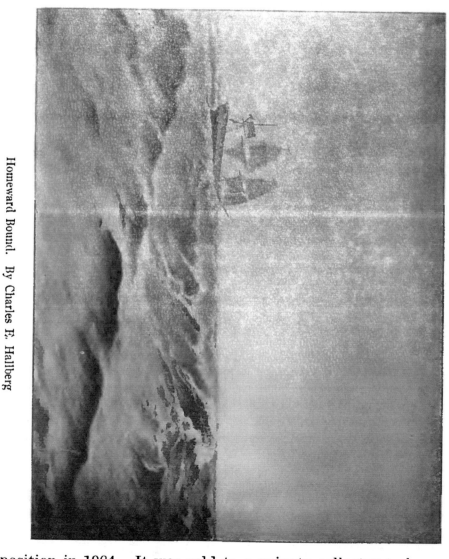

Homeward Bound. By Charles E. Hallberg

Exposition in 1904. It was sold to a private collector to be presented to the Art Gallery of Oakland, Cal. In the spring of 1906 Mr. Hallberg had a separate exhibition of forty-one pictures in one of the rooms at the Art Institute. They were all marines—Hallberg can paint water and, except for an occasional fishing smack or schooner, he paints nothing else. Here was a splendid opportunity to judge of the artist's work. The variety of canvases was unusual, showing coloring and light effects under the varying aspects of the day, the clime and the seasons. Having painted entirely according to his own art instinct for several years, Hallberg, after having had his work accepted by the Art Institute, set to work to gain an understanding of the craft of other painters—Woodbury, Homer Richards, Harrison and Whistler—as shown in their canvases. This study has helped him to a better definition of his talent, and so positive has been his own personality, that in no instance may a picture be said to reflect the style of another man. Thus, in a little over five years this artist has made such progress as to acquire a national reputation. Among his later pictures, which tend to illustrate the advance made by him, may be mentioned, "Summer Morning", a study in opalescent water and morning mists, "Morning After the Storm", with ragged clouds and angry breakers giving way to approaching calm; "Ocean Wave", imparting a sense of the vasty deep; "The Coming Storm", "In the Teeth of the Gale", "Off the Isle of Wight", "Returning Fishermen", now owned by the Clio Association of Chicago; "Evening at Sea", "Moonlight Spin", "Storm on the Sea of Galilee", "Summer Evening on the Atlantic", and "A Northeaster on Lake Michigan."

In 1908 Mr. Hallberg's paintings were exhibited for two weeks in the art rooms of Marshall Field & Co. in Chicago. Among purchasers was Mr. A. E. Johnson, of New York, who added three of Hallberg's marines to his extensive private collection. Another was purchased for the Field art department.

At the outset, Hallberg, in a stuffy little basement den, far from the pounding breakers and the rolling surf, painted the ocean of his youth, as memory brought again the salt breeze to his nostrils and the dashing spray and tumbling brine to his sight. Of late, however, he has worked mostly in the open air, with his easel planted on some commanding point along the shores of Lake Michigan.

Frank A. Lundahl

In point of priority among Swedish-American artists of Illinois, Frank A. Lundahl, of Moline, Ill., has a place next to the early artists, the two Blombergsons and Almini. He is best known as a painter of altar-pieces being one of the earliest in that class of artists in the West. In treatment and coloring these works betray a generous measure of talent, but his figures frequently are disproportionate, showing a lack of that training which might have placed him in the first rank of Illinois artists of the Swedish nationality.

John Paul Jones. Statuette by Jean LeVeau

The Viking. Terra Cotta Statuette by Jean LeVeau

Lundahl's work in crayon and oil has been seen at numerous occasions both in Moline and Chicago. By trade a decorator, Mr. Lundahl displays great skill in that line, combining craftsmanship with genius.

Alfred Jansson

Alfred Jansson came to the United States and to Chicago in the year 1889, equipped with an art education acquired in the schools of Stockholm, Christiania and Paris. Before long, he became recognized in local art circles for his fine landscape work, his subject being usually

Frank A. Lundahl

Alfred Jansson

chosen from around Chicago. Jansson's canvases have hung in many annual art exhibitions not only in Chicago but in Philadelphia, St. Louis, Denver and elsewhere. One of the striking pictures in the local exhibition in Chicago in 1902 was Jansson's "Winter Approaching," which was purchased by the Clio Association. Mr. Jansson is a member of several organizations of artists, including the Palette and Chisel Club.

Gustaf Adolf Strom

A struggling young artist of Chicago who paints wagons for bread and pictures to satisfy his ideal cravings is Gustaf Adolf Strom. In 1897 he had the good fortune to see his first paintings hung in the exhibition of American artists at the Art Institute. The subjects were, "The Fisherman's Hut" and "The Suburb." Since then he has been successful in having his work accepted for almost every local exhibition.

The following named canvases, most of which have been exhibited, are some of his best: "Early Moonrise," "The Old Mansion Gate," "Twilight Tones," "Autumn, the Sad and the Gay," "The Homestead," "The Dreamer's Retreat" and "The Golden Hillside." This laborer-artist has qualities which have gained for him favorable comment in various newspapers and art journals. Strom is a native of

Gustaf Adolf Strom

Sweden, born at Skillingaryd, Småland, March 2, 1872. Not until he came to Chicago in 1892 did he begin to devote himself to art, and then only in spare moments. As the breadwinner for a family of ten, he is compelled to turn his talent to practical use, while following art merely for the love he bears it.

Other artists and designers whose skill may well be recognized but of whom there is little to be said here, are Gus Higgins; Bror Julius Olson Nordfelt, now on the staff of illustrators of "Harper's Magazine;" August Swenson, who was in Chicago in the nineties and died

The Art Studio at Augustana College

here about 1897; Jean LeVeau, a sculptor, who spent a year or two in Chicago; Johannes Anderson, Richard Swanson and Elmer C. Blomgren, all architectural designers, and one DeMaré, of whose art no data are available. One or two churches have altar-pieces painted by Higgins, but his brush was employed much more frequently in rendering attractive the interiors of Chicago's dram shops and cheap music halls. In the years just prior to the universal reign of the halftone, Higgins held lucrative positions on Chicago dailies as an illustrator. He had

The Homestead. By Gustaf A. Strom

marked talent as a sketcher of portraits and has drawn many cartoons and comic pictures of a peculiarly bizarre type. The picture here shown, entitled "War News," is probably a specimen of his most creditable work, outside of portraiture.

Were one to make note of all commercial artists and of those persons who as amateur painters have attained a fair degree of skill in handling the artist's brush and palette, the list of Swedish artists in Chicago and Illinois would be materially extended. From the mural decorator and architectural sculptor it is not a far cry to the architect, and in the field of architecture the Swedish-Americans boast quite an array of masters of the craft.

War News. Wash Drawing by Gus Higgins

The Swedish-American Art Association

Of a score or more of the most notable Swedish artists in the United States, the majority have been located in Chicago for a greater or lesser period of time. A desire on their part to conserve their com-

Winter Landscape. By Alfred Jansson

mon interests prompted the organization of the Swedish-American Art Association of Chicago. At the initiative of Carl Johan Nilsson, a sculptor, the association was formed February 17, 1905, and Nilsson was chosen its first president. In the fall of the same year the association felt strong and confident enough to arrange an art exhibition of its own. So great was the interest in their enterprise, that the exhibition was kept open one week over the allotted time, or from October 23rd to November 11th. It was a small but choice collection that was placed on view, comprising eighty numbers in all, seventy-two of which were by Swedish-American and eight by Swedish artists.

The success attending the exhibition, led Mr. Nilsson and his colleagues to plan their next exhibition on a larger scale. An invitation was accordingly extended to the Swedish Society of Artists at Stockholm to participate in such an exhibition, at the Chicago Art Institute, in the fall of 1906, but circumstances placed obstacles in the way.

The Linné Monument

In the middle eighties, after the Lincoln statue had been erected in Lincoln Park, and the Chicago Germans had given like tribute to

Group of Children. Portrait Plaque by Henning Rydén

the memory of Schiller, while the Danes were planning a statue of Hans Christian Andersen, the idea of rearing a monument to Carl von Linné was brought up for serious consideration by the Swedish-Americans of Chicago. Discussion matured into action, and on the 7th of June, 1887, a meeting was held, when the first step toward the organization of the Linné Monument Association was taken. On this occa-

sion C. J. Sundell presided and C. F. Peterson acted as secretary. At
a subsequent meeting to complete the organization, 45 directors were
elected and a constitution and by-laws adopted. According to a rule
subsequently adopted, any member became a director upon donating
a minimum sum of twenty-five dollars to the cause. At the first meeting of the directors, held July 26th, these officers were elected: Joh.

Linné. Plaster from Marble by Christian Eriksson in National Museum of
Stockholm. Presented to the Art Institute of Chicago by P. S. Peterson

A. Enander, president; C. J. Sundell, Robert Lindblom, P. S. Peterson,
O. G. Lange, P. M. Almini, Andrew Chaiser and P. W. Nilsson, vice
presidents; Lawrence Hesselroth, recording secretary; Victor Tengwald, corresponding secretary; H. P. Brusewitz, C. Eklund, assistant
secretaries; C. Widestrand, financial secretary; John R. Lindgren,
treasurer. Dr. Josua Lindahl was elected the first honorary member
of the association.

King Oscar II.   Bust in Plaster by Carl J. Nilsson

A call for public contributions was issued in August, and 10,000 membership diplomas were printed, to be awarded to all persons subscribing at least one dollar to the monument fund. The same year four of Chicago's Swedish writers, viz., Joh. A. Enander, C. F. Peterson, Jakob Bonggren and Ernst Lindblom, published a volume of their verse, entitled ''Linnea'', which was sold for the benefit of the fund.

The enterprise was of national scope, and no less than five hundred solicitors were appointed throughout the United States. The Swedish-Americans in the East wanted the monument erected in New York, those in the Northwest, in Minneapolis, and other locations were suggested, and when the Swedes of Chicago, who originated the plan, and took the first active measures towards its realization, refused to yield, it was left largely to themselves to carry the undertaking through to success.

The work of raising the money was vigorously pushed in 1888. Three public entertainments, given in Chicago, each netted over one thousand dollars, and others yielded sums running into the hundreds.

The proposed monument was to be a replica of the statue of Linné, modeled by C. J. Dyfverman and erected in Humlegården, in Stockholm. In November, 1888, the association let the contract to Otto Meyer & Co., of Stockholm, for the casting of the main figure of the monument. From the sculptor a new model, with such improvements as art critics had suggested, was ordered for the sum of 5,000 crowns. The bronze figure was to cost 23,000 crowns. The plan was to substitute jardinieres for the four allegorical female figures of the Stockholm monument, but this was abandoned, and the directors decided to make the replica complete. Thereby they incurred an additional outlay of 4,000 crowns for models of the allegorical figures and relief panels, and 30,000 crowns for the casts, making a total of 62,000 crowns for the statue and accessories, not including the cost of the ornate granite pedestal.

In March, 1889, Dr. Enander resigned the presidency and was succeeded by Robert Lindblom, who retired one year later to go abroad. Much work still remained to be done, before the monument could be completed, and this was done under the direction of Andrew Chaiser as acting president.

Finally, sufficient funds were at hand to have the main statue erected, leaving the auxiliary figures and decorative details to be added at a later date. The heroic bronze figure arrived, was mounted on its gray granite pedestal, and on May 23, 1891, the 184th anniversary of the birth of the Swedish ''Flower King'', the monument was unveiled with appropriate ceremonies in the presence of a great concourse of Swedish-Americans.

The association continued to raise funds up to July, 1893, when the subscriptions had reached a total of $18,970, or a little more than 70,000 crowns. It appears that by eliminating the bronze reliefs and reducing the estimates, the total cost of the monument was brought within that limit.

The monument to Carl von Linné, located near the conservatories and flower gardens in Lincoln Park, is, next to the Grant monument, the most imposing one in Chicago. A photographic reproduction of this fine example of Swedish plastic art fittingly serves as the frontispiece of this volume.

CHAPTER XV

Organizations

The Svea Society

T HE pioneer of Swedish-American social, fraternal and beneficiary organizations is the Svea Society, of Chicago, which in January, 1907, celebrated its fiftieth anniversary. In response to a growing demand among the non-churchly element for a society of Swedish Chicagoans, organized on a fraternal basis alone, C. J. Sundell, the Swedish vice consul, issued a general call for a preliminary meeting to be held Jan. 22, 1857, in Hoffman Hall on North Clark street, to discuss the project. The temporary officers of the meeting were, C. J. Stolbrand, chairman, C. J. Sundell, secretary, and C. F. Billings, treasurer. Mr. Sundell called attention to the need of an organization such as had been privately talked of, the purpose of which, he said, should be to strive for the education and ennoblement of its members by means of good entertainments and the collection and maintenance of a library, and to render every assistance to the Swedish people in the city. Their plan met with general favor and a society was immediately organized, to be known as Svea. The temporary officers were made permanent. A constitution and by-laws adopted at a subsequent meeting embodied the plans and purposes of the society mainly as outlined at the organization meeting.

In December of the same year the society arranged its first public entertainment, a fair, when the sum of $130 was realized for the purchase of books. Shortly before, Rev. Unonius of the St. Ansgarius Church had donated a small collection of books, to which later was added a collection originally meant for the church. Thus, a library of four hundred volumes was secured. The leading Swedish daily newspaper, "Aftonbladet" of Stockholm, was kept at a cost of no less than $56.00 per year, until the price to the society was reduced by one-half through the kind offices of Mr. Hellberg, Swedish director of posts at Hamburg. Other papers from Sweden were secured at less cost.

The meetings during the first year were held in P. M. Almini's building on Kinzie street, then for several years in the Newberry build-

Charles J. Sundell

ing, at Wells and Kinzie streets, subsequently in the German Hall on Wells street and in 1868 the society removed to 45 N. Clark street, where it was located at the time of the great fire.

During the first seven years Stolbrand and Sundell alternated as presiding officers, while F. E. af Jocknick served as librarian. A beneficiary provision was early added to the by-laws, granting members a sick benefit of $5 per week during illness. In 1859 Svea procured its first banner, costing $130.

At the outbreak of the Civil War a number of the members of the Svea Society enlisted, joining the Swedish corps under Captain Silfversparre, known as the Silfversparre Battery. While encamped at Savannah after the victorious battle of Atlanta, the battery was given a furlough and the Swedish boys went home for a brief visit. They were given an enthusiastic reception in Chicago, and a festival arranged in their honor by Swedish ladies was held at German Hall. On this occasion a flag of blue satin, on which was embroidered the American eagle and the names, Shiloh, Vicksburg and Atlanta, was presented to the battery, the presentation speech being made by Miss Lena Larson. This highly cherished trophy was burned in 1871.

In 1866 O. G. Lange during a visit to Sweden procured an addition to the library, comprising 500 volumes and sundry art portfolios, a large part of these being donations from the royal family. The society now owned a library of one thousand volumes. In consideration of his valuable services, Captain Lange was elected an honorary member and presented with a jewel-studded gold medal. The greatest loss sustained by the Svea Society in the Chicago fire was the total destruction of this valuable library.

During the famine year of 1867 in Northern Sweden the society sent 7,000 crowns to the sufferers, that being the net proceeds of a fair arranged by Svea in the face of considerable opposition from the Swedish churches who, while favoring the cause, disapproved of the method.

The same year Svea, with commendable enterprise, undertook the founding of an emigrant hotel or home for the care and protection of Swedish newcomers. After the close of the war Swedish immigration to this country greatly increased, reaching the floodtide mark in the years 1866 to 1870. There was a large and steady influx to Chicago, which served as a distributing point for the entire west and northwest. These people were an easy prey to a class of swindlers termed emigrant runners, self-appointed "agents," who met the unsuspecting newcomers at the trains and, representing themselves as guides, advisers and friends, sought to fleece them at every turn. Some were the paid emissaries of steamship companies, others were in league with hotel and boarding house keepers, while still others operated on their own account. Hundreds upon hundreds of innocents were thus swindled in the most brazen fashion, these sharks and vultures attacking their victims openly and fearlessly, under the guise of officialdom or philanthropy.

After flourishing for several years the system grew intolerable and public opinion was aroused. The rascals were denounced at mass meetings and in the press, Isidor Kjellberg leading the attack through his paper, "Justitia," while "Hemlandet" and "Nya Verlden" maintained a steady fire. This public anti-runner campaign, however, was not started until about 1871. It devolved upon the various church organizations and the Svea Society to aid and protect the Swedish immigrants long before that.

The pastors had taken the initiative in this work, Erland Carlsson, Unonius and others having labored arduously for the welfare of the newcomers ever since the early fifties. The Swedish churches, aided by other Scandinavians and several Americans, in 1867 built an emigrant home where newcomers in distress were lodged and fed free of charge. They also maintained an agent, invested with police authority, to keep an eye on the runners and warn immigrants against them.

Not long after, the Svea Society took similar measures. The prime mover was Charles Eklund, and his proposition that the Svea Society erect and maintain an emigrant home was warmly seconded. A cooper shop at Franklin and Ohio streets was leased and remodeled into a lodging for Swedish newcomers and S. Trägårdh was engaged as the society's representative. These arrangements were merely provisional. To procure funds for a suitable building of its own the society started a general subscription which netted $2,500. A lot was purchased at 120 Illinois street, for a sum of $4,000 and a building was put up at an equal cost. In 1869 thousands of immigrants found shelter there. A ladies' auxiliary was organized to assist in raising the funds needed to house and feed such numbers. During the same year seven immigrants were provided burial and 87 were sent to the county poorhouse.

At length dissensions over this laudable but expensive enterprise arose among the members themselves and the upshot of the feud was that the home was sold for the benefit of the creditors on Sept. 6, 1871, for the sum of $6,000, only to be reduced to ashes one month later. About this time the society numbered 300 members.

The gala event in the history of Svea was the reception tendered Christina Nilsson, the renowned Swedish singer, on her first visit to Chicago in December, 1870. In the evening of the 22nd a great national celebration took place in the German Theater at Wells and Indiana streets, under the auspices of Svea, with whose committee of arrangements other representative persons co-operated. The hall was crowded to the doors by men and women who had cheerfully paid five dollars for admission. The great singer was feted in splendid style, crowned with a golden wreath, given homage in speech, verse and song and finally toasted at a banquet board spread in her honor. The banquet was followed by a grand ball. Some time after, the arrangers were chagrined to learn that the wreath, for which a prominent jewelry house was paid $1,000, was not genuine. Nevertheless, the Svea Society

had cause for satisfaction and pride in the fact that the affair proved
a most brilliant success.   This was the first great celebration by the
Swedish population in Chicago.

The following summer Christina Nilsson gave a benefit concert
in Chicago, the proceeds of which were to be divided among the various
Swedish churches and the Svea Society.   The latter, being allotted only

Christina Nilsson

a twelfth part of the net receipts, the directors in protest against what
they deemed niggardly and ungrateful treatment refused to accept
their share.

In 1872 Svea rallied from the stroke dealt it by the great fire.
Its meetings were held in various halls for the next five years, and
thereafter it secured permanent quarters at Chicago avenue and Larrabee street.   By 1880 it had collected a new library, numbering over
500 volumes, in charge of Anders Larson, who had served as librarian

since 1867. The presidents during the first quarter century of Svea's existence, were: Stolbrand, Sundell, J. P. Hussander, J. A. Nilson, Oscar Malmborg, C. Blanxius, Th. Engström, C. Stromberg, C. F. Billings, Gerhard Larson, O. G. Lange, N. Torgerson, Konrad Göthe, Berglund, P. M. Almini, J. M. Schönbeck, Gylfe Wolyn, C. G. Linderborg, A. Aspman, Sven Olin, A. J. Westman and Knut Nilson.

The Svea Society in 1881 provided for death benefits for its mem-

Anders Larson

bers. The twenty-fifth anniversary of its organization was celebrated with an imposing festival Jan. 22, 1882. Other notable data of its history are, the sending of a congratulatory cablegram to A. E. Nordenskiöld, the Swedish explorer and discoverer of the northeast passage, upon his reaching Yokohama in 1880, and the election of Paul B. Du Chaillu an honorary member upon the publication in 1882 of his work entitled, "The Land of the Midnight Sun." Nordenskiöld sent a letter to the Svea Society, which is preserved as a memento. Since 1901 the society has met at Schott's Hall on Belmont avenue, where its library of some 2,000 volumes is installed. In recent years the membership has dwindled down to about fifty.

Among Svea's earliest members was Anders Larson, one of the pioneer Swedish Chicagoans. He came to the United States in 1846 and then located in Chicago instead of going to Bishop Hill with Erik Jansson's party with which he crossed the ocean. He was a soda water manufacturer in the city for ten years, subsequently locating at Jefferson as a farmer. Larson served as librarian of the Svea Society from 1867 until about 1882. He was born June 11, 1801, at Torstuna, Westmanland, Sweden, and died in Chicago Sept. 1, 1884. His union with Sarah Brita Mårtensdotter, dating from 1829, was blessed with eight children, one of whom is Mrs. Emma L. Peterson, a singer who won repute in the '70s and '80s. When Jenny Lind visited America, Mrs. Larson and Mrs. Unonius elicited her promise to give a benefit concert for the St. Ansgarius Church. Illness prevented the singer from keeping her word, but the action of the two ladies paved the way for Jenny Lind's subsequent generous gifts to this church. Mrs. Larson passed away June 18, 1898.

The latter half of Svea's existence has been less eventful than the first. In the seventies and especially in the eighties quite a number of Swedish organizations of similar character sprung up, dividing the field and thereby decreasing Svea's former sphere of influence.

Knox Svea Bildningsförening

Knox Svea Bildningsförening was the name of a literary society that was formed in April, 1858, and existed about one year. Its president and secretary were, Sven Peterson and Dan J. Ockerson. The undertaking was revived in December, 1865, by the organization of Svea Bildnings- och Läseförening, whose aim was identical, namely, to afford opportunity for self-development through reading and intellectual exercises. Its work was largely along popular science lines, and, although opposed by the most intolerant church members on this account, the society persevered until 1872, when it succumbed. It appears that Pehr Mattson was president and Torkel Nilson secretary during the greater part of its existence.

The Freja Society

The Freja Society was organized in Moline in September, 1869, as a social and beneficiary organization. It flourished for eight years and reached a membership of about one hundred. In 1874, with $2,000 in the treasury, it erected its own building, at a cost of $8,000. The debt thus incurred proved too great a burden, and in 1877 the hall was sold and the society dissolved. Those of the most active members who served as president were: John A. Samuels, Gustaf Swenson, C. A. Westerdahl, Andrew Swanson, F. O. Eklund, and Eric Asp. Under the auspices of Freja was organized the Moline Swedish Band, which in its day was a popular musical organization in this part of the state.

The First Swedish Lodge of Odd Fellows, No. 479

The First Swedish Lodge of Odd Fellows, No. 479, was organized in Chicago, Feb. 22, 1872. At the time only three of its ten original members were of Swedish birth, but when the lodge had got well under way the others withdrew. The lodge grew rapidly to an average membership of 150, including many well-known Swedish-American citizens of Chicago. In the list of its early leaders we find the names of P. A. Felt, Henry Allen, J. T. Appleberg, D. W. Modeen, A. L. Gyllenhaal, John Mountain, P. M. Nelson, P. G. Bowman, Aug. Nieman, E. O. Forsberg, W. T. Eklund and Charles J. Strombeck.

The Scandinavian Benevolent Society

A beneficiary fraternal organization known as the Scandinavian Benevolent Society, antedating the Freja Society, was formed in Moline in 1866 and outlived the latter. It did not enjoy so vigorous a growth, having attained a membership of but 70 during the first twelve years of its existence. Its finances were more conservatively managed, however, the funds being devoted exclusively to the original purpose of sick benefits and funeral aid.

The Independent Order of Svithiod

Organizations similar to the Svea Society were formed from time to time among the Swedish population of Chicago and other communities in Illinois, but not until the '80s did the idea of forming a federated body of Swedish societies or lodges patterned after the American beneficiary orders, reach the point of realization.

The first step in this move was taken by one Simon Hallberg, who took the initiative in the organization of the Independent Order of Svithiod. On Dec. 3, 1880, he called together a few friends, eight in number, who took favorably to the plan he laid before them. They then and there constituted themselves into a society, or the nucleus of a society, which adopted the name of Svithiod. The name had been borne by a prior Scandinavian society, then on the point of dissolution. The new society increased and prospered and soon felt the need of a charter. Articles of incorporation were submitted, and on Sept. 2, 1881, the secretary of state issued incorporation papers for The Independent Order of Svithiod. The charter, granted under the Revised Statutes of 1874, is a liberal one and all the more valuable as later legislation has narrowed the rights and privileges of similar orders.

The constitution adopted laid down these fundamental provisions: The purpose of the order shall be to unite in brotherly love and co-operation Swedish men of sound health and good character, to exercise among its members an influence for moral betterment and to render material benefits, to give assistance to members in need and affliction and to pay, upon the death of members, certain beneficiary sums to their nearest kin.

The aforementioned Simon Hallberg was the first president, or Grand Master, of the order, serving up to Jan. 1, 1882, when he retired from office, but not from active work in behalf of the order. His career, however, was unexpectedly cut short by his death on the following 7th of July, at the age of thirty-two years.

In spite of the loss of its organizer and energetic promoter, the order continued its wholesome growth by the aid of other leaders. Among the men who have since carried forward the work no one has earned more credit than Axel Blomfeldt, who succeeded to the post of Grand Master. By New Year's, 1885, the Order of Svithiod numbered 200 members and its funds amounted to $4,000. That year John P. Johnson was elected Grand Master, succeeded later by Bernard Peterson, both of whom are still active members of the brotherhood.

During succeeding years the members by removals became scattered far and wide throughout the city, making it less convenient for them to meet in a common hall. Up to 1889 they had met in the North Side Turner Hall, but at this time members living in Lake View and on the west side, petitioned for authority to organize branch lodges in their respective neighborhoods. Extension work was then taken up with the result that Manhem Lodge No. 2, I. O. S., was organized Oct. 11th, and Verdandi Lodge No. 3, Oct. 25, 1890. Within the next three years as many other new lodges were added, the first lodge during that time acting as grand lodge, under which were subordinated the other five. These additions were, Mimer No. 4, Oct. 3, 1891, Frithiof No. 5, Dec. 25, 1891, and Gylfe No. 6, March 25, 1893.

At this stage of development the members began to realize the need of a representative central organization or grand lodge, to transact the common affairs of the order. This agreed, a committee was set to work revising the constitution with the desired end in view. After three months the work was completed, and on June 25, 1893, the Grand Lodge of the I. O. S. was organized with appropriate ceremonies. Its first set of officers were the following: High Grand Master, Axel Blomfeldt, Verdandi Lodge, High Grand Secretary, Bernard Peterson, Svithiod Lodge, High Grand Treasurer, John Peterson, Verdandi Lodge. The following named gentlemen constituted the first executive board:

Gust. Oman, H. E. Hanson, S. Franson, Frank Lindquist and John P. Johnson. The Grand Lodge met in annual convention in February, 1894, for the first time.

The organization of the grand lodge marks the beginning of a period of greater progress for the order. Up to this time the membership had reached only 750, although the organization dated its existence back a dozen years. Its growth during the subsequent period of almost fifteen years is far beyond comparison, as shown by the records up to November, 1908, when the total membership exceeded six thousand and the number of lodges had reached thirty-nine.

On July 22, 1894, the order was extended beyond the limits of Chicago and the boundaries of the state of Illinois, by the organization of the Björn Lodge No. 7, in East Chicago, Ind. While the membership grew constantly, no new lodge was formed for nearly three years from that time, the Ring Lodge No. 8 being organized May 29, 1897. This was followed by the Hilding Lodge No. 9, of Roseland, March 20, 1898. From now on new lodges were started in more rapid succession, namely, four in 1899, two during each of the following two years, three in 1902, five in 1903, two in 1904, one in 1905, six in the banner year of 1906, three in 1907, and two in the present year. The order has not adhered to the original practice of designating its lodges by names from the Norse mythology, but genuinely Swedish names are commonly adopted, a few local names forming exceptions to this rule.

The subsequent lodges, with location and date of organization of each, are as follows:

Odin Lodge No. 10, Joliet, Ill., Sept. 16, 1899; Thor Lodge No. 11, Chicago Heights, Ill., Oct. 22, 1899; Balder Lodge No. 12, Cragin, Ill., Nov. 11, 1899; Stockholm Lodge No. 13, Chicago, Dec. 30, 1899; Svea Lodge No. 14, West Pullman, Ill., May 19, 1900; Linden Park Lodge No. 15, Moreland, Ill., Oct. 6, 1900; Frej Lodge No. 16, Moline, Ill., March 16, 1901; Vasa Lodge No. 17, Galesburg, Ill., May 25, 1901; Nore Lodge No. 18, Chicago, March 9, 1902; Andree Lodge No. 19, South Chicago, Ill., Aug. 17, 1902; Irving Park Lodge No. 20, Irving Park, Oct. 19, 1902; Linné Lodge No. 21, Hegewisch, Ill., Jan. 27, 1903; Tegnér Lodge No. 22, Harvey, Ill., Feb. 7, 1903; John Ericsson Lodge No. 23, Rockford, Ill., June 28, 1903; Götha Lodge No. 24, Kansas City, Mo., Sept. 12, 1903; Norden Lodge No. 25, Kewanee, Ill., Oct. 3, 1903; Gustaf Adolf Lodge No. 26, Rock Island, Ill., April 16, 1904; Skandia Lodge No. 27, Evanston, Ill., Oct. 28, 1904; Monitor Lodge No. 28, Elburn, Ill., April 1, 1905; Brage Lodge No. 29, Peoria, Ill., Jan. 14, 1906; Thule Lodge No. 30, Chicago, May 12, 1906; Valhalla Lodge No. 31, Galva, Ill., May 30, 1906; Sten Sture Lodge No. 32, Maywood, Ill., June 9, 1906; Ymer Lodge No. 33, Minneapolis, Minn., Sept. 17, 1906; Engelbrekt Lodge No. 34, La Grange, Ill., Dec. 31, 1906; St. Paul Lodge

Delegates to the Grand Lodge, I. O. S., 1905

No. 35, St. Paul, Minn., Jan. 21, 1907; Spiran Lodge, No. 36, Danville, Ill., April 30, 1907; Vega Lodge No. 37, Kansas City, Mo., Dec. 28, 1907; Oscar II. Lodge No. 38, Minneapolis, Minn., April 26, 1908; Englewood Lodge No. 39, Chicago, Oct. 23, 1908.

Under the original charter the order had no authority to levy assessments for the creation of a reserve fund. Many members saw in the absence of such a guaranty fund a danger, which ought to be removed. This was done when on April 17, 1901, the order agreed to comply with the new insurance law of 1893 and thereupon obtained a license to do business under its provisions, including legal reserve regulations.

On June 2, 1901, the constitution was so amended as to provide for the creation of a reserve fund by setting aside for that purpose five per cent of the proceeds of each and every assessment. At the annual meeting of the Grand Lodge in February, 1903, this amount was changed to ten per cent.

Up to December, 1898, each member of the order was insured for $500. At this time the amount of insurance per capita was raised to $1,000. In 1902 Class B. was added, for those desiring to have $500 insurance policies. Four years later, in 1906, Class C. was instituted for those desiring a $100 policy.

The Svithiod order pursues the plan of furnishing insurance at actual cost. The average cost per $1,000 is about 85 cents per month. The current expenses of the grand and subordinate lodges are defrayed by income from other sources. The quarterly dues to lodges average $1.50, making $6 per year. From these funds sick and funeral benefits and lodge expenses are paid. The sick and funeral benefits are the same to all members, regardless of the insurance class to which they belong. The amount of the assessments is not permanently fixed, but may be varied according to necessity, whereby ample funds are always assured. The privilege of determining the amount of sick benefits and other aid to be paid to members is vested in the individual lodges, which likewise have full charge of their own treasuries and property.

The most recent reports show the following status of the order: Total membership, 6,015; insurance in force, $4,746,000; reserve fund, $23,677.93; other funds, $9,857.09; cash assets of subordinate lodges, about $68,000; insurance paid out during the existence of the order, in 308 death benefits, $293,455; sick benefits, about $144,000; funeral benefits, about $32,000; charitable donations, about $14,000.

The chief officers of the order have been: High Grand Master— Axel Blomfeldt, John Wolgren, John P. Johnson, Olof Pearson, Fred Franson, H. E. Hanson, Joseph G. Sheldon, C. A. Carlson; High Grand Secretary—Bernard Peterson, John Wolgren, Hjalmar Hedin, John A. Sandgren; High Grand Treasurer—John Peterson, Gust Johnson, Linus Olson, Axel Blomfeldt, H. E. Hanson.

The Swedish-American Press Club

In the year 1890 a plan long talked of among the Swedish newspaper men of Chicago was realized by the organizing of a press club
for their mutual pleasure and profit. At a preliminary meeting held on
May 29th, and attended by a dozen men, A. L. Gyllenhaal presiding
and Herman Lennmalm acting as secretary, the feasibility of bringing
the Swedish writers and publishers into closer social intercourse, was
discussed. The result of the deliberation was that the proposed club
should be organized, and at a meeting held at the Sherman House on
the 12th day of July, 1890, Svensk-amerikanska Publicistklubben was
called into existence. The members for a time fraternized cordially
and for a period of three years or thereabout, the club held fairly
regular weekly meetings, whereupon meetings grew less frequent and
ultimately ceased altogether. Waning interest in general and personal
friction in particular cases seem to have been the disintegrating factors.
Alex. J. Johnson, publisher of "Svenska Kuriren," as said to have been
the last president, and the last official act of the club on record was
the sending of representatives to attend the funeral of a colleague in
Minneapolis. The obsequies of the club itself, however, were never
held and it might be revived at any time, without prejudice to its
constitution and by-laws.

The Independent Order of Vikings

Second in size among the purely fraternal Swedish orders of
Chicago and the state of Illinois stands the Independent Order of
Vikings. It dates its origin from the year 1890, when on June 2nd the
Viking Society was organized with an original membership of eleven
persons, as follows: Charles Carlson, G. A. Carlson, Charles Henry,
N. Hallerts, Aug. Johnson, Gust. Johnson, V. Muerling, Ed. Muerling,
C. H. Victorin, R. Waldén and Aug. Waldén. Their purpose was no
other than social intercourse on the basis of universal brotherhood. In
a short time they added the sick benefit and funeral aid features,
realizing the value of mutual assistance as a factor in knitting a close
fellowship.

For the first few months the society met at the homes of members,
but by October of the same year, having outgrown the capacity of the
homes, it engaged a hall at Sedgwick and Sigel streets for the monthly
meetings.

The uniforms and regalia adopted by the Viking Society were
patterned after the costumes of the Viking age, and at their first public
appearance, in the parade that took place on the day the Linné monument was unveiled, the Vikings mustered a large force and made a
splendid showing for a society but a year old.

When the membership had reached four hundred the society set about changing its organization for the purpose of enlarging its scope. The revised constitution and by-laws were adopted in September, 1892, and on the third of October the Grand Lodge of the Independent Order of Vikings was organized to become the central organization of subordinate lodges. Among its principal purposes were also the establishment of a readingroom, promoting the circulation of wholesome . literature among the members and the founding of a common death benefit fund, amounting to life insurance.

Two months after the reorganization a second lodge was started, known as Brage Lodge No. 2. During the course of the winter three other lodges were organized, namely, Drake Lodge No. 3, Angantyr Lodge No. 4 and Frej Lodge No. 5. The names selected were Norse, and this system of nomenclature has been consistently adhered to ever since.

When the time was ripe for the establishment of the insurance plan it was found advisable to secure a new charter, the old one being deemed inadequate to safeguard the rights and privileges of members. In the spring of 1895 a new charter was applied for, under the insurance law of 1893, the requirements of which were full met on the 30th day of November following, when the Independent Order of Vikings was given a certificate of incorporation as a legally organized fraternal beneficiary society. The incorporators under the new plan were: Andrew A. Carlson, Otto Anderson, Alexander Holm, Nels L. Anderson, Gustavus J. Bird, Gustavus Myhrman, Peter G. Almberg, Andrew Söderlin, John Anderson and Bengt A. Wester. The new insurance plan of the order was put in force Jan. 1, 1896.

The first roster of officers of the grand lodge was as follows: Grand Chief, A. Holm; Vice Grand Chief, C. Victorin; Grand Secretary, Alfred Carlson; Grand Treasurer, P. A. Noren; Grand Organizer, G. Carlson.

In 1901 the order extended its activities beyond the confines of Chicago and Cook county by organizing the Thor Lodge in Moline. Later it went outside the state and now extends west as far as Omaha, Neb. On July 29, 1908, the thirty-first lodge was organized, completing the following list:

Vikingarne No. 1, 1890, Brage No. 2, 1892, Drake No. 3, Angantyr No. 4, Frej No. 5, 1893, Frithiof No. 6, Runan No. 7, 1899, Odin No. 8, 1900, all in Chicago, Thor No. 9, Moline, Svea No. 10, Chicago, Norden No. 11, Waukegan, all in 1901, Balder No. 12, DeKalb, Harald No. 13, Chicago, Götha No. 14, Roseland, Ragnar No. 15, Chicago, Hilding No. 16, Aurora, in 1903, Bele No. 17, Chicago Heights, Ring No. 18, Batavia, in 1904, Thorsten No. 19, Joliet, Björn No. 20, South Omaha, Valhalla

R. Walden   Aug. Johnson   N. Hallerts   Chas. Henry   V. Muerling

Chas. Carlson   Ed. Muerling   C. H. Victorin   Aug. Walden

Gust Johnson   G. A. Carlson

The Viking Society, 1890

No. 21, Chicago, Niord No. 22, Kewanee, Hjalmar No. 23, Evanston, Orvar Odd No. 24, Omaha, in 1905, Ellida No. 25, Rockford, Yngve No. 26, Chicago, Ivar No. 27, Chicago, Vasa No. 28, Hammond, Ind., in 1906, Thyr No. 29, Galesburg, Sigurd No. 30, Kenosha, in 1907, Brejdablik No. 31, Milwaukee, Wis., in 1908.

The men who have held the chief offices in the order are: Grand Chief—Alex. Holm, Alfred Carlson, Eric Forsell, Axel Borg, A. W. Johnson, Herman Carlson, Frithiof Malmquist; Grand Secretary— Alfred Carlson, Otto Anderson, Nils J. Lindskoog, Eric Forsell, Anders Hessel; Grand Treasurer—P. A. Noren, Gust Bird, N. L. Anderson, A. W. Johnson, O. F. Sandstedt, Eric Forsell, Herman Carlson, John Anderson; Grand Organizer—Gustaf A. Carlson, Otto Anderson, Alex. Holm, P. A. Anderson, Nils J. Lindskoog, Fred L. Pearson, Anders Hemwall.

The order publishes a monthly paper, "Vikingen," as the common organ of the lodges. Its first number was issued May 15, 1899.

There exists a woman's auxiliary known as the Grand Lodge of the Independent Order of Ladies of Vikings having nine lodges under its jurisdiction.

The reports for Oct. 1, 1908, show a total membership of 4,538, a reserve fund of $6,198.06, an assessment fund of $14,835.94 and a total balance in the lodge treasuries of $40,045.12.

The Swedish Societies' Old People's Home Association

The initiative to the formation of a federation of Swedish societies in Chicago for charitable purposes was taken in 1893 by Dr. C. W. Johnson, a physician, and Hans Anderson, a jeweler. This was in the time of great need among the laboring population, and after the definite organization in April, 1894, of the federation, which was named The Swedish Societies' Central Association, its first care was to provide for Swedish workingmen who were suffering want as a result of the prevailing hard times. On May 19th the association gave an entertainment at Svea Hall, netting about $28—the first money realized by it for benevolent purposes. In August a state charter was secured and that fall, with the proceeds of an excursion to Milwaukee and a popular concert at the Auditorium, the association entered upon the aforesaid charity work.

With improved conditions in 1896, the association began to map out another field of work, that of caring for indigent Swedish people in their old age. For the purpose of founding a home for the aged, a fund was established May 17, 1896, starting with the sum of $700. With the net proceeds of picnics, excursions, concerts and other entertainments, as also by individual donations, this fund was kept growing

The Swedish Old People's Home at Park Ridge

for the next few years. In 1898 a committee was appointed to look up a suitable site for an old people's home, and on March 19, 1899, they were instructed to purchase a building and grounds at Park Ridge, which have since been occupied by the institution known as the Swedish Old People's Home at Park Ridge. The deal was closed April

Prominent Workers of the Old People's Home Association

26th, and on Oct. 7, 1900, the home was dedicated and in readiness for the reception of occupants. Miss Anna Anderson, a trained nurse, was engaged as superintendent and housekeeper. The first inmate was admitted the following December, others being received from time to time until the institution, which has accommodations for a score of persons, was taxed to its full capacity. The last payment on the property was made in April, 1905, and an inventory of the institution, as it stands today, shows a property value of about $12,000.

The property purchased in 1900 comprised a two story brick building of nineteen rooms and a block of ground 150 feet square. The purchase price was $4,500. Considerable sums of money were expended in renovating and furnishing the building for occupation and a number of societies and individuals undertook to furnish certain rooms at their own expense. A new heating plant was installed, cement walks have been laid and other costly improvements made. In 1908 about $9,000 for the home was realized through a bazaar, making a total of over $10,000 in the treasury of the home at the present time. Plans are under way looking to the extension of the institution either by building an addition on the present site or erecting a structure on acre property in some other locality near Chicago.

In 1908, to specify the object for which the organization exists and works, its name was changed to the Swedish Societies' Old People's Home Association, while a change was made in the constitution so as to admit to membership not only societies and lodges but individuals of a charitable bent. Beyond raising funds for the purpose above named, the association has made several contributions to other charities, including the sum of $166, in 1894, to the Pullman Fund, and at a subsequent occasion $500 to the Swedish Home of Mercy in Bowmanville, Chicago.

A Ladies' Guild was organized in 1899, which has ably seconded the efforts of the main organization.

The Swedish National Association

The organization which has existed for fifteen years under the name of the Swedish National Association of Chicago was called into existence by a tragedy. On Christmas eve, 1893, Swan Nelson, a Swedish-American, was murdered in cold blood by Moran and Healy, two ruffianly members of the Chicago police force. The crime stirred the fellow countrymen of the victim, and a movement was set on foot to raise funds for the prosecution of the culprits. Heading the movement and most active in the cause were F. A. Lindstrand, the publisher, and Frederick Lundin. These two men appeared in a large number of Swedish churches and lodge halls in all parts of Chicago for the purpose of enlisting general interest. By this method quite a sum was raised, but it proved inadequate and other means had to be resorted to. It was then that the plan for an association to fight the battle of justice took shape, and on May 25, 1894, the Swedish National Association was organized, with F. A. Lindstrand as chairman and Erik Thelin as secretary. In the same month a musical festival was held which filled the Auditorium to overflowing and yielded a substantial addition to the fund. After a long and costly trial, in which the prosecution was conducted by Luther Laflin Mills and Harry Olson, the association triumphed by securing the conviction of the criminals.

As a permanent reason for its existence, the association later in the year 1894 established a free employment bureau, which it has maintained ever since. From the outset this has been managed by Mrs. Othelia Myhrman. The organization is composed of an active and executive membership, together with delegates from local organizations in Chicago and Cook county. After some time Mr. Lundin's interest in the association flagged, but Mr. Lindstrand remained its chief backer. Time and again he has gone down into his own pocket to cover deficits in its treasury, and it is more than likely that but for him the association would not now be in existence.

Mr. Lindstrand served as president until January, 1897, when, contingent on his foreign travels, he resigned the place and was succeeded by O. C. Peterson. In 1900 he was again elected to the place and served until 1906. Upon his resignation, George E. Q. Johnson served as acting president that year and was elected for the following year. In 1908, G. Bernhard Anderson succeeded to the presidency.

The association has had no fixed income, depending on public festivals for means to carry on its work. A midwinter and a midsummer festival have been held regularly every year. The first winter festival was an international tournament of song, male choruses of seven nationalities participating and the Swedish Svithiod Singing Club winning the championship. Subsequent winter festivals have been of the following character: 1896, historical tableaux; 1897, commemoration of the silver wedding anniversary of the King and Queen of Sweden; 1898-9, historical tableaux; 1900, "Frithiof och Ingeborg," an opera presented three successive evenings; 1901, "Vermländingarne," a popular drama, with Ragna Linné and John R. Örtengren in the leading parts; 1902, "Engelbrekt och hans dalkarlar," an historical drama; 1903, concert by the Düring Ladies' Quintette; 1904, dramatic production of Jules Verne's "Around the World in Eighty Days;" 1905, concert by the Swedish Singers' Union of Chicago and historical tableaux; 1906, lecture by Dr. Otto Nordenskjöld on his antarctic explorations; 1907, exhibition of Swedish national dances by a troupe of dancers from Skansen in Stockholm; 1908, historical drama, "Gustaf Adolf och Regina von Emmeritz," with John R. Örtengren and Ida Östergren in the title roles. The midsummer festivals have been in the nature of picnic excursions to out-of-town parks. That of 1907 was made especially notable by the presence of Herman Lagercrantz, the Swedish envoy at Washington. The foregoing two were held jointly

with the Swedish Singers' Union. Extra entertainments and concerts
have been arranged by the association as follows: 1902, benefit concert
to provide funds for the defense of Anton Nelson, arrested for shooting
one Prendergast, indicted for manslaughter and acquitted on the ground
of self-defense, through the efforts of the association; 1905, concerts
by students' chorus from the Lund University; 1906, concerts by the
chorus of the Young Men's Christian Association of Sweden; 1908,
concerts by the military band of the Kronoberg Regiment of the
Swedish army.

The third fight for justice wherein the association has been engaged
was in the case of John Nordgren, who, after having been sentenced to
thirty years in the penitentiary for the alleged crime ·of poisoning his
wife, was given a new trial and acquitted of the charge after having
remained in jail two years. In connection with the free employment
bureau the association extends charity in various forms to unfortunate
and needy Chicagoans of Swedish extraction.

The Swedish-American Republican League

The Swedish-American Republican League of Illinois was organized in December, 1894, and incorporated on the 31st day of the same
month. Its has for its general purpose the propagation of the principles
of the Republican party, while its specific object is the political education and advancement of the Swedish-Americans.

For years the Swedish-Americans, generally loyal Republicans,
performed the duties of citizenship without belonging to any specific
organizations of their own. In time, they found it expedient to organize
themselves into local clubs wherever the number of Swedish voters
warranted such a step. In Rockford, Moline, Galesburg, and at other
points such clubs sprang up and in Chicago a number of ward clubs
were combined into a central Republican club of Cook county. The
suggestion was next made that a state organization be formed, with
ramifications in the various counties, this to be a representative body
that might speak for the great bulk of the Swedish voters of the state.
In the fall of 1894 this idea, at first broached tentatively, ripened into
action. A meeting was called for Dec. 4th, and that day saw the birth
of a Swedish state league. Among those who were present and took
active part in the proceedings of the organization meeting were:
Edward C. Westman, Will S. Hussander, Charles H. Hoglund, C. A.
Edwardts, and Gustaf L. Nelson, of Cook county; M. O. Williamson and
A. W. Truedson of Knox county; A. L. Anderson and John S. Smith of
Henry county; Rev. C. O. Gustafson of Will county; George W. John-
son, Frank A. Landee, Alfred Anderson, Frank A. Johnson, C. G.
Carlson and G. L. Peterson, of Rock Island county, and A. J. Anderson,

L. M. Noling and Carl Ebbesen, of Winnebago county. An organization was perfected by the election of officers, as follows: president, Edward C. Westman, Chicago; vice president, Hjalmar Kohler, Moline; secretary, Will S. Hussander, Chicago; treasurer, A. L. Anderson, Andover. The league was first planned by the leading men of the central club of Cook county, the most active and energetic of whom was Mr. Westman, and his election as the first president of the new organization was merely just recognition of his activity in bringing it about.

The league is a body made up of delegates from local clubs and from communities where a considerable number of Swedish-American

Edward C. Westman

citizens reside. The basis of representation is one delegate for the first one hundred voters of Swedish descent and one additional delegate for every three hundred such voters. The representation is by counties, and wherever an organization exists among them, it governs the selection of delegates.

In determining the time for holding the annual convention the organizers hit upon the happy idea of combining with it the celebration of some memorable event, and in selecting March 9th, the day on which was fought in 1862 the historic battle between the Merrimac and the Monitor, they found in the greatest single achievement of a Swedish-American, an excellent cause for celebration. Thus was instituted the commemoration of John Ericsson Day among the Swedes of Illinois. The sequel to every convention of the league, and the feature of the occasion, has been a banquet at which the name of the great engineer and inventor is invariably toasted. These banquets, planned on a grand scale, are always largely attended, and many of them have been brilliant affairs, at which governors, senators, members of the President's cabinet, the famous orators and wits of the nation, and even rival candidates for high offices, have fraternized under the intertwining flags of Sweden and the United States. Moreover, many favorable opportunities have been offered for representative Swedish-Americans to appear, as it were, in an open forum, to plead their cause and air their grievances, if any, before men of large calibre, open minds, high station and a wide sphere of influence. Generally speaking, the social and intellectual intercourse at these political feasts have proved profitable to both the hosts and the guests.

The league convened for the first time on March 9, 1895, at Chicago. The business sessions were held in an assembly hall in the Masonic Temple. One hundred and nineteen delegates were seated and an equal number of alternates were accredited, representing the Swedish voters of eighteen counties of the state. The first officers of the league were all re-elected for the succeeding year. The convention was followed by the John Ericsson memorial banquet, given at the Grand Pacific Hotel under the auspices of the Swedish-American Central Republican Club of Cook County. Subsequently conventions have been held in the following cities in the order named: 1896, Rockford; 1897, Chicago; 1898, Paxton; 1899, Aurora; 1900, Joliet; 1901, Galesburg; 1902, Bloomington; 1903, Princeton; 1904, Moline; 1905, Peoria; 1906, Chicago; 1907, Rockford; 1908, Aurora.

A list of the presidents of the league from its inception follows: Edward C. Westman; M. O. Williamson, Galesburg; Frank G. Stibb, Rockford; Frank A. Landee, Moline; C. A. Nordgren, Paxton; Edwin A. Olson, Chicago; A. W. Truedson, Galesburg; Carl R. Chindblem, Chicago; M. A. L. Olson, DeKalb; Julius Johnson, Lynn; P. A. Peterson, Rockford; Justus L. Johnson, Aurora; Oscar D. Olson, Chicago.

In the great campaign of 1896 a committee from the league was in charge of a Swedish bureau at the headquarters of the Republican national committee in Chicago. An idea of the work accomplished by this bureau is gained from the fact that from it were sent out 7,300 letters, 789,975 books and documents and 700,000 copies of newspapers. But for this committee the Swedish Republican vote in Illinois and other states in that election doubtless would have been materially lessened. In 1900 the league aided in the election of M. O. Williamson, one of its ex-presidents, to the office of state treasurer, and it has made its influence felt in a number of instances.

Twelfth Annual John Ericsson Day Banquet, Auditorium, Chicago, March 9, 1906

At the outset the league undertook to publish a paper to promote its interests. G. Bernhard Anderson was chosen editor, and one issue of the paper, which was named the "Monitor News," was published in 1895, but a second number never appeared. A few years ago the league began to plan for the erection of a monument to John Ericsson, and an organization was formed to solicit funds. Some progress has been made, but the project is yet far from a realization.

Probably the most brilliant event in the life of the league was the great Ericsson memorial banquet in 1906, at the Auditorium Hotel, Chicago, when about 800 persons sat at table and Charles J. Bonaparte, secretary of the navy, graced the occasion with his presence.

The Swedish Historical Society of America

Cultured Swedish-Americans years ago realized the desirability of having the records of their nationality written and preserved for posterity and the need of an organized body to make systematic efforts to that end. In the year 1889 a number of representative men in Chicago sought to fill this want by associating themselves into an organization which was named The Swedish-American Historical Society. Several of its members are known to have engaged in historical writing both before and after that time, but the society as such never went on record except in the list of Illinois corporations.

In 1905 other persons, sensible of the need of immediate and active work for the preservation of all things historical pertaining to the Swedes of America, took up an identical project. One or two of the founders of the first society joined in the movement for a second, manifestly acting on the assumption that the prior organization had passed out of existence. A preliminary meeting was held in the early summer of 1905, at which the plan was outlined. Among the participants in the action then taken were: Aksel G. S. Josephson, L. G. Abrahamson, J. A. Enander, Louis G. Northland, Anders Schön and Ernst W. Olson. An organization committee headed by Dr. Abrahamson was appointed, and it was resolved to meet again during the Swedish singers' convention in July to perfect the organization. This was done at a meeting held on July 22, 1905, in the rooms of the Chicago Historical Society, Dr. Abrahamson presiding and Mr. Josephson acting as secretary. At that time a constitution was adopted, setting forth the objects for which the society was formed and the mode of operation. The name adopted was, The Swedish-American Historical Society. The objects, as briefly defined are:

To promote the study of the history of the Swedes in America and their descendants;

To collect a library and museum illustrating their development;

To issue publications relating to the history of the Swedish people in Sweden and America;

To encourage the study of Swedish history and literature in American universities.

Membership is conditioned on the payment of an annual fee of two dollars, and life membership is granted upon the payment, in one

Dr. Josua Lindahl

sum, of fifty dollars. The affairs of the society are in the hands of a council of fifteen members, empowered to elect among their number the customary officers.

The council selected on this occasion first met on August 29th, when as the first set of officers of the society, the following gentlemen were elected: President, Dr. Johan A. Enander, Chicago; vice president, Dr. Gustav Andreen, Rock Island; secretary, Anders Schön, Chicago; treasurer, Aksel G. S. Josephson, Chicago.

In January, 1906, the council took action looking to the immediate establishment of a library in Chicago and inviting donations of books, newspapers, manuscripts, engravings and photographs of value as material pertinent to Swedish-American history or of interest for their associations with Swedish and American culture.

The first annual meeting was held in the Chicago Historical Society building on March 28, 1906. On that occasion Eric Norelius and Johan A. Enander, were elected honorary members in recognition of their achievements in the field of historical writing. As a guide for those willing to aid in building up the proposed library, a schedule designating what it should contain was made up and approved, as follows: 1) books dealing with Swedish colonization on and immigration to the American continent and its adjacent islands; 2) books by Swedish-Americans; 3) publications of Swedish-American publishing houses; 4) publications of Swedish-American institutions, churches, schools, societies, lodges, etc.; 5) Swedish books dealing with America; 6) American books dealing with Sweden; 7) translations of works of Swedish authors into English, and of works of American authors into Swedish; 8) original records, or manuscript copies of such records, if not already printed, of Swedish-American churches, societies, lodges, labor unions, etc.; 9) photographs of Swedish-Americans who have made their mark in this country, as well as of buildings of interest on account of their associations with the Swedish people in America, such as churches, school and college buildings, hospitals, homes of old settlers, etc.; 10) a selection of the most important works on Swedish history and literature, so that this library might in time become the recourse for all who desire to make a study of the history, literature and civilization of Sweden.

A total of 118 members for the first year was reported. Eliminations for failure to fulfill the pecuniary obligation, however, reduced this number to a net total of about 80. The present membership is about 140.

At the annual meeting in 1908 it was resolved to change the form of the name and to incorporate as The Swedish Historical Society of America, which was done. There was then a nucleus for a library which has since grown to over one thousand numbers, inclusive of smaller pamphlets and periodicals. The first yearbook had been issued, embracing the first two years of the society's existence, and the young society was shown to have made at least a fair start. Hampered by a dearth of funds, its progress heretofore has been slow, yet there is evidence that both men and means may be counted on for the furtherance of a cause so vital to the interests of the Swedish people everywhere on the American continent.

As president of the society each of the following named persons have served in turn: Johan A. Enander, C. G. Lagergren, C. G. Wallenius, Josua Lindahl; as vice president, Gustav A. Andreen, J. S. Carlson, C. G. Wallenius, Ernst W. Olson; as secretary, Anders Schön, A. G. S. Josephson, Joseph G. Sheldon; as treasurer, A. G. S. Josephson, John R. Lindgren.

The Swedish Historical Society of America has taken up a field of activity as wide as the continent and reaching back almost to the beginning of civilized order in America. It is planned on the broadest lines and to it no political, social or sectarian boundaries exist. It looks to all Swedish-American men and women of intelligent interest in the history and achievements of their race and nationality to aid in the attainment of its high aims.

BIBLIOGRAPHICAL REFERENCES

Alvord, C. W., Collections of the Illinois State Historical Library. Vol. II. 1907.
Alumni Record of the University of Illinois. 1906.
Annual catalogues of the Swedish-American colleges.
Archives of the Vendes Artillery Regiment of Sweden.
Årsbok för Svenska Baptistförsamlingarna inom Amerika.
Bateman, W., and Selby, P., Historical Encyclopedia of Illinois. 1901.
Berg, P. G., Svenska Minnen på utländska orter. 1874.
Biografiskt Lexikon öfver namnkunnige svenske män. Vol. V., 1861.
Bishop Hill Colony Case. Answer of the Defendants to the Bill of Complaint.
Blanchard, Rufus, Discovery and Conquest of the Northwest. I-II, 1900.
Blue Book of the State of Illinois, 1903, 1905.
Bowman, C. V., Missionsvännerna i Amerika.   En återblick på deras uppkomst
    och första verksamhetstid. 1907.
Bremer, Fredrika, Hemmen i Nya Verlden. I-II. 1866
Charleston News and Courier, February 4, 1894.
Chicago-Bladet.
Chicago Inter Ocean, May 28, 1880.
Chicago Tribune, 1861; Nov. 15, Dec. 9, 10, 1862.
Cornelius, C. A., Svenska Kyrkans Historia efter Reformationen. 1887.
Crooker, L. B., Nourse, H. S., Brown, J. G., and Haney, M. L., The Story of
    the Fifty-Fifth Regiment Illinois Volunteer Infantry in the Civil War. 1887.
Edgren, J. A., Minnen från Hafvet, Kriget och Missionsfältet. 1878.
Enander, Joh. A., Förenta Staternas Historia. 1874-1880.
Erik Jansonisternas Historia. (Anonymous defensory pamphlet.) 1903.
Gamla och Nya Hemlandet.
Gerberding, G. H., Life and Letters of W. A. Passavant. 1906.
Hall, A. G., Svenska Baptisternas Historia under en tid af femtio år, 1848-1898. 1900.
Hemborg, C. A., Jubelalbum med en kort historik till minne af sv. ev. lutherska
    Moline-församlingens 50-årsfest år 1900.
Herlenius E., Erik-Jansismens historia. 1900.
Historik öfver Första Svenska Baptist-Församlingens i Chicago, Illinois, Fyra-
    tioåriga Verksamhet. 1866-1906.
History of De Kalb County. Ill., 1868.
History of Monroe, Randolph and Perry Counties, Illinois, 1883.
Iduna.
Illinois-Konferensen, 1853-1903.
Johnson, Eric, The Viking. 1906-07.
Johnson, Eric, and Peterson, C. F., Svenskarne i Illinois. Historiska anteckningar.
    1880.
Jubelalbum till minne af Första sv. lutherska församlingens i Galesburg, Ill. 50-
    årsfest, år 1901.
Kaeding, George, Rockfords svenskar, historiska anteckningar, 1885.
Koch, Col. Charles R. E., Illinois at Vicksburg. 1907.
Korsbaneret.
Kurre Kalender.
Lindh, O., Minnen och iakttagelser från en förfluten lefnad. 1907.
Linnström, Hjalmar, Svenskt Boklexikon. 1868.
Lundqvist, P. N., Erik-Jansismen i Helsingland. Historisk och Dogmatisk fram-
    ställning jemte Wederläggning af Läran. Published anonymously. 1845.

Lundstedt, Bernhard, Svenska tidningar och tidskrifter utgifna inom Nord-Amerikas Förenta Stater. 1886.

Mattson, Col. Hans. The Story of an Emigrant. 1890.

Mellander, Axel, De svenska Missionsvännerna i Amerika. Manuscript.

Mikkelson, A., The Bishop Hill Colony. 1892.

Minne af Princeton sv. luth. församlings 50-årsfest den 17-19 juni, 1904.

Minneskrift, illustreradt album utgifvet af Sv. Ev. Lutherska Immanuels-församlingen i Chicago, med anledning af dess femtioårsjubileum år 1903.

Missions-Wännen.

Montague, E. J., Directory, Business Mirror and Historical Sketches of Randolph County. 1859.

Nelson, A. P., Svenska Missionsvännernas Historia i Amerika. Första delen: De Svenska Kongregationalisterna. 1906.

Nelson, O. N., History of the Scandinavians, and Successful Scandinavians in the United States. 1893.

Newman, S. B. Autobiography.

Norelius, Eric, De Svenska Luterska Församlingarnas och Svenskarnes Historia i Amerika. 1890.

Hasselquist, T. N. Lefnadsteckning. 1900.

Nya Wecko-Posten.

Officers of the Army and Navy, who served in the Civil War. Philadelphia.

Örebro Tidning. November, 1894.

Peterson, C. F., Ett Hundra År, 1892.

Sverige i Amerika. 1898.

Pierre Menard Papers.

Portrait and Biographical Album of Henry County. 1885.

Prärieblomman, 1900, 1902-1908.

Proceedings of the Conventions of the Swedish-American Republican League of Illinois, I, 1896, II, 1897, III, 1901.

Protokoll öfver Methodist-Episcopalkyrkans Svenska Central-Konferens.

Protokoll öfver Svenska Evangeliska Fria Missionens årsmöten.

Reed, Major D. W., The Battle of Shiloh and the organizations engaged. 1902.

Referat öfver Augustanasynodens årsmöten.

Referat öfver Illinois-konferensens årsmöten.

Referat öfver svenska metodistkonferensernas i Amerika årsmöten.

Reports of the Supreme Court of Illinois, Vol. 121.

Report of the Adjutant General of the State of Illinois, Vol. 1-9. 1900-02.

Rockford i ord och bild.

Schaack, M. J., Anarchy and anarchists. 1889.

Schön, A., Svenska läroverk och barmhertighetsinrättningar i Amerika. Printed as a serial in Hemlandet, 1894.

Schroeder, Gustavus W.. History of the Swedish Baptists in Sweden and America.

Skarstedt, Ernst, Svensk-Amerikanska Poeter i ord och bild. 1890.

Våra Pennfäktare. Lefnads- och karaktärsteckningar. 1897.

Skogsblommor.

Svenska Amerikanaren.

Svenska Evangeliska Missionsförbundets rapport till församlingarna.

Svenska Nyheter.

Svenska Tribunen.

Swensson, C. A., and Abrahamson, L. G., Jubelalbum. 1893.

Transactions of the Illinois State Historical Society, Nos. 3, 7, 9, 11.

Ungdomsvännen.

Unonius, Gustaf, Minnen från en sjuttonårig vistelse i nordvestra Amerika. 1861.

Bihang till "Minnen från en sjuttonårig vistelse i nordvestra Amerika." 1896.
Valkyrian.
Vintersol.
Wallenius, C. G., Liljegren, N. M., and Westergreen, N. O., Svenska Metodismen i Amerika. 1895.
War of the Rebellion. A Compilation of the Official Records of the Union and Confederate Armies.
Witting, Victor, Minnen från mitt lif som Sjöman, Immigrant och Predikant. 1902.
Year-Book of the Swedish Historical Society of Amerika, 1907.

ACKNOWLEDGMENTS

The publishers beg to acknowledge contribution of valuable data from Mr. Andrew L. Anderson, Rev. C. A. Björk, Mr. Samuel E. Carlsson, Mrs. Elizabeth Engberg, Mr. Olof Forsse, Capt. Eric Johnson, Mr. Emil Larson, Mr. Oliver A. Linder, Prof. Axel Mellander, Mr. Nels Nelson, ex-lieutenant of Co. C, 43d Inf. Ill., Mr. Gustaf Norberg, Dr. Eric Norelius, Mr. Emil Olund, Mrs. Sarah Corning Paoli, Mrs. Henry E. C. Peterson, Rev. J. G. Princell, Mrs. Lottie Rudman, Mr. Ernst Skarstedt, Mr. Philip J. Stoneberg, Mr. John L. Swenson, Dr. Mauritz Stolpe and Rev. C. G. Wallenius.

For the use of a number of engravings the publishers are indebted to the following: Augustana Book Concern, Illinois State Historical Society, Immanuel Swedish Lutheran Church, Col. Charles R. E. Koch, A. L. Löfström, Hon. James A. Rose, Swedish M. E. Book Concern, Rev. E. Wingren and Trustees of Chicago Sanitary District.

ERRATA

Page
163. For "Lundquist" read "Lundqvist."
190. For "odius," read "odious."
192. For "eighteenth century," read "nineteenth century."
207, 209, 235. Footnotes are quoted from Lundqvist, P. N., and not, as stated, from Landgren.
274, 276. For "Kassel," read "Cassel."
413. For "Epicopalian," read "Episcopalian."
437. For "captain," read "second lieutenant."
601. For "Missions Friends," read "Mission Friends."
729. For "Gustaf Stolape," read "Gustaf Stolpe."

INDEX

INDEX